THE Chorti are an agricultural people whose self-sufficient society maintains itself in an oval area some sixty-five miles long in eastern Guatemala. Their daily lives are largely built around the cultivation, harvesting, and storing of such crops as maize and beans; and their most important festivals are celebrated as part of the agricultural cycle.

Mr. Wisdom analyzes the cultural and social organization of these Indians and gives the fullest account ever made of the primitive economic system from this part of the world.

Particular attention is given to the interesting fusion of Spanish, Catholic, and native Indian religious beliefs and practices, divination, primitive remedial practices, and black magic. Illness, political organization, and folk patterns are studied; and, in every aspect of daily life, the author traces the extreme dedication of a whole people to one principal food—maize.

THE UNIVERSITY OF CHICAGO
PUBLICATIONS IN ANTHROPOLOGY

ETHNOLOGICAL SERIES

THE CHORTI INDIANS OF GUATEMALA

THE UNIVERSITY OF CHICAGO PRESS
CHICAGO, ILLINOIS

—

THE BAKER & TAYLOR COMPANY
NEW YORK

THE CAMBRIDGE UNIVERSITY PRESS
LONDON

THE MARUZEN-KABUSHIKI-KAISHA
TOKYO, OSAKA, KYOTO, FUKUOKA, SENDAI

THE COMMERCIAL PRESS, LIMITED
SHANGHAI

THE CHORTI INDIANS
OF GUATEMALA

By

CHARLES WISDOM

THE UNIVERSITY OF CHICAGO PRESS
CHICAGO · ILLINOIS

AUTHOR'S PREFACE

M Y FIRST trip to eastern Guatemala extended from May to October of 1931, during which time I worked principally in the *aldea* of Tunucó, about ten miles south of Jocotán pueblo. This is one of the most conservative of all the *aldeas*, containing many *lenguajeros* (Chorti-speaking Indians), and is a center for much sugar-making and manufacturing. My principal informants were Señor Juan Hernandez, a man of about sixty; his son Juan, who was about twenty; and his daughter Magdalena, who was about twenty-five. Juan Senior gave me much material concerning religious beliefs, together with many Chorti texts, and his son dictated many Chorti texts, as well. Another valuable informant was Don Juliano Cervantes, the most influential Indian in Tunucó. He was about sixty-five, and thoroughly Indian in every way, although because of his position he had many Ladino friends. My second trip lasted from June to September of 1932 and was spent largely in Jocotán pueblo, from which place I made short trips to the outlying *aldeas*. The same informants were used that year. Señor Hernandez died in August of elephantiasis, and my best informant was lost. The third trip, lasting from June to October of 1933, was spent almost altogether in Olopa *municipio*, where I worked principally with Juan Vásquez, an Indian soldier stationed at that *comandancia*. He was about twenty-eight years old and constantly checked his information with his large family who lived in the *aldea* of Tuticopote (Olopa *municipio*). He gave me many texts, as well as most of the native stems and grammatical material still used in Indian speech.

I am much indebted to Señor Don Manuel Vásquez, the Ladino druggist in Jocotán, for his many suggestions and leads concerning native medicines and Indian customs in general, all of which were easily and quickly checked with various informants. He proved himself far more familiar with and sympathetic to the Indians than the average Ladino, most of whom know little about them and whose contacts with them have not extended far beyond the market place on Sundays. His brother, Don Domingo, who lived in Camotán, was also helpful in this way.

Acknowledgment is also due to Marjorie Williams Wisdom for assistance in proofreading and for making the drawings; to Miss Dolores Thelma Ochoa, of the Tucson Senior High School, for help in Spanish orthography; and especially to Dr. Sol Tax, of the University of Chicago, for aid in the general preparation of the manuscript.

Results of studies in the Chorti language will appear in a separate publication; but, since some Chorti terms are mentioned in the text, a description of the phonetic alphabet employed will be useful.

The symbols used in writing Chorti are: *a, c, e, h, i, k, k', l, m, n, o, p, p', q, q', r, s, t, t', tc, t'c, ts, t's, u, w, x, y,* and glottal stop ('). The vowels are: *a* as in Spanish (neither "front" nor "back"); *e* as in English *met; i* as in Spanish *si*, except in two or three stems,[1] where it is like English *i* in *sit; o* and *u* as in Spanish, initially before a vowel as *w*. Only four stems were found in which *o* and *u*, when final, were nasalized. Long vowels, of the same quality, are written with a following raised dot (*a·*, etc);

---

[1] An example is *qi·wi'* (achiote), the first *i* being like that of Spanish and long, and the second as in English *sit*.

they were often confused with vowel plus glottal stop (see below). Diphthongs consist of *a*, *e*, and *o* plus *i* or *u*, and of *u* plus *i*, with stress on the first element (falling diphthongs), even when final or before final *x* or *h* (as in *puhui*, "nightbird"; *laux*, "banana leaf"). *w*, especially initial, is like Spanish *gu* before a vowel. This was for a long time written as *gw*, the sound of *g* being faintly heard. It is possible that this pronunication of *w* has been acquired by the Indians from their long use of Spanish. *y* is as in Spanish; both *w* and *y* are voiceless, with *i*-timbre, when final.

Of the consonants, *l* (in a few cases), *m*, *n* (after *h*, as in *mwahn*, "hawk"; or after a diphthong, as in *mein*, "spirit"), and *r* (prolonged, with strong hissing) are voiceless when final. Only in very few stems does *l* appear initially. In nearly all cases the Chol *l* has become *r* in Chorti, although Chorti retains the former *l* in certain compounds; e.g., "earth" is *rum*, but the name of a volcanic peak near San Juan Hermita is still called *ti' q'an lum* ("mouth of yellow earth"). Similarly, the transitivizing suffix *res* appeared as *les* in a few verbs. *h* is a weak aspirate, *x* is midpalatal, with more friction; both have a rounded *i*-timbred offglide when final after *o* or *u*; between vowels in coalescence both are usually replaced by *y* (*u cay-ir* from *u cax-ir*, "its plain area"). *k* is usually midpalatal, but when final is fronted (dorsoalveolar); *q* is lenis. *k'* and *q'* are glottalized, *q'* being even more lenis than *q*, with very weak glottalization. *p* is nonreleased when final; *p'* is glottalized. *r* is as in Spanish, but prolonged and voiceless when final. *s* is as in Spanish; *c* is like English *sh* in *show*; both *s* and *c* are prolonged when final, as are *ts* and *tc*, or all four have a voiceless *i*-glide. *t* is as in Spanish; *t'* the same, with glottalization; *ts* as in English *pots*, both initial and final;

tc as English *ch* in *church;* *t's* and *t'c* glottalized. The glottal stop, after and between vowels, is very weak; vowel plus glottal stop seems to vary freely with long vowel, with a faint rearticulation after the glottal stop (*t'co'k* or *t'co'ᵒk* or *t'co· k,* "rat"; *ha'* or *ha'ᵃ.* "water"). All final consonants except *h* and *l* (and *c, s, tc, ts* when prolonged) have a usually voiceless off-glide *i.*

Stress is always on the last syllable and is unmarked.

This study was made possible by funds granted through the Department of Anthropology of the University of Chicago.

CHARLES WISDOM

TUCSON, ARIZONA
August 1939

TABLE OF CONTENTS

LIST OF ILLUSTRATIONS

PHOTOGRAPHS

FIGURES

xiv LIST OF ILLUSTRATIONS

CHAPTER I

INTRODUCTION

THE present habitat of the Chorti-speaking Indians (Fig. 1) is an oval area about sixty-five miles long from north to south and forty-five or fifty miles from east to west, lying roughly between 89° and 90° west longtitude and between 14° and 15° north latitude. It is located in eastern central Guatemala, principally in the department of Chiquimula, but its eastern boundary extends over the frontier of Honduras for about ten miles to include the *municipio* of Copan. The Copan region, however, forms a small islanded area, since between it and the main habitat to the west in Guatemala there is an area extending north and south which contains only whites and mixed bloods. The majority of the Indian population today lives in the *municipios* of La Unión, Jocotán, Camotán, San Juan Hermita, Olopa, Quetzaltepeque, and Copan, all of which, excluding Copan, comprise a contiguous Indian area, with the pueblos of Jocotán and Quetzaltepeque the most important centers of Indian life. The *municipios* that surround this area are populated for the most part by Ladinos;[1] their few Indians seem and are said to be culturally more Ladino than Indian, and the *municipios* themselves are not considered by most of the Chorti as a part of their native area. Beyond the Ladino area to the southwest there is an island of Pokoman-speaking Indians with whom the Chorti have trade contacts; but aside from

[1] "Ladino" is the term applied in Guatemala to one who is not an Indian (see p. 223).

I

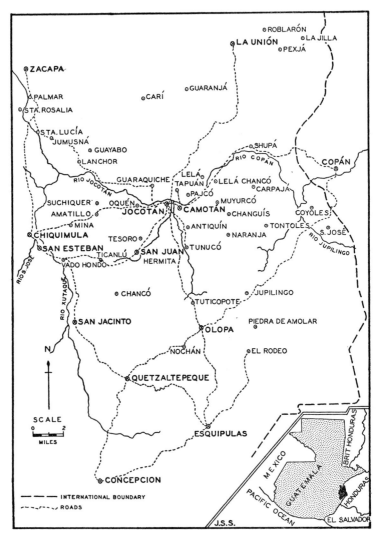

FIG. 1.—Map of Chorti-speaking area

them, if one excepts the occasional Indian traders from western Guatemala, the Chorti have no connections with other Indian groups.

The Chorti area was the locale of the Old Empire Maya civilization of which Copan was the culture center.[2] Excepting the Ladinos, it is now occupied only by Chorti, who may well be direct descendants of the pre-Conquest Copan people and whose language may be fundamentally the same as that spoken at ancient Copan.[3] Before the coming of the Spaniards the area of these Indians was probably much larger than at present, since Chorti place names are still used far outside the present habitat. At that time it must have reached into El Salvador on the south, some distance west of the city of Chiquimula on the west, almost to the Golfo Dulce on the north, and probably east of the present pueblo of Copan. Juan Galindo, in a report on the Copan ruins in 1834, deduces that the "king" of Copan must originally have dominated the area stretching from the Gulf of Honduras almost to the Pacific Ocean.[4]

[2] For a detailed description of the pre-Spanish history of this region see S. G. Morley, 1920, chaps. i and v.

[3] See Thompson, 1938, pp. 584–85.

[4] "From the analogy of their language, writing, and places where sacrifices were made, it is deduced that Copan originated from a Toltec colony, and that its king dominated the country extending to the east of that of the Mayas, or Yucatan, reaching from the Gulf of Honduras almost to the Pacific Ocean, and comprising an area of over 10,000 square miles, at present included in the modern states of Guatemala, Honduras, and Salvador. . . . . Throughout this extent of land the Chorti language was spoken and is still spoken, and from these and other data it is inferred that the peoples of Cuaginiquilapa, Los Esclavos, Quesaltepeque, San Jacinto, Santa Elena, San Esteban, San Juan Ermita or del Río, Jocotán, Camotán, San José, Chimalapa, Sacapa, and San Pablo, in the state of Guatemala, formed a part of this empire. Chiquimula and Esquipulas were governed by subordinate princes of the king of Copan. In Honduras, Omoa, the mineral district of San Andrés, Sensenti, Ocotepeque, Tipalpa, La Brea, and other places were comprised in their dominions. In Salvador, the large empire comprised Texis, Dulce Nombre, Metapas, Tejutla, and Sitalá. . . . . The large city of Copan, Copante, or Copantli was the capital of the nation

Fuentes y Guzmán, writing in 1689, placed present-day Copan as one of the villages of the province of Chiquimula de la Sierra, a unit of the kingdom of Guatemala. This part of the colonial empire of Spain consisted of the greater part of Central America and the state of Chiapas in southern Mexico. It was governed by a captain-general and governor who were stationed at the capital, now called Antigua Guatemala, a few miles from the present Guatemala City.[5] The province of Chiquimula de la Sierra was subdued in 1524 by three Spanish captains, Juan Perez Dardón, Sancho de Baraona, and Bartolome Bezerra, acting under orders from Pedro de Alvarado, the lieutenant of Cortes and conqueror of Guatemala. They, together with Conciso Hernandez, introduced the Christian religion for the first time into this section, preaching intermittently to groups of Indians as they marched through the country.[6] Nothing is mentioned, however, in the works of the early historians of any permanent work which these priests may have done. Apparently they abandoned the region in 1530 and never returned. In that year the Indians of Chiquimula declared their independence of the Spaniards, and Hernando Chaves and Pedro Amalín were sent with troops from the capital to put down the revolt. With the taking of Esquipulas, one of the Indian capitals, the whole province of Chiquimula was subdued by April of the same year. Copan was next besieged and, with the aid of an Indian traitor, was soon taken, and the revolt ended. The church

---

and residence of the monarch" (Juan Galindo, written in a report on the ruins of Copan to the commander-in-chief of Guatemala, 1834, and quoted in Mo. ley, 1920, p. 595). Galindo is, of course, incorrect in his deduction that Copan originated from a Toltec colony (see Morley, chaps. i and v).

[5] Fuentes y Guzmán (1689), quoted by Morley, p. 16.

[6] Fuentes y Guzmán (1689) and Juarros (1808), quoted by Morley, pp. 16–27.

has apparently been established throughout the Chorti area ever since.[7] It was believed by Juan Galindo that the present-day pueblos of Jocotán and San Juan Hermita were founded shortly after this revolt by Indians who were dispersed from the Copan region and that Camotán was founded many years afterward by Chorti-speaking Indians from El Salvador.[8]

According to La Farge, the Chorti-speaking Indians belong culturally and linguistically to the southern Maya group and thus are more closely related to the Maya of Yucatan, British Honduras, and northern Guatemala than to the highland tribes of southern Guatemala, who are usually referred to as the Quiché-Pokom group. The Chol, who live in Chiapas, southern Mexico, are first cousins to the Chorti, linguistically and culturally, and the two languages are almost mutually intelligible. These two tribes had already separated by the time of the Conquest, the Chol moving northwestward and the Chorti remaining in what was probably the original habitat.[9] Gates states that Chol and Chorti are almost equivalent languages[10] and

[7] The pacification of the Chol began in 1603 and was fairly complete by 1628, at which time they revolted, burned their churches, and abandoned the towns in which the Catholic priests had persuaded them to live. They were soon repacified, but fled to the forests again in 1678, burning more churches. By 1695 all the Chol area was subdued, and Spanish domination has been maintained since that time.

[8] Morley, p. 603.

[9] La Farge and Byers, 1931, pp. 1–9; see also Thompson, 1938, for an excellent map showing the areas occupied by the Chol and Chorti.

[10] "Cholti and Chorti constitute but one language . . . . , and the two combined almost constitute a branch to itself among the Mayance tongues, stretching from the Sensenti Valley in Honduras, including Copán and Quiriguá, through the tierra caliente north of the Guatemalan highlands, a stretch of country some forty leagues broad, quite to Ocosingo and Palenque, the Tulhá and Nachán, respectively, of Ordoñez. It is bounded on the south by the three southern Mayance branches, the Pokóm, the Quiché, and the Mame, on the

that these two are much more closely associated with the Yucatec than with the Pokom-Quiché languages.[11]

The native language (*tcor ti'*;[12] Sp. *Chortí*) seems to be identical in the *municipios* of Jocotán, La Unión, Camotán, and Olopa, and the Indians claim this to be the case. No linguistic observations were made in Quetzaltepeque *municipio*, but all the informants stated that the language there differed slightly in phonetics from that of Jocotán. Phonetic differences were observed when talking to Quetzaltepeque Indians in the Jocotán market but were not recorded. According to the informants, however, there are no structural differences over the whole Chorti-speaking area. Spanish today is essentially the trade language, since nearly all the Indians tend to use it, even when dealing with one another, in the market plazas, and especially when dealing with Ladinos and Pokoman Indians. None of the Ladinos knows more than a few dozen Chorti words or is able to carry on even the most limited conversation. Of the Indians, only a small proportion of the older women are unable to speak Spanish, and even these seem to understand fairly well what is said to them. The Indian men speak it well, some excellently, although some of them

north by the Yucatecan Maya, and on the west by the Tzental district. Its closest affiliation is with the last, and it must either be treated as a separate branch altogether or as part of the Tzental or Chiapan branch" (Gates, p. 610).

[11] Some two hundred Chorti stems were compared with their Chol equivalents as given by Francisco Moran. They were very similar and showed a fairly constant shift from Chol *l* to Chorti *r*. A comparison of the same stems with their Maya equivalents as given in the Motul dictionary indicated also a close connection between Chorti and Yucatec, although the Chorti similarity to Chol is much greater. No similar comparison was made between Chorti and any of the languages of the southern Guatemala highlands.

[12] *tcor*, "milpa"; *ti'*, "mouth," "language"; thus, "milpa language" (cf. Seler, 1904, p. 81).

require an Indian interpreter when being questioned at the
juzgado, and nearly all the older children and the young
men and women seem to speak it about as well as do the
less-educated Ladinos of the same age. Chorti is the domestic language, being used almost exclusively in the
aldea[13] homes. The few *aldeas* situated close to the towns
of Jocotán and Olopa contain a small number of Indian
families who use Spanish more than Chorti for all purposes.
These families usually pride themselves on their degree of
Ladino culture; their older members still speak Chorti
fluently, but the younger adults can barely converse in it,
and most of their children know only a few words. In the
more distant *aldeas*, however, every Indian speaks Chorti
and uses it exclusively in family life; the children seriously
begin to learn Spanish when about seven or eight, at which
age they usually enter the *aldea* school and begin to meet
Ladinos in the market places.

Racially, the Indians are typically Middle-American,
with skin color usually of a light red. The men seem to
average about five feet six inches in height, and the women,
five feet three inches. Obesity is extremely rare, even the
very old retaining a slender figure. The hair is cut short
and allowed to hang in bangs over the forehead. The brim
of the hat, in the case of males, presses against the hair in
front, flattens it out, and causes the hair to rise to a peak
at the top of the head. This gives the effect of artificial
head deformation, which is not practiced. The forehead is
high, although it seems low because of the bangs; the nose
is high and wide and thin nostriled, and the lips only
slightly full. The face is not extremely wide, and the chin
seems to have greater development than that of most
North American Indians. The musculature is good. As

---

[13] The *aldeas* are rural settlements (see pp. 216–20).

would be expected in a mountain-dwelling people who have no animals for riding or carrying, the legs, back, and neck are extremely well developed, while the arms and shoulders are much less developed and seem puny in some individuals. The back of the neck especially shows great musculature, from the constant carrying of heavy loads with the tumpline. The feet are large, and the toes spread considerably from the wearing of sandals.[14]

The region which the Indians now occupy in Guatemala comprises one lowland and two highland areas. The lowland area extends from east to west in the form of a wide valley through which runs the Copan River. At its western end is the city of Chiquimula, and at its eastern end, the town of Copan, in Honduras. About midway between the two, possibly slightly nearer to Chiquimula, is Jocotán pueblo, which is the social, political, economic, and religious center of Jocotán *municipio*.[15] This lowland area is usually called in Spanish "low country," or "the low places," and occasionally "hot country."[16] Both north and

[14] Load-carrying and mountain travel have given the Indians, especially the men, a sort of dogtrot gait. The foot is lifted high and placed flat on the ground with each step, and toes first, probably because of the wearing of sandals.

[15] Guatemala is divided into *municipios*, or townships. The main settlement of each is called a *pueblo*, *villa*, or *ciudad* in official documents such as the census (where Chiquimula, e.g., is a *ciudad*; Jocotán, Quetzaltepeque, and Esquipulas are "villas"; and the remaining towns of the department of Chiquimula are "pueblos"). But locally and unofficially *ciudad* is used only in reference to Guatemala City, and "villa" is to my knowledge never used. The religious, political, and marketing center for a group of surrounding *aldeas* is always called a "pueblo," except when it is a political center for a group of pueblos, when (as in the cases of Chiquimula and Zacapa) it is called a *cabecera* ("capital").

[16] The principal Chorti terms are "plain area" or simply "plain" or "valley" and "hot area." The word "plain" is also used adjectively to describe anything belonging to the lowlands, such as lowland maize and lowland people. It is applied to the lowlands because only the lowlands have level spaces of any considerable size.

THE COUNTRY NEAR JOCOTAN PUEBLO, SHOWING MILPAS ON THE HILLSIDES

south of this valley the land gradually rises and becomes more hilly; the streams are narrower and swifter, and the natural vegetation becomes less profuse. These are the middle-highland areas, called in Spanish "temperate country" or "midway country."[17] The Indians and Ladinos, however, usually make reference only to the two climatic extremes of their region and so think of it as being either high and cold or low and hot. Beyond the middle highlands, both north and south, the land rises higher to form mountains; streams are very small and infrequent, and their water extremely cold; and the small hills give way to high peaks, mountain ridges, and deep gulches. These are the two highland areas, usually called in Spanish "high country" or "the high places."[18]

The low country has a general altitude of less than two thousand feet and contains the pueblos of Chiquimula, Jocotán, Camotán, and Copan.[19] Chiquimula, capital of the department of Chiquimula, has an altitude of 1,167 feet.[20] Jocotán is about thirty miles east of Chiquimula, on the road to Copan, and is in the center of the Indian country. During the dry season the road to it can be covered by auto from Chiquimula in about two hours, but during the rainy season a day by muleback is required. It has a population of one thousand or less and a fairly typical lowland climate. Copan, at a slightly higher altitude, is a day-and-a-half journey by mule farther east, lying just over the Honduranian frontier.[21] The northern highlands

[17] There is no Chorti term.

[18] The Chorti term is "mountain area," or simply "mountain." Another Spanish term is "cold country" (Ch. "cold area").

[19] For a general description of the climate, altitude, topography, soil, and important plants of the Copan Valley see Wilson Popenoe, 1919.

[20] This is the figure given by the railroad company.

[21] The automobile road from Chiquimula was extended to Copan in 1938.

contain the one pueblo of La Unión, and the southern highlands, the *municipios* of Olopa, Esquipulas, and Quetzaltepeque. Parts of the latter no doubt approach four thousand feet altitude, with sparsely inhabited mountains reaching much higher; the Ladinos claim that Olopa pueblo is as
high as Guatemala City, which is around five thousand
feet. Olopa *municipio* lies directly south of Jocotán, the
two pueblos being about a day's journey apart. The connecting road is little more than a trail, and a few spots are
impassible even for mules. In the area where these two
municipios join are a number of Indian *aldeas* with an
average altitude of possibly twenty-five hundred to three
thousand feet, and with typical middle-highland climate
and topography.

The entire region, and especially the high country, is extremely rough and mountainous and covered with large
boulders, exposed rock formations, and clay beds. The latter are to be seen usually on the sides of steep hills, where
considerable erosion has gone on. A bluish limestone seems
to prevail, with some volcanic tufa near the extinct craters.
Clays, usually red and yellow, abound in the upper hills.
The large rivers seem to be old geologically, since in many
places they have cut their beds through several hundred
feet of limestone. The rivers are not extremely large, and
most of them are no more than creeks. The Copan River is
perhaps the largest. It takes its source in west-central
Honduras, where it is known as the Jupilingo, flows west-
ward past the pueblos of Camotán and Jocotán, where it is
called the Jocotán, veers northward near Chiquimula, and
joins the Motagua near the city of Zacapa. The Lempa
River, near Quetzaltepeque in the south, is next in importance. Hot and cold springs are in great abundance.[22]

[22] Many of the hot springs have sulphurous water which is much used as a
body wash to relieve rheumatism.

All the pueblos secure their water from near-by cold springs, as it is said to be purer than river water. Only two volcanoes, both extinct, are known. These are called Ticanlúm (Ch. *ti'q'an lum*), near the *aldea* of the same name, in the west-central part of the region, and La Jigua, situated in the north, near the pueblo of La Unión. There are probably many of these extinct volcanoes in the region, but their names and all legends concerning them have disappeared.

In both the high and the low country the year is divided, according to rainfall, into three seasons: the rainy, near-dry, and dry. The first is called in Spanish "winter" and in Chorti, "rainy season."[23] Although it corresponds in time to the North American summer, the Spanish term refers to amount of rainfall rather than to temperature. All over the area it begins by the first week of May, the first showers being referred to as "the beginning of winter," and seems to be considered the real beginning of the year by the Indians and Ladinos. This is also called the "planting season," as it is the time for the first important planting of the year. The high country has only one continuous rainy season annually, which lasts from May to October or November. During these months the precipitation is almost continuous from day to day. This is the agricultural season in the high country, when its most important crops

[23] A government station in the city of Chiquimula read temperatures and measured relative humidity in 1937. The results, as given in the Department of Agriculture's *Memoria* (Guatemala, 1938), pp. 432–37, follow:

Month	Mean Temp. (° F)	Rel. Hum. (Per Cent)	Month	Mean Temp. (° F)	Rel. Hum. (Per Cent)
January	77.7	75	July	84.5	50
February	79.7	67	August	85.6	54
March	82.0	59	September	85.8	54
April	84.5	58	October	84.2	57
May	85.1	59	November	77.2	67
June	86.0	55	December	76.1	73

of maize and beans are produced. In the low country there are two rainy seasons. The first, lasting from May to September, is called in Spanish "the first" and in Chorti, "first rainy season." This is followed by a month or so of comparative dryness, called the *canícula* (Ch. "little dry season"), during which time the first crops of the year are harvested and the second crops planted. A second rainy season begins in October and lasts for about a month. It is called in Spanish "the second" and in Chorti, "second rainy season." These names refer both to the two rainy seasons and to the crops produced in them.

During the rainy season the precipitation is great in the entire area and, according to the Ladinos, slightly heavier in the high country than in the low country. The rains begin in the early afternoon of each day with clocklike regularity and continue until the early morning. The next day breaks clear and dry, and all the outdoor activity of the twenty-four hours must be carried on between sunrise and about two o'clock in the afternoon. The rain is expected to come at that hour, and the day's activity is planned accordingly. Travelers take the trail long before sunrise and plan to reach a certain house or pueblo before two o'clock in the afternoon, as the trails are almost impassable once the rain starts.

The near-dry season extends roughly from November to February, during which time the rains are light and intermittent. It is called in Spanish "spring" and in Chorti, "harvesting season." This is the principal harvesting season of the year, when the last maize, beans, and other vegetables of the year are gathered and placed in the storehouses to last the families until the following July, when the first new crops come in.

The dry season lasts from February to May. It is called

in Spanish "summer" and in Chorti, *q'in* ("sun," "day," "time," "season"), or "clear season."[24] During these three months the rainfall decreases considerably in both the high and the low country, the smaller streams dry up, and the natural vegetation thins out except along the banks of streams. In the extreme highlands rain may fall once a week or more, and in the lowlands, not more than once in every three weeks. This is the manufacturing season, when articles are being made in all the *aldeas* and sold in great profusion in the Jocotán and Olopa markets, and when no agricultural work goes on except the irrigating of sugar cane and the raising of a few irrigated vegetables.

The same seasonal classification is made on the basis of temperature, although temperature has little economic significance in the minds of the Indians and Ladinos. The warm season (Ch. "warm weather," "warm season") lasts from April to about October and is equivalent in time to the rainy season. The cold season (Ch. "cold weather," "cold season") extends over most of the near-dry and dry seasons. The average temperature for the low country seems to be about 85° during the warm rainy season and about 75° during the cold dry season, although it is much warmer at midday than at midnight. The temperature in the high country is probably 15°–20° lower for each season, and in that area there is sometimes frost in the early mornings, although snow is never seen.

The wild flora grows more luxuriantly in the lowlands than in the highlands; but, owing to the heavy population and the lack of uncultivated land, in neither section are there any great stretches of virgin forest. Except on the summits of the highest hills, where no one lives and where there are pine and cedar forests, and in spots too steep or

[24] Also called in Spanish and Chorti "dry season."

too rocky for cultivation, such as the sides of cliffs and along the banks of some of the streams, there is no untouched land or vegetation. The principal wild trees in the uncultivable spots in the lowlands are the oak, the palms, the gigantic ceiba, the *madre cacao*, the copal, and many others. On these trees parasitic plants abound, and from their limbs are suspended a large variety of vines and runners which form in some places an almost impenetrable network between the larger trees. Bushes and shrubs of many species grow beneath. On the land which is lying fallow the vegetation is small and bushy, since it does not go unmolested for more than four years at a time. In the highlands the cultivated spots resemble those of the lowlands, but there is a thinning-out of wild vegetation; it is less luxuriant and varied. This section contains more large trees than the lowlands, but there is a noticeable scarcity of smaller plants, such as ground and tree runners, vines, and bushes. The less important cultivated plants are in most cases restricted to one climatic section or the other, but the most important staples, like maize, beans, squash, and pumpkins, are grown extensively in both, each having varieties which will grow successfully only in it.

The fauna is not nearly so diversified and abundant as it is in the tropical coastal regions. The domestic animals are the same in both highlands and lowlands, but the wild fauna exists in much greater abundance in the highlands than in the lowlands. This is probably not so much due to climatic differences as to the fact that the heavily populated lowlands contain less forested area. The Indians say that the wild animals, especially deer, have been pushed to the higher hills, and it is in such localities that the professional hunters operate. Fish seem to be rather scarce, except in the large lowland rivers, the principal one of which is the Jocotán.

The cultivation, harvesting, and storing of the domestic food and industrial plants consume the greater portion of the working time of all the Indians. Their daily lives throughout the year are largely built around the production and handling of such plants, and they consider this by far their most important work. They look upon the techniques connected with the domestic plants as the most basic and necessary of the whole technical system for maintaining their social and economic life as it now exists. The family education of boys consists almost altogether in learning them, and they begin early in life to master them by working along with the men.[25] Of the domestic plants, maize and beans are probably more important than all the others combined and are the only foods considered absolutely indispensable. *Tortillas* and beans symbolize food, and their native names are often used to mean "food."[26] In some of the temperate-country *aldeas*, sugar cane seems almost as important as maize, as many of those families devote a third or a half of their land to it, but even there cane is merely the principal money crop, while maize and beans are considered, as elsewhere among the Indians, as the principal subsistence crop.

The domestic animals are not nearly so important. The keeping and using of animals, except for chickens and turkeys, seems to be an occasional activity, receiving little attention and planned work, and the food animals are considered only as a supplementary source of food supply. Not many Indians eat them or their by-products, but usually sell them to the Ladinos and use the money thus ob-

[25] Other techniques, such as textile- and pottery-making, are of course highly important, and many could not be dispensed with, but they are either engaged in only occasionally or are restricted to professional workers and therefore are not activities in which the entire Indian community is completely and continually engrossed.

[26] See p. 87, n. 2.

tained to buy the more valuable maize and beans. The work animals are important to the sugar-makers, sandal-makers, and professional hunters, but the Indians in general know very little about them, almost never use them, and have few techniques for their use, handling, and consumption.[27] The collecting of wild plants and animals is at best an occasional activity, since three-fourths or more of the plant foods consumed throughout the year are grown in the milpas, gardens, and orchards, and nearly all the food and industrial animals are domestic. Wild vegetables are more important than wild fruits; wild fruits are not considered necessary foods, being usually eaten out of hand, while wild vegetables are placed somewhat in a class with maize and other cultivated food plants. Although wild plants are eaten much more than wild animals, and are collected more seriously, the techniques of animal-collecting, especially of hunting and fishing, are more highly perfected and consume more of the collector's time. Trapping provides very little food, being used principally to protect the milpas and gardens from marauding animals. Except for a few professionals, hunting, trapping, and fishing seem to be engaged in as much for diversion as for acquiring food. Honey-collecting is of least importance, sugar being less expensive and more easily secured than honey.

For this report the principal low-country area studied was Jocotán *municipio;* the principal high-country area, Olopa *municipio;* and the temperate-country area, the *aldea* of Tunucó and the region surrounding it, which is in the southern part of Jocotán *municipio.* No observations

[27] Their handling of large animals is clumsy and timid, in contrast to the skill with which the Ladinos, long accustomed to domestic animals, handle their mules and cattle.

were made in the northern high country, although information was secured from time to time from La Unión
Indians who made market trips to the Jocotán plaza.

Jocotán and Olopa *municipios* are more or less self-
sufficient economic units, since each produces most of its
economic goods within its area and distributes them in its
own market. They are dependent upon one another only
for those goods which are not produced equally in both
highlands and lowlands; and, since these two sections produce nearly everything the Indians require, the two *municipios* comprise a larger economic unit within the department of Chiquimula. Every Sunday a few Jocotán Indians
journey to the Olopa market, carrying with them strictly
lowland products which they sell, and bringing back highland products which could not be bought in Jocotán. A
few Olopa Indians buy and sell in the Jocotán market as
well.

Each of the *municipios* is a large area, twenty-five to
forty miles wide in every direction, with a single pueblo of
the same name which serves as its religious, political, and
marketing center.[28] The pueblo contains the one Catholic
church, the political officials who govern the *municipio*,
and a large plaza in which the Indians congregate for
marketing every Sunday and festival day throughout the
year. Surrounding the pueblo are the various satellite
aldeas which make up the *municipio*. The pueblos are principally inhabited by Ladinos,[29] although they contain a

[28] The census of 1921 reported the populations of Jocotán and Olopa, respectively, as 14,385 and 7,308; the populations of the pueblos are given as
894 and 622, respectively, the remainders representing the rural, and Indian,
populations.

[29] The census reported 612 Ladinos in Jocotán *municipio* and 452 in Olopa;
since all the Ladinos live in the towns, they apparently constituted some 70
per cent of the town populations.

few Indian families who serve as hired laborers. The *aldeas* contain only Indians and are primarily the areas of production, since nearly all the goods sold in the market places are grown and manufactured in the *aldeas*. The Ladino merchants import the few articles, such as cloth and matches, which the Indians cannot produce for themselves and sell these in their stores on market days. Each *aldea*, which is no more than a rural settlement, is made up of a number of fairly self-sufficient families, each with its group of houses and surrounding milpas, gardens, and orchards. Most of the families are of the single-household type, consisting usually of a man, his wife, and their own and adopted children; but a few are of the multiple-household type, containing the chief household of the headman and his wife, and the subsidiary households of his married sons and daughters who have remained as members of his family group. These live and work together as a physical, social, and economic unit.

Indian religion represents a fusion of pagan and Catholic elements. The church and the saints are important, but they are adapted to a religious ideology permeated with non-Catholic concepts and deities. The Indian ceremonial organization is based upon an Indian priesthood of *padrinos*, who fill also the function of professional shamans but who are in some degree distinguished from professional diviners and curers. The most important festivals are celebrated as part of the agricultural cycle, but they often occur coincidentally with festivals of the Catholic calendar. In no case is there Indian consciousness of difference of origin of any religious or ceremonial elements in the culture.

CHAPTER II

REGIONAL SPECIALIZATION AND TRADE

REGIONAL DIFFERENCES

THE Chorti are an agricultural people, growing chiefly maize and beans, sugar cane, tobacco, and rice, and a variety of garden vegetables. They supplement their cultivated foodstuffs with fowl and some beef and pork, with greens that are gathered, and with game and fish. On the whole, little in the way of foodstuffs need be imported, the area being for the most part self-sufficient. Likewise the houses and furnishings are for the most part built locally of native materials. Only for clothing are the Indians largely dependent upon outside sources. Conversely, little agricultural produce, except processed sugar and tobacco, is sold in the markets to outsiders; however, surpluses of manufactures such as musical instruments, soap, copal, pottery, and textile products are produced and sold. But since within the Chorti area there is considerable regional specialization, marketing and money are of no little importance.

In spite of the differences in topography, climate, rainfall, and available natural resources between the highland and lowland sections, the mode of economic life does not vary fundamentally throughout the two *municipios* of Olopa and Jocotán. The most important of the food and industrial plants are produced in both sections, most being of a single variety which grows equally well at any altitude.[1] Maize and beans, however, are of many varieties, and these are divided between the highlands and the lowlands. The less important plants are confined to either highlands or lowlands and are distributed from the one to the other through the markets. The important manufacturing activities are carried on at least to some extent in both sections, although to a greater extent in the one in which the required raw materials are more available. Each section is divided into manufacturing areas, or districts, depending upon the allocation of its natural resources.

In highland Olopa *municipio* the houses are built of clay walls and grass roofs because of the cold and the lack of palms; only one crop of maize is produced each year, owing to the shortness of the rainy season and the low temperature; and this crop is largely supplemented by a great production of beans, since maize is often scarce, and a second and third crop of beans can be grown. This is the principal hunting area, as deer are to be found only in the highlands. The highlanders are more devoted to garden culture than the lowlanders, since they can grow vegetables the year round, although maize is their predominant crop. Pottery is principally made in the highlands, as this section is said to contain finer and greater quantities of clay.

In lowland Jocotán *municipio*, where the climate is warm, the houses are covered with palm and sugar-cane leaves, since these two are abundant; two crops of maize are harvested annually, as the rainy season is long; beans are less important, because maize is plentiful the year round; and the Indians are preponderantly given to milpa

[1] These include maize, beans, the pumpkin, sweet potato, tomato, mustard, chili, pineapple, papaya, mango, cassava, citrus fruits, sapodilla, avocado, *zunza*, agave, gourd plants, and hay plants.

culture, although every family raises beans and other vegetables.[2] Fishing is principally a lowland activity, as most of the large fish-bearing streams are in the lowlands.

The Tunucó Indians, who live in the middle highlands, are the principal sugar-cane growers and sugar manufacturers, and they also produce nearly all the pine torches sold in the markets, since the best pines for this purpose grow only in the middle highlands. This section, however, produces as well all the important crops of the other two.

Northwest of Jocotán is the area of native-type baskets, and south of that, or west of Jocotán, is the area of braided hats and mats. Most of the lowland fruits and vegetables sold in the Jocotán market come from the region southwest of Jocotán. The *aldeas* south of San Juan Hermita constitute the area of woven hats and palm-frond baskets, professional lime-making, and tanning. South of Jocotán, and including most of Olopa *municipio*, is the area of fiber-working, and included in this region is the area of woodworking. Midway between Jocotán and Olopa is the principal pottery area. The coffee and tobacco areas cover most of Olopa and La Unión *municipios*, as well as the southern part of Camotán *municipio*, as these regions have a highland climate. The fish area is around Jocotán pueblo, along the Rio Jocotán. Slightly east of Jocotán is the soap area. All the pine charcoal sold in the Jocotán market is made in Matasano; the oak charcoal, in La Mina; and the *tashiste*

---

[2] The strictly highland domestic plants, occasionally grown in the lowlands but only with irrigation, are rice, coffee, the potato, cilacayote, cabbage, huisquil, tobacco, and certain medicinal plants. These are regularly carried to the Jocotán market for sale. The strictly lowland domestic plants, seldom or never grown in the highlands, are *maicillo*, the large tomato, watermelon, muskmelon, onion, lemon, wild annona, cacao, coconut, cashew, *jurjáy*, jobo, banana, plantain, mamey, nanse, *piñuela*, izote, matasano, jocote, tobacco, cotton, palms, *jiquilite*, and certain medicinal plants.

charcoal, around Changuís, in Camotán. Most of these areas are not clearly demarcated, a few overlap, and some are superimposed upon others. Thus, the large fiber-working area includes in its northern part the area of woodworking and one of the areas of sugar-making.

According to the Indians, these areas have been formed on the basis of such factors as climate, slope of the terrain, nearness to trading centers, and the presence of streams, special soils, and minerals. Such highland products as coffee, tobacco, and highland fruits, vegetables, and maize are regularly carried by the highland Indians of Olopa, La Unión, and Camotán *municipios* to the Jocotán market for sale, and the lowland products of Jocotán *municipio* are carried to highland markets as well. The proper slope for cane-growing is said to be found only in the middle highlands, so that sugar is made principally in such areas. Such articles as fruits, hay, and firewood, which are said to be too bulky to pay for long transportation, are supplied to each market from the *aldeas* which are nearest to it. All the hay and firewood sold in the Jocotán market, for example, come from the *aldeas* of Oquén and Los Bados, about three miles away. Most of the prepared foods also come to market from adjacent *aldeas*. The one fishing area is near the Jocotán River, since the other streams of Jocotán and Olopa *municipios* are too small to contain large fish, and the *aldea* of El Morral, near Jocotán, supplies all the fish for the Jocotán market. The type of soil in each area is thought to determine the type of plants which will grow in it. The Indians state that the region around the *aldeas* of Oquén and Amatillo is best for growing carrizo, sedge, and palms, which accounts for its mat, basket, and hat industries, and that the woodworking area has the type of soil which produces the most desired trees.

The area around the pueblo of San Juan Hermita contains the best and greatest quantities of limestone, and the pottery-making area contains the finest clays.

Most of the occupational areas are made up of groups of contiguous *aldeas*, and there is a tendency for each *aldea* to specialize in only a part of the general occupation of its area. In the woodworking area one *aldea* makes all the violins, two or three others make only such household objects as chairs and tables, and another makes all the wooden canoes. In the pottery area one specializes in pitchers, another in pottery with handles, another in pottery without handles, etc. The weaving *aldeas* are similarly divided, one making mats, another hats, and another baskets. Each of the *aldeas* carries on more than the one occupation, but it specializes in at least one, and sometimes in two or three, and is known as being a center for these occupations. Almost every article sold in the markets is associated with the few *aldeas* in which it is especially made, or in which it is best made, and it is generally said not to be made elsewhere. Some of the occupational areas consist only of one or two neighboring *aldeas*. The woven hat, for example, is made only in Tesoro; indigo dye, only in Brazilar; tanned leather goods, in Chiramáy and Yocón; pine torches, in Matasano; and soap made from animal fat, in Tapuán.[3]

[3] The Indians are commonly referred to by the names of the principal occupations of their *aldeas*. Those of Oquén are called hat-makers; those of Amatillo, mat-weavers; and those of any basket-making *aldea*, basket-weavers. The Tunucó Indians are known as potters or as sugar-pressers, these being the principal occupations of Tunucó. The Matasano Indians, who are said to work principally as hired hands for Ladinos and other Indians, are referred to as laborers and very often as "pigs," since those who work regularly as laborers have no social standing. The Indians of *aldeas*, such as Naranjo, who have no professions and work only at agriculture, are called milpa-makers or maize-growers, and such families have only slightly more community prestige than the laborers. The occupational areas are similarly named, with the use of some form of the locative. A pottery area is a "place of pottery, or clay," a "place of clay molding," "a clay molding place," or "its place the clay molding."

The pueblos are the areas for the manufacture and distribution of articles which the Indians cannot produce. The Ladino merchants import salt, iron and steel, cotton cloth, cheap shawls and jewelry, kerosene, matches, and prepared medicines, all of which the Indians now use to some extent. The Ladino seamstresses make most of the clothes the Indians wear, although many of the women's skirts are bought from traders who bring them from western Guatemala to sell in the Jocotán and Olopa markets. The venders say the shirts are made and bought in Sololá, but they must be mistaken.[4] The Indians buy all the iron points for their implements from the Ladino blacksmiths, and they buy most of their tanned leather sandals and tumplines from the Ladino and Indian tanners of San Juan Hermita. The Pokoman Indians in Jilotepeque make the wheel-made coffeepot, metate,[5] water filter, and *cántaro* water jar, none of which is made by any of the Chorti-speaking Indians. Every family buys these articles from the Pokoman traders who bring them on Sundays to the Jocotán and Olopa markets for sale. The Pokoman, in return, buy native sugar, cigars, and textile products which they are said not to produce.

MARKETING

The Chorti do not make distant or prolonged trips and seldom go outside the area made up of the contiguous *municipios* of Jocotán, Camotán, La Unión, San Juan Hermita, and Olopa, which comprise a region of close

[4] McBryde, 1933, does not mention the manufacture of such shirts in Sololá, and Sol Tax (personal communication) says definitely that they are not made in Sololá but that they may be made in Quezaltenango.

[5] The area around Jilotepeque, Jalapa, is said to contain great quantities of the granite used in metate-making, none of which is found in the department of Chiquimula. These Indians supply much of eastern Guatemala with metates.

social and economic relations. The usual trip of the Indian, made almost every Sunday, is from his *aldea* to his pueblo two or three to perhaps fifteen miles away. Every month or two he may go to the pueblo of an adjacent *municipio*, both for trading and for visiting; and he may journey to Chiquimula, Zacapa, or Gualán once or twice a year for marketing or taking part in a festival. The professional Indian traders make regular trips to all parts of the Chorti-speaking area and even as far south as Jilotepeque and the frontier of El Salvador, but the average Indian has never been so far from his *municipio* and seems to have no desire to travel outside the area in which Chorti is spoken. Traveling within this area is facilitated by the custom of providing food, a bed, and pine torches to anyone, even strangers, who may request them. The giver does not expect to be paid but in turn may request the same hospitality in the future when he needs it, and from any family. Every family keeps a supply of torches in its kitchen to give to travelers to light their trail when caught by nightfall before getting home.[6]

The Indians seldom travel alone but in small groups. The men of several families often collect along the *aldea* trail and proceed in a group to the pueblo, resting often, exchanging loads, and making the arduous trip more pleasant by conversation and merrymaking. They usually walk in single file; no doubt the narrowness of most of the trails has made this a habit, since it is done as well when

[6] Many of the Indians seem offended when an offer of payment for hospitality is made. The professional traders are usually charged for food, since they are said to be constantly on the road and not at home often enough to return the favors and to be traveling merely in the way of business. The giving of torches to passers-by is almost a symbol of generosity, and one of the most uncomplimentary remarks to make about one's enemy is that he would not give a torch to a traveler (*ma·tcu· q'an-i u-y-ahq'-u in-te' tic-ar takar e ah p'i·r-se-y-ax*, "He will not give a torch to one on the trail").

walking in the pueblos and along wide trails, where walking abreast would be possible. The entire household usually attends market on Sundays, the men carrying the heavier goods which are to be sold, and the women carrying lighter articles and the infant children. The Indians use no pack animals, in spite of the fact that the Ladinos have for centuries used them for riding and transport. The men carry most loads in large fiber bags or cane crates, which are supported on the back with a tumpline which passes over the hairline of the head, and they carry firewood and hay in bundles which are held together with the straps of the tumpline. The women carry articles in baskets, ollas, or gourds, which rest either on the right hip or on a cushioning cloth on the head. They transport mats to market on their heads, each carrying several done up into a single roll. The women carry their infants astride the right hip for short distances, but for longer distances the child sits either in a wide shawl the ends of which are tied around the mother's forehead, or in a fiber bag the strap of which is used as a tumpline.[7] At every half-mile or so along the trails which run to and between the pueblos are resting-places where the heavily burdened Indians stop to rest, smoke, and cool off.[8]

[7] For head-carrying, a hand is held against the container to steady it when walking, and for hip-carrying, the arm of the same side is held around the container, usually a bottle-necked jar, or around the infant's waist.

[8] These spots are under shade trees, at one side of the trail, and consist of a natural bench, or shelf, upon which the Indian can let down his load and retrieve it once more without difficulty. For getting a very heavy load off level ground and onto his back, the carrier must be helped to his feet by others, but he can do it alone if the load is resting on a ledge above his feet. The carriers, if traveling alone, can rest only at such spots, all of which are well worn from long use. A few have been made by stacking logs or stones to a height of about two feet all around the base of a shade tree. Such a bench or ledge is called *xihr-ip'* (*xir-i*, "to rest"), and the spot, *ta xihr-ip'*, or *tur-uk'* ("a seat"; from *tur*, "to sit down").

SUNDAY MARKET IN JOCOTAN PLAZA

The principal marketing center which the Indians know about is Chiquimula, but it is outside the Indian area and therefore too distant to attract many Indians except once or twice a year on festival occasions. It is primarily a Ladino trading center. The principal marketing pueblo of the Jocotán-Olopa area is Jocotán, which is also a marketing center for most of the Indians of the *municipios* of Camotán, San Juan Hermita, and La Unión, which have poorly attended markets of their own every Sunday. Olopa is an important highland market and attracts many Indians from Esquipulas and Quetzaltepeque. The Copan market is fairly large but is too far to the east for the Jocotán and Olopa Indians. The most important market occasion of the year in any *municipio* is that of the four-day titular celebration[9] which is attended not only by the *municipio* Indians but by Ladinos and other Indians from many parts of the Republic. Every Sunday throughout the year is market day as well, the open plaza of the pueblo being used for this purpose. Only Chiquimula and Copan have special buildings, located on one side of the plaza, for trading.[10] These are unroofed in the center to admit light, with the stalls of the sellers ranged all around the walls and around the central patio.

The hours of selling are from early morning, a little after daylight, until about two o'clock in the afternoon. Shortly after sunrise all the trails leading into Jocotán are thronged

[9] Described on pp. 449–53.

[10] Chiquimula, now a large city, has transformed its mercantile plaza into a botanical park, and Copan is said by Jocotán Ladinos to have confined its plaza trading to a separate building about fifty years ago. An expensive market building which was put up in Jocotán pueblo about forty-five years ago was never used and soon went to ruin because the traders in the Jocotán market were and are preponderantly Indians from the *aldeas* and have consistently refused to sell their wares anywhere but in the open plaza, even during the rainy season.

with Indians bringing their wares to market. They usually refuse to sell anything on the trails, or will sell only after a buyer insists.[11] All proceed to the plaza, and by nine o'clock it is so crowded that the new arrival has difficulty finding a spot in which to sit down and deposit his articles. The sellers group themselves into selling sections, each containing all those who sell the same article, such as hats, mats, fruit, sandals, etc. These sections are grouped to form larger ones as well, each consisting of those who sell articles of the same general type. Thus, each fruit-seller, who normally sells only one kind of fruit, groups himself with those who sell the same fruit and with all the others who sell every variety of wild and cultivated produce. These are in the center of the plaza and constitute the "produce" section. The mat-makers, also, gather roughly into a unit, as do the mat- and rope-makers, and all these form a larger unit at the southwest corner of the plaza, constituting the "textile" section. The basket-sellers, for some reason, form a separate group by themselves, always next to the church wall. Those who sell prepared foods range themselves on the north side of the plaza, the soap- and copal-sellers are at the west side, and the candle-makers are usually at the church door. The Ladino tanners, who sell sandals, and the blacksmiths group themselves at one edge of the plaza, at a dignified distance from the body of Indian sellers. All the sellers from outside the Chorti-speaking area form separate groups, the Pokoman who sell metates and *cántaros* staying well outside the local Indian group.

This grouping seems to be done because the sellers,

[11] No reason was given for this, beyond the statement that it was "better" to sell in the plaza and that the plaza was "the place for selling" (*u tur-tar tua' a-tcon-ma*).

nearly all of whom make their own wares, come from the same or contiguous *aldeas* and are therefore friends and relatives. The market occasion is as much a social as an economic one, and such grouping facilitates gossip and repartee, much of which goes on during the hours of selling. It may also be that each seller feels more secure and at home when in the plaza by associating with others from his own rural district who are selling the same product as himself. These cannot be the only reasons, however, since a potter, for example, who comes from a nonpottery-making area will always take her place with or near the pottery-sellers if none of her *aldea* friends happens to be in the plaza. This she does in spite of the fact that the other potters are mostly strangers to her. But if her *aldea* friends, who will be selling other wares, are present, she usually sits with them. The selling groups occupy the same relative positions in the plaza throughout the year.[12]

All trading is done in the open, although the Ladino merchants sometimes construct temporary stalls for themselves, covered with canvas or thatch. The Indian women sit on the ground next to their wares, with their legs bent at the knees and crossed in front, and, if carrying infants, suckle them while carrying on their business. The men sometimes stand but more often squat near their wares, with both feet flat on the ground, the knees separated and the outstretched arms resting on them, which is the typical male posture when resting. The Indians do not bargain over prices as the Ladinos invariably do. The husband often leaves his wife to attend to selling while he mills

[12] The Indians state that grouping is done because the sellers, being friends, "like to be together" (*q'an-i a-tur-p'-o·p' kom-on*), and because those who sell the same article or type of article "like to sell in one place" (*u-q'an-i a-tcon-m-o·p' tama·n-te' tur-tar*).

through the crowd to buy the goods needed at home for the ensuing week and to inspect everything offered for sale. There is much conversation and quarreling, the latter among the older women, many of whom are known to be long-time enemies. The men gather around and encourage them, provoking much laughter from the bystanders. During these verbal fights insults are constantly shouted across the plaza.[13] By two or three o'clock in the afternoon most of the selling is over, and many of the men have gathered at the pueblo *chichería* to spend the rest of the afternoon in drinking *chicha*, talking, and having a general good time, while their wives wait patiently on the outside to assist them home.

A great variety of products are offered for sale, fruits being the greatest in quantity. Maize, both shelled and on the cob, is an important article of trade, especially during the winter months when it is scarce. There are many sellers of fiber articles, usually men, who walk around through the plaza with their wares thrown over their shoulders, looking for customers. The hat-makers usually congregate in a selling group, but many walk around, each with eight or ten hats stacked precariously on his own. Pottery is one of the most important articles sold. Most of it is made by the Chorti-speaking Indians, but the Pokoman merchants sell many large water jars. With the tumpline these men make the two-day trip on foot from Jilotepeque to Jocotán, each carrying sixteen of the jars on his back. They usually bring from Jalapa the small greenish-gray coffee pitchers which

[13] These often contain indelicate references to the opponent's presumed origin and filthy personal habits. Every market plaza has two or three well-known characters, usually poor and mentally unbalanced Indians who make a precarious living in the pueblo, who are the butts of much repartee and practical joking, and whose answers to stock questions always set everybody around in an uproar.

are partially made on the wheel, and which are preferred by the Indians because of their cheapness. The Pokoman traders also bring the stone metates, each carrying two on his back. Much native sugar is sold, as many Indians make it for the market; white sugar is seldom seen. Most of the soap sold is made of animal fat; vegetable soap is seldom sold, and imported soaps are unknown. Tamales, wrapped in banana leaves, are sold cold by many of the women, principally to the Ladinos. Powdered lime is carried by the women in large gourds and sold by weight. There are many lime merchants, since many Indian families do not make it, and all require it daily for softening maize.

A large number of stalls serve cooked food over the counter. This is usually meat which is boiled with vegetables in a large olla over an open fire, served with *tortillas* or sweetened wheat bread. Many beverages are sold, usually highly sweetened and rather weak, such as colored lemonade, pineapple-ade, and a number of sweetened drinks made from artificial syrups brought from Chiquimula. Ice is never available in Jocotán except on July 24, the day of the patron saint, when it is brought by muleback from Zacapa. Bread, usually sugared and always dry, is made by the Ladino bakers and sold to the few Indians who like it and can afford to buy it. Fresh meat is an important commodity and is sold only by the Ladinos. They butcher their steers and hogs on Saturday afternoon, cut the meat in wavy strips, and hang these on long ropes in front of their houses on Sunday morning, from which places they are sold to the Indians. A type of ground sausage, stuffed into intestinal skins, is much sold.

The Ladino dressmakers of Jocotán and Olopa who make most of the clothes of the Indians and the Ladino tanners from San Juan Hermita who make most of their

sandals have their selling areas in the plaza. The dressmakers also sell cotton blankets, cotton shawls, towels, and
other cheap textiles, most of which are imported from the
United States. Textiles from other parts of Guatemala are
not sold except in the festival markets, as the Indians cannot afford to buy them. Tobacco, especially cigars, is sold
extensively, as almost all the Indian and Ladino men use
it. It is sold secretly, owing to a recent law prohibiting the
sale of tobacco without a license, but the trade in 1933
seemed to go on mostly undisturbed. Agricultural implements are manufactured by the Ladino blacksmiths and
sold without handles. Many pine torches are sold, especially to those Indians who stay too late in the pueblo and to
others who live in areas where the pitch pine does not grow.

MONEY

The Indians use silver coins in all their trading in the
plazas, and money exchange usually prevails in the small
amount of trading which goes on in the *aldeas*, although in
the more remote ones there is some bartering during the
week between Sunday markets. There is little *aldea* trading, however, since nearly all the families are largely self-
subsistent and usually buy their few needs and exchange
their small surpluses only in the plaza market. When barter exchange occurs, it is based upon the money value of
the various articles, since these are standardized and
known to everyone. For example, a pitcher is exchanged
for about a pound of shelled maize; both sell for one peso in
the market. During any time of crisis when very little
money is circulating, barter exchange increases, even in
plaza trading, and this is the only time when the Indians
engage in any haggling over prices and values.

Money is called in Chorti *tumin*,[14] and the term refers to any of the silver and copper coins of the Republic, although primarily to the small Guatemalan peso, sometimes called the realito, which was coined by the government only in the years 1899 and 1900. They are about the size of an American dime and worth one-sixtieth of a dollar. They began to be withdrawn from circulation with the monetary act of 1924, which authorized the present quetzal money. The Chorti-speaking Indians, however, retained pesos as their own medium of exchange and refused to accept anything but pesos in their dealings with one another and with Ladinos. The Ladinos of their area were, of course, forced to accept them, since most of their trade was with Indians. The Indians in 1933 still refused to give them up, with the result that they remained in circulation in most of Jocotán, Camotán, Olopa, San Juan Hermita, and La Unión.[15] The Indian lays his pesos in the center of a cloth, ties up the

[14] A corruption of the old Spanish *tomin*, the name of a sixteenth-century Spanish coin (personal communication from Dr. Manuel Andrade, University of Chicago). The Sp. *peso* is more often used than *dinero* ("money"). It is used in the plural form to denote actual pesos, and in the collective form to mean "money," as *no tengo peso* ("I have no money"; Ch. *ma-tuq'a· yan ni tumin*), and *¿Cuanto peso?* ("How much money?"; Ch. *xai-te' e tumin*).

[15] In 1933 the government appointed local agents in the pueblos to collect them and to pay the owners an equivalent in quetzal money. Signs were posted on all the public buildings to the effect that after a certain date the old pesos would be valueless, but the Indians were slow to believe that their money could lose its value simply by government decree. They believed that only their pesos had real value, but were gradually being won over by the example of the Ladino merchants, who were advised by the government bank to stop accepting them as money. Such a crisis as that mentioned above occurred during the summer of 1933 because of this forced change of Indian money. Because of the government's action the Indians began to doubt the value of their pesos, and of course the new quetzal money could not instantly assume real value for them, with the result that they merely bartered with one another as much as they could. This continued for the rest of that year, although it was obvious that they were gradually accepting the new money as legitimate.

four corners, and thus carries them in his shoulder bag. Small coin bags with drawstring are sometimes used for this purpose also. The men carry single coins in the ear when at market as a sign to the sellers that the wearer has a peso or two to spend.

Cacao seeds were used before and after the Conquest as a medium of exchange by many Maya groups, and, according to several aged informants, the Chorti-speaking Indians used them in this way until about fifty years ago.[16] They are still used in formal gift-making, as between the mother of a newborn child and the *padrino* in Quetzaltepeque *municipio;* the cacao is said to be a gift rather than a payment, but its present-day ceremonial use is probably a vestige of its wider use as money in the past.[17] Maize is somewhat used by the Indians today as a medium of exchange, especially when shelled and therefore of known quantity. The maize unit is usually a gourdful, weighing about a pound, and is often used, especially during the dry season when many families are forced to buy maize, as a substitute for its money value, which is one peso. Maize is always acceptable to any Indian except the few wealthier ones who have a large surplus to sell, since it is eaten every day and can be easily exchanged anywhere for other things. The maize-sellers in the plaza usually merely exchange a portion of their shelled maize for the articles they wish to buy, without bothering to sell the maize first. The Indian buyer often asks the seller whether

[16] According to a Ladino in Jocotán, the Indians would come early in the morning on market days to his father's house, buy cacao seeds from him or exchange other goods, principally maize, for them, and use the seeds later in the day in the plaza as a medium of exchange in buying from other Indians.

[17] The ceremonial use of cacao is found at Mitla, and Parsons raises the question whether it was once used as a medium of exchange in that area (Parsons, 1936, p. 147). See also Thompson, 1933, p. 67.

he wishes pesos or maize for his articles, or states that he has maize but no pesos, and the seller is usually willing to take either. There is a slight preference for pesos, as they are more negotiable and more easily carried home, but almost any seller will accept maize for his wares toward the close of a bad market day rather than carry them home unsold. The Ladino merchants use maize in much of their trading with the Indians.

Most divisible goods are sold in the markets in one-peso quantities, although manufactured objects, such as furniture, bags, and metates, are sold for from ten or fifteen to ninety pesos each. The Indians seem to dislike to spend more than one peso for each purchase or with each seller. On market day they buy a peso's worth of lime, a peso's worth of coffee, etc., and then repeat their purchases from the same or different sellers until they have bought as much as they need. Because of the tendency to spend only one peso at a time, the sellers use measuring gourds which hold only one peso's worth, or weighing stones which equal in weight a peso's worth of the commodity sold. Less expensive commodities, like shelled maize and beans, are sold merely by quantity, a peso a gourdful, but more expensive ones, like ground coffee and cacao, are sold by weight, a crude native-made balance, probably of Spanish origin, being used.[18] The manufactured objects such as furniture, bags, and metates vary greatly in price[19] from ten or fifteen

[18] It consists of a small stick, about one foot long, suspended in its exact center from a cord which is held in the hand. Cords hang from each end, the bottom ends of which are attached to the gourds on three sides. One of these contains the weighing stone, and the other, the commodity.

[19] Pottery containers sell for from one to four pesos; bags, three to twenty; hammocks, fifteen to eighty; hats, six to ten; thirty-foot ropes, six; baskets, one to three; fishing nets, twenty to eighty; household furniture, one to thirty; a woman's skirt, about eighty; and a metate with mano, fifty to eighty.

to ninety pesos each, but smaller articles like cigars, pellets of copal, soap, indigo dye, starch, and candles are mostly made of a size which can be sold for one peso.

Aside from their obvious exchange value, the silver pesos have for the Indians an intrinsic value that does not depend upon such a thing as government backing. Long use has habituated the Indians to their shape, size, "feel," and appearance, and they are accustomed to think of them as being actually worth the goods for which they are exchanged. The quetzal money, being new, does not have this inherent value or genuineness; the paper currency especially does not, since this lacks even the value of being made of a precious metal. And, lacking inherent value, its exchange value is doubtful. The notion that the new money has value because of government decree is foreign to the Indians, and few of them seem to understand it. They take the word of the Ladino merchants and officials that such is the case and that the pesos have lost their value, but they are not fully convinced.[20] They have always refused to accept anything but pesos, and, when forced to accept other Guatemalan coins, rushed to a Ladino store to exchange them for pesos. Only the few middlemen, who are accustomed to marketing in Chiquimula and Zacapa, will accept currency.

As a general medium of exchange, the pesos are used in the *aldeas* in payment for labor in the milpas and at the sugar presses, in payment for professional services from the *padrinos*, curers, diviners, and others, as a substitute for the communal labor which is exacted by the *municipio* officials, and in paying fines to the alcalde's office. The

[20] It seemed in 1933 as if several years would be required for the Indians to be able to transfer the inherent value of the pesos to the new money, after which time the latter would automatically take on enough exchange value for the Indians to make full use of it.

first two are just as often paid for in kind, usually in maize, although most of the Indian laborers prefer pesos. Light fines are usually paid in pesos, although heavier ones are wiped off the books by imprisonment, a certain sum being allowed for each day in jail. Some of the wealthier Indians pay the alcalde five pesos for each of the ten days which every Indian man is required to work repairing the trails of his *municipio*, and thus avoid this work. The pesos are used as gifts between individuals, as between the families and *padrinos* during transition rites, and they are offered to the deities as gifts in return for sending the favors asked for. The ceremonial gift is in the form either of actual pesos or of copal pellets made in the form and shape of pesos and is always called a "payment."

The pesos have aesthetic, protective, and curative value in themselves. The men wear a single peso in the outer ear-opening both as an ornament and to prevent and relieve earache. A peso is perforated, strung on an agave twine, and worn as a neck or ear pendant by men, women, and especially children, both as an ornament and as a charm, like the pendant cross, for warding off sorcery, evil spirits, and apparitions.[21] Many of the Indians provide for future security by burying quantities of pesos against drought, loss of property, and old age,[22] since there is no individual or

[21] The prevalence of this practice is shown by the fact that about a third of the coins collected by the bank agent at Jocotán were perforated. The holes were filled with copal gum to make them appear whole, since neither the Ladino merchants nor the bank agents would accept or pay for perforated coins.

[22] This practice increased after the pesos were being called in. The Indians were confident that before long the government would see its "mistake," after which the pesos would have their former value. The agents knew of this, but could do nothing beyond issuing more and sterner warnings. After many of the wealthier and more conservative Indians began turning over their pesos, the agents were astonished to discover how many of them showed signs of having been buried for a long time. According to the agents, no one had suspected that the Indians owned so many pesos.

institution in any of the pueblos with whom money could be deposited. The city of Chiquimula contains a branch office of the government bank, but at the time of this study the Indians feared the government too much to intrust their money with it. The wealthier Indians derive a small income from lending pesos to others, especially to the professional traders, at an interest rate of 50 per cent a month, but this is not a general practice.

CHAPTER III

AGRICULTURE

THE MILPA

THE Indians cultivate food and industrial plants[1] in milpas, gardens, orchards, the courtyards of the houses, and in earthenware and wooden vessels. The method of cultivation is that of tillage: the only implements used are the machete, the planting-stick, the ax, and the hoe,[2] and no working animals whatsoever are used, except that dogs guard the milpas when the ears of corn begin to form. In both the highlands (Olopa *municipio*) and the lowlands (Jocotán *municipio*) the same agricultural methods are used, although the types of plants grown in each section are slightly different, owing to the differences in rainfall and temperature.

Wherever possible, the milpas and gardens[3] are made square or rectangular, each plot square with the cardinal

---

[1] The generic term for plant is *te'*, which specifically means "wild tree," as *wai te'*, "conacaste tree," "conacaste plant." Any cultivated tree is *te·r*, or *te·r-ar*, as *u te·r-ar e kakau'* ("its tree the cacao"). For plants which grow both wild and cultivated, the cultivated variety is *arak te'* (*arak*, "tame," "domesticated"; from *ar-i*, "to give birth"), and the wild variety, *q'opt-ar te'* (*q'opot*, "wild vegetation," "forest"; *q'opt-ar*, "wild"). Thus, *arak itc*, "cultivated chili," and *q'opt-ar itc*, "wild chili." The cultivated name is applied to wild plants after they have been transplanted in the courtyards and orchards. See Glossary for the generic terms for plants.

[2] The agricultural tools are described on pp. 172–73.

[3] The milpa is called *tcor*, and a field of *maicillo*, cane, or rice, *rum*. *tcor* denotes only a plot the principal plant in which is maize. A maize field worker is *ah tcor*, or *ah tcor-w-ar*. The garden is *ut rum* (*ut*, diminutive, *rum*, "earth," "soil").

points, the corners, pointing to the northeast, the south
east, the northwest, and the southwest. The square shape
is said to be necessary because the altar is square, the altar
and milpa being considered equivalent.[4] But this is not always possible, because most of the cultivable land is extremely hilly and covered with stones or large boulders. In
laying out a new milpa,[5] a coral tree is planted at each of
the four corners to serve as boundary markers (*mo'*, *oix*).
Running in straight lines between the trees on all sides are
usually to be found *piñuelas* or other spiny plants, set close
together to form an impenetrable fence. Milpas, measured
with a stick (*p'ihs-ip'*) said to be as long as both the arms
outstretched, have no standard size, which depends rather
upon the wealth of the owner and the amount of available
land which can be cultivated in his vicinity.

The milpa crops are maize, vine beans, pumpkins, and
other vine vegetables. Maize is grown in many varieties.
Certain types are grown only in the lowlands, certain types
only in the highlands, while others grow in both sections.
The highland types include a reddish maize called in Spanish *barroso* (Ch. "red maize"), a yellow maize, a type called
in Spanish *maíz bayo*, a white spotted maize (Sp. *maíz
sangre de Cristo;* Ch. "blood maize"), and "forty-day
maize" (Ch. "tiny maize"). The last is very small and is
planted in separate milpas at the beginning of the rainy
season, principally in the highlands. It yields in about
forty days, thus providing the highlanders with fresh
maize until their major crop ripens. The lowland types
include a red maize and a greenish-black maize (Sp. *maíz*

[4] See p. 430.

[5] Milpas are often made in or near spots where the *cucaracho*, a wild shrub, or
the *sinquín*, a tall wild cane, grows in abundance, as these are said to enrich the
soil and to grow only in soil most suitable for maize.

negro; Ch. "green maize"). The types which grow in both sections are black maize, *tepezinte* maize, *majoco* maize, white maize, and a whitish maize called in Spanish *maíz pushagua,* or *maíz raque* (Ch. "white maize"). Some of the Ladinos and a very few of the Indians plant a second crop of maize in the highlands in November and December; it ripens by the following February or March. It is called in Spanish *apante maíz,*[6] and in Chorti, "dry-season maize." Dry-season maize, however, is said not to grow well at any altitude.

The ears are in general rather small. The principal colors are red, white, yellow, and black, although many shades of these colors are produced. The black is used mostly in making *atol,* the ceremonial drink, and the white, for making *chilate.*[7] The yellow is made into foods and remedies for strengthening the body. Any maize is used in making *tortillas,* the principal maize food. The ears usually contain grains of several colors, a fact which the Indians cannot account for, as they are ignorant of the process of pollination.

Beans, the varieties of which differ, as in the case of maize, in the highlands and lowlands, are of the vine and shrub types. Shrub beans are almost always planted in separate gardens, grow to about two feet in height, and yield eight or ten pods each. Two crops can be planted without irrigation in the space of a rainy season. Vine beans are planted always with maize or sugar cane, and there is only one crop annually, since they require more time than the shrub beans to ripen. Both types of beans are planted in the first part of May, with the advent of the

---

[6] The term is applied to any dry-season crop, as *apante* beans and *apante* pumpkins.

[7] See p. 430.

rainy season. The vine beans are harvested usually in November, and the shrub beans in August. The second crop of shrub beans is planted in September and harvested in December. In the latter part of January a third crop of shrub beans is planted on land which can be irrigated, and this is harvested usually in March.

The vine beans are of six varieties. A black bean (*frijol talete*, *frijol pacho*), a black, violet, and spotted bean (*frijol pocajul*), and the Mexican string bean (*frijol perome*, *ejotillo*, *ejote*, *cachito*) are commonly grown in the highlands. The last is quite small, of a dull black or ashy color, and is sometimes grown in the lowlands as well. The *frijol Chaján*, or *frijol enredador*, is also grown in the highlands and is of four colors: black, red, white, and spotted. The two lowland vine beans are a black bean (*frijol de rienda*) and a variety which resembles the Lima bean (*frijol Chapaneco*, *frijol gigante*), which is both light red and black. The shrub beans, all of which grow equally well in both highlands and lowlands, include a black bean (*frijol Terezo*), a red bean resembling the navy bean of the United States, a white bean also resembling the navy bean, a small black bean (*frijol arbolito*, *frijol siete caldos*, *frijol chapín*), another small black bean, and a black bean which is covered with down (*frijol vellano*). All types are made into a great variety of foods, rivaling maize in importance in the diet, and are used medicinally as well.

Pumpkins are grown in both highlands and lowlands, planted in May and harvested in September and October. The three varieties are black, dark white, and yellowish. They resemble those of the United States but are smaller. The shapes are round, flat, and elongated; all are eaten. The flower is large and edible. Pumpkins and pumpkin seed are especially eaten on ceremonial occasions, such as the Day of the Dead. Two other types of pumpkin grown are the *guicóy* and *pepitoria*. The former is a squash, grown mostly in the highlands. The latter is not edible, although its seeds are ground and mixed with tamales as a condiment. The cilacayote, or *chiberre*, is a ground vine with large fruit, green and slightly sweet, resembling a watermelon. It is planted in May, only in the maize and cane fields, and yields fruit in January. It is probably of Asiatic origin and is of little importance to the Indians. Watermelon is planted in the maize and cane fields in May and yields from September through November. The large sweet fruit is much liked. The muskmelon is planted in May and yields in September and October. The fruit is small and green and not very sweet. Neither watermelons nor muskmelons are of much importance and are planted only occasionally. The *melocotón*, or *melón de olor*, is occasionally cultivated in the highlands.

There are four important cultivated gourd plants: two vines and two trees. The gourd vine is usually planted in the milpas and yields a bottle-shaped fruit with long neck which is made into water canteens. The calabash vine yields an elliptical fruit which is made into dippers, ladles, and spoons. Another variety of this is the *barco*, the round fruit of which is made into bowls, saucers, and drinking cups.[8]

The clearing of wild vegetation[9] from the milpas and gardens begins and ends during the dry season which precedes the planting of each crop. In both highlands and lowlands the clearing season usually begins in January and is

---

[8] Gourd containers are described on pp. 144–45; calabash trees, on p. 65.

[9] Wild vegetation, especially that which is small and useless, is called *q'opot* (Sp. *monte*), a term which seems to be of Nahuan origin. It probably means forest, as well.

continued spasmodically until some time in April,[10] at which time the dry season is drawing to a close. In Jocotán *municipio*, where a second rainy-season crop of maize is planted, the second clearing of the milpas is done at the end of August. The vegetation cut down is allowed to dry for several weeks and is then raked into piles and burned when a strong wind is blowing. The larger trees are left standing, to be cut down later after repeated firing has dried the sap out of them. Since each milpa is cleared and burned several times, by the time planting begins the ashes have accumulated to a depth of several inches; they are left on the ground to serve as a fertilizer.

At the conclusion of the rain-making ceremony of April 25, and the ceremony to the earth-gods and consecration of the planting seed,[11] both of which are held on May 3, the planting of maize begins early on the morning after the first heavy shower.

Although each household or small family individually clears off the wild vegetation from its milpas prior to planting, weeds its milpas after planting, and tends and guards them during the ear-forming season, the planting, harvesting, and storing are always co-operatively done and are the most important of the co-operative economic activities. All the family males work at these tasks until finished, after which they begin helping neighboring families, until every family in the *aldea* has them out of the way. A half-dozen families may plant all their milpas together, the entire group working on one milpa at a time until all are planted, after which the men of each family

[10] The wild vegetation is somewhat denser in Jocotán than in Olopa, but in neither *municipio* is clearing as much work as it is in areas nearer sea-level, where the jungle growth makes clearing an extremely difficult task.

[11] These three ceremonies are described on pp. 437–44.

CHORTI MEN WITH PLANTING-STICKS, MACHETES,
AND GOURD CONTAINERS

visit others, partly as a way of being neighborly, to help in various ways.

The planting group of five or six or more begins at about five-thirty in the morning and continues until about eleven. A siesta of about two hours is then taken, during which time the noon meal (Ch. "midday") is eaten. Work continues until about five in the afternoon, when all go home to supper. This daily routine is followed by both Indians and Ladinos during the maize-planting season. Maize is planted with the planting-stick, the planter digging five or six holes all around himself while standing in the same position.[12] There is no attempt to plant in rows. The seed is carried in a small gourd which hangs from the left shoulder by a fiber strap. Five or six grains are dropped with the left hand into each hole[13] while the right hand manipulates the stick. The stick is driven four or five inches into the soil, swayed from side to side to open the hole, and the seed dropped in. The maize cobs from which the seed was taken are carried by one of the men of the family to a secret spot at some distance from the houses and hidden. In Jocotán they are buried in the

[12] Milpas and gardens are often cultivated on mountainsides so steep as to be very dangerous. In many cases the planter holds by one hand to a stone protruding from the soil and gouges out footholds with his machete on which to stand. In some cases the grade is so steep that the Indian ties a rope around his waist, the other end secured to a near-by tree. He plants all around this tree and then ties the rope to another.

[13] The holes are usually four *cuartos* apart, a *cuarto* (Ch. *q'ap'*, "hand") being the English span. If four *cuartos* apart, four grains are planted in each hole, and if five, five grains are planted. The former is more common and illustrates the ritual value of the number four (see p. 429). Bishop Landa (chap. xxiii) describes a similar method of planting in Yucatan: "This they do carrying a bag on their shoulders, and making holes in the ground with a pointed stick. In these holes they place five or six seeds, covering them up with the same stick" (quoted by Thompson, 1930).

ground, whereas in Olopa and Quetzaltepeque they are hidden in dense shady underbrush.[14]

The seeds of climbing beans, gourd vines, pumpkins, and other vine vegetables are planted in the same holes with the maize, so that several months later all these plants are growing from the same spots. The beans entwine around the maize stalks, using them as supports, and the pumpkins and other ground vines utilize the space among the stalks.

Eight days after the planting, the ceremony to the wind-gods[15] is performed. The planting of other cereals, sugar cane, vegetables, and fruits is not accompanied with ceremony, since it is felt that the earth-spirit and wind-god ceremonies serve for all the crops of a given year. As soon as the maize has sprouted, about a week after the planting, a replanting is done in the same milpas. Seeds are planted in the spots where no sprouts appear, so that within another week the milpas are thickly covered with young maize. A replanting of beans is done in the bean gardens at the same time. Other vegetables are seldom replanted. Until the maize is waist high the Indians are almost continuously occupied with destroying weeds, which if left alone would grow shoulder high and nearly impassable in a few days. The first weeding is done around June 1 and is repeated at the end of the month. By this time the maize is about three feet high, and no more weeding is done. The machete is used in this work. The Indian squats and drives the end of the instrument under the soil, thus cutting the weeds and digging up their roots. He moves across the milpa in this fashion, cleaning a whole swath as he goes. Vegetables are also weeded until they attain sufficient growth to be left to themselves. The orchards are seldom

[14] See pp. 337, 339.   [15] See p. 444.

weeded, except around the base of the trees, although coffee groves and banana orchards are always kept clean.

Traps[16] are set in the milpas, gardens, and orchards as a protection against marauding birds and animals. Crows are the most destructive pests, with the exception of weevils, with which the Indians have to contend, since it is said that a small flock of them can clean out a milpa in a few hours.[17] During the sprouting stage thin strips of plantain bark are stretched in zigzag fashion from the ends of sticks set upright in the ground all over the milpas and are left there until the maize grows about them. It is said that the birds will not light on a milpa thus protected, as they fear the strips to be a trap. The snare, deadfall, and rat trap are used for capturing small mammals, and the bird trap is used for birds.[18] All the traps are left in the milpas until the maize has become hard and ripe. They also protect the maize during the roasting-ear season from hungry dogs which, not being fed at home, take to stealing the young ears. All dogs, except those which have been trained to watch property and to hunt, are tied up near the houses during this season and are not released until the ears have ripened. Poison is also set in the milpas and gardens to kill marauding animals.[19]

[16] See pp. 74–77.

[17] Other bird pests include the blackbird, hawk, blackhawk, raven, duck-raven, *shesheque*, and sparrow hawk.

[18] These seem to be used more as a protection for the milpas than for securing edible meat, although the latter is usually eaten.

[19] The poisons used are all native grown, some producing temporary convulsions while others are fatal. Maize, of which the animal pests are fond, is the principal base for the poisons. It is ground to a paste and the ground parts of the poisonous plants mixed with it. These consist of roots, seeds, fruits, sap, bark, and leaves. The preparation is placed in ollas and left in the trails leading to the

After the ears begin to form, the milpas are guarded day and night by the men of the families, who take turns sleeping in a temporary shed which is built in or near the milpas. It is built like the ordinary house, except that it has no walls and is low. It is used for sleeping at night and as a protection from the sun and rain for the day watchers whose special task is to frighten away crows and hungry dogs. The watcher sometimes keeps a shotgun, and his food is brought to him by the women of his family. During the night a fire is sometimes built in each milpa and wood piled on to keep it burning until morning. This is said to scare away all pests and is a very common method of milpa protection.

Harvesting is of greatest importance in connection with maize, sugar cane, beans, cacao, coffee, and rice, since these are the most valuable crops. Other plant foods, being of much less importance, are harvested in rather desultory fashion.[20] For example, it is seldom that an entire potato patch is harvested. The family who owns it will secure a few from time to time for their own use; but, unless someone else wishes to buy potatoes, which is rare, the rest are left to rot.

Maize is harvested around the middle of August in the lowlands and in November in both highlands and lowlands. Two or three weeks before harvest time the stalks are cut about halfway through just below the ears and the tops allowed to hang downward in order to dry properly. This renders the maize comparatively safe from weevils

---

milpas. The most important of the animal-poisoning plants (*tcam-san-i-ar te'*) are the *chiltepe* chili, *chilillo*, *chilindrón blanco*, *chipilín*, *jabillo*, *loroco*, *madre cacao*, *higuero*, and jimson weed.

[20] This may be because of the extreme predominance of maize and beans in the diet and because the Indians have no methods of preserving for a long period any foods other than maize, beans, rice, cacao, and coffee. These, however, are harvested with great care and completely utilized.

and mold when stored. Harvesting continues for ten to fifteen days and is done by the men only. While several of them cut the ears off the stalks with the machete, others transport them in large agave bags[21] and carrying cases to the near-by storehouse. The carrying case,[22] which is carried on the back with the tumpline, is used principally for transporting maize on the cob, vegetables, and fruits. The ears are piled on the ground in front of the storehouse where they remain to dry until the harvesting is finished. On the last day of the harvest the families provide feasts for themselves and the others of the *aldea* who helped them in their work. Next day the ears are stacked in the storehouse, at which time the storage ceremony is performed.[23] The best and largest ears are laid aside, tied by their shucks in pairs, and slung over the kitchen rafters and beams to be used as seed the following year. The stalks are left to dry in the milpas, after which they are pulled up and brought home to be used as fodder for the cattle during the dry season.

Many families shell their maize before storage. For this a special thresher[24] is set up temporarily in front of the granary or sleeping-house; this thresher is also used for

[21] See pp. 160–61 for the manufacture of these.

[22] It is made of various light canes and dried sunflower stalks and is rectangular in shape, being about two to three feet long, one foot wide, and two feet deep. At the corners the ends of the stalks are notched to fit one over the other in alternate order, as in the construction of the corner of a log wall. An agave twine is then passed from the top of each corner to the bottom, being wrapped around the joints of the side and end pieces so as to bind the joints together. The bottom pieces are tied on in the same manner. This case corresponds in type and use to the carrying box with four legs used in the western Guatemalan highlands.

[23] See pp. 446–47.

[24] Four five-foot poles are set up in the ground to form a five- or six-foot square. Across the tops of these are laid connecting poles, and over the latter is laid a reed or cane covering of the sort used for covering beds (see pp. 132–34). The canes which form the cover surface are placed closely enough together so that the threshed grains may drop through while the ears and shucks remain on

beans and rice, both of which are always threshed before storage. A helper shucks the ears and lays them on the thresher, while the operator beats them with a heavy stick. The cobs are used as firewood. The thresher is torn down after the harvesting. Sometimes threshing is done by placing the husked ears in a large agave bag of the type used in carrying maize on the cob. The bag is then placed on a mat on the ground and beaten with the stick. The openings in this bag are too small for whole ears and cobs to slip through.

In harvesting beans, the entire vines are pulled up with the hands, carried to the houses, and placed in the sun for several days to dry. They are then laid on the thresher and beaten until all the pods have fallen through to the mat below. The thresher cover is then exchanged for one the vertical strips of which are much closer together, and on this the pods are beaten until the beans have broken loose and fallen below. They are winnowed on the first windy day in the courtyard by pouring them from one basket into another, allowing them to drop four or five feet through the air. The beans are then "cured," placed in ollas, and stored in the storehouse and kitchen. Shrub beans are usually picked by hand in the gardens and threshed and stored in the same way.

FIELD, GARDEN, AND ORCHARD CROPS

The important field and garden crops are sugar cane, tobacco, rice, forage grasses, and vegetables.

Sugar cane, introduced to America shortly after the Conquest, is planted at any time of the year, although

---

top. A short stick is set up on each of the vertical poles and to these are tied banana or cane leaves on three sides, leaving the operator's side open. This wall is about a foot higher than the thresher itself. A mat is placed on the ground underneath to catch the maize.

usually in August, and special fields are devoted to it. A single planting is said to serve for four or five years and, if properly weeded and irrigated, for an even longer time. Only one crop a year is produced. It is grown by the Indians principally in the middle-highland *aldeas*, of which Tunucó is the most important in the *municipio* of Jocotán, although some of the lowland Ladinos of Jocotán raise it and manufacture sugar with modern machinery.[25]

Tobacco is planted in October and November, and the leaves are cut in April for curing. The seed are first sown in large ollas, in wooden "canoes," or in special plots of ground, after which the young sprouts are transplanted to the tobacco fields. Great care is taken to protect them from ants. It is said that very few of the Indian tobacco planters are able to keep their plants alive until maturity. Tobacco has many medicinal uses and is one of the most important plants which the Indians possess. It grows to about five feet in height and is harvested once a year. Tobacco is principally a highland plant but will grow in the lowlands if irrigated. Nearly all the Indian men smoke it in pipes, but it is almost never chewed except in curing ailments.

Rice, grown only in the highlands, around Olopa and La Unión, and brought to the lowland markets for sale, is planted in separate fields after the milpas have been planted, in May. In the harvest, in November, the stalks are cut in the middle, and the upper portions tied together in small bundles. These are transported to the houses and spread out on tables, mats, or the roofs of the houses to dry for several days in the sun. After the drying the bundles are untied, placed on the thresher, and beaten until all the grains have separated from the stalks and fallen through.

[25] See pp. 99–104.

For threshing rice the cane strips of the thresher cover are placed extremely close together. The seeds are then placed, a handful at a time, into the coffee mortars and beaten with a pestle to remove the husks. They are winnowed on the first windy day. If the rice is to be stored, the bundles of stalks are tied in pairs, as in the case of maize, and hung on the kitchen rafters. Rice, which is very commonly eaten, can be kept in this way for two or three years.

The hay and forage plants grow wild, but most of them are also cultivated to some extent in separate fields. The wild stalks are gathered in the hills in May and transplanted to plots near the houses. One planting suffices for several years. The Indians seldom use them as forage, as they have no beasts of burden and few cows, but they regularly sell hay in the pueblo markets to the Ladinos, many making most of their living in this way. The most important is the *zacate amargo*, which is semicultivated and resembles sugar cane. The stalks are cut principally in July and August, as they are fresh and green at that time of the year. Important as cattle food are the dried maize stalks taken from the milpas after the harvest.[26]

Maicillo is a tall grass or cane which grows both wild and cultivated to about ten feet in height. The fruit, which grows at the top of the stalk, is round and white and about half the size of the chickpea. It is planted in May, after maize-planting is out of the way, in separate fields and yields in November and December. The wild variety, *maicillo montés*, resembles the cultivated one, except that it has black seeds. The plants are used as a forage for cattle, the flowers are tied in bundles to make brooms,

---

[26] Other important hay and forage plants are the *camalote, conejo (mesmético), coronita, mozote, teosinte, parpar, pará, habanero,* and *pelo de mico* grasses, the *conte* vine (*hoja de conte*), and *güisquilete*.

and the tough stalks are used in fence-building. The seeds are eaten like maize and made into a delicacy.

The vegetable gardens, which contain only vegetables of the herb or shrub type, are planted in the same way as the milpa, and the planting-stick is used. They are usually planted in May, a week or so after the maize. The gardens, laid out like the milpas, but usually smaller, are located wherever there is available space, often in small spots between the milpas. They are usually nearer the houses, probably because the women sometimes weed and harvest them. Vegetables are often seen growing in plots two or three feet square all around the houses. The garden normally is planted with only one kind of vegetable, if the owner is well to do, but the poorer families usually plant two or three kinds together. The herb vegetables are never grown in the milpas.

Without irrigation, dry-season tillage would be impossible. Maize is never irrigated, since it is a rainy-season plant, but plants which grow only during the dry months, nonperennials of which three crops a year are planted, and annual plants such as coffee, sugar cane, and fruit trees, must be irrigated during the dry months. Water for irrigation is obtained from streams and springs, and all crops requiring irrigation are planted conveniently near them. Sugar cane and dry-season vegetables are often planted in the same fields to facilitate their irrigation. The main ditches, of which the average *aldea* has two or three, pursue as straight a course as the terrain will permit as they run from a stream at the upper end of the *aldea* to rejoin some stream again, perhaps several miles away, at the lower end. Each leaves the stream at an oblique angle and runs from it in the general direction of the current. The opening is filled with earth and stones which can be pulled away with a hoe when desired. A solid row of stones, and sometimes piled logs, stretches partly across the stream to divert the water. The main ditches are often built along the summits of small ridges as well as along the sides of hills, each with a trail next to it so that it can be constantly repaired. It is dug by pulling the earth out on both sides with hoes to form embankments, until the ditch itself is two to three feet wide and about a foot deep.

Radiating from both sides of each main ditch are the smaller subsidiary ditches, which connect with the cane fields, gardens, and orchards some distance away. These orchards are usually located on steep inclines, the upper rims of which have a narrow flat surface along which the smaller ditches may run. The small ditches meander considerably in order to pass above as much irrigated land as possible before rejoining the main ditch at a lower level. When an Indian wishes to irrigate, he taps the main stream by pulling the earth out of the opening of the main ditch, and then opens the wall of the subsidiary ditch in a number of places just above his own fields. After his land is thoroughly soaked, he closes the entrances above his fields so that others below him may irrigate without flooding his own land again. No sluice gates of any kind are used.

The chief vegetables grown are sweet potatoes, potatoes, tomatoes, chili, cassava, and mustard.

Sweet potatoes are planted early in May and ripen by November. They are reddish yellow and whitish in color and not exceptionally sweet. They do not grow wild but are cultivated in all parts of the Indian country. The Indians are especially fond of them and consider them an important vegetable. Almost every family in Tunucó plants one or more sweet-potato gardens every year.[27] The

[27] The Indians do not grow yams, although they were grown in the Copan Valley until a few years ago.

jícama, a vine resembling the sweet potato, is occasionally grown. Its fruit is eaten raw. The potato is small, round, and about an inch in diameter. It is planted, usually in separate gardens, in May or June, and ripens in October. It is strictly a highland plant and is brought to the Jocotán market from the *aldeas* of Olopa. A few are grown around Jocotán, but they are of poor quality. The Indians are very fond of them, but they are usually too expensive to buy in large quantities.

A variety of tomato, the tomatillo, is about one-half inch in diameter and is planted in separate gardens. If not irrigated, it must be planted in May and yields in November. The irrigated crop is planted usually in September and yields in March, although it is sometimes planted the year round. This variety grows both wild and cultivated, in both highland and lowland regions. A large variety, the *tomate de riñón*, resembling the ordinary large tomato of the United States, does not grow wild. When planted in May, it yields in August. These tomatoes are grown principally in the lowlands, as the Jocotán market is supplied with them from the Zacapa Valley, a very low area.[28]

Chili is grown in six varieties. The *chocolate* is red and fairly sweet. The *diente de perro* is grown in the lowlands and yields a small, green, and very piquant fruit. The *chile de zope*, or *lengua de gallina*, resembles the *diente de perro*. The *chile de relleno* is the so-called "sweet chili" and is the type used in the United States. It is the most commonly eaten. The *chileguaque* is always cooked with other foods. The *chiltepe* is the largest of the chili plants and yields a piquant fruit. Its leaves and shoots are eaten as greens. All are shrubs which grow to five or six feet in height and all are cultivated only, except the *chiltepe*,

[28] The small tomatoes are no doubt of American origin, but the large variety was probably imported into eastern Guatemala in fairly recent times.

which is found also in the wild state. Chili is usually
planted with other vegetables and can often be seen growing around the houses. If irrigated, it bears the year round,
but otherwise it yields only during August, September, and
October. It grows to some extent at all altitudes. Most of
the fruit is extremely piquant, and very little of it is required as a condiment. At least half the foods which the
Indians eat are seasoned with it.

Cassava, of South American origin, is a small tree or
shrub, about eight feet high, with a trunk about one inch
in diameter. The roots have a white meat which strongly
resembles the potato in taste and color. They are three to
four inches in diameter and as long as two feet. Cassava is
planted, usually in separate gardens, in August, and yields
edible roots within a year. It is normally cultivated, although it is occasionally found growing wild. The Indians
and Ladinos are very fond of the root (*u wi·r*). Also from
the root, starch is made, and it is the only type known to or
used by both the Indians and the Ladinos. The Indians use
it medicinally and surgically, as well as in making the
maize drink called starch *atol*. They sell it to the Ladinos,
who use it principally to stiffen clothes. The bark is removed from the root and the latter soaked in water for
eight days. It is then dried in the sun, ground to a powder
on the metate, and stirred in an earthenware pot of water
for about a day. The pure cassava, which settles to the
bottom, is squeezed in a cloth to remove the remaining
water and impurities. It is then patted into round pellets
and dried in the sun.

The cabbage is rather large but resembles lettuce. It is
planted in gardens with other vegetables late in April and
is ready to eat by July and August. It is principally grown
by the Ladinos. Onions are of a white and purple variety.

Both grow to about a foot in height and yield a small head which is slightly larger than garlic. The white onion is planted in November and ripens in two months. The purple, which is the rainy-season variety, is planted in April and yields in August and September. Both are planted in gardens, usually with other vegetables. The Indians usually buy the few onions they eat from the Ladinos. The cucumber, or pepino, is grown to some extent in the highlands. It is planted in both May and November and is eaten raw. Mustard, a cultivated plant of European origin, rarely grows more than six inches high. The seed are small and round and of a purplish color. It is planted at all altitudes in May and yields in November. The seed are used as a condiment and are regularly sold in the Jocotán market by the Indians.[29]

The medicinal plants are often grown in separate patches, each household or family having a small patch near its houses, but usually they are planted in the family courtyard in any available space. They are described principally in chapter xiv.

Pot plants are grown both in large earthenware vessels and in hollowed-out logs called canoes. Containers are used because the plants are said to be too frail to be planted in the ground and because they would be quickly devoured by the pigs, chickens, and turkeys unless set above the ground. A few holes are broken through the bottom of the olla to permit stale water to pass through. The vessels are kept aboveground, usually in the fork of a large

[29] Very few of the Indians plant beets, turnips, and radishes; but all the Ladinos raise and eat them. Beets and turnips, planted in November and December, ripen by April, and radishes, planted in November, are eaten from December to March, so that all three are dry-season vegetables. The peanut is also largely a Ladino plant. A few of the Indians around Olopa raise them and toast them on the *comal* for eating.

stick about five feet high which is set up near the houses. The canoe is set aboveground on several large stones, and its bottom is also perforated. The plants are watered by the women and girls of the household. The three important pot plants are garlic, peppermint, and coriander, all of which grow only with cultivation. They are used principally as condiments.

The orchards[30] are usually square, like the fields and gardens, and are often inclosed with fences, although they have no boundary markers. Nearly all are located conveniently near springs, so that irrigation can be carried on during the dry season.[31] Small ditches run from the nearest spring and are interlaced among the trees in order to keep the soil flooded day and night during the dry months. Many orchards are planted along the banks of streams in sandy soil and in such cases require no irrigation. Throughout the Indian country orchards are to be seen along both banks of all the streams, and these usually contain such trees as produce fruit throughout the year. Fruit trees, and sometimes small orchards, are occasionally planted around the houses, and these are watered by small ditches which run from a main irrigation ditch not far away. The average orchard contains at least a dozen varieties of fruit trees, the most important being the banana and plantain, upon which the Indians rely considerably during the dry season when maize is scarce. Every household has a banana and plantain orchard at the nearest stream or spring or growing near its courtyard.

Small saplings are secured from the hills or from other

[30] The orchard is denoted either by the term *pahq'-ip'* or by attaching the locative *ta* to the name of the plant grown in the orchard.

[31] The *sirasil* shrub is planted around these springs, since it is believed to prevent their drying up during the dry season.

orchards and set out about a dozen feet apart. The transplanting of wild trees and shrubs goes on constantly. Almost every Indian, when on a hunting, fishing, or trading trip, digs up interesting and useful plants which he brings home to replant in his courtyard or gardens. Most of the family courtyards contain many such plants. The trees bear fruit in a comparatively short time, especially in the lowlands, where the climate is warm and the rainfall heavy. Not much work is done in the care of fruit plants beyond irrigation and an occasional clearing of weeds. Bananas and plantains, because of their importance as foods, are usually well taken care of. The lower leaves are regularly cut from the trunk and the dead bark pulled off from time to time. Most of the other trees, except for an occasional watering, are uncared for. Orchard plants consist of all the fruit trees, coffee,[32] and a variety of plants which are used for industrial and medicinal purposes.

Bananas are of seven varieties. The *manzano* produces a small fruit. The *majoncho*, *cantiado*, and *habanero* grow to about twenty feet in height. The fruit has a reddish peel, and, unlike the other bananas, it grows downward. The *dátil* and *criollo* produce a medium-sized fruit which is usually boiled. The *mínimo*, or *guineo de seda*, is the best of the bananas and is the type generally exported to the United States. The plantain is grown in all the orchards and, like the bananas, is an important food during the dry season; it is also used medicinally. The banana-plantain resembles the banana more than the plantain and is eaten raw. It is not important.

The citrus fruits, which grow only when cultivated, include oranges, limes, lemons, and grapefruit. The sour

[32] Coffee, requiring constant shade for proper growth, is always planted under fruit trees or specially planted shade trees.

orange bears in August and September. The fruit is large and sour and is usually eaten with salt. The sweet orange is a small tree which bears from August to October. Its fruit resembles the orange of the United States and is principally used in making beverages and preserves. The lime yields a very acid fruit from August to December. The juice is nearly always mixed with chili before the latter is used as a condiment and has so many medicinal uses that it can properly be called a panacea.[33] The sweet lime, which bears in November and December, yields a fruit which tastes like an orange but looks like a lemon. It is very commonly grown and eaten. The lemon, grown only in the lowlands, yields from August to November. It is occasionally made into lemonade but is not common. Grapefruit is sometimes grown in the lowlands. The fruit is large and slightly sour. It is grown mostly by the Ladinos. The citrus fruits are usually planted around the houses and seldom in separate orchards.

The sapodilla, probably not native, is a semicultivated tree which bears in March and April. Its greenish-brown fruit is about the size of a lemon and has reddish, stringy meat. It is very commonly eaten. The white annona is a cultivated lowland tree, of American origin, which bears in September. It is planted usually in orchards but is never irrigated. The sweet fruit is much liked and is commonly eaten. It is one of the few plants used for surgical purposes. The mamey is extensively grown. The fruit, about the size of a *guacal*, has a yellow meat.

Cacao is a native cultivated lowland tree which bears annually. A frothed drink made from the roasted seeds is much consumed ceremonially. Until about fifty years ago

---

[33] It is said to be a very "cool" plant and so is used to reduce fevers, swelling, and inflammation.

the dried seeds were used as a medium of exchange among the Indians in the Jocotán and Olopa markets.[34] Cacao is picked and carried to the houses in large fiber bags. The seeds are cut out with a knife and spread on a table or mat in the courtyard to dry for several days. When thoroughly dry and hard, they are roasted like coffee on the griddle, ground on the metate to a powder, and stored in gourds.

The *patashte* tree, which is related to the cacao, is occasionally grown in the lowlands. A cacao drink is made from its seeds, but is not much liked. The fruit is not eaten.

Coffee, which is grown only in the highlands and usually at an altitude of about three thousand feet, is usually planted in separate orchards and always in the shade of other plants.[35] It bears for five or six years, beginning after the second year, and yields from October to February. The beans are pulled from the shrubs and brought in gourd containers to the houses, where they are spread on mats to dry. They are then husked in a wooden mortar especially used for coffee-husking, winnowed with baskets, cured in various ways, and stored in mat bags.

The coconut, a cultivated lowland palm, bears the year round and is usually planted in separate orchards. The fruit is not often eaten but is much used medicinally. The pineapple, a cultivated highland plant about three feet high, bears in May and June. The fruit, which is eaten raw, resembles the *mescal*. The sweet pineapple is grown in the lowlands, and another variety, called "water pineapple," is grown in the highlands.

The avocado, one of the most common fruit trees, is a

[34] See p. 34.

[35] The *cuje* tree (also called *cujín* and *cujinicuil*) is planted in the coffee *fincas* for shading. It yields a fruit which is eaten raw.

large tree which bears from June to September. It is irrigated during the dry season. The fruit is eaten raw with meals and is made into salads by the Ladinos. Many Indians regularly bring the fruit to the Jocotán market for sale. The *chucte*, which resembles the avocado, is a semicultivated tree, planted in irrigable orchards in the lowlands. It bears from May to June. The huisquil is a native clinging vine which resembles squash. It is planted in orchards near the trees, up which it climbs. It is planted in May and is eaten in August and September. The fruit resembles the avocado and is very commonly eaten. The nanse is a cultivated native shrub which bears in July and August. The small fruit has a sweet yellow meat which is eaten raw as a delicacy. The bark is much used in tanning hides. The *piñuela* is a cultivated coarse herb which resembles agave but is closely related to the pineapple. It yields fruit and shoots three times a year—in February, April, and September. The bulb, fruit, and shoots are very commonly eaten. *Piñuelas* are often planted in straight rows to serve as fences around milpas and courtyards.

The izote is a cultivated plant about fifteen feet high, usually planted in or near the courtyards. The edible crest of the trunk is eaten from April to July, and the flower is boiled and eaten as greens. The izote is also planted to serve as fences. The papaya is a very common native cultivated tree which grows at all altitudes and bears in March and April. Irrigation is said to spoil its roots. The fruit, which resembles the cantaloupe, is eaten raw. The zapote, a native cultivated tree, bears in March and April. It is planted in irrigable orchards and is watered during the dry season. The large red fruit is much liked. The matasano, also native, is semicultivated and bears a white mushy fruit in April and May. The *membrillo* is also semicultivated and resembles the zapote. It yields an extremely acid fruit from August to November. The *alberja*, or *arbeja*, yields a fruit resembling English peas, in November and December. It is grown mostly in the lowlands.

The jocote is of five varieties. The *corona* is semi-cultivated and grown in the lowlands. The fruit, which has a sweet yellow meat, is eaten raw. The *zamarute*, or *amarillo*, is cultivated only, and bears in July and August. The fruit is very sour and seldom eaten. The *San Jacinto* is cultivated and yields in March and April. This is the only one of the dry-season jocotes. The *agrio*, or *pitarillo*, is a wild variety. Its acid fruit is not eaten but is used medicinally. The *jocotillo* is wild and not commonly used for any purpose. The shoots and buds of the jocotes are eaten as greens during the rainy season. Two other cultivated trees which yield greens are the *copapayo*, or *chayo*, and the bay tree, or *laurel*.

The cashew is a lowland, semicultivated, native tree with red and yellow fruits which ripen from May to July. The seeds are toasted and eaten, and the Ladinos make a wine from the fruit. The *jurgáy* is a semicultivated lowland tree which bears a small fruit in May and June. It is usually planted along stream banks. The jobo is a semi-cultivated lowland tree which bears around June. It is especially planted in the coffee groves to provide shade for the coffee plants. The fruit is acid and is commonly sold in the markets. The mango is semicultivated and grows at all altitudes, bearing in the lowlands in May and in the highlands in August. It is one of the commonest of fruits among the Indians and, like bananas and plantains, is one of the principal means of subsistence after the maize stores are exhausted. It is much used medicinally. The *zunza*, or *zunzapote*, is a semicultivated native tree which bears in July. The fruit resembles the mamey apple but is much sweeter. It is commonly planted in cane fields, in orchards, and near the houses. The achiote is semicultivated and is usually planted in orchards. It bears a green spiny fruit in January and February. The seeds are ground and boiled and made into a red sauce which is used as a coloring for foods, especially tamales and rice. The achiote is grown extensively in both the highlands and lowlands.[36] The vanilla vine is planted in the orchards and yields a year after planting. A vanilla beverage is much drunk by the Ladinos.

Agave is grown in separate orchards by each fiber worker. The average orchard contains from fifteen to twenty plants. The leaves contain fiber which is netted and woven into a variety of articles. The three varieties grown are the *Castilla* (*henequén*), *cimarrón*, and *mescal*, of which the first, which is cultivated only, is the most important. Cotton is not extensively grown, as the Indians do no cotton-weaving. Almost every family cultivates five or six plants in its orchard or around its houses, principally in the lowlands. The fiber is made into candlewicks and spun into a thread which is netted into bags and fishing nets and used for mending clothes. The plant grows to six or seven feet in height. The royal palm yields shoots at its crest which are somewhat bitter, although edible from September to April. These, called *pacayas*,[37] are baked in hot coals or cut into pieces, boiled to remove the bitter taste, and commonly eaten in the dry season. The

[36] Less important orchard fruits include the guanaba, guamá, huskcherry, *poshte*, breadfruit, tamarind, *guaicume*, peach, *yemas de huevo*, sour pomegranate, *chan* shrub, and allspice. Most of the important fruits grown by the chorti are described in detail by Popenoe, 1920.

[37] See under "Pacaya" in Glossary.

unopened fronds are sewn together and worn as raincloaks and are woven together to make brooms. The "hat palm" also yields *pacayas*, which are much eaten. Its fronds are especially used in weaving hats, twined baskets, and brooms. The palms are sometimes found growing wild, but more often have been transplanted to the fruit orchards. They grow only in the lowlands.

The calabash tree is semicultivated and of two varieties. One yields an oval fruit about a foot long and six inches in diameter (Sp. *jícaro;* Ch. *simax*), the other, a round fruit (Sp. *guacal;* Ch. *rutc*); both are made into bowls.[38]

Jiquilite, from which indigo dye is made, is the most important of the dye plants. It is lowland and semicultivated and grows to about ten feet in height. The dye, which is taken from the leaves, is a deep blue.[39] The *cuajatinta*, a cultivated highland shrub, also yields a blue dye, inferior to indigo. The *tinta de monte*, also called *saca-tinta* and *hierba de tinta*, is a cultivated native shrub about six feet high. The leaves are boiled with clothes as a bluing. It is seldom used as a dye, as the color is not fast.

[38] Gourd vines are described on p. 43; the manufacture of gourd utensils, on pp. 144–45.

[39] Until about thirty years ago a great deal of it was exported from Jocotán *municipio* to all parts of Guatemala, but the general preference for analine dyes has now ruined the industry. Indigo dye-making is described on pp. 183–84.

CHAPTER IV

ANIMALS AND WILD PLANTS

THE Indians do not domesticate any wild animals at the present time, except for an occasional parrot, parakeet, or dove which is taken in a trap, tamed by the children, and kept as a pet about the house.[1] Monkeys and parrots, brought from the lowland coastal regions, are sometimes sold in the markets as pets, although the Indians seldom keep them. The domestic animals include cattle, pigs, dogs, chickens, turkeys, and honeybees, of which fowls and bees are of the greatest value. The Indians know of goats and sheep but do not keep them. No Indian owns or uses any riding or carrying animal but always transports on the back with the aid of the tumpline or on the head with the basket, and walks when traveling, regardless of the distance.

Most families keep from one to half-a-dozen pigs. They are usually disposed of through sale to the Ladinos in the markets and nearly always on the hoof, since the Indians

---

[1] No doubt in the past a number of wild animals were captured and domesticated, as is shown by terms in the native language. The prefix and noun *arak* is attached to the names of domestic species, while the prefix and noun *q'opt-ar* is attached to names of all wild species (see n. 1, chap. iii). These prefixes are used only in the case of animals which exist both in the wild and in the domesticated state and not in the case of those which live only in the one state. For example, any piglike animal is *tcitam;* the domestic, or European pig, *arak tcitam*, and the wild pig, or peccary (Sp. *javalí*), *q'opt-ar tcitam*. Similarly, the European chicken is *arak aq'atc*, and the wild mountain hen, which is native, is *q'opt-ar aq'atc*. The Indians probably thus transferred the names of native animals to similar ones which were introduced after the Conquest.

do not butcher to any great extent. Pigs are bought when weaned, kept tied to a long rope in small cleared spaces until they are grown, and then led to market to be sold. The breeding of pigs is principally a Ladino activity. The raising of pigs is considered a means of making money and not often as a means of providing meat food for family use. This may be partly caused by the fact that the Indians have no thorough meat-preserving techniques. However, soap is made from hog grease as well as from a number of wild and domestic plants.[2]

Cattle are of little importance, probably due to the fact that the steep inclines which are everywhere to be found and the thickness of the natural vegetation make impossible the keeping of many large animals. Cows are kept by very few of the Indians. Those who have them usually have only one, and the milk is invariably made into cheese[3] to be sold in the markets. The cows are milked (Ch. "to squeeze") once daily, the average giving two quarts or less a day. Young boys stake them out to graze wherever an open spot is to be found and bring them home at night. Cows are too few and valuable to be frequently butchered, but the meat is always eaten or sold whenever a cow dies of disease or age.[4] The Indians usually sell their few pigs and cattle on the hoof to the Ladino butchers. A few butcher for their own needs, in which case the owner invites the men of neighboring families, perhaps eight or ten, to assist him and gives each a chunk of meat for his help.

Aside from their money value as a food, cattle are valuable for their hides, which are sold to the leather-makers

[2] The manufacture of both kinds is described on pp. 181–82.

[3] It is said that one reason for this is to protect the cows from sorcery (see p. 339, n. 33). The manufacture of cheese is described on p. 106.

[4] The Ladinos suspect all the meat they buy from the Indians to be diseased.

for the manufacture of sandals, bags, and leathern tumplines.[5] Oxen and bulls are used only by the sugar-makers for drawing sugar presses. Most of the bulls are castrated[6] when about two years old. The finest which the owner possesses is not castrated but is kept for breeding purposes, although this is much more an activity of the Ladinos. Many of the wealthier sugar-makers own six or seven oxen and one bull, but the poorer ones merely hire oxen from other pressers in the same *aldea* during the pressing season.

Nearly every family has at least a dozen turkeys and perhaps half as many chickens, while the wealthier Indians own large flocks. Both fowls and eggs are almost never eaten secularly by the Indians, being used principally for ritual purposes, although they are regularly sold in the markets to the Ladinos. Fowls are made to forage for most of their food but are usually fed maize every other day.

A number of families, mostly in the *aldea* of Matasano, supply the Jocotán market with honey which they secure principally from wild bees, of which the *talnete* is the most important.[7] These are small and black, have no sting, and are native to eastern Guatemala. A few families keep domestic bees of the European type, which are large and yellow, although these are owned principally by the Ladinos. Since the wild bees do not remain long in one place, the bee-keepers are continually on the lookout for new swarms. They are called "wild" before being caught but receive the domestic name as soon as they are set up in a hive. Bee-keeping is engaged in to some extent by nearly

---

[5] Leather-working is described on pp. 178–80.   [6] *cur-i u qu·m*, "to castrate."

[7] Wild black bees, called in Spanish *chicote*, are dug from the ground (Ch. "earth hive") when young and carried home to be boiled and eaten. They produce no honey.

all the Indians. The bees, which live principally in hollow pine trees, logs, and stumps, are discovered in the hills and their honey taken home in a jug or gourd to be eaten or sold. If the finder is a bee-keeper, he cuts the tree in two above and below the bees themselves and carries the log, which is about four feet long, to his house to serve as a hive.[8] A number of flowering plants, usually wild shrubs but occasionally fruit trees, are planted near the houses to increase the honey yield. The honey is taken from the hives only once or twice a year, since the bees produce very slowly. The owner takes out the mud from one end, inserts his hand, and pulls out the comb. The comb is squeezed in the hands, and the honey strained through a basket sieve several times to clean it. It is finally strained through a cotton cloth and brought to the markets in small pitchers and bottles. The comb is boiled until it solidifies and is used as a substitute for copal wax. The Indians occasionally boil honey with foods and drinks, but they usually sell it (since it brings a good price) and use native sugar as the principal sweetening.

Every family owns at least one dog, which is kept to guard the premises, and some families have four or five which are used for hunting. Some are obviously of European origin, but most are small, with little hair, and very likely are aboriginal varieties. Hunting dogs are trained by the professional hunters to bring down small animals and birds and especially to assist in deer-hunting. Good hunting dogs bring a high price to the owner, although they are

---

[8] He fills the ends with mud and stones, ties a rope around each end, and suspends the log from the eaves of the sleeping-house. In some cases two poles are set up in the ground, about five feet high, and the log laid in their forked ends. The whole is usually covered with a layer of banana leaves to keep it dry. Some bee-keepers have five or six such hives, which are constantly replaced with newly discovered ones.

seldom sold. They are the only dogs which are at all cared for, being well fed and given medicine when ill.[9] Untrained dogs are seldom fed, with the result that they become community pests, and special poisons are set in the milpas to destroy them during the ear-forming season.

HUNTING, TRAPPING, AND FISHING

Hunting is done principally with shotguns and only very occasionally with the bow and arrow.[10] The latter is sometimes used for birds and for killing animals caught in the traps, but it is primarily considered a toy. Until about forty years ago, blowguns were made and used for hunting purposes, but are now unknown to any but the older Indians. They were used principally for killing birds, small darts being blown from them.[11] Most of the shotguns are antiquated and nearly worn out. As they are expensive to buy and use, only the professional hunters own them.[12] For hunting large animals, such as deer and mountain lion, a single large lead bullet is used. On the outer end of this a cross is cut with a knife and the lines filled with beeswax. This is called "curing the bullet" and is said to be done to insure correct aim. Deer and coyote, above all other animals, are said to be shot only with cured bullets.[13]

[9] A necklace of lemons or limes strung on a cord is placed around the animal's neck to cure it of a variety of ills, especially colds.

[10] See p. 296 for the manufacture of bows and arrows.

[11] Blowguns are still used at Jacaltenango (La Farge and Byers, 1931, p. 64).

[12] The Indians do not buy shells, as they are too expensive, but buy the powder in bulk form and stuff the shot, powder, and wad into a breach loader. The powder is carried in a steer's horn strung on a twine which hangs from the shoulder. The wad consists merely of agave fiber. The caps and shot are bought from the Ladino merchants.

[13] At Mitla, "enchanted deer" must be shot only with a bullet which has a cross scratched on it (Parsons, 1936, p. 476).

Game-hunting is done individually, but deer-hunting is usually done by groups of two or three to a dozen men, the man who owns the one gun in the group being usually a professional hunter. Deer are nearly always hunted at night, although this is said to be difficult because of the underbrush and roughness of the trails. It is not necessary in most of Jocotán and Olopa *municipios* to go far in search of edible animals; the hunters usually merely go to the nearest mountaintops out of range of the houses, although they sometimes journey eight or ten miles from home. The principal hunting season is during February and March, at which time the deer, because of the comparative drought, are forced down from the higher hills in search of food and so can be easily found.

The hunting ceremony is performed only in the case of deer and is said to be repeated before each hunt. It is done at midnight, and early the next morning the hunters set out for the locality where deer might be found. The man who owns the shotgun stations himself in the underbrush, a few feet from the trail. His companions spread outward from his position, perhaps for several miles. They form into a line, each several hundred yards from the next, and proceed toward the gunner, driving all the game before them. Much of the small game escapes, but the deer are forced along the trail, where the gunner shoots them as they run by. For night hunting, torches are carried to light the trails and for blinding the deer. The light is reflected in the animal's eyes, and the gunner, who stands to one side and in front of the torchbearers, is thus enabled to aim at its head. The Indians say that the torchlights act as a charm upon the deer and prevent their taking instant flight at the approach of the hunters. The meat is divided among the group equally, except that the gunner gets the largest share of all, or if there is more than one gunner present, the larger share goes to the one whose shot brought down the animal.

The hunting ceremonies are directed principally to the deer-god,[14] who is the patron of deer, to propitiate this deity, to make payment to him for the animal about to be taken, and to secure information from him as to where deer may be found. Before the hunter sets out he must have a dream, in which the deer-god informs him of the price he must pay for the animal. He is told that he must pay a certain number of pesos, and this is done by burning in an incense burner an equal number of "pesos" of copal gum. Many Indians say that, if hunters do not make proper payment to the deer-god, they will have no luck, and the deer, because of the god's anger, may leave the locality. The hunter prepares his copal pesos and burns them at midnight before his altar, offering them to both the saints and the deer-god. At midnight of the next day the hunter or group of hunters go to any of the hills which the deer-god inhabits and pray to him, asking again if they may have one of his animals. In some way they are said to receive his answer. The deity is then asked where one or more deer may be found the next day, and the petitioners are told.[15]

Next morning at dawn the hunting party set out for the locality to which they were directed, usually in the higher

[14] See p. 400.

[15] It is said that no professional hunter would dare hunt until he had his dream, even over a period of months. A hunter stated that he might travel into the hills looking for deer, perhaps "just for fun," but if he had not had his dream and made the proper payment, he would not touch any of them. If he is unable to have the dream, he can hire a *padrino* (see pp. 373–74) to do it for him for about fifteen cents. The *padrino*, who is said to be much more able to have dreams than other people, gets the required information and passes it on to the hunter. None of the informants could explain how the deer-god's answers are given or interpreted.

mountains. While the men are away, the women at home burn copal and pray to the family saints that the hunt be successful, sometimes burning candles on the altar. The hunters, on returning, shout to the women when within a half-mile or so of the house that they are bringing a deer. The women immediately heat copal gum. The deer is laid on the floor of the kitchen or in front of the house; if it is a doe, a man's hat is placed on its head, but, if a buck, a woman's shawl is used. The men then incense the carcass with copal fumes to purify the meat. The incense is said to drive out evil spirits from the dead body.[16] In order to insure success in the hunts thereafter, the horns are sometimes hung from a rafter in the sleeping-house. Most sleeping-houses, especially those of professional hunters, contain a set of deer horns.

The Indians who live in the *aldeas* near Jocotán pueblo, where there is very little wild game, do almost no hunting, but those in the remoter *aldeas*, where game is plentiful, engage in it to a greater extent. The former usually buy the little meat they eat, which is more often pork or beef than anything else, in the Sunday markets. The hunted animals are eaten,[17] and the hides of many are used for making bags, sandals, and belts.[18] Other animals are occa-

[16] The hat probably represents the male aspect of the deer-god, and the shawl, the female aspect, and in either case is said to be an act of thanks and respect to the deity (cf. the treatment of a dead deer by the Zuñi [Parsons, 1939]).

[17] Those used for food are the armadillo, bullfrog, deer, the iguanas, *micoleón*, *musaraña*, opossum, peccary, *perro de agua*, *pizote*, rabbit, raccoon, spotted agouti, squirrel, *taltuza*, tapir, tepesquintle, and tortoise. The armadillo and tortoise shells are made into basket-like containers.

[18] The tapir hide is made into sandals. The hides of the anteater, coyote, guanas, jaguar, *micoleón*, *oso colmenero* bear, peccary, *pizote*, puma, raccoon, skunk, spotted agouti, squirrel, tiger, *tigrillo*, weasel, and wild cat are made into shoulder bags. Snake hides are made into belts worn by the men to support their drawers, although snakes are primarily used medicinally.

sionally killed, but they have no use.[19] Birds are not often eaten, although most of them are considered edible;[20] the plumage of the tail feathers of a few birds are used to adorn altars.[21]

Trapping is done to protect the milpas from marauding birds, wild animals, and stray hungry dogs who steal the young ears and to provide an incidental supply of fresh meat. The traps are usually set in or near the trails which lead to the milpas or gardens, as the animals frequent the milpas at night, and are sometimes set in the mountains near springs. They are used for capturing all wild animals except deer. The traps (Fig. 2) include the snare, deadfall, rat trap, and bird trap; the snare (*f*) is the most commonly used. A small sapling the top of which can be bent to the ground is found on one of the trails leading to the milpa. Two posts are set up in the ground, about three feet apart, and a crosspiece is tied into their forked ends. Another crosspiece is placed against the uprights, on the inner side of the trap, and a foot or so from the ground. The upper end of the trigger stick, which stands vertically, presses against the outer side of the upper crosspiece, while its pointed end at the bottom presses against the inner side of the lower crosspiece. The sapling is bent down and con-

[19] These include the *charancaco, cotete, lagartija, salamanquesa,* and land snail.

[20] The edible birds are the *aurora, chacha, chaparral, chorcha gato,* wild duck, *garcita, guarda barranca, guava, guía de león,* heron, loriot, macaw, martin, mountain hen, mountain turtle dove, partridge, patacoon, *paujil, perico ligero, posoroco, preuchillo, pucuyo,* quail, *quebranto hueso,* quetzal, ringdove, *shara,* swallow, toucan, turtle dove, woodcock, woodpecker, and *zenzontli.* The bat (believed to suck the blood of white cows at night), jay, blue-bottle bird, *caballero, chacola* (a black vulture), *chipe cabeza canela, chunchuncillo,* cuckoo, eagle, nightbird, *pijije, pijúy, piscóy,* sparrow, and thrush are considered of no use, although a few of these are sometimes eaten.

[21] These include the *chacha,* woodcock, peacock, and quetzal.

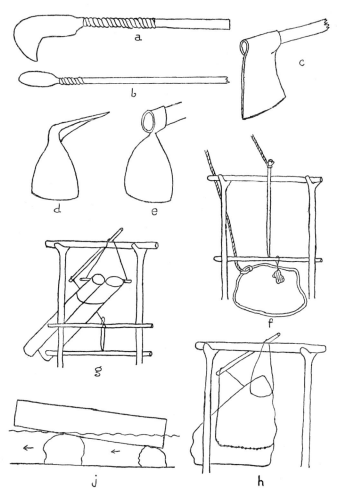

Fig. 2.—Agricultural implements; traps

nected to the upper end of the trigger with a rope. Thus, the upward pull of the sapling holds the lower crosspiece in place. The bait is tied to the latter. A noose, one end of which is tied to the bent end of the sapling, is laid on the ground in front of the trap, in such a position that the animal will probably be standing in it when the trap is sprung. The animal pulls at the bait, thus pulling the lower crosspiece downward and releasing the bottom end of the trigger; the sapling flies upward, taking the noose with it, and the animal is usually caught by one of its legs. The noose is sometimes hung downward in front of the trap with the bait directly behind it, so that the animal will have its head within the noose when it pulls at the bait. Poles are usually set up all around the snare trap in order to force the animals to get at the bait from the front side where the noose is.

The deadfall (g) is used principally in capturing raccoons,[22] whence its Spanish name. It employs the same principle of trigger release as the snare, except that the upward pull of the sapling is provided for by the downward pull of two heavy logs, the front ends of which are suspended several feet above the ground. The trigger is held by two crosspieces, the lower one just high enough above the ground so that the animal, in order to enter the trap, will probably step on it, thus releasing the trigger and allowing the logs to drop on the animal directly below.[23] The rat trap (h) is set principally in the maize storehouses to kill field rats, and sometimes in the kitchens and sleeping-houses. It is of the deadfall type but makes use of a heavy flat stone, the front end of which is held above the

[22] Raccoons and crows are the worst of the milpa pests and are especially dreaded by the Indians when the ears begin to form.

[23] This same deadfall trap is used by the Bachajon of Chiapas (Blom and La Farge, 1927, pp. 352–53).

ground. A twine, strung with pumpkin seeds as a bait, is passed around the center of this stone, and the rat, gnawing at the seeds, bites the string in two, thus releasing the trap and allowing the stone to drop. The seeds are placed on its underside, in order to get the rat in the proper position. The bird trap is used both to capture crows and other birds in the milpas and by children at play. It is like that used in the United States. The box is an ordinary carrying crate, one side of which is tilted slightly aboveground so that the birds may enter it to secure the bait.[24]

Fishing is done in nine ways, most of which are used according to the season and the consequent condition of the streams. During the dry season, poisons, lime, dams, seines, and dynamite are used, as the water is low and too clear to make direct capture possible. When the streams rise and become muddy and turbulent after the rains have set in, the fish trap, nets, basket, and diving are employed. The hook and line, though unimportant, is used the year round. Poisoning is the most common method. No ceremony is performed in connection with fishing, although there may have been in the past.[25]

Poisons are used only from January to May (*Ch.* "fish-poisoning season"), when the streams are low and quiet and the water can be poisoned thoroughly. They are used principally at the sides of streams and preferably in deep, quiet spots. The poisons are obtained from a large number of wild plants, all of which contain a sap or milk which produces toxic effects in varying degrees without being fatal.[26]

[24] The boys whose work it is to guard the milpas often divert themselves by setting these traps all over the milpas and, from a hiding place, watching with great glee as the birds walk into them and imprison themselves.

[25] Cf. Thompson, 1930, p. 90.

[26] The most important are the *bejuco de barbasco* vine, *bejuco de pescado* vine, *camote silvestre* vine, *camotillo* vine, *ceibillo* shrub, conacaste tree, *matapescado* shrub, *zopilote* tree, and the *siete pellejos*. Slaked lime (*tan tcix*) is also much used.

The stalks and leaves of the desired plant are tied in bundles and laid on a rock which has been placed in the water. One of the fishermen beats the leaves on this rock with a heavy stick, at the same time throwing water on them with his left hand. The sap thus trickles into the surrounding water. Sometimes the plants are beaten in the wooden mortar and carried to the stream to be thrown in. Several of the fishermen stand all around in the water and stir it continuously with long sticks as a means of spreading the poison. After a half-hour the fish are completely paralyzed and floating on the surface.[27] Other fishermen pick up the fish and carry them home in small shoulder bags which they carry.

The fish trap (*j*) (Ch. "fish bed") is especially used during the rainy season, as its success depends upon a swift current. It is built mostly of light cane so that it can be easily carried from one stream to another, and is rectangular, having two vertical sides and a flat bottom, but no top covering. It is about ten feet long, two feet wide at the front end and six or seven at the rear, and is about a foot high along the sides, thus resembling a flat-bottomed boat with pointed bow and wide stern. The framework is of small limbs, tied at the joints and intersections with bark string, over which the canes are laid lengthwise, as in the manufacture of bed coverings.[28] The canes are about a half-inch apart, sufficiently close together to prevent the

[27] It is said that the sap of these plants burns the eyes of the fish, causing them to thrust their heads above water to escape the pain. They are also said to be temporarily "put to sleep." Poisons must be used only when the moon is in the quarter-stage or they will have no effect, since during that time the plants are said to contain the strongest and greatest quantities of the sap. For fish-poisoning only the hands may be used, since it is said that, if a net or other contrivance is allowed to touch the water, the fish will immediately revive and swim away.

[28] See p. 132.

fish from passing through but not so close as to restrict the current. The trap is laid, with the wide end facing the current, in a mountain stream where the current is swift and narrow, the object being to force as many fish into it as possible. It is set upon rocks, with the wide end partly submerged and the narrow rear end slightly raised above the water. The fish enter the open wide end and, owing to the force of the current at this spot, are carried forward along the bottom of the trap to the inclosed rear end, where they are out of the water and helpless. The current prevents their turning back to escape at the front. The fisherman stands at the rear end and stows them in bags or pots to be taken home.

The fishing nets are of three types: the *ataraya*, a throwing net; the *chinchorro*, a dragging net; and the seine (Ch. "shoulder net").[29] All three are used only during the rainy season, when the turbulence of the streams permits the fishermen to stand in the water without frightening off the fish. The *ataraya* varies from three to about six feet in diameter. A retrieving rope about ten feet long is attached at one end to its center, and at the other end to the fisherman's left wrist. A heavy twine is attached to the outer rim of the net, and strung on this, necklace-like, about two inches apart, are stone or lead weights which carry the net to the bottom. Another twine is run in zigzag fashion all around the rim and is drawn somewhat tighter than the netting itself, thus causing the rim to be slightly constricted and allowing the interior of the net to bulge outward. The fisherman stands in the stream, folds the net in half, and lays it across his right forearm, with the weighted end nearest his hand. He hurls it forward, the weights fly outward from the center, and the net settles

[29] For a description of netting see pp. 156–61 and Fig. 10, *a* and *b* (p. 157).

on the water like an open parachute, trapping all the fish under it. With the retrieving rope he slowly raises it, dragging the weights, and the fish with them, toward the center. When the weights have all come together, the net is lifted clear. The restriction of the rim and interior bulging of the net, plus the weight of the leads, prevents the fish from falling through. He opens the net on the bank, transferring the fish to earthenware vessels, or remains in the stream and places them in a netted bag hanging from his waist.

The *chinchorro* is a small limb bent into a circle, over which is loosely spread a net. It is usually about two feet in diameter and resembles a butterfly net. The netting is allowed to hang seven or eight inches downward from the rim and is secured to the rim all around with strong twine. The hoop is attached with twine to the end of the handle— a small limb about eight feet long. The fisherman stands in three or four feet of water and drags his net around himself in a half-circle, imitating the sweep of a scythe.[30] As he scoops up fish he transfers them to the netted bag at his waist.

The seine is used only by those who live near the Jocotán River, as it is not practicable in small streams. It consists of two nets, each about forty feet long and seven or eight feet wide, which are netted from large agave twine as in the case of all the netted bags. They are weighted on the bottom with leads or stones. The nets are stretched across the stream, with several men holding the ends of each. They drag the nets toward each other, allowing the weights to scrape the stream bed. When the two are brought together,

[30] *tcihr, hur tcihr, "ataraya* net"; *hur-i e tcihr,* "to throw the *ataraya"; tcint'cox,* "*chinchorro* net"; *kerehp'-a e tcint'cox,* "to drag the *chinchorro"; kerehp' tcihr,* "seine."

they are lifted clear, opened on the bank, and the fish placed in large bags or pots.

In diving, the fisherman descends into a deep spot at the side of the stream and retrieves the fish with his hands (Ch. "hand-fishing"). This method is used only in the dry season when the streams are quiet and clean, as the fisherman must open his eyes to locate the fish. The men of the party take turns at diving, the diver throwing the fish up to the bank and his companions retrieving them. Women sometimes do the work on the bank.

The hook and line is never used by professional fishermen and seldom by others, except boys. Earthworms, bits of *tortilla*, and the buds of certain trees are used as bait on the hooks. Dynamiting is seldom used, as the cost of dynamite is prohibitive to most of the Indians. The game laws of Guatemala prohibit its use, but in 1931–33 the law was said to be seldom enforced. During the dry season the Ladinos did a great deal of dynamiting in the Jocotán River at night.

Dam and basket fishing are engaged in principally when maize and beans are scarce. The dam is built in the bed of a stream which is only a few feet wide and very shallow. It is of stones laid on top of one another to a height of about two feet, with clay forced into the cracks to make it almost watertight. The dam first crosses the stream diagonally, passes along the bank in the same direction as the current for a few feet, and then recrosses the stream. The two walls are then about seven or eight feet apart. The wall facing the current is slightly below water, while the second is built several inches above. The fish pass over the first wall and are thus caught between the two, where the women easily catch them with their hands. Both the walls are sometimes built above water, thus diverting the small stream from its bed, after which the space between the two walls is partially emptied with large ollas, and the fish which happened to be in it caught. This is too laborious a method for common use, however. The dam is used only in the dry season, when there is little water to contend with.

Basket-fishing is done during the rainy season, as it requires muddy water and a swift current. Each fisherwoman uses a single large basket, about three feet in diameter. She walks upstream in the middle of the current, holding her basket under water in a vertical position, and lifting it clear every few minutes to retrieve the fish caught in it. Because of its close weave even minnows cannot pass through it. This is the same method as that employed by the women to cleanse the maize kernels after they have been boiled with lime to soften the husks.

Fishing with nets and the hook and line is done individually, but fishing with poisons, dams, seines, traps, and by diving is done by groups of a dozen or more men. Usually five or six men co-operate in dragging a seine or paralyzing fish with dynamite, and as many as a dozen women may build a fish dam together. The catch is divided equally. The larger families do most of their hunting and fishing by themselves, each family constituting the cooperative group, although the smaller ones nearly always team up with others.

The Indians are not familiar with many species of fish and do not eat them with any regularity. Most of the catches are sold in the markets to the Ladinos. The average fish sold in the Jocotán and Olopa markets are scarcely larger than minnows, but they are easily sold. Occasionally a fisherman comes in with fish eight or ten inches long, in which case there is a mad scramble to buy his supply. The Jocotán River is the only stream in Jocotán *municipio* which contains many fish, and there are perhaps three smaller streams in Olopa which are regularly used.[31]

PLANT AND MINERAL COLLECTING

Greens are collected principally during the rainy season, from May to November, during which time the leaves, shoots, and buds of the greens plants are tender. After November the edible parts become tough and usually of bad taste and so are seldom collected until May of the following year. Wild fruits are, of course, collected throughout the year, and principally during the dry season, from November to May, since there is less maize, beans, and fresh greens during that time, and the wild fruits available are much needed. The women of the family, often six or eight, usually journey in a group, each with a basket on her head or hip, to the hills and stream banks in search of every kind of edible plant. They are often accompanied by small boys whose work it is to climb the trees and shake down the fruit. They may travel five or six miles from home, leaving early in the morning and returning shortly before night. Such co-operative collecting is done especially in May and June, when the fresh greens and fruits are available and much desired. During the rest of the year the women of each household make short trips alone to collect the few they can find.

The most important of the wild food plants are those which produce leaves, buds, shoots, and flowers which are boiled as greens, and those which yield fruits. A few of the wild fruits are especially edible and as much liked as any of the cultivated fruits, but most are either of bad taste or more or less tasteless and are eaten only when other fruits

[31] The important fish include the *cacaricu*, catfish, *cucaracha*, *cuyamel*, crab, crawfish, eel, *jute*, *jutuja*, *machaca*, *pecháy*, *pepemechín*, perch, *pescadito*, *pescado blanco*, *platiada*, shrimp, tadpole, *tepemechín*, trout, and water snail.

and foods are not available. Greens are the most desired of all wild vegetables, almost no meal during the rainy season being complete without a bowl of boiled greens. Of the many dozens of plants which produce edible greens, those highest in favor are the wild amaranth, the coral tree, the *chipilín*, the *loroco*, the *palo jiote*, and the jocote. Wild amaranth is a small weed with reddish stalk and light-green leaves, which is eaten as greens from May to August; a similar species, called *bledo rojo*, or *quilete rojo*, also provides edible leaves and shoots. The coral tree, yielding heart-shaped leaves the year round, is occasionally planted near the houses and in the milpa corners as boundary markers. The leaves and buds are edible throughout the year, but the flowers can be eaten only in November and December. The leaves are said to induce sleep if placed under the pillow at night. Many articles woven of agave fiber are dyed yellow with the coral bark.

The *chipilín*, or *chipilín de comer*, is a shrub of American origin about ten feet high, which yields small leaves and dry pods from August to November. It is sometimes transplanted to the gardens and courtyards and is said to live about three years. Its greens are perhaps the most commonly eaten, usually boiled with beans or rice. The flowers are much eaten with maize preparations. The poisonous roots are mixed with maize paste and placed in the milpas to kill marauding animals. The *loroco* is a native vine which entwines around trees. The long leaves are said to be edible the year round, and the flowers are eaten in July and August. The poisonous roots are also used to kill marauding animals. The *chayote*, a variety of *loroco*, also yields edible greens. The *palo jiote* tree yields leaves and shoots which are eaten in May and June. It is often planted in the courtyards, as much to provide shade as food. The living trunk is used as the vertical bar of the family yard cross, for which purpose it is planted on May 3 each year. The jocotes, especially the wild varieties, yield many edible leaves and shoots during the dry season.[32]

The following are the most important wild fruits. The wild annona is a native lowland tree which bears in March. The fruit resembles the cultivated annona, but is not so well liked. The *capulín*,[33] a native tree which yields red fruit about the size of an olive, ripens in the summer. The *pacaya* is a small highland palm which produces edible shoots on its trunk. They are slightly bitter but are eaten from December to April. The *huiscoyol* and *palmiche* palms also yield crests which are eaten. The wild grape is a clinging vine with fruit slightly larger than peas and very sweet. It is eaten raw in May and June. The *guana* nanse is a wild shrub with yellow acid fruit which bears in March and April. The allspice tree yields seed which are boiled with vegetables as a condiment. The *chununa* is a climbing vine the fruit of which resembles a pear. It is sweet and ripens in November and December.[34]

Two types of mushroom are gathered, chopped up, and mixed in maize dumplings, or *shepes*. The *canturul*, or *canturuque*, is yellow and is found principally in pine forests. Another type, of white, yellow, and purple varieties, grows in decayed wood.

Firewood is collected throughout the year, as it is needed

[32] Other wild greens plants include the purslane, *quilete, quilete de zope, quilete de danta, Santo Domingo* herb, *chufle, guachipilín, yagüirir*, and *culantro de tripa*.

[33] The Spanish name of two varieties of wild cherry.

[34] Other wild fruits are the *irayol (jagua)*, guava, *moco de gallo, suncuya, jilotillo (seisoco), aguacate de mico* (a wild avocado), *zapotillo, pepeto, palo de llorón, cirín de pava, cordoncillo, piña de garrobo* (a wild *piñuela*), and the aceituna, the fruit of which resembles the jobo.

every day in the kitchens for cooking, as well as at various times for sugar-making and many of the manufacturing processes. The men usually collect it individually for their own kitchens. Almost all the smaller wild trees and shrubs are used, although the few long-burning species are preferred.[35]

Many of the wild remedial plants are bought from the herbalists, although most are secured by the family of the sick person, the women and girls going out to the hills to find the plants they need.[36] Wild industrial plants are collected usually only by the professionals who use them in manufacturing; they are described under other headings.

Most of the minerals[37] are collected by the professionals. Only one mineral, salt, is used as a food, and it is not obtained in either Jocotán or Olopa *municipio*. Lime, important in the preparation of maize for food, is found and made by most Chorti families.[38]

[35] The principal of these are the *aguja de área, marío, plumajillo, chaperna, cojón, cucaracho, tepemiste, tempisque,* and *shaguáy*.

[36] The most important remedial plants are described in chap. xii.

[37] The important minerals include salt, large river stones upon which clothes are washed, flintstone (Ch. "cloud stone," "stone-fire"), black paintstone, limestone, granite (Ch. "metate stone"), red sandstone, pumice stone (Ch. "white stone"), greenstone, yellow sandstone, sand, ordinary sandstone, and various transparent stones.

[38] Its manufacture is described on pp. 177–78.

CHAPTER V

FOOD PREPARATION AND STORAGE

COOKING AND EATING

THE four cooking techniques, in the order of importance, are baking and toasting on the griddle, boiling, baking in hot coals and ashes, and roasting on the spit. As the inclosed oven is not used, toasting is done on the *comal*, or griddle, as in the case of unprepared foods like coffee, cacao beans, shelled maize, and fish, and prepared foods like *tortillas*. Boiling is used in preparing most vegetables and cooked fruits, such as greens, tamales, *shepes*, and unshucked spring maize, and in preparing all the drinks, such as *atol*, *chilate*, coffee, and cacao. Baking in the open fire or in hot ashes is done without the use of containers, as in the case of spring maize to be eaten on the cob, pumpkins, *pacayas*, and other fruits, and foods which are reheated before being eaten, such as the *totoposte*. Roasting[1] on the spit, notably of wild meats and certain fruits, is done with a special stick which has been hardened in hot ashes. Frying in fat is seldom done.

Maize in some form is eaten three times a day every day of the year, and it is used as a base in a great variety of other foods. Almost every food has some maize in it, and even the important coffee and cacao drinks are made with equal amounts of maize. The *tortilla*,[2] the most important

---

[1] Chorti, "to bake with the stick."

[2] Food is called *we'*, which also means "to eat," but often the Indian refers to his food as *ni pa'* ("my tortillas"), as *u-q'an-i im-patn-a tua' in-mor-i ni pa'*,

of the maize preparations, is made usually of only maize paste and water and is virtually the only type of bread eaten.[3] Prior to cooking, the ears of maize are brought by the women from the storehouse and shelled in the court-yard, in large agave bags (as described on p. 50), in the coffee mortar, or by hand, the latter being the most common method. The women press the base of the palm, or the part near the wrist, against the grains, thus prying them off. The fingers are not used. Shelling in the mortar is not often done. Nearly all the maize which is shelled from day to day for family use is done by hand in the kitchens. The shelled maize is boiled overnight on the fire-place in an olla of lime water to soften the husks. Early next morning the water is poured off, the boiled grains (Sp. *nistamal*) placed in a basket, and fresh water poured over them to cleanse them of the lime. This is often done in a near-by stream, in which case the basket of maize is held with its open side against the current and the water al-lowed to pass through until the maize is clean.

The operator places two or three handfuls of the grains on the metate at the end nearest her and grinds them to a paste with the handstone, or mano. The metate rests at one end of the grinding table, at a level slightly below the operator's waist. Several grains are caught under the mano each time it is rubbed back and forth on the metate, so that a thin sheet of paste is continuously spread from one end of the metate to the other. This gradually collects at the op-

---

"I have to work in order to get food." Sometimes *ni p'u·r* ("my beans") has the same meaning, though not often, and at times food is referred to as *ni pa' ni p'u·r* ("my maize, my beans").

[3] In the pueblos there are bakeries which make wheat bread, but the price is prohibitive for most of the Indians, and even those who can afford to buy it seldom eat it, since it is believed to cause stomach disorders.

CHORTI WOMAN GRINDING MAIZE IN OLOPA

posite end and falls into a basket or olla. The paste which collects at the sides of the metate is caught up with the fingers and placed in the center. Every few minutes the hands are dipped in water and the mano sprinkled to prevent the paste from clinging to it. After enough maize has been ground for the day, the paste is reground and sprinkled with water so that it will hold together more firmly. The operator works with stiffened arms, doing most of the work from the shoulders and back.

In shaping *tortillas*, the paste is not thrown from one hand to the other but is pressed by the base of the right hand against the palm of the left and given a final shaping with the fingers. Some of the women press them on a banana leaf which is laid over a bench or stool.[4] They are toasted on the *comal* as fast as they are made, each for a few minutes until it is slightly brown on both sides. No grease is used. Those not eaten for breakfast are wrapped in a cloth and covered with gourds. For later meals they are warmed up in hot ashes at the fireplace. The women usually prepare enough in the early morning to last the household for the rest of the day. Two women usually do this work, one grinding the maize and the other shaping and baking the *tortillas*.

Tortillas are made principally from hard ripe maize (Ch. "yellow maize"), since only ripe maize is to be had during most of the year. These are about a quarter-inch thick and five or six inches in diameter and are called "dry *tortillas*."

[4] The Ladino women in Jocotán lay a pinch of the paste in the left palm, flatten it with the right hand, and then proceed to slap it with the base of the right hand. After each slap the cake is turned slightly with the right fingers and thus goes clockwise around the left palm until it is of the desired thickness. The final slaps are given with the palm. This is the method used in Mexico. It is nearly impossible to sleep in the open after sunrise, when the loud clapping can be heard all over the neighborhood.

Two types are made from *elotes* (spring maize), one from young *elotes* and the other from spring maize just after it has begun to harden (Ch. "hard maize").[5] They are made much larger and thicker than those of the hard ripe maize and are softer and more palatable. The maize used in making them is boiled without lime, as the husks do not require softening. They are eaten, of course, only in the *elote* season.

The *totoposte*, a very thin cake usually made of hard ripe maize, is toasted to an extreme crispness and is the regulation food to be taken on journeys. Much salt is added to the paste before making them, no doubt as a preservative, since the Indians say they are not especially fond of salted maize. This is the only maize cake in which salt is used. *Totopostes* will keep for several weeks and are merely rewarmed when eaten. They are carried in a cloth in the shoulder bag. Indian travelers seem content to have eaten nothing but *totopostes* even after a week or more on the road.

Four gruels—*atol*, *atolágrio*, *chilate*, and *pinol*—and one cold beverage are made from maize. The gruels are considered more as foods than drinks. *Atol* made of spring maize is much consumed. The maize is ground raw on the metate and boiled with sugar and ground toasted cinnamon bark, after which it is strained to remove the paste. *Atol* made of ripe maize, which is much liked, is prepared in the same way, except that the maize is first boiled with lime. The boiling lasts until the liquid is thick and whitish. It is left to cool and solidify into a jelly and is often eaten with *tortillas*. *Atol* is much eaten as a daily food and at all feasts given in celebration of marriages, deaths, and saints'

[5] The first of these is called in Spanish *sispaque*, and the second, *sacuaz*. Both are called in Chorti "cold *tortilla*" or "fresh *tortilla*."

days. *Atolágrio* is merely unsweetened *atol*. *Chilate* is made only from ripe maize which is toasted, ground, and boiled with sugar. If consumed ceremonially, it is not sweetened, powdered cacao is added to it, and the mixture beaten until it froths.[6] The *pinols* are made of ripe maize which is toasted, ground, boiled, and flavored with the proper ingredient. They are not strained. For cacao *pinol*, the maize is ground with toasted cacao and the mixture boiled with sugar. It is then frothed and is principally drunk at meals. For pork *pinol*, the maize is ground with *pimienta gorda* and the mixture boiled with the soup taken from boiled pork. It is stirred to prevent the maize from forming into balls. Greens *pinol* is made in the same way, except that *chatate* greens and soup are used instead of pork. The maize beverage (Sp. *orchata de maíz*) is made from dry-ground maize which is left to soak in cool water, sweetened, and strained before being drunk. This is especially liked when made of spring maize.

Tamales are of three kinds: the chicken tamale, *elote* tamale, and bean tamale, or *shepe*. The first is probably a fairly recent importation among the Indians, as they seldom make them, but the second and third, which are commonly made, are doubtless native. About two dozen chicken tamales are made from one chicken, a small olla of maize paste, a handful of pumpkin seeds, a little chili and salt, a few tomatoes and onions, and about four ounces of grease.[7] Usually, achiote coloring is added to provide a

[6] This is made in great quantities by the women at the Jocotán *cofradía* and usually served gratis to the Indians on July 24, the patron saint's day (see pp. 449-50).

[7] The paste is boiled with the grease and salt, and the other ingredients are ground together and boiled with chicken soup. A layer of the boiled paste is first laid on a part of a banana leaf; on this is laid a small amount of chicken; a layer of the other materials is laid on the chicken; and the whole is wrapped and tied in the leaf and boiled.

red color. The *elote* tamale is made only of ground spring maize and so is prepared only during the spring and early summer. The boiled maize, which contains no other ingredient, is shaped into a pellet about half an inch thick and five or six inches long. It is wrapped in a banana leaf and boiled for two or three hours. During the spring maize season it is eaten at nearly every meal.

The *shepe*, like the *totoposte*, is carried by travelers, as it remains fresh for a long period. Dozens of *shepe*-sellers attend the Jocotán market every Sunday, and other Indians buy them for the midday meal. *Shepes* are made principally of maize, but other foods are added for flavoring. For the bean *shepe* (Ch. "dry bean *shepe*"), equal amounts of maize paste and boiled ripe beans are mixed together, heavily salted, and then mixed with the ground flowers of the *chipilín* shrub. The pellet is wrapped in a strip of banana leaf and boiled for two hours. It is then wrapped in maize shucks for preservation until eaten or sold. For the *ticucu shepe*, uncooked shelled green beans are mixed with the paste, wrapped in sugar-cane leaves, and boiled. A third type, called *p'ut' nak*,[8] is made of maize paste, hard ripe beans, and pumpkin seed. The ground seed are boiled with the beans and a small quantity placed inside an uncooked *tortilla*. The *tortilla* is rolled, wrapped in sugar-cane leaves, the ends tied with leaf string, and boiled. This type of *shepe* is much eaten ceremonially.

Maize on the cob is eaten mostly during July and August, when the first ears of the crop become edible. It is boiled with the shucks on, or baked with the shucks removed, in hot coals and ashes. The former is usually eaten cold, as it remains fresh, and is much sold in the markets. The baked ear is eaten hot. The kernels are never bitten

[8] *p'ut'*, "to fill"; *nak*, "stomach," "interior."

off, but are pulled off with the thumb and transferred to the mouth. During the roasting-ear season the average adult Indian eats more than a dozen ears a day.

The *maicillo* kernels are toasted on the *comal*, mixed with a thick syrup made from boiled cane juice, and patted into round balls which are eaten as a delicacy. These are sold extensively in the markets. *Maicillo* is often mixed with weevilly maize and made into *tortillas*, *totopostes*, and *shepes*.

Rice is boiled in a bean olla until the water evaporates and is eaten rather dry, usually unsweetened. Salt is always added, and chicken meat is boiled with it if it is to be eaten for a ceremonial occasion. Rice is ground on the metate to a powder and soaked in cool water to make a beverage (Sp. *orchata de arroz*). Powdered cinnamon is usually added.

Vegetables are eaten raw, boiled, baked, and used as condiments. Beans, next in importance to maize in the diet, are usually eaten separately, although, like maize, they are often cooked as a base with other foods. The most common meal among the Indians, at any time of day, is one of *tortillas* and beans, with water, coffee, or a maize gruel to wash them down. During the spring and summer, when the first beans are gathered, they are eaten in the pods, but are always shelled after becoming ripe and hard. Ripe beans are boiled overnight with salt in a specially made olla, which is used only for beans. A great deal of thick, black soup, which seems to be the principal part desired, is made and taken at meals as if it were a beverage. Beans may be boiled with almost any food. Boiled beans are crushed and while still moist are baked over an open fire to make *fritos*.[9]

[9] This is a Spanish term meaning "fried." This preparation is called in Chorti *hut'c-p'ir p'u·r* (*hut'c*, "to crush"; *hut'c-p'ir*, "crushed"). The Ladinos fry crushed beans in hog lard, whence the Spanish name.

Greens are one of the commonest of foods during the rainy season. They are boiled without flavoring to be eaten, and the liquid is drunk.

Pumpkins are cut into strips and boiled or else baked in hot coals or on the *comal*. The flowers are pounded up, squeezed dry, placed in a *tortilla* or mixed with cheese and salt and placed inside a *shepe*, and the whole baked on the *comal*. The flowers and shoots are often boiled as greens. The toasted seeds are ground to a powder and mixed with other boiled foods, such as beans and rice. This powder is flavored with ground cinnamon and soaked in cool water for several hours to make a beverage (Sp. *orchata de ayote*) which is much liked.

Potatoes are usually salted and boiled with other vegetables. Sweet potatoes are boiled with the skins and eaten usually with honey or syrup. They are sometimes baked in the fireplace and eaten out of hand. The cassava root is peeled, cut into small cubes, and boiled like potatoes. The unpeeled root is also toasted on the *comal* to be eaten. Starch made from cassava[10] is boiled with sugar and cinnamon to make starch *atol*. Chickpeas, though seldom eaten because they are imported, are boiled like beans. Cabbages and onions are cut into small bits and usually boiled with meat and other vegetables. Both varieties of tomatoes are generally boiled, alone and with other vegetables, and are often toasted on the *comal*. The Ladinos fry them in grease. Watermelons, muskmelons, cilacayotes, and melocotons are always eaten raw. Cilacayote seeds are ground, boiled with sugar, and made into a preserve.

The condiments are used mostly for flavoring and are often mixed with wild chili. Mustard leaves are boiled with other foods as greens, and the seeds are boiled with foods as a condiment. The domestic and wild chili fruit is dried

[10] See p. 56.

in the sun or toasted, ground to a powder, and sprinkled over foods. Only a small quantity is used, as most of the chilis are very piquant. It is often cut up, slightly toasted, and soaked in lime juice before being used. Chili leaves and shoots are boiled as greens. Peppermint leaves are boiled as an aromatic, especially with chicken meat. Coriander seeds are cut up and mixed with chili and garlic and much used for flavoring beans. The leaves and buds of many of the wild condiments are ground up and mixed with tamales and *shepes* before cooking.

Most of the fruits are eaten raw and between meals and so are not considered by the Indians as necessary foods, but there are about a dozen which are much cooked and eaten and which are considered of great value.

The pulp of the cacao fruit is eaten raw; the cacao beverage is not often drunk with meals, being reserved principally for ceremonial occasions. It is always prepared with maize: one part of cacao seeds is mixed with two of ripe maize, the mixture toasted and ground, and boiled with sugar into a hot drink on a special part of the fireplace. The maize is strained out, and the liquid frothed with the chocolate beater. The drink is weak and tastes strongly of maize.

Coffee, like cacao, is toasted on the *comal* with an equal amount of maize, usually until almost burned. The mixture is stirred with a hand scraper, made of a piece of dried gourd. Coffee is boiled with a great deal of sugar in a specially made pitcher, and is much drunk, especially for breakfast.[11] No Indian would start the day without a bowl or two of coffee. Coffee and cacao which are meant to be sold in the market, where they bring good prices, are ground and toasted without maize.

[11] The *te de limón* is sometimes used as a substitute for coffee. It is a cultivated grass, the leaves of which are boiled.

Bananas and plantains are much eaten the year round, and especially during the dry season. Bananas are eaten raw, boiled, and toasted. The Ladinos often split them into strips and fry them. Plantains are never eaten raw, but are fried, boiled, or toasted. Unripe plantains are toasted, ground, and boiled with sugar to be drunk as a substitute for coffee, especially by the sick and anemic. Ground plantain is sometimes mixed with coffee as well. Huisquils are usually eaten raw, but are sometimes boiled. Mangoes are one of the mainstays during the dry season, when there is little maize. They are much eaten raw and boiled with other foods. The flowers, fruit, and shoots of the *piñuela* are cut into small pieces and boiled with beans, or are cut into larger pieces and roasted in the fire or on the *comal*. The fruit is sometimes eaten raw. The jocote is eaten raw, and the leaves and shoots boiled as greens. The seeds are baked in hot coals and eaten as a delicacy.

Lime juice is occasionally drunk as a beverage (Ch. "savory water"), with sugar. The Indian women use the juice in every way in which the Ladino women use vinegar. It is cooked with all kinds of greens, with the bitter *pacayas*, and with beans, meat, and sometimes *tortillas*. Lemons are not of importance, being used only occasionally to make a lemonade. The sweet orange is eaten raw and is made into a beverage. The rind is boiled with sugar and made into a preserve, called in Spanish *matagusano*. The cashew is soaked in water to make the much-liked cashew beverage (Sp. *orchata de marañón*).[12] The cashew seeds are toasted and eaten between meals.

Wild meats are usually cooked on the spit and only

[12] The Ladinos make a certain *aguardiente* from the fruit and make what is called *marañón* wine from the fermented fruit juice.

occasionally boiled. Domestic meats are boiled, generally with vegetables and fruits. The Indians are fond of meat soups and take them as beverages at meals. Boiled pig blood (Sp. *moronga*) is much liked and is extensively sold in the markets.[13] All meats are highly salted, and so much so that the Ladinos boil meat to remove the salt before cooking it. Fish are always cooked with salt and are boiled with tomatoes, rice, and other vegetables, or are toasted on the *comal*. The spit is not used for fish.

Milk is never drunk raw, and seldom even when boiled, as most of it is made into cheese. Only the well-to-do regularly eat cheese.

The Indians seem to crave sugar and eat it in some form as often as they can get it. It is almost the only sweetening they have to offset the excessive starch in their diet. Raw cane is much eaten, especially by children. They cut down the stalks, peel them with the machete, and chew them all day long during the pressing season. Indians of all ages are seen in their courtyards and on the trails chewing cane incessantly. The brown sugar is mixed with a great many foods in the kitchen, the molded cake[14] pounded into small lumps and the desired quantity boiled with the food. It is never mixed with foods after they are cooked. It is boiled and allowed to coagulate to make what is called sugar-honey, a sort of molasses.

The amounts of the various important food preparations consumed by the average male was determined in Tunucó

[13] The blood is caught in a gourd from the throat gash and mixed with salt, chopped onions, peppermint, and garlic. The Ladinos add grease. The intestine is cleaned and cut into lengths of five or six inches. The lengths, with one end tied, are filled with the blood. The other ends are then tied and each length allowed to coagulate in an olla of cold water. They are then brought to the boiling-point over the fire, taken out, and allowed to harden.

[14] See below, p. 104.

during the summer of 1932. The daily consumption of
about fifteen men was observed, and the food of each
weighed at various times with a native scale over a period
from June to October. Their consumption was said by
themselves and other Indians to be typical for the adult
male. The tests were made during the rainy season when
maize, beans, greens, and a great variety of other foods
were plentiful, but the subjects claimed they ate equal
amounts, especially of maize and beans, during the dry
season, as well. This is no doubt true of the average family,
which stores away a sufficient amount of maize and vegetables to last over the dry months until the first spring maize
is ready to be eaten in July, but it would not be true of the
small proportion of poorer families who have too little land
to raise enough to last them, and who are reduced, from
about March to midsummer, to a starvation diet of wild
fruits, greens, and the little maize and beans they can work
for or afford to buy. The figures arrived at give maize
roughly 65 per cent of the total diet, and beans, 22 per
cent. The former, however, should be even higher, since
the Indians eat great quantities of fresh maize on the cob
during the summer months, and they eat maize gruels at
least several times every week throughout the year.
Maize, then, easily constitutes 70 per cent or more of the
diet. The annual consumption of greens and other vegetables was also difficult to estimate, as these are not eaten
regularly, and the variation in quantities among families is
too great.[15]

[15] The averages for the men were: twelve *tortillas* at each of the three meals,
or two pounds daily; two-ninths pound of beans at each meal, or two-thirds pound
daily; one-fourth pound of meat weekly; one pound of fruit weekly for about
seven months, after which very little fruit is eaten; two pounds of greens weekly
for about three months during the rainy season; and possibly one pound a month
for the rest of the year; about seven-eighths pound of native sugar weekly; two

The Indians, when eating, sit on a low stool in the middle of the kitchen floor or on a bench in the courtyard and place the two or three gourd or pottery containers which hold their food on the floor between their feet. They seldom hold food in their laps, and very few eat at tables. Most of the wealthier families have low eating-tables in their kitchens, but this is not the general custom. One container may be filled with hot beans or bean soup, another with boiled greens or other vegetables, and another with maize ears baked in the fire. On a cloth or banana leaf is a stack of *tortillas*, which comprise more than half the meal. One of the women brings these hot from the fireplace as the men eat them. Aside from bowl containers, the average Indian family owns no eating utensils, solid foods being eaten with the fingers and liquid foods drunk. The stiff-baked *tortilla* is, however, a kind of eating utensil, especially in eating beans.[16]

COMMERCIAL FOOD PROCESSING

The preparation of honey has been discussed above.[17] The processing of sugar cane into both sugar and *chicha* and the making of cheese are more professionalized. Sugar is the most important.

In the areas where cane is grown and pressed most of the large families have their own presses, which they use themselves and lend to smaller families who usually do not own

---

pounds of cheese monthly; and fifty to one hundred pounds yearly of other vegetables.

[16] A small piece is torn off, a few beans pressed against it with the thumb until they stick, and the part covered with the beans bitten off. The Indians and Ladinos are adept at this and eat a whole meal of *tortillas* and beans without much soiling of the fingers. Partially liquid foods are scooped up with the *tortilla* and eaten.

[17] Pp. 68–69.

them, for which they receive a part of the sugar as payment. Each large family is a co-operative unit in this work,
and it is done only by the men. The smaller families who
have presses often press co-operatively with other families
who do not own them, the owning family receiving a small
share of all the others' sugar for the use of the press.

The sugar-making equipment consists of the press, boiling oven, oxen yokes, sugar molds, gourd strainers and dippers, and various large pottery ollas.[18] The presses are built
on a level spot, since the circular path used by the oxen in
turning it must be level, and are as near as possible to the
cane fields, since the cane is transported to the press on the
back with the tumpline. Usually they are covered with
specially constructed sheds as a protection against the sun
and rain. If no shed is used, the press is covered with a
layer of palm fronds, tied together with liana, which is removed when the press is in motion. All the presses are fundamentally alike, although those of the wealthier Indians
are larger than are others. They are, of course, of Spanish
origin.[19] Directly under the press rolls, about eighteen

[18] The ollas are described in chap. vi.

[19] Its four corner posts are set up in the ground, about six feet high, and forming a rectangle about six feet long and three wide. These are held together at
each side and end by two heavy timbers, one laid across the tops and the other
laid about midway between the tops and the ground. Short timbers, which
extend between the four side timbers, support the rolls. The large roll, about a
foot in diameter and three long, is set vertically in the center, with one smaller
roll, about eight inches in diameter, on each side of it. All three are fitted together with wooden cogs, so that when the center roll is turned the other two
are turned with it. The center roll has a shaft which extends above the press,
and to this is tied a long pole, about twenty feet long, to which the oxen or bulls
are yoked. Many of the presses are built by professional woodworkers, who
especially make the rolls, although the average Indian does most of the work for
himself. No nails are used, as all the joints are securely fitted and held together
with wooden pegs. After being used for several seasons the wood warps and the
bearings of the rolls loosen, so that a loud squeaking noise can be heard from all
the hillsides during the pressing season.

inches above the ground, is laid a specially built wooden canoe,[20] which is square at one end and pointed at the other. The pointed end contains a small opening through which the cane juice may run into the large olla placed beneath it.

The sugar oven is set up under a shed a few feet away from the press and contains the three large boiling ollas (Fig. 5, C) in which the juice is cooked. Halves of broken or worn-out ollas are laid on the ground end to end, with their convex sides up. These support the weight of the oven above, the space they leave being used as the firebox, which is open at both ends. The three vats are laid in a row on this, and the oven built up around them. The material used is a composition of wet clay, large and small stones, and a great quantity of dried grass and vines. The oven is built up solidly to about three inches from the rims of the ollas, and is about four feet wide and six feet long. When an olla is broken, it is taken out, and a new one sealed into its place with wet clay.

The oxen yoke is about five feet long, carved from a single timber, and is made to fit the necks of two oxen. It is carved with the machete only, and in some cases is smoothed down with a handstone. It is no doubt of Spanish design.[21] Many are made by the professional carpenters who manufacture household objects. The sugar mold is a single board, about five feet long, four inches thick, and a foot wide. On one side it contains thirty-three circular molds, each of which is three inches in diameter at the top, two at the bottom, and two and a half in depth. They are carved out in three straight rows of eleven each. The cone

[20] See p. 147 for a description of these canoes.

[21] Yokes are principally made of the wood of the wild annona, *churumuya*, guanaba, guamá, the three varieties of *cortez*, and the *cortez coyote*.

shape of the molds permits the syrup to be easily knocked
out after it hardens. The strainers and dippers[22] are made
of large half-gourds, usually nine or ten inches in diameter.
A handle about three feet long is attached with string to
the rim of each across its center. Two holes are bored on
each side of the rim directly beneath the point where the
handle is to be attached; string is passed through these and
up and around the handle several times, thus holding it
securely in place. For strainers, the gourd is perforated
with small holes.

Sugar-making (*tce-y-ax tcap'*) begins as soon as is convenient after the cutting of the crop. Five men are required to operate the press and equipment. The family
male head directs the work and helps the others at their
tasks; two heads of his households feed the cane through
the rolls; another carries the juice to the boiling vats and
superintends the boiling; another coagulates the hot syrup
and molds it into round pellets; and a boy of the family
drives the bulls which turn the press. The stalks are carried from the fields to the press and cut into lengths of
about two feet. Each is hacked on all sides to make pressing easier. If there are not enough men in the family group,
two or three laborers may be hired to do this work, for
which they are paid either in pesos or in sugar. The very
old men and boys of the family collect firewood for the
vats, wrap the sugar pellets in maize leaves or shucks, and
carry drinking water. Some of the juice is set aside without boiling to be made into *chicha*, and this, together with
the sugar, is divided among the family's households, the
family head keeping the larger share.

In the early morning a fire is built under the boiling vats.
Two oxen or bulls are yoked to the press pole and turn the

---

[22] The strainer is shown in Fig. 3, *f* (p. 117).

press by walking in a circular path around it. The two operators feed the cane stalks into the rolls from both sides, passing the same ones back and forth several times until they are thoroughly dry. The juice drops into the wooden vat below, from which it runs through a hole in one end into a large olla. The cook carries this as it fills to the large vats, where the juice is boiling. This goes on for a half-hour or more, until one *tarea*,[23] or six jugs, of juice is extracted, at which time everyone rests while the hot cane is exploded.

Six cane stalks, one for each olla of juice, are heated in the oven and exploded against the uprights of the press. The two pressers stand on top of the press, one at each end; the stalks are handed up to them when sufficiently hot, and they bring them down with a resounding whack against the press, filling the air all around with vapor. The explosion can be heard for many miles and is said to be done to notify the *aldea* that a *tarea* of juice has been extracted and that sugar will soon be offered for sale. When the pressing is finished, eight stalks are exploded, by way of notifying the *aldea* that the work is done and that the oxen and press may be used by others. After each explosion, the pressers smoke, rest, and play for a half-hour or so before resuming. Pressing is done usually from about ten in the morning until about eleven at night; but, when the pressing season is in full swing, it is kept up day and night. It is said that the work cannot begin until the day has become warm. Each batch of juice is boiled from twelve to possibly sixteen hours. Every half-hour or so during the boiling a handful of some kind of defecator is poured into

[23] Six jugs of juice are boiled in the three vats at a time. As the latter are placed in a line in the oven, the amount of juice which can be boiled in them at one time is called *in-tsohr* (*in*, "one"; *tsohr*, numerical classifier denoting objects placed in a line, thus, "one line"). *in-tsohr* is equivalent to Sp. *tarea*.

the vats to bring the bits of stalk and other impurities to the surface. The defecators consist of lime and the parts of certain plants.[24]

During the boiling, the cook constantly skims the impurities from the surface of the juice with the large perforated gourd dipper. When the juice has boiled down to about the thickness of molasses, it is dipped into an olla, carried outside to cool, and beaten with a stick until it coagulates. It is then poured into the molds, where it hardens to the density of lump sugar in a few minutes. It is packed by placing the large ends of two molds together, wrapping them in maize shucks, and tying the ends with a twine made from split palm frond. Each package is about six inches long and three in diameter and weighs about a pound. This is one of the most extensively sold articles in the Jocotán and Olopa markets. It is not really sugar, since it is never ground, and is little more than hardened syrup. In Quetzaltepeque *municipio*, however, a white sugar is made by the Indian and Ladino sugar-makers. Indian merchants bring it to the Jocotán market regularly for sale.[25]

[24] The important plants so used are the mango, caulote, *aguacate cimarrón*, *guapinol* (*copinol*), acorn oak, *mozote de caballo, pimientillo, sálamo, zapotón*, and quebracho. In most cases, the wood of the plant is burned in the kiln, and the ash, which contains potash, is used. The entire *mozote* shrub, as well as the caulote bark, is pounded on a stone, soaked, and the liquid used as a purifier.

[25] The cane juice is placed in large ollas and diluted with water. It is then placed in the boiling ollas, either lime or wood ash added as a defecator, and the whole boiled. The syrup is then transferred to a large cone-shaped olla in which it is kept for eight days to harden. It is taken out, pounded in a mortar, and replaced in a cone-shaped olla with a small hole in its base. Over the sugar is placed a layer of black clay about two inches thick, and this covered with water. The clayish water seeps for about fifteen days through the sugar to purify it, thus hardening it again into a cake. It is then removed and left in the sun for several weeks to dry and bleach. The upper half of the cake is white and completely purified, while the lower half is brown. The clay water thus used is caught in an olla, left to settle, and drunk as an intoxicant, called in Spanish *miel de purga*.

Chicha, a sucrose wine, is made principally from sugar cane and is the only intoxicating beverage the Indians make.[26] It seems to be about as strong as ordinary beer. A supply is kept on hand by every family, as great quantities of it are drunk on all ceremonial and festival occasions, and it is usually offered to guests. The *chichería* in Jocotán, which caters to Indian trade, sells nothing but *chicha*, which is handed out to each customer in a gourd. It is made in five ways: of pure sugar-cane juice, of native sugar and water, of native sugar and maize, of maize and honey, and of pineapple juice only. The first three are the most commonly made. For maize *chicha*, the maize is toasted, ground to a powder, placed in a *bongo* olla,[27] covered with water, and left for four or five days until the maize has fermented and has a strong odor. The olla is then filled up with water and powdered native sugar poured in and left for about three days more until fermentation is complete. The maize has settled at the bottom; the skum is dipped off with a gourd, and the pure *chicha* dipped out, strained, and transferred to another *bongo* where it is kept until drunk. Most of the *chicha* is made in this way, especially that which is drunk ceremonially. For honey *chicha*, honey is added in place of the native sugar.[28] This is not often made, as honey is expensive and difficult to find in large quantities. During the pressing season *chicha* is made altogether of the pure cane juice and is con-

[26] The Indians occasionally drink *aguardiente*, which seems to have a higher alcoholic content than whiskey, but the price of it is prohibitive for most of them. A distillery in Camotán pueblo sells it to most of the pueblos of eastern Guatemala.

[27] Described on p. 140.

[28] An alcoholic beverage of fermented honey and water was made by the ancient Maya (Thompson, 1927, p. 77).

sidered the best-tasting of all.[29] A great deal of the juice is set aside at the presses and is quickly made into a supply which lasts the family for the next two or three months. Pineapple *chicha* is seldom made, but is said to be very good. The fruit is crushed, and the juice is caught in an olla and allowed to ferment. *Chicha* of native sugar and waste is made only during the dry season and at other times when better ingredients are not available. The sugar is merely pounded up, mixed with water, and left to ferment in the *bongo*.[30]

Cheese[31] is prepared for sale in some of the *aldeas*. The milk is placed in a gourd or olla and mixed with a pinch of *cuajo*.[32] This is stirred and left to coagulate for a half-hour. The palms are laid on to force the coagulating parts downward, after which the latter are lifted out and squeezed in a cloth. Much salt is added as a preservative, and the whole is ground down with the palms on the metate. It is then pressed into molds made from the inner bark of trees. A thin strip of bark, two to three feet long and three to six inches wide, is bent into a circle and the ends tied together by a cord which is passed several times through them. It has no top or bottom but is set upon a flat surface when being filled. Or the cheese is patted with the hands into round pellets of about the size of a tamale and wrapped in maize shucks, or in the leaves of the *hoja de queso* tree, and

[29] A drink of fermented sugar-cane juice is made at Jacaltenango (La Farge and Byers, 1931, p. 73).

[30] Maize *chicha* is called *tcitca' nar;* honey *chicha, tcitca' tcap';* *chicha* made of pure cane juice, *tcitca' si k'ap* (Sp. *chicha de caña*); pineapple *chicha, tcitca' sak'ir;* and *chicha* made of native sugar and water, *tcitca' ha't's-p'ir tcap'* (Sp. *chicha de dulce*).

[31] The Indians use the Spanish term, *queso,* although *in-cuk' tcu'* ("fermented milk") was occasionally heard.

[32] A lacteal substance taken from the stomachs of cows.

stored in the kitchen or carried to the markets, especially to Zacapa, which is famous in eastern Guatemala as a cheese center. It is preferred when about a week old, after it has turned sour and strong. The whey (Ch. "the milk's water") is boiled to make the second curds, which are eaten with *tortillas*.

FOOD PRESERVATION AND STORAGE

The Indians do not have many techniques for preserving perishable foods, but they do not greatly need them, as most such foods are eaten soon after being prepared. Any surplus that cannot be eaten quickly, such as of venison, *tortillas*, *shepes*, fresh maize and beans, and fruit, is usually carried to market and sold to other Indians or to Ladinos. This is especially done during the warm rainy season, during which time perishable foods cannot be kept in good condition for more than a day or two; but during the cold dry season, from November to about March, they can be preserved and kept in the kitchens for as long as two or three weeks.

Nonperishable foods, like ripe cereals and beans, will preserve for a long time, and there are many techniques for protecting them against rot and destruction. The preservation techniques are curing and wrapping. The term "curing" (*puts-se*) is applied to any process in which food is treated with another substance, and which makes it less liable to destruction, and includes drying, heating, smoking, the use of lime, sand, and ash, salting, and spicing.[33] These are used both to prevent destruction and to salvage what is left of the stored foods after it has started.

Drying is done either on the *comal* or in the sun. Shelled

[33] The term refers also to the preservation of nonfood materials, as in the curing of hides and leather, new pottery vessels, and many others.

cereals are dried on the *comal*, especially if weevilly, after which they are usually eaten. Sun-drying usually extends over a period of four days. All cereals, beans, coffee, and cacao are spread out on large tables or mats and placed in the courtyards where the sunlight is not impeded. The foods are stirred until completely dry and shriveled. Coffee beans and rice are stored in their husks. The cereal seed to be used the following year is dried with the husk or shuck on. The shucks of pairs of maize ears are tied together and the pairs strung over ropes stretched in the courtyard for drying. Stalks of seed rice are tied in pairs of bundles and dried in the same way.

The smoking of foods is done in the kitchen. The kitchen storage shelf is situated usually above the fireplace, so that the foods stored on it are continuously subjected to smoke. The maize hung on the rafters is often shifted around throughout the year in order to subject all the ears to as much smoking as possible. Smoke is said to prevent the appearance of weevils and mold. Cereals or beans are heated on the *comal* to kill the weevils, then placed in a container of water where the floating weevils are skimmed off. The partially spoiled foods may be placed in an olla of boiling water, and the weevils skimmed off the surface.

Liquid lime is much used as a preventive against weevils in the storehouses. The unshucked ears of maize are laid in rows from the floor to the roof, and layer of each row covered with the lime as it is laid down. The lime is mixed with water in a gourd and applied with a shuck. Powdered lime (Ch. "dry lime") is mixed with all shelled foods when weevils are discovered, after which they are restored to the granaries. It is said that powdered lime destroys the weevils and keeps away rats. Dry sand is used in the same way and for the same purpose. Ash is secured from the fireplace and from cattle manure. The latter is dried and burned in a kiln. Both are mixed thoroughly with shelled maize and beans to kill weevils and to prevent molding. Beans are placed in mat bags or large ollas and covered over with a layer of wood or manure ash. The mixing with dry lime, sand, and ash is done in a large hollowed-out log which is especially made for this purpose. A long paddle is used for stirring.

The maize weevil is the most destructive and feared pest with which the Indians have to contend. It is black and small and has no wings. The bean weevil is of a grayish color and has wings. Cacao is attacked by a white worm. These insects eat out the heart of the kernel, leaving only the husk intact, and work so rapidly that most of the stored food of a family can be destroyed before they are discovered. The Indians are careful to examine their maize and beans every few days during the storage season because of this danger.[34] Mold appears on the cereals, beans, cacao, and coffee when these are stored in damp spots where ventilation is poor. This is avoided by the use of matted floors in the storehouses and clay walls and suspended floors in the granaries, and by the use of heating and drying both before and after mold appears. Field rats are often very destructive and are said by some of the Indians to be the worst of all the pests. They are guarded against by traps and poisons.[35] The storage places include the family storehouses and granaries, the kitchen storage shelves and rafters, and various kitchen containers.

[34] They believe that the maize and bean weevils are born of the maize and beans themselves and are certain they could not have got in from the outside.

[35] Human thieves are much feared, especially during the dry season when many of the families have exhausted their maize and are living on wild fruits and greens.

The family storehouse[36] is used principally for maize on the cob, since maize is the most important crop, but it is often used as well for rice, beans, *maicillo*, and vegetables. A short time before the harvest a specially built floor is made in it. Limbs are laid from one side wall to the other, four or five inches apart, and across these is placed a thick layer of dried maize stalks upon which the maize ears are stacked. In the highlands very low benches are placed side by side to support the maize above the ground. They are laid in rows and with the shucks on, the width of each row being the length of an ear. The rows extend from one side of the house to the other and usually up to the roof. Because of their conical shape, the ears are laid alternately in the same row, in order that both sides of the row will be of the same height. The storage ceremony[37] is performed as soon as one row on each side of the storehouse has been stacked to about a foot in height. To the Indians this ceremony is the most powerful preventive they know against rot and destruction of stored foods. It is performed for maize only and is especially directed against the personified weevil, but it is said to protect all the stored foods against any kind of nonhuman danger. As soon as mold or weevils are discovered, the ears are taken out, shelled on the thresher, winnowed, the partially eaten grains cured, and then placed in a granary, or, if the family does not have one, in large mat bags. If almost completely eaten, the grains are mixed with *maicillo* and made into *tortillas*. Stored maize is never shelled until attacked by weevils, as it is said to preserve better if left unshucked and on the cob.

The granaries are usually built in one corner of the sleep-

[36] For a description of housebuilding see chap. vi.

[37] Described on pp. 446–47.

ing-house and are used only for storing shelled maize and beans, one being built for each of these. They are especially used for storehouse maize that, having been attacked by weevils or mold, has been shelled and treated and is restored in the much dryer granary. Every Quetzaltepeque family has a granary,[38] although it is less often seen in Jocotán and Olopa *municipios*, where large bags made of mats are more commonly used to store the grain.

The kitchen storage shelf is used for storing bags of shelled beans, potatoes, sweet potatoes, nonperishable fruits, and perishable fruits which are ripening in storage. It is especially used for storing native sugar, which is wrapped in banana leaves and kept for as long as two years. The kitchen rafters are used for ears of maize that are to be used as seed for the next year's planting and for rice. One shuck of each ear is pulled back and tied to the shuck of another, and all the pairs are hung side by side over all the rafters. Bundles of rice, with the stalks, are tied in pairs and suspended in the same way until eaten. The kitchen containers include jars, pitchers, ollas, gourd vessels, mat bags, tables, and food hangers. Many of the vessels, such as *chicha* jars, sugar ollas, and gourds for salt, ground coffee and cacao, *tortillas*, *shepes*, and cheese, are especially made for the storage of a single food. Most of the gourds hang from the rafters; fresh foods are also kept on hangers[39] and hooks suspended from rafters. Every kitchen contains at least one large table on

[38] The granary is about four feet square and reaches from the floor almost to the roof. The walls and floor are of clay and limbs, like that used in the clay houses, and the floor is built about a foot above the earth floor of the house. The top is uncovered. A hole about two feet square is left in one of the walls as an entrance. This is sealed with thin horizontal strips of wood, on the inside, which extend up to the level of the stored maize.

[39] See below, p. 137, for description of hangers.

which containers with stored food are kept, and benches in the sleeping-house are used in the same way. A common storage container is the mat bag, which is made by doubling a mat and sewing up the two sides and top with vine string.

Salt is used for preserving cooked foods, especially *toto-postes*, *shepes*, cheese, and raw meat. Salt is not often eaten except with such foods as require it for preservation. During the cooking a great quantity of it is added, and this keeps certain foods edible for two or three weeks. Meat is usually eaten or sold immediately, if possible, but if not it is completely covered with salt for several days, hung on ropes in the courtyard for a week to be dried in the sun, and stored hung on the kitchen rafters.[40] Fish are split open and the interior salted, but they are not dried. Spicing is used only for raw meats, and especially pork. Spiced meats are said sometimes to be preserved during the dry season for almost a month. Strong *chicha* is slowly poured over meat until much of it has been absorbed. Various spices, especially cloves and peppers, as well as onions and garlic, are crushed in a bowl and spread over the meat. It is then placed in a large olla and tightly covered.

Cooked foods are often wrapped in fresh leaves. Fresh maize shucks and the fresh leaves of maize, banana, and plantain are especially used for wrapping. *Shepes*, cheese, and native sugar are wrapped in the maize shucks. These are wrapped for sale or preservation by placing two of the pellets end to end, extending shucks all around them from one end to the other, and tying the ends with split shuck string. The package resembles an ear of unshucked maize. Many foods, such as tamales, are boiled in the leaves of banana and plantain and preserved for a week or longer in

[40] The meats sold in the Jocotán market are so salty it is nearly impossible for a non-native to eat them. The Ladinos often preboil them.

the same leaves. Ears of spring maize are often boiled with the shucks on in order to preserve them without wrapping.

Native sugar molds are wrapped in banana leaves and bark and stored on the kitchen shelf. Each package of them is about two feet square and six inches deep.

Fruits are stored principally during the ripening stage, in order to hasten the ripening and make it more uniform. Controlled ripening (Ch. "to make ripen") is done by all the fruit-sellers. The fruits, especially oranges, mangoes, zapotes, avocados, limes, sapodillas, and *chuctes*, are picked green and placed in large fiber bags which are lined on the inner side with *madre cacao* or banana leaves. The bags are suspended from rafters in the sleeping-houses while the fruit ripens. Bananas are hung by themselves on their stalks. They are cut at the beginning of the ripening stage, as they acquire a bad taste if allowed to ripen on the plant.

CHAPTER VI

CLOTHING AND SHELTER

CLOTHING AND ACCESSORIES

THE clothing of the Indians, since they do not weave cloth, is either made locally of imported muslin or woven in other parts of Guatemala. Since the Indians do not own sewing machines, Ladino seamstresses sew all the men's and women's shirts as well as the men's drawers. The Indian women merely mend their clothes, using the hand needle. The children's clothes are exactly like those of adults, differing only in size.

The men wear a single white cotton shirt or blouse of the slip-over type which hangs well below the hips, and which is worn outside the drawers. There is no decoration except a number of small pleats which extend vertically down the front center, with a small flap hanging from the bottom. The drawers are of the same material and reach to within about six inches of the ankles. They are held up by a strip of cloth which is sewn to the waist and tied in front above the hips.[1] As the drawers have no pockets, the men carry their personal articles in a small fiber bag slung from the left shoulder. Sometimes a large cotton handkerchief, the four ends tied together, serves for this purpose. Every man and boy wears a hat at all times, often with a bright red or purple strip of cloth tied around the

---

[1] The men and boys seldom wear the shirt when working in the milpas during the warm months, using instead a cotton shawl which is laid on the back, with its two upper corners pulled over the shoulders and tied in front. This is cooler and less expensive than the shirt and protects the back from the sun.

CHORTI WOMEN

The woman covers her child's head and face with a red cloth to protect him from the "evil eye" of the camera.

crown. On market and festival days a wild flower may be
stuck in the hatband. Most of the men own a second costume which is kept in good condition and worn on dress-up
occasions. The men's clothes do not vary from the shirt
and drawers costume, except in the case of the few who
are sufficiently Ladinoized to prefer wearing the European
shirt and trousers when visiting the pueblos.

The women wear white cotton blouses[2] and skirts of a
bluish material with cross-hatched decorative lines. The
skirts are woven in western Guatemala; the most common
type is a wrap-around style sewed in the form of a very
wide skirt into which the woman steps and then wraps the
additional material from the back around to the front and
stuffs the upper corner of it into the front waist. Since the
skirt is about three feet wide, there is a great bulge at that
point. A less common type is made of the same material, but is made form-fitting at the waist by the Ladino
seamstresses. It is pleated all around at the waist and contains a sewn strip, like the men's drawers, for tying. This
type is said by the Ladinos to have been recently introduced from Quezaltenango. The skirts are worn extremely
long, almost touching the ground. No undergarments are
used, and very few of the women own Ladino-type clothes.
They never wear the hat, except when at home and working in the sun, but wear the shawl or go bareheaded.

Leather sandals are a part of the men's costume. They
are removed and slung over the shoulder when traveling
along muddy trails, as the clinging mud causes them to
flap uncomfortably against the soles of the feet. They are
principally worn merely to protect the feet from sharp
stones in the trails and usually are not worn at all when at

[2] These have the large "mutton" sleeves similar to those worn in the United
States a generation ago. The huipils of the Guatemala highlands are not worn.

home. The women never wear sandals except when taking long trips, as to the pueblos. Wooden sandals are occasionally worn by both sexes on muddy trails or when working in milpas on extremely steep hillsides.[3] The machete is carried so invariably by the men that it may be considered an article of costume. When not being used in the milpas or around the houses, it is always carried on the trails for protection. No man is ever seen away from his home without his machete. The handle is held in the right hand, with the blade end resting on top of the forearm. The Indian reaches automatically for it when he moves from one place to another, even in the pueblo where he is safe from harm, and even though he may be carrying a heavy load on his back and in both arms.[4] A very few of the Indians have adopted the Ladino custom of carrying the imported cutlass (Sp. *corbo*), which rests in a leather scabbard hanging from a belt around the waist.

Tobacco pipes[5] have bowls which are made to fit a bit of cigar, as tobacco is generally bought in this form. The most common elbow type (Fig. 3, *v*) is of one piece except for the cane stem. The pipe is about five inches long, and the flanges, above and below, about three-eighths of an inch thick. The shaded portions represent holes. The cylindrical pipe (*t*) is nearly straight and is of one piece. Another type of elbow pipe (*u*) always has the small knob at the

[3] This sandal is of copal wood, of the shape of the foot, and about three-eighths of an inch thick. It is left about an inch thick below the heel and below the ball of the foot. The projections raise it above the ground and prevent slipping. It is attached to the foot as is the leather sandal.

[4] Even boys of nine or ten, who live only a short distance away, come to the *aldea* school every morning carrying their small machetes on their arms, as the men do. These are all stacked in a corner of the room while the class goes on.

[5] Pipes are made principally from the *guachipilín* and quebracho woods, although any hardwood may be used.

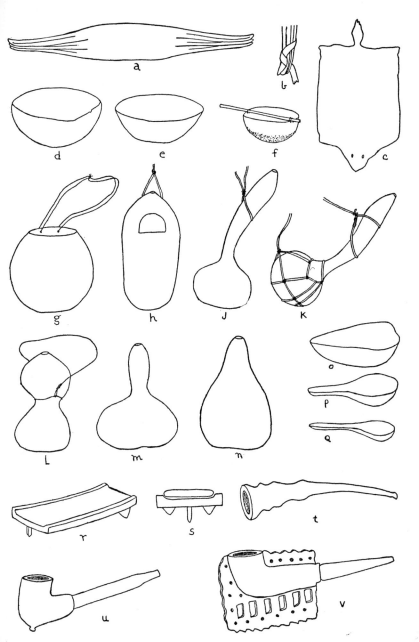

FIG. 3.—Gourds, metate, and smoking pipes

base of the bowl. Pipes are carried either in the shoulder bag or suspended around the neck on a twine. New ones are usually buried in damp soil for a week or so to give them a slightly brownish color, or are rubbed with the root of the *camotillo*, mixed with lime, to stain them red. Nearly all tobacco is smoked in pipes, although the Ladinos principally smoke cigars and cigarettes.[6]

A flint outfit, the steel of which is made by the Ladino blacksmiths, is used for striking fire. The men carry it in their shoulder bags, when on trips, to light their pipes. It is seldom used in the kitchens, as continuous fire is kept in the fireplace or can be brought from a neighbor's house with a pine torch. At one end of a small chain or agave cord is attached a small flat piece of steel, and, at the other, a metal container resembling a thimble, into which is stuffed very tightly a wad of cotton or the inner bark of the *papelillo* tree. The flint rock is carried separately and is held in the left hand when struck with the steel. The burning is extinguished with an airtight cap which fits over the thimble.

Jewelry is not extensively made or worn. Small crosses are carved from wood and worn as neck pendants and charms by the women and children. The red beans of the coral tree are hardened in the sun, strung on a fine agave thread, and worn as a necklace. The white seed of the *lágrimas de San Pedro* bush, called "pearls" because of their whiteness, are bleached in the sun and also worn as necklaces. The old silver pesos are the most commonly used pendants and are often perforated and strung on twine to be worn around the neck.[7] The men carry the

---

[6] The use of tobacco is confined largely to the men. Many of the older women smoke at home but seldom in public.

[7] When the Guatemalan government began recalling them in 1932, it was found that nearly a third of them had been perforated.

pesos stuck in the outer ear opening, both as a decoration and to prevent the entrance of evil wind.[8]

HOUSES AND BUILDING

With the exception of the few distant milpas which the *aldea* family may own, its house sites and cultivated land form a contiguous area. Trails connect all the households with one another and with the chief household, and a larger trail runs from the latter to the main trail which connects with other families, with other *aldeas*, and with the pueblo.

The chief household of the family[9] usually consists of two or three sleeping-houses, a kitchen, several store-houses for maize, vegetables, and agricultural equipment, a privy for the women, a sugar press and pressing equipment, an altar-house, and the family burial plot. The principal houses and sheds are set in a rough circle, thus inclosing a central courtyard which is kept free of weeds and useless shrubs. The whole is inclosed usually with a fence-like row of tall spiny plants. Since the land is extremely hilly, most of the houses are set at different levels, some being above the roofs of others. The sleeping-houses contain all the beds and the wooden chests in which personal belongings are kept, and manufactured articles are stored in them until sold in the markets. Several hammocks are swung near the doors, in which the men take their midday siesta. The sleeping-houses are the lounging place for the men when there is no milpa work to be done.

The kitchen contains the fireplace at the end opposite the door, and a few tables and benches, built into the earth floor, which are used for sitting and for the preparation of

---

[8] See pp. 317–26.

[9] Speaking of the multiple-household, or extended, family; some families consist of but one household. See pp. 246–50.

food. The kitchen is said to be the house of the females, since their work centers almost entirely in it. The main storehouse is located near the houses, and smaller ones are often built farther away, at the edge of the milpas. The privy is outside the courtyard, hidden in the brush, and reached by a narrow path. The lime and pottery kilns are dug in the ground at the edge of the courtyard, and near them is the sugar press and boiling vats, covered with sheds. The altar-house contains the family's ceremonial equipment. The burial plot of the family is usually not far from the houses of the chief household. Within the courtyard are some of the family's fruit trees and shrubs, medicinal plants, and a number of large trees used for shading the workers during the warm months. Under these are set up the poles on which agave fiber is cleaned and made into articles. The family's land usually adjoins the house site, although a few of its milpas and gardens may be a half-mile or more away, depending upon the density of the population in the locality and the competition for available land. The orchard is located near by on the banks of the nearest stream or at the nearest spring.

The other households of the family are much smaller, consisting only of one sleeping-house, a kitchen, one store-house, a privy, and perhaps a shed or two. The sleeping-house and kitchen are always placed end to end, about twelve feet apart, and in this small court the household lounge during the day when there is no rain, talk with neighbors and relatives, and entertain visitors with coffee, *atol*, and hot *tortillas*. It contains several *butaca* chairs and two wooden benches which are built against the facing walls of the two houses. The household's land usually immediately surrounds its house site. The chief household is

the social center for the family, and all the households congregate in its courtyard for all social and ceremonial occasions. Much of the family work is done in the courtyard as
well. The households of the sons and sons-in-laws of the
family head are located all around the chief household,
from a few yards to a quarter-mile away.

The houses of the *aldea* Indians seem to be native in
every detail (Fig. 4) and to contain no Spanish elements.[10]
As the country is extremely mountainous, few houses can
be built on naturally level ground, so that in most cases
the house sites must be leveled off. This is done by excavat-
ing into the side of the hill and throwing the earth to the
edge of the opening, thus providing a floor (*u wa·r-ip'*)
which is half-excavated and half-raised. The level site is
usually just large enough to accommodate two houses
placed end to end, the space between, and about two feet
of level space extending out from the walls on both sides.
The open sides of the foundation, being nearly vertical,
are sometimes faced with stones to prevent erosion. The
typical house group consists of the sleeping-house and the
kitchen facing each other with a patio eight or ten feet
wide between them; and the outhouses, usually at a lower
level, consisting of the storage-houses, the women's privy,
and one or two sheds. The storehouse is built like the
sleeping-house. If the household makes sugar, a shed in
which this is done is built near by, although sometimes
farther away at the cane fields.

A large and a small type of house are built, the former
for kitchens and sleeping-houses usually, and the latter for
storage-houses, sheds, and temporary structures. The

[10] The pueblo Indians sometimes build tile floors, tile roofs, and walls of clay
bricks (Sp. *adobe*) like those of the Ladino houses.

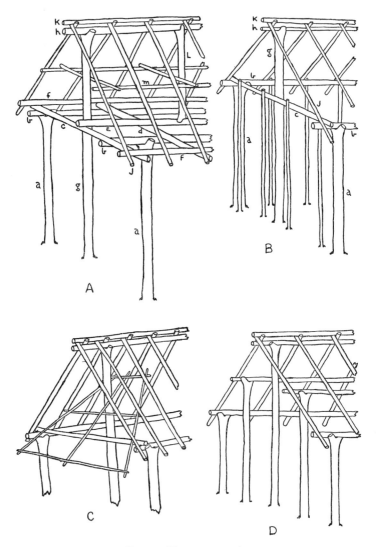

Fig. 4.—House construction

larger timbers are taken from a number of wild trees,[11] the smaller limbs of which are used as rafters, braces, wall studs, and roof and wall laths. The tying materials are the various bindweeds, all of which have fibrous vines which are tough when dry, and split sections of the bark of certain trees.[12] The bark is split into fine strips about a quarter-inch in width and thickness and is extremely tough and durable.

The large house (Fig. 4, *A*) is about twenty feet long, ten or twelve wide, and six high at the eaves, and nine or ten at the ridge. It is supported at the corners by four oak posts (*a*), each set in the ground and with a forked upper end in which rest the two side plates (*b*). Additional posts may be set up in the side walls to support the center of the roof. The end plates (*c*) are laid across the ends of the side plates. Two, and sometimes three, joists (*d*) are laid across the side plates, parallel with the end plates and of equal distance apart. These support the center beam, which in turn supports the center of the roof. Over the end plates and joists, in the center of the house and running its full length, is laid the center beam (*e*). Running parallel with this, and lying on the ends of the end beams about two feet out from the wall plates, are the secondary wall plates (*f*), one on each side of the house. These support the lower ends of the rafters and the upper ends of the wall studs. All intersections are tied with split bark or bindweeds.

The two ridgeposts (*g*), each ten to twelve feet high, are set in the ground, one at each end of the house and against

[11] The most important are white oak, black oak, yellow oak, evergreen oak, acorn oak, white pine, torch pine, mahogany, ceiba, cypress, *madre de cacao*, brazil, *nacascahuite* (*guaje*), *pimiento*, walnut, *guayabilla* and *cortez*.

[12] The important bindweeds (Sp. *bejuco*) are the *bejuco amarillo*, *bejuco blanco*, *ata corral*, and *bejuco de cinaca*. The pliable bark is taken from the *capulín*, banana, plantain, *gualmeco*, *mecate*, and other trees of less importance.

the inner side of the end plates. These support the roof, since the latter is not a self-supporting arch.[13] The ridge-pole (h) is laid across the forked ends of these posts and extends about two feet out from the ridgeposts at the ends to provide for the wide end eaves. The rafters (j) are laid on crosswise, being tied at the center of the roof to the upper side of the ridgepole and at the eaves to the second-ary side plates. Each is notched at the point where it inter-sects the wall plate to prevent it from sliding down. At the center of the roof the rafters of the two sides meet to form a small fork, just large enough to contain the false ridge-pole (k), to which is attached the ridge cap. Additional support for the roof is provided by the ridge support (l), the forked end of which rests on the center beam. It is notched at the top end to fit under the ridgepole. Several of these are put in if the house is long. The roof stringers (m), about one inch in diameter, extend for the entire length of the roof, usually one on each side. They are tied to the underside of the rafters to keep the latter in place. Inward sagging of the rafters is prevented by the cross-braces, which extend from the stringer on one side to that on the other. There are usually as many cross-braces as ridge supports, so that pairs of them can be tied where they intersect.

The smaller houses (B) are ten to fifteen feet long, six to eight wide, five high at the eaves, and eight or nine high at the ridge. They are built of smaller timbers and are not nearly so well constructed. The corner posts are a part of the wall, so that the wall itself supports the edges of the roof. The secondary wall plate is not used, and the lower ends of the rafters and the upper ends of the wall studs rest

[13] As it is in the Mopan Maya house (Thompson, 1930, p. 92).

SLEEPING-HOUSE

directly on the wall plate. As the house is not large, the inner bracing for the roof is left out; only two end plates are used, and the joists, center beams, and ridge supports are not required. Roof stringers are seldom used.

Both house types, especially those used as kitchens, contain storage shelves at the rear end. Two joists are laid from one side wall plate to the other, about two feet apart; across these are laid five or six small sticks as supports, and over these, running lengthwise, are laid lengths of cane or reed, placed close together, to form the shelf surface. This is used for storing utensils, foods, and odds and ends.[14]

In Jocotán *municipio* the roofs and walls are covered with either sugar-cane leaves or the fronds of various palms, as these plants grow abundantly in the lowlands.[15] The highland houses in Olopa *municipio* are covered with dried grass, clay, or small saplings, since neither palms nor sugar cane grow in most of Olopa. The clay wall is described later. For the wall made of plant parts, the studs are set in the ground on all four sides, about a foot apart, and tied at the top to the main or secondary wall plates. Various types of canes and reeds[16] are tied horizontally to the rafters and wall studs, at right angles to them and about a foot apart, and to these laths the roof and wall coverings are tied. The palm fronds are laid on with the stems pointing upward and the concave

[14] In some cases the shelf is made separately, of large limbs and covered with a matting, and is suspended with ropes from the rafters.

[15] The cohune palm frond is commonly used among the lowland Maya (Blom and La Farge, 1927, p. 346), but is seldom used in this region, as the cohune does not grow abundantly.

[16] The most important are the carrizo (a wild reed grass which grows along the banks of streams), *tanij* (a wild cane), and the *vara de bandería*. *Caña real*, a cultivated bamboo, is sometimes used.

surface of the fronds facing outward. A single outer seg-
ment of each is split back a few inches and is used for tying the frond to the lath. They are laid on in horizontal
rows, each row placed slightly above the last, so that every
part of the wall and roof is covered with three or four
thicknesses. The wall is thus covered from the ground up
to the wall plates. The first row on the roof is tied on at the
eaves and allowed to hang almost to the ground, to keep
rain water away from the walls. The roof is covered in
the same way to the ridge. Similarly, sugar-cane leaves are
laid on vertically in overlapping horizontal rows, each
bunch of leaves being about four inches thick, and each
row about two feet wide. The wall and roof of dried grass
is laid on in bunches in the same way. The rows of fronds,
leaves, or dried grass are held secure by canes which are
laid horizontally along their outer sides, a foot or so apart,
and tied with agave string to the studs and rafters underneath.

A ventilated type of wall is built in the kitchens to permit the smoke and heat from the fireplace to escape. Either
canes or cohune palm stalks are set up at the base of the
wall, about one inch apart, and are tied at the top to the
secondary wall plate. Smaller canes are laid horizontally
on the outer side of these to hold them rigid and are tied to
the vertical pieces at all intersections. The rear of the
house is covered up to the ridge. Canes are laid horizontally against the end rafters, about a foot apart, and the
wall covering attached to them.

The roof is finished by laying the ridge cap, which is
made of banana, plantain, or sugar-cane leaves. These are
laid across the ridgepole, five or six inches deep, and their
ends on both sides of the roof center held down by a long

pole which is tied to the nearest rafters. The two poles prevent the cap from blowing off during high winds.

The front end of the sleeping-houses and kitchens usually has a rain shed inserted into it (*C*). Three canes or small limbs are made into a triangular frame and held together with a number of canes which are attached horizontally to it. The apex reaches almost to the ridge of the roof, about three feet in from the rafters. The base, which is wider than the house itself, projects outward from the end plate for about three feet, thus providing a wide eave to keep rain away from the door. The shed is covered like the walls and roof. The door frame is usually made of saplings which form a rectangle about six feet high and three wide. This is covered like the rest of the walls, although a few are covered with canes or reeds, like the bed covering.[17] Short pieces of rope, looped around one of the uprights of the door frame and a wall stud, serve as hinges.

For the clay wall, the studs are set up, and canes attached horizontally to their inner and outer sides, each about four inches above the other, from the ground to the wall plates. All intersections are securely tied with bark string. The clay is mixed with an equal part of river sand which serves as a temper and prevents too much cracking. The builder piles his clay and sand on the ground, mixes the two with his hands, and adds water as he tramps it with his feet, making it into a thick paste. He then mixes dried rice stalks or dried hay and grass plants with it to give it added strength. Two men apply the mixture, one standing on each side of the wall, each pushing his handfuls against those of the other. The wall is made from four to six inches thick and is then scraped smooth. The clay walls of sleeping-houses and storehouses are built solidly

[17] Described on p. 132.

up to the roof, but those of the kitchens are usually built up to about two feet of the wall plates, the intervening space consisting merely of the uncovered wall studs. This opening runs all around the kitchen, admitting light and permitting smoke to escape. In some cases this wall is built up solidly, and only a window, consisting of four small square openings which are placed in the form of a square, is left in the wall nearest the fireplace as an escape for the smoke.

The floor is five or six inches above the outside level, usually built up of clay and hardened with water. The better floors are covered with a two-inch layer of clay which has been mixed with straw. The house foundation is kept drained at all times by shallow ditches which run along both sides of the house, each about two feet out from the wall. The earth from the ditches is piled against the bottom of the wall to about a foot in height. The ditches converge at the rear and run for a short distance downhill.

The sheds are built like the smaller type of house, but usually have two instead of one row of posts on each side of the central ridge, since the width requires additional support for the rafters (D). The corner posts are four or five feet high, with the overhanging roof reaching nearly to the ground. The walls are not covered. The privy for the women consists merely of a half-dozen or so small upright posts, each about four feet high, which are set up in the ground to form a square. The walls are covered and a small opening left for entrance. It has no roof. It is usually set up at one edge of the courtyard and is kept clean by vultures and pigs. The men have no toilet but merely walk a short distance from the houses to a small clearing which they use for this purpose.

The fences, which are built to inclose milpas, gardens, house groups, and sometimes orchards, are constructed of limbs, growing plants, and stone. For the first, pine posts are set up in a straight line about fifteen feet apart. All are forked at the top and have small limbs on both their sides which form forks. Horizontal limbs are laid in the forks, and between these are stuffed many brambles and thorny plants to make a solid fence. Fences of growing plants are either of the bushlike varieties of cactus, which are thorny and impenetrable when closely planted, or are composed of plants which grow in a single stalk, thickly covered with spines, and twelve to fifteen feet high. These are planted in a solid line and are held in vertical position by cane strips which are laid horizontally on both sides and tied together between the plants.[18] The stone fences, which are seldom used, contain no mortar, the stones merely being laid on top of one another to form a wall about two feet thick and four or five feet high. The hanging fence is merely an extension of the fence where it crosses a stream and stretches between the nearest fence posts on either side. A pole is laid across the tops of these two posts, and short poles with hooked ends hang from it to the stream bed, about six inches apart. They are about a foot longer than the distance from the horizontal pole to the bottom of the stream bed, so that they incline outward from the field or garden at the bottom and thus prevent animals from pushing their way through from the outside. The vertical poles are held in place by strips of cane which cross them horizontally and which are tied to them at every intersection. Pole gates and hinge gates are made, mostly by the carpenters, but are used only by those families who keep large domestic

[18] The important plants which serve as fences are the *piñuela*, *orégano*, Indian fig, *pitahaya* (*espina de tejer*), nettle, wild bay tree, *aguja de área*, *ishcanal*, *subín*, *tempisque*, *vara de bambú*, and *shaguáy*.

animals which must be taken through the fences to pasture. Both may be of Spanish origin.[19]

Each family builds its smaller houses and sheds, all the men working together and rather spasmodically, but the building of larger houses is always a community affair, especially in transporting the larger timbers from the hills and laying them in place. A man who is known for his skill in making joints with the machete and in leveling the structure is especially invited, since the average Indian has little skill at these two tasks. Usually the group continue at the work for a week or more until it is finished, although the family for which it is built may lay on the thatch roof and walls without help. Houses are usually built during the dry season when, since there is little rain, there is no rush to get them finished. During these months most of the men have little work of their own to do, and so combine visiting with all kinds of co-operative labor.

The new-house ceremony is performed each time a new house is built, for the purpose of accepting it into the community and of driving evil spirits out of it. The entire *aldea* is expected to participate in the dedication, as well as to attend the festival, which goes on for either four or eight days afterward. At the completion of the house, the owner invites the wives of several *padrinos* to come and prepare it for the blessing. They hang curtains over the doors and colored paper, resembling crepe, inside the

[19] The pole gate consists of two upright posts and six or seven horizontal poles, each five or six feet long. Holes large enough to admit the poles are bored in the inner sides of the uprights, five or six inches apart. The uprights are set in the ground, about five feet apart and forming a part of the fence, with the poles laid horizontally through the holes. One who wishes to pass through slides three or four of the center poles out of one of the posts and climbs through the opening. The hinge gate is used mostly by the Indians near the pueblos. All the pieces are joined together by notches or wooden pegs. It resembles the European hinge gate in that it is suspended from a post at one end, but in place of hinges it moves in open sockets.

room. A *padrino*, invited and paid a fee by the owner, comes soon afterward with a small gourd of water which he has taken from a sacred spring. This he sprinkles in the four corners of the kitchen and sleeping-house, both inside and out, all the while calling on any evil spirits who may be present to depart. The wives of the *padrinos* buy sky-rockets, it being considered their duty to pay for them, and while the *padrino* is blessing the house a group of men on the outside shoot them off at intervals of a few minutes. After this, invitations are formally sent to friends and relatives to come to the ensuing festival, although anyone who wishes may come, even strangers, and the owner provides festival foods and drinks for everybody. Accordion players provide music, and everyone dances, the celebration usually lasting until dawn of each day.[20]

HOUSE FURNISHINGS

The typical house groups are invariably furnished with a built-in fireplace, bed structures, tables, chest and altar supports, benches and stools, a special grinding table, mats, hangers, and ladders.[21]

The fireplace consists either of three stones which are set on the floor in the form of a triangle, upon which the cooking pots rest, or of a large clay and stone structure which

[20] In Quetzaltepeque the Catholic priest often performs this ceremony for the pueblo Indians, using holy water from the church.

[21] Fig. 5, *A* (p. 133), shows a ground plan of the sleeping-house and kitchen which the average household occupies. The kitchen contains the fireplace (*a*), the built-in table on which food is prepared (*b*), the lime olla (*c*), the eating table (*d*) with a bench or stool on both sides, the storage shelf at the rear (*e*), the implements stacked near the door (*f*), the metate at one end of the kitchen table (*g*), and the door (*h*). The sleeping-house usually contains two beds (*j*), two or three chests to hold personal belongings (*k*), benches at its front end (*l*), the altar table on which the saints are kept (*m*), and behind which there usually stands a large wooden cross, and the door (*n*). The courtyard between the two houses usually has two benches (*o*).

may be of Spanish origin. The former is found in the poorer houses. The stones are slightly separated to allow for the insertion of firewood. The latter (Fig. 5, *B*) is built by the wealthier families and by those of some Ladino culture. It is about three feet wide, six long, and four high at the high end. The Indians build them on the floor, although the Ladinos set them up on a framework of limbs, about three feet above the floor. The walls are four or five inches thick and are built in three horseshoe forms (*a*, *b*, and *c*), each inclosing a firebox. The *comal* (*d*) rests on the wall of the higher firebox and is a permanent part of it. A fire is kept under the *comal* for toasting all sorts of foods. An opening (*e*), the bottom of which is flat, is made to contain a small pitcher for boiling drinks, especially coffee. The higher flat surface (*f*) is about two feet high, and the lower one (*g*), about six inches. Hot ashes and coals are raked out from the fireboxes, and on them are set ollas of food to be kept hot until eaten. All foods are boiled in the two lower fireboxes. They are also much used for roasting spring maize on the cob.

The bed structure is used for sleeping, as tables, and as chest and altar supports. It is fixed permanently in the floor. Four small limbs, each about two feet high, are set up in the ground to serve as corner posts. The top ends are forked to contain the two side limbs which run lengthwise. The bed surface, which is made separately, is made of various reeds and canes[22] which are as long as the bed structure itself. These are laid side by side to a width of about three feet, with six or seven heavy crosspieces of cane laid about a foot apart on their underside. The crosspieces

[22] The most important are carrizo, *jimilile, vara de cama, vara de canasto,* and sunflower. The canes and reeds used in the walls and roofs of houses are sometimes used for this purpose as well.

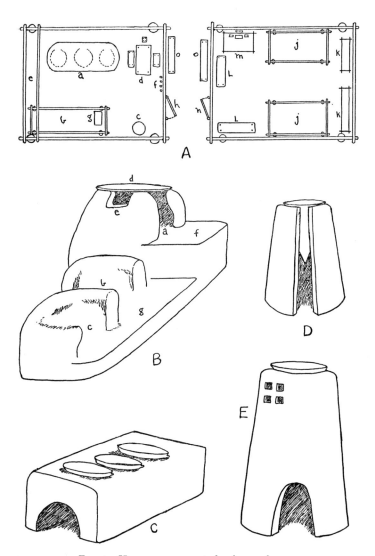

Fig. 5.—House arrangement; fireplace and ovens

are tied to each strip at the intersecting points with a heavy fiber twine which wraps around the crosspiece, up and over the strip, down and under the crosspiece, up and over the next strip, and so on for the entire width.[23] This framework is laid on the bed structure but is not attached, and on it is laid a reed mat to provide a smooth surface.[24] Beds are used for sleeping at night, although hammocks, strung in the courtyard under shade trees or in the sleeping-house, are often used for resting during the day and evening. Each adult usually has one bed and one chest in which to keep his personal belongings. The children often sleep on mats laid on the floor. The built-in tables, set up in the kitchen near the fireplace, are made like the beds. All the handling of food is done on them, and, in the absence of a grinding table, the metate rests at the end of one of them. The rest of the space is filled with gourds, small pottery vessels,[25] and food. The chest supports are about three feet long, one wide, and one high, and are used to support wooden chests above the floor in the sleeping-house. The altar support is set up in the sleeping-house or in a specially built altar-house and is about four feet long, three wide, and four high. On it are placed the altar cases, candles, foods, crosses, and other sacred objects.[26]

The wooden household articles (Fig. 6) are made prin-

[23] The same type of covering is used to cover the threshing tables, fish traps, and doorways and other openings.

[24] A few of the wealthier families buy Ladino-type carpenter-made beds of planed lumber, held together with pegs. Small ropes or thin strips of cowhide are stretched in lattice fashion across it to provide a flexible surface.

[25] Kitchen utensils are washed with a bundle of the dried fiber of the fruit of the *paxte* (*pashte*) vine, which is also used as a bathing cloth.

[26] Movable tables are occasionally bought from the Ladino carpenters and used for this purpose.

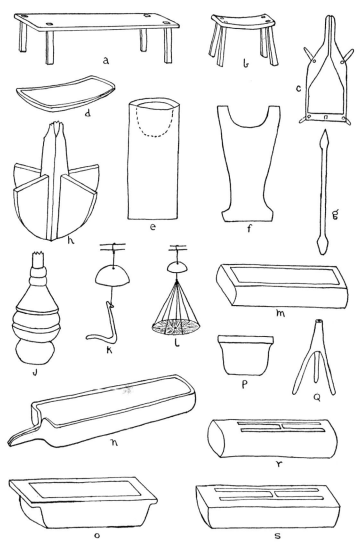

FIG. 6.—Woodworking

cipally of the hardwoods.[27]   Benches and stools consist
merely of a top board, about two inches thick, nine or ten
wide, and from one to seven or eight feet long, in the corners of which are cut four square holes for the insertion of
the legs. The legs are from six to about eighteen inches
high. No nails or pegs are used. The benches are used for
sitting and as supports for chests and other articles (a).
Two long ones are found in every courtyard, one under the
front eaves of each house. The stools are often made with
a slightly concave top board (b) to allow for greater com-
fort. The water-jar stand is a long bench which contains a
number of round holes, each five or six inches in diameter,
in which round-bottomed jars are set. Tables, used principally when eating, are made like benches and stools,
but are usually three feet long, two wide, and two high.
Ordinarily the Indian eats his meal sitting on a stool, with
his bowls of food on the floor between his feet, while the
table is set only for visitors. A small table about three feet
long, two wide, and eight or nine inches high, is used in
Quetzaltepeque for serving gourds of *chilate* during ceremonies. The top is perforated with three or four rows of
holes in which the gourds are set, so that the assembled
Indians can help themselves. Chairs are sometimes made
which resemble the European-type camp chair, except
that they do not fold up. They are very low and have a
large piece of cowhide or deerhide which hangs loosely from
top to bottom to support the sitter.[28]

A grinding table is used to support the metate. It is a
single large wooden slab (c), with four inserted legs which

[27] The most important are the oaks, pines, mahogany, brazil, *pimiento, cortez,
palo amarillo, matilisguate,* and *hormigo.* The *peine de mico* vine and the *vara
de bambú* are occasionally used.

[28] This chair is called "back stool," or "leather seat," and in Spanish, *butaca.*
It is probably of Spanish origin.

spread outward, and stands about three feet high. It is about two feet wide at the operator's end and comes to a point at the other end. The top surface is hollowed out to about an inch in depth, leaving a rim running all around its edges. This connects with a groove which runs to the pointed end. The metate is placed at the wide end for grinding, and excess water runs through the groove to a pot placed there to catch it. A square hole is carved out of the operator's end for insertion of the single leg of the front end of the metate to prevent the stone from sliding forward during grinding.

Chests, probably of Spanish origin, are used as containers for clothing and valuables and are kept in the sleeping-houses. They are about three feet long, one and one-half wide, and two deep. The lid is hinged and has a convex top, and the joints are usually pegged. Most of these are made by the Ladino carpenters.

Hangers, suspended from the house rafters, are used to protect food and objects from rats, dogs, insects, and roof snakes. The *garrapato* (*k*) is a small limb, in the shape of an acute angle and about a foot long, which is suspended with a rope. A foot or so above the limb an inverted gourd is strung on the rope to prevent the descent of animals and insects. It is used for hanging up pots of food, for clothing, and for strips of meat. The *yagual* (*l*) is made by bending a small limb into a circle about two feet in diameter, tying the ends together, and stretching any tree bark across the center in all directions to form a flat surface. It is also strung on a rope and protected with an inverted gourd, and is used for supporting ollas without lugs, fruits, and *tortillas*. Several of them are hung in the sleeping-house to contain pipes, tobacco, needles, thread, and other personal articles.

Ladders are made of single limbs, usually about ten feet long and five or six inches in diameter. Notches are cut on one side at intervals of about eight inches to serve as steps. They are cut so as to have a flat surface when the pole is set up at an angle of about 45°. These poles are used in housebuilding when laying the roof, in houses for ascending to the shelf at the rear, and principally for climbing over fences. One is placed on each side of the fence, the upper ends of both resting against the same fence post.

HOUSEHOLD UTENSILS

Household utensils consist of basketry articles, described in chapter vii, pottery, gourds, and stone metates, and a number of wooden articles.

Earthenware utensils are cups, ollas (cooking pots), water jars, bowls, pitchers, and incense burners. All except a few types, notably a kind of water jar and a glazed coffeepot, are made by the Chorti in the pottery-making *aldeas*.[29]

Nearly all the pottery types (Figs. 7 and 8) have handles, solid lugs, or ring lugs. The first is grasped with the hand, the second with the thumb and forefinger, and the third by inserting the forefinger into the lug opening. The pieces are both slipped and unslipped, decorated and undecorated, and are made with flat bases only. The only round-bottomed pieces used are the large *cántaros* which the Indians buy in the markets from the Pokoman. Cups are three to five inches deep, about five inches wide at the orifice, and three at the base (Fig. 7, *a*, *b*, and *c*). They are used for drinking liquid foods, such as maize gruels, and

---

[29] The manufacture of pottery is described below, pp. 167–70. No European ware is sold in the Jocotán and Olopa markets, although the Ladinos buy a few metal containers in the city of Chiquimula and from the few peddlers who visit the pueblos. Very few of the Indians own them, their reason being that they have no way to repair leaks in them.

for such beverages as coffee and cacao. They are probably of Spanish origin and are not much used. The cups are

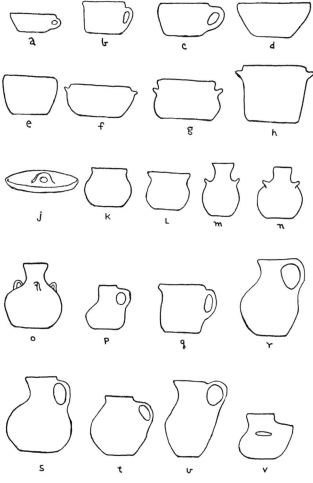

Fig. 7.—Pottery types

never decorated and are slipped with either light or dark red. Bowls vary in size from two to five inches deep, four to eight inches in diameter at the orifice, and two to four inches in diameter at the base (*d* and *e*). They are usually slightly constricted at the orifice. All are slipped inside and out with light and dark red, the outer surface left with an "onion" finish.[30] Nearly all are decorated with the black straight and wavy lines on the inner side. Bowls are used as eating utensils, as drinking cups, and as dippers with which foods are scooped from the cooking pots.

The cooking ollas (*f*, *g*, and *h*) are used only for boiling solid foods, the first for maize, the second for beans, and the third for miscellaneous foods. Some have vertical walls without constriction, others are constricted like bowls, and still others have rounded walls with flared orifices. All have solid lugs. They are neither slipped nor decorated, as they quickly blacken in the fireplace. They vary in size from five to nineteen inches in diameter and from six to twelve inches in depth. Every family owns a dozen or so which are in constant use for boiling foods. The olla cover (*j*) is laid over the ollas during cooking. Its side rim varies from one-half inch to one inch deep and flares outward. All have handles in the center.

Two types of open ollas used for noncooking purposes are the *bongo* (*k*) and the *burna* (*l*). The *bongo* is used as a container for *chicha* while it is fermenting. It sometimes has three vertical ring lugs placed equidistantly around the base of the neck and is slipped in red and brown. Its neck is slightly smaller and shorter than that of most ollas. It is usually about a foot deep, ten inches in diameter at the center, and six or seven in diameter at the orifice. The *burna*[31] is a small olla used by the women especially for carrying beans and bean soup to the men who are at work in the milpas. It is about eight inches deep and six inches in

[30] See below, pp. 169–70. [31] Called *p'u'rna'* in Chorti.

diameter and has two horizontal ring lugs to which a rope is attached so that it can be slung over the shoulder. It has a flared orifice and is slipped in red.

The bottle-necked jars are used only for holding and carrying water (*m, n,* and *o*). The women carry them on the right hip to the nearest spring to secure water for use in the kitchen, where they are usually kept on a separate table. They vary in depth from ten to fourteen inches, in greatest diameter from nine to eleven inches, in diameter at the neck from three to four inches, and hold three gallons or more. All bottle-necked vessels have either two or three ring lugs; if two, they are placed horizontally; if three, they are placed vertically. All are slipped in red or brown, usually with the "onion" finish. The bases are flat. A round-bottomed water olla, several of which every family owns, is made only by the Pokoman and is said to be of superior quality. These are kept in the kitchens on tables which contain holes into which the ollas are set.

The pitchers are principally used for boiling liquid foods. One type is used for boiling milk (*q*), and others are used for boiling coffee, *atol, chilate,* and cacao (*p, r, s, t,* and *u*). All have handles of various sizes and slightly constricted spouts. Most have the general shape of ollas[32] and vary from five to about twelve inches in depth and from four to ten inches in greatest diameter. A peculiar type is the "duck effigy" pitcher (*Ch.* "bird olla"), in which the rear side projects outward as a tail, with two useless solid lugs on the sides which suggest the wings. The duck head is omitted (*v*). These are seldom made now, although several potters stated that they were commonly made until a generation ago.

[32] This suggests that they are merely native ollas with Spanish handles and spouts attached.

The largest of the pottery containers are used principally for boiling cane juice. One type (Fig. 8, *a*) is set at
the spout end of the wooden canoe under the sugar press

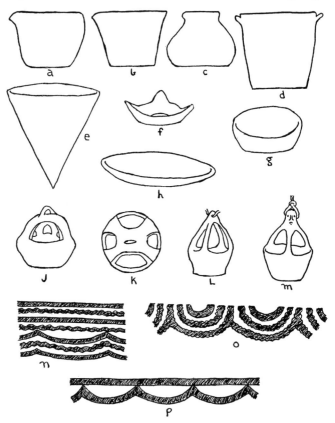

Fig. 8.—Pottery types and decorative designs

to catch the juice as it comes out of the rolls. Other types
(*b* and *c*) are used for stirring the boiled juice until it hardens sufficiently to be poured into the sugar molds. All
three types have two horizontal ring lugs. Another type

POTTERY

(d) is built permanently into the boiling vat (Fig. 5, C), usually three to each vat, in which the cane juice is boiled. It is about thirty inches high and has two small solid lugs on its sides. The sugar ollas are often used for storing foods and other objects in the kitchen. Each kitchen has one for lime, one for shelled maize, and perhaps one for beans, usually stored under the tables or in the corners. The olla used for boiling soap (e) is cone shaped and is built solidly into the crown of the soap oven (Fig. 5, D).

The water-jar supports, used under the Pokoman jars, are usually unslipped. The sides flare outward to fit the base of the ollas which are set in them. One type (Fig. 8, f) has three points, while another (g) resembles a bowl. Both types are left open at the bases. They vary in height from three to four inches, and in top diameter from three to about eight inches. The comal, or griddle, varies in diameter from ten to twenty inches, and in central depth from one to three inches (h). It is round and saucer shaped and is never slipped or decorated. It is attached permanently to the rim of the highest of the fireboxes of the fireplace, and on it are roasted maize, cacao, coffee, tortillas, and many other foods.

The incense burners have either three or four arms, are round, and have flat bases. Through a small hole at the top is passed a cord the other end of which is usually tied to a rafter. One type (j) has four "windows," with the largest one in front through which the copal wax is inserted. A ring lug is attached at the top for the suspending cord (top view shown at k). The type at l is the most commonly used, as it is easily made and sells cheaply in the market. The most elaborate type (m) has a human face etched at the top with indented lines, and a hole passing through the head for the cord. All incense burners are made in a single piece and are unslipped, slipped in red, or slipped in black. They have no other decoration.

Gourd containers (Fig. 3, p. 117) are made from the wild and cultivated gourd vines and trees. The gourd fruits are round or slightly oval, extremely oval or oblong, elliptical, and bottle shaped, either with a long slender neck or of two compartments with a joining neck. If to be made into open vessels, the fruit is cut in half while still fresh and green. The halves are boiled for about an hour, the inner portion cut out, and the inner sides of the husks rubbed with a small handstone. The boiling is said to stop shriveling. The husks are then dried and bleached for eight days. In making closed vessels, a small hole is cut in one end, the gourd boiled, and the contents gouged out as much as possible. The husk is then partly filled with pebbles and shaken in order to break loose the rest of the meat, soaked in water for eight days, and dried in the sun for four more. A maize cob is inserted as a stopper.

The round or oval fruit is halved and made into two bowls (Sp. *guacal*; Ch. *rutc*), which are also used as drinking cups, eating dishes, and saucers (Fig. 3, *d* and *e*). If perforated all over the underside, and with handle attached, it is used as a strainer (*f*) for cane juice at the sugar oven, and if merely cut off at the smaller end, with a shoulder rope inserted on one side (*g*), it is carried on the shoulder by the men as a seed container when planting maize and beans. The oblong fruit is halved and made into two elongated bowls (Sp. *jícara*; Ch. *simax*), or is left whole and used for storing small quantities of salt, ground cacao, and ground coffee in the kitchen. An opening, large enough to admit the hand, is cut on one side near the top (*h*), and at the top end the cord which is tied to a house beam is inserted through two small holes. The elliptical fruit is halved and made into two pointed bowls (Sp. *morro;* Ch. *tsimax*). The bottle-shaped fruit is usually made into canteens (Sp. *tecomate;* Ch. *murur*). These are wound around in various ways with agave twine or small rope (*j, k,* and *l*), and can be slung on the shoulder. They are carried by the men as water canteens when on journeys or working in the milpas. Other shapes (*m* and *n*) have shorter necks and fairly flat bottoms and are kept in the kitchens to contain water and liquid foods. The smaller *tecomates* are halved and made into dippers, ladles, and spoons, the neck end usually being used as a handle (*o, p,* and *q*).

The Indians do no stoneworking but buy all their stone articles from the Pokoman, the most important being the metate, handstone, and water filter. The metate (Fig. 3, *r*) has three legs,[33] a long pointed one in the center of the end next the operator, and two shorter ones at the corners of the other; the resulting slope permits excess water to drain off during the grinding. The two sides, each about an inch wide, are slightly raised to prevent the water and ground maize from sliding off. The inner width is about one foot; the length varies from eighteen inches to two feet. The grinding surface is somewhat concave in cross-section, thus permitting a slight dipping motion in the grinding. The handstone, or mano, is a polished piece of similar stone, about two inches wide and thick, and of a length about equal to the inner width of the metate.[34]

The water filter is a porous cone-shaped stone with an opening at the top which is filled with water. It is supported with point downward in a wooden frame. The

[33] *tcu'* ("breast"), leg of metate (so called because each leg has the shape of a woman's breast).

[34] An end view of the metate, with mano attached to indicate how it fits, is shown in Fig. 3, *s* (p. 117).

water filters through seven or eight inches of stone, drops out at the bottom point, and falls into an olla kept underneath. A few of the Indians keep these in their houses, although they are mostly sold to the Ladinos. The Pokoman also make and sell stone pillar supports to the Ladinos, who use them as foundations for the upright timbers of their houses.

Wooden utensils include mortars, platters and "canoes," candle-holders, and chocolate beaters.

Mortars are extensively used for husking coffee, cacao, and rice, for pounding up fish poisons, and occasionally for shelling maize. They are about three feet high and one to one and one-half in outside diameter. The grinding cavity is sufficiently less in diameter at the top to leave a wall all around which is about two inches thick. The cavity, about a foot deep, narrows as it goes down, barely fitting the end of the pestle at the bottom. The cheaper mortars have perpendicular sides (Fig. 6, *e*), but a more graceful form (*f*) is made with a small base and slender neck. The cavity is burned out with a charcoal fire. The top and inner surfaces of the wall are covered with earth and sprinkled constantly as the fire burns in order to prevent the wall from burning through. The pestle (*g*) is about four feet long. The ends are rectangular, with the sides tapering slightly toward the ends. The wider end is used for breaking the husks, and the narrower end, for removing them completely. They weigh from ten to twelve pounds.[35]

Wooden platters are made of a slab of wood, two to five feet long, about half as wide, and about two inches thick (*d*). The top surface is carved out to leave a rim around the edges, giving it the appearance of an oblong plate. It

[35] Mortars are principally made from oak and tamarind wood, and pestles, from the wood of the *madre cacao* tree.

is used principally for washing clothes and may be of Spanish origin, as the Indians more often use a large rough rock, located in a small running stream, for this purpose.

Wooden canoes resembling European bathtubs more than canoes are used as containers. The smaller ones (*m*) serve as feed and water troughs for domestic animals and fowls. One of the larger type is used as a container under sugar presses to catch the falling juice (*n*), and another, for shelled maize and beans when these are being mixed with ash or sand in the curing process (*o*), as well as for pot plants, such as coriander and peppermint.[36] Its end view is shown at *p* in Figure 6. The canoes vary in length from one to twelve feet, in width from one to three, and in depth from one to two. The original log is shaped to four square sides and hollowed out with the adz to leave a thick wall and bottom. A rope is passed through a hole bored in a projection left at one end of some of the larger ones and the canoe dragged by oxen to wherever it is required. The canoe used under the sugar press projects at one end to a small spout, through which the cane juice runs to the vessel placed underneath it.

Candle-holders are set up at the four corners of the altars to support the large candles which are burned during ceremonies. They are of wood only (*q*), although it is said that pottery ones were made until about forty years ago. A limb, two to four inches in diameter, with either three or four smaller limbs branching off from it is cut about six inches back from the smaller limbs. The smaller branches, which serve as the legs, are left from two to three feet long. The cut end serves as the holder: a hole is bored for several inches down its center, and the candle inserted in the hole.

---

[36] In Quetzaltepeque a small one is placed near the altar of the patron saint in the *cofradía* and contains live frogs (see p. 384, n. 29).

The wood is smoothed down and polished with a hand-stone.

The chocolate beater is made of cedar, as this wood is said not to give a foreign taste to foods. The cheaper type (*h*) is much sold in the markets. Its handle varies from eight inches to two feet in length, is rounded, and has its bottom end carved out so that only its four corners are left. The two wings, each about five inches high, are notched halfway across in their centers, fitted together, and inserted tightly into the bottom end of the handle. A type more commonly used (*j*) is made on the lathe and only by the Ladino carpenters. It contains five or six bands of raised design and is made from a single piece. The two rings at the top of the base are carved away from the handle and left free.[37] The beater is used principally for beating and frothing liquid cacao and for beating *chilate* to thicken it. It is revolved by placing the handle between the palms and rubbing them back and forth.

[37] It is said that many years ago this was the only type made, and that all were shaped by hand.

CHAPTER VII

INDUSTRY

THE important industries[1] are textiles, pottery, sugar (described in chapter v), and woodworking. Less important manufactures, described later in this chapter, include lime, leather goods, charcoal, pine torches, soap, glue, copal, candles, indigo dye, and cigars.

TEXTILES

The textiles made are nets, bags, hammocks, rope, tumplines, mats, hats, baskets, and brooms. Involved are a number of special tools and implements and a variety of techniques.

The implements (Fig. 9) include the rasping stick and pole, hand twister, machine spinners, shuttle, and spindle. The rasping pole is a single large timber, about seven inches in diameter and six feet long, one side of which is planed down to a flat surface for its entire length (*a*). It is stood against a tree or house corner post when used. A small stick, about eighteen inches long, is suspended by two ropes from a peg at the top end and allowed to hang against the flat surface. Agave leaves are tied to this stick when being scraped. The rasping stick is about eighteen inches long and two inches in diameter (*b*). About six inches of each end is rounded off to serve as handles. The inner portion contains a deep groove on one side which is cut out with a knife (*c*). The two upper edges of the groove are

---

[1] For a general discussion of the manufactures and professionalization of industry see below, pp. 187–203.

sharpened to a fine line, and with these the scraping is done. The sticks are made of oak or quebracho wood.

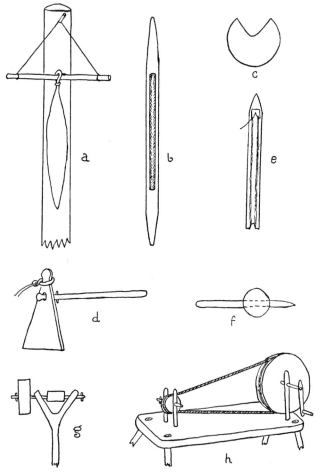

Fig. 9.—Textile implements

The rope and twine twister is used for twisting several strands of fiber into rope and heavy cord and consists of a revolver and handle (*d*). The revolver is about eight inches long and four wide at its base. Its top end is shaped into a knob, and directly below this a hole is bored through. The handle, a foot long, has a wide knob on its end which passes through the revolver, and a peg is passed through it just behind the revolver to prevent the latter from sliding back. The agave strands to be twisted are attached to the revolver knob, and the other ends tied to a tree or other object. The revolver can be easily made to turn on the handle, as most of its weight is at its bottom end.[2]

The machine spinners are operated either by a rope or by a crank. The rope type (*g*) is a forked pole about five feet long, the unforked end of which is set firmly in the ground. A wooden shaft passes horizontally through the two ends of the fork, the inner portion of the shaft being left four or five inches in diameter to serve as a pulley around which the operating rope is wrapped. A heavy wooden flywheel is attached to one end of the shaft, and in the other end is inserted a wooden peg to which the fiber to be spun is attached. The operating rope is eight or ten feet long and at its center is wrapped once around the pulley.[3] The crank type (*h*) consists of a heavy board which is set up on four spreading legs and contains a shaft at its front and rear ends. The pulley of the front shaft is five or six inches in diameter; this shaft contains a peg in one end to which the fiber is attached and has a flywheel attached to its other end. The rear shaft contains a pulley about eighteen inches in diameter. This is placed in the center of the shaft, with

[2] A similar hand twister is used at Mitla (Parsons, 1936, p. 58).

[3] The operator, usually a boy, sits in front of it, holds both ends of the rope taut, and, by pulling the end in his right hand, causes the pulley and flywheel to revolve. He loosens the rope until the right end is near the pulley as before, and pulls it again. The flywheel keeps the shaft turning while the rope is re-winding around it between the pulls.

a handle attached to one end. The two pulleys are connected with a rope belt, so that the twisting of the strands is greatly accelerated. Many of the professional ropemakers, as at Tunucó, use this type of spinner.

The shuttle is used for tying knots in fishing nets and for netting all articles of agave fiber. It is a pointed stick (*e*), about ten inches long, a half-inch wide, and a quarter-inch thick. Two inner spaces are carved out, leaving the tongue at one end and the two end prongs at the other. Its size depends upon the netting done with it; for netting fishing nets it is of the size given above, but for maize bags it is much larger. The thread is wound around the tongue, down between the end prongs, up and around the tongue, and so on. A round stick, about a foot long, is used as a gauge in netting and knotting. The thread is wrapped around it each time a loop is made, so that all the loops in the finished piece are of the same size. Its diameter varies according to the size of the loops desired.

The spindle is a small stick, about five inches long and a quarter-inch wide, which is passed through the center of a ball of fired clay (*f*). It is used only for spinning cotton thread. The bottom of the shaft is sharpened to a point, upon which the spindle whirls when in use. The clay ball is placed near the pointed end in order to maintain its balance. The cotton to be spun is tied to the upper end of the shaft, and the latter is spun with the fingers in a gourd vessel. Spindles are seldom seen, as very little cotton is spun.

The most important of the textile materials are agave, cotton, carrizo cane, sedge, other reeds and canes, palm fronds, and the *saraque* bush.

The large agave leaves are cut close to the trunk and brought to the work shed. Each is beaten on a flat rock until the sap has run out and most of the pulpy covering broken off. Both ends are whacked against the top until the leaf is in shreds. It is then tied at one end in a single knot to the holder of the rasping pole. The remaining pulp is then scraped off with the rasping stick, which is applied lightly in order not to break the fiber. The lower half is scraped until only fiber remains, after which the leaf is reversed on the pole and the other half scraped. The worker stands in front of the pole and scrapes with a downward stroke,[4] thus producing a bundle of yellowish fiber about two and a half feet long. It is spread out in small bunches, usually on the housetops, to dry and bleach for several days, usually four. Drying is said to be necessary since undried fiber would straighten out after being twisted.

Cotton is picked, laid out in the sun to dry, and spun. The seeds are removed and stored.

The carrizo stalks are cut near the streams, sliced with a knife from one end to the other while green, and flattened out with a handstone to a width of about one inch. Before drying, these are sliced to the desired widths, varying from one-eighth to one-half inch. The former are used as weft strands in baskets, and the latter, as warp strands in baskets and for the weaving of certain mats. The strands are then dried in the sun for several days. The *vara de canasto* stalks are prepared in the same way for basket-weaving.

The sedge stalks, which are triangular in cross-section, are cut in the fields or along the stream banks and dried in the sun for three or four days. They are then tied in bundles and placed on the rafters of the sleeping-house until used. The weaver peels back the three outer surfaces of

---

[4] In Chan Kom, Yucatan, the leaf is laid horizontally on a board or rock, and the worker applies the rasping stick by means of an outward stroke, i.e., away from himself, as in washing clothes (Redfield and Villa, 1934, p. 40).

each stalk at one end with a bone knife and then pulls the surfaces off for the entire length with her hand. The hearts of the stalks are laid aside for other purposes.[5] With one end of the knife she flattens out each strip against a flat stone, thus smoothing the inner sides, and the strips are ready to be woven into mats.

The palm fronds are cut at the end of the stalk while young and therefore pliable. These are dried in the sun and split with the bone knife into shreds of the desired width. The center stalks of the *saraque* bush, which has an inflorescence at the summit, are cut from the plant but are not prepared in any way.

The important plants from which dyes are made are the campeachy, brazil, fustic, and coral trees, the *camotillo* herb, and the *mashaste* vine.[6] The wood of the first two are used for dyeing, and for the others, the roots, leaves, buds, twigs, and stalks are used. The textile strands are dyed before being made into finished articles. The limbs or inner portion of the tree are cut into sticks; these are split with the machete into thin strips or shavings, and a quantity of them boiled in an olla. After boiling they are removed and the textile strands are boiled in the same water for several hours. The other plant parts are usually boiled with the strands for dyeing. Lime is usually added to soften the outer coverings of the strands, and ash is sometimes added to produce different shades of color. The mashaste furnishes a reddish brown; the brazil, a red; and the campeachy, fustic, and coral, a yellow. Brazil wood boiled

[5] These are plaited into lengths of four or five feet each, a quantity of them twisted together, and the ends brought together to form a circle. Three of the braids are tied equidistantly from one another to the circle, and the other ends are tied to a rafter. The circle lies horizontally and is used to hold containers of food or other articles.

[6] Besides *jiquilite*, from which indigo dye is made. See below, pp. 183–84.

with ash gives a purple. The *camotillo* roots are boiled with lime and used for dyeing red. This dye is rubbed on wood, especially tobacco pipes, to produce a red stain. *Jiquilite*, from which indigo is made, and the *tinta de monte* and *cuajatinta* shrubs are used only as bluings for cotton cloth. Textile decoration is done by weaving dyed strands with undyed ones in various patterns, and by variations in the textile techniques. In some cases both are used in the same articles.[7]

The textile techniques include the spinning of cotton and agave fiber, rope-twisting, knotting, braiding, netting, and weaving.

Cotton is spun[8] for use as sewing thread and candle-wicks, and in the smaller fishing nets. A small bundle of fiber is stretched thin and about a foot in length. One end is attached to the upper end of the spindle and the other held in the hand of the spinner. The spindle is spun in a gourd until the cotton is reduced to a thread. Agave fiber spinning is done both by hand and on the machine. For machine spinning, the operator attaches two small bundles of fiber to the shaft pin and twists them into a single strand by hand for a foot or so. With her right hand she constantly holds the twisted portion taut as the machine does the twisting, while she splices on new strands with the left. She releases the hold of her right hand every few moments to allow a few inches of the untwisted strands in her left hand to twist, and in this way slowly walks away from the machine until a twine about two hundred feet long is spun. Hand-spinning requires more skill. The worker rolls each

[7] Dyeing is largely done at the present time with imported aniline dyes of green and red, especially by the Indians who live nearest the pueblos. The native dyes are more commonly used in the remoter *aldeas*, however.

[8] *t'sohnok*, "cotton thread" (usually of about the weight of the No. 20 thread sold in the United States).

bundle on his leg and strikes it in the air with his hand to make it fluffy. He holds two bunches of strands in his left hand, keeping them separated with his thumb, and rolls them with the right hand down the upper leg or down the calf. The strands under his hand are about two inches apart. With a single rolling he spins each strand into a single twine and then allows the two to twist together before lifting the hand. A skilful spinner produces about five inches of twine or small rope with a single rolling of his right hand. Machine-made twine is usually made into cord and rope, while that made by hand, which is much finer, is made into bags and straps.

Rope-twisting is done with the twisting machine and the hand twister, which are at opposite ends of the rope. After the fiber is spun into a single strand on the machine, one end is taken off and placed around a forked pole. Two operators are required. They hold the strand taut as they lay it in the fork, one walking in a circle around the pole until the two ends are brought together, after which they are tied to the knob of the hand twister. The end at the pole is attached to the machine, so that the double strand is twisted at both ends. After this, the length is pulled around the forked pole as before, and twisted with the hand twister into four-strand rope. The ropes vary in thickness from about one-quarter to three-quarters of an inch in diameter. Most are of four strands, made of two lengths of two-stranded rope twisted together. All are of the same length, about thirty feet. A small two-stranded rope is sometimes made with dyed fiber, one or two strands being dyed and the others left undyed, resulting in a spiral decoration. The twine is of two strands only.

Knotting is used only in the manufacture of fishing nets. In fishing-net design (Fig. 10, *a*), the squares are about

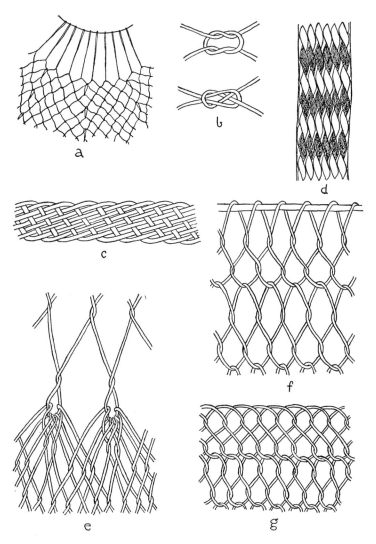

Fig. 10.—Knotting, braiding, and netting techniques

one-half inch on all sides, and are knotted together at every intersection. The two types of knots are shown at *b* in Figure 10. The squares are kept of uniform size by being tied around the bamboo stick. All the threads radiate outward from the heavy cord shown at the top of the drawing. The threads are looped around it, and its ends tied into a knot after the net is finished, thus forming the net's closed center. As the net must lie horizontally when opened, new threads are added, as shown, at every third or fourth knot all around its circumference. These are merely looped around knots already tied. The new threads are dispensed with some eight or ten inches before the operator reaches the outer edge of the net, thus leaving an outer band which is restricted, and which causes the net to settle in the water like an open parachute.

Braiding is used in making bag straps, tumplines, hammocks, and the coverings for food hangers. The braided shoulder strap for small bags (*c*) is usually about an inch in width. Each strand serves as both warp and weft, since each is braided out to the edge of the strap and then turned back and braided as before, crossing and recrossing in zigzag fashion. These straps are attached to all the shoulder bags of the single-compartment type and are braided of an even number of strands, usually eight. If the latter is desired, four long strands are looped around the topmost horizontal strand of the bag, at any point on its circumference. The four double strands are then braided into a strip about three feet in length. Four shorter strands are looped in the same way directly opposite the longer ones and are braided into a strap six or seven inches long. A hole is left in the free end of it, into which the end of the long strap can be tied in a simple knot, so that the entire strap is adjustable in length. The end of the longer strap and the hole in the end of the short one are sewed with a buttonhole stitch, a fine agave thread being used for this purpose.

In the braided headbands for tumplines (*d*), each strand is a slightly twisted bunch of fibers, about one-fourth inch in diameter. A twine serves as the warp; at every point where the vertical double strands twist, the warp twine is run horizontally between them to hold them together. A single twine is used; it runs through the first horizontal band, down and through the third, up and through the second, down and through the fourth, and so on. The strands are usually alternately plain and died with brazil coloring to a bright red. The bands are about eighteen inches long and have a small hole in each end, sewn around with the buttonhole stitch, through which the carrying ropes or straps (Ch. "its arm") are passed. Other articles similar to the tumpline, such as girths and cinches for saddles and bands for tying merchandise to pack saddles, are braided in the same way.[9]

Hammocks (*e*) are not braided with the shuttle, the twine being looped in and out by hand, and in some cases with a long wooden needle. One end of the long twines are tied to a corner post of the house and are braided with the hands as in braiding the hair. The hammocks are usually of the ten-strand type, although this is sometimes increased to twelve or fourteen. Most are undecorated, but occasionally the strands are dyed in alternating groups of three. For the larger ones, a type of false loom is used.[10]

[9] The fiber tumpline is fast giving way to the more durable leather tumpline (see p. 179). Both types are called in Spanish, *mecapal*. Girths and cinches are, of course, sold only to the Ladinos, since the Indians use no carrying or riding animals.

[10] The loom consists of four boards held together in the form of a rectangle. The end pieces are movable and can be brought together or moved apart, depend-

They are principally sold to the Ladinos and are of all sizes, the average being about nine feet long and six wide. A small hammock, about three feet long, is made for infants for day sleeping.

Netting is used for making most of the bags and is done with the large shuttle, the size of the openings being kept uniform by the insertion of one to three fingers. For the large maize bags, as well as the smaller ones which are carried with the tumpline, the bands are about two inches wide (*f*), and the openings just large enough to prevent ears of maize from slipping through. A heavy cord runs around the opening of the bag, on which is hung the first horizontal band of small twine, running from left to right. The second and remaining bands are hung in the same way to the bottom of the bands directly above them until the desired depth is obtained. The bottom band of the finished piece is strung with a heavy cord, as was done at the top, and this is tied into a knot, thus closing the opening. The larger maize bags have wide straps attached, which serve as tumplines for carrying them. They are used for transporting and storing fruit and maize ears and contain about as much as a man can carry. They are sometimes made in the form of saddlebags and sold to the Ladino carriers for transporting maize by muleback.

A more elaborate netting (*g*) is used for the smaller shoulder bags. The top cord is dispensed with, since the top band is given sufficient strength by additional looping. The bands are about three-fourths inch in width. These bags are usually four or five inches wide and about eight

---

ing upon the length of the hammock to be made. They are held firm with pegs which fit into holes on the upper rims in the side pieces. The end pieces have small nonremovable pegs around which the strands are strung. A number of strands are stretched the length of the loom and around the small end pegs. The remaining strands are braided around these, according to the design desired.

deep. As the native trousers have no pockets, they are carried, especially by the men, to contain such personal articles as tobacco, pipe, money, flint outfit, unfinished hat strips, etc. No man is seen away from home without one, and women sometimes carry them. Drawstrings are sometimes added, though not usually. Many are decorated in brazil red, with red and plain bands alternating.

Weaving is used in making the double-compartment bags of agave fiber, baskets, mats, hats, and brooms.

In weaving agave bags a long wooden eye needle is used for pulling the warp threads alternately over and under the weft threads. The strands used are of stiff heavy cord, as stiffness is required to keep the strands apart in the loosely woven pieces (Fig. 11, *a*). A false loom similar to that used in braiding hammocks is used for agave weaving and is about a foot wide and two long. The entire frame is covered with a single warp strand which runs around the end pegs from one end of the loom to the other until the desired width is obtained. A single weft strand is then run from one side to the other, over and under each of the vertical strands, until the desired length is obtained. The finished piece is taken off the frame, its ends brought together, and the sides sewn together to form a bag. The carrying strap is usually a tumpline which is attached to both sides. The double-compartment bag (Ch. "double handbag") is used for carrying personal articles and is worn over the right shoulder, one bag hanging in front and the other behind.

In basket-weaving six to ten warp strands of carrizo or *vara de canasto* are used for each basket. These are laid across one another in a circle, all transversing in their centers (*b*). As near the center as possible, two weft strands are woven over and below the arms of the warps in a spiral pattern. Two strands are woven simultaneously in order

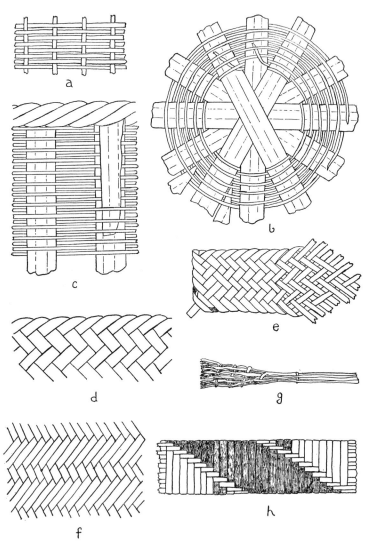

FIG. 11.—Weaving techniques

that as each circle is made any given weft strand will be alternately passed over and under all the warp strands without exception. Additional warp strands are added as the basket widens. At the orifice the warp strands are bent down on the outer side and the last inch or so of them woven into the weft strands (c). This holds the warps in place and seems to serve as a decoration. All orifices are wrapped for a half-inch downward with palm frond strips which are about a half-inch wide. These are passed under the second or third weft from the top, up and over the orifice, down under the weft, and so on around the basket. For the larger baskets, warp strands are used for this wrapping. The decoration consists of dyed bands, about a half-inch wide, which run horizontally, alternating with undyed bands. Brazil red and an artificial green are commonly used. A fine type of twined basket is made by the Ladinos and a few of the Indians near the pueblo of San Juan Hermita. The twining element consists of narrow strips, about one-fourth inch wide, of split palm fronds, which are wrapped and tied around horizontal reeds which serve as the base.[11]

Nearly all the baskets are bowl shaped, about twice as wide at the orifice as deep. Other shapes, taken from pitchers, water jars, and bowls, are made, especially at Olopa. For pitcher-shaped baskets, lids are made which fit down into the orifice and are made like the bottoms of the baskets. Handles are stretched in an arc shape over the tops. These are made of several layers of warp strands which are wrapped with palm frond strips. Bowl-shaped baskets are used to hold fruit, maize, and beans, and the women carry

[11] This type of basket-weaving is done by the Jacalteca (La Farge and Byers, 1931). Several Ladinos in Jocotán stated that the twined basket was introduced into the area not many years ago. The Indians have not taken to making them extensively.

them on the head in transporting goods to market. They are especially used for straining liquids, such as honey and gruels, for washing the lye out of cooked maize, and for winnowing maize, rice, and coffee. Pottery-shaped baskets are used principally to contain personal articles.

In mat-weaving the sedge strands run diagonally across the piece, each woven alternately over and under every two strands it crosses (*d*) A selvedge is left on all four sides by turning the last two or three inches of each strand back and under the piece, and weaving it into two or three of the cross-strands to hold it in place. Each mat is woven in two halves, the two being spliced together to form the finished piece. The strands on the sides which are to be spliced are left unwoven for eight or ten inches, and these are woven together so that the central joint cannot be detected. No loom is used; the woman sits on the ground and weaves her mat with the strands laid out before her, using no instruments. To weave in a new strand she lifts the strands which run in the opposite direction with her left hand and with the right hand lays the new strand in place. With her fingernails she keeps the woven strands pulled down tight as she proceeds. A few of the mats are decorated with dyed strands which run diagonally toward the four corners, alternating with undyed ones. They are usually the size of beds, three or four feet wide and five to seven feet long. All beds are covered with mats, which serve as mattresses, and one is placed on the floor near it to stand on while dressing. They are placed under threshers to catch the grains which fall through and are spread out in the courtyards to be covered with foods which are drying in the sun. Bags are made of them by ringing the two ends together and sewing up the open sides with heavy agave cord, which is also looped over and under the two edges at the top to close it up. These vary from one to four or five feet square, and are used for storing foods and for carrying goods to market with the tumpline. Mats are used for covering doors, altars, wall cracks, and other openings, are spread on the earth floors, and are hung from the rafters in the sleeping-houses by the women to provide privacy while dressing.

Two types of hats, the sewn and the strictly woven, are made. The former is the more common and is quickly put together. To make it, a single long strip, about one inch wide (e), is woven in an "over two and under two" technique[12] like that used in mat-making. Thin strips of palm frond are used in weaving the strip, each being turned back at the edge and woven diagonally across, as before. New strips are woven in with the ends of the old ones as the latter run out. The sewing of the hat is started by twisting the strip in a horizontal spiral, the beginning of the spiral being the center of the hat crown. With a small needle, the spiral is sewn on both sides to the spirals next to it, from the center to the brim. Every second shred in the strip is sewn to every second one of the spiral next to it. A spiral can be made to flare downward by sewing every third or fourth of its shreds to every second shred of the spiral already sewn, and to flare upward, by attaching every second shred to every third or fourth shred of the spiral already sewn. In this way the proper shape is given to the hat.[13] The woven hat is made in two pieces, the crown being first made and then sewn to the brim. The bottom edge of the crown, as well as the outer edge of the brim, are selvedged in the same way as are the mats, by turning the

[12] An identical hat strip is made at Jacaltenango (*ibid.*, p. 60).

[13] The sewn hat sells for eight pesos in the markets (about twelve cents American).

strips back and under and fastening them under two or three cross-strands. It is excellently woven and is said to be watertight. Only the woven hat is decorated, and usually by colored bands, about an inch wide, which run horizontally, alternating with plain bands. A weaving decoration is often made by allowing a series of strands, usually three, to pass over or under another series before the "over two and under two," or "over one and under one" technique is resumed again (*f*). This results in a series of angular bands running all around. Most of the hats have a relatively low crown, the top of which is rather flat, and the brim of which turns upward around the edge. A few have the high pointed crown and wide brim of the Mexican sombrero. The hat-makers make them in different sizes for market sale, so that purchasers can find their exact fits.

Brooms are made mostly from whole palm fronds and are the only type used by both Indians and Ladinos. They are about four feet long. The fronds are cut so that each has a stalk two to three feet long. Four or five of these are tied together by weaving several frond strips in and out around the fronds themselves. The stalks, which serve as the handle, are tied around with agave cord (*g*).[14] A small whisk broom is made from the *saraque* grass. The stalks of the plant are gathered together to form the handle, and these are bound into a circular form with thin strips of sedge bark which pass in and out around the handle (*h*). The shaded bark strips are dyed red, while the uncolored ones are left plain. At those places along the handle where the vertical stalks are exposed, the bark wrapping is passed under those stalks, thus producing the decorative form as shown. The same type of broom is made from the *vara de escoba*, a wild cane.

[14] A large broom is also made in the same way from the stalks and leaves of the *escoba amarga* shrub and the *maicillo montés*.

POTTERY

Pottery, the forms of which have been described in chapter vi, is made by both molding and coiling, the first of which is more commonly done. Sand is brought from a dry stream bed and sifted through a basket to remove all the larger pebbles, after which it is winnowed to remove the dust and fine dirt. The pure sand is used as a temper. Clay is brought from the nearest clay bed and the pebbles and other foreign matter removed with the fingers. The clay is left to soak overnight in a large olla to make it more pliable and cohesive. The pottery-maker begins the next morning by grinding down the clay on a flat board with the base of her palms. She places a couple of handfuls of the clay on the board, sprinkles it with water and a quantity of the sand, and grinds it with a movement like that used in grinding maize. This breaks up the hard clots and mixes in the temper, until the whole is a sandy paste. Each batch is ground five or six times on the board, rolled into a ball, and laid aside until about three jugfuls are prepared.

A banana leaf is laid on a low stool and a ball of clay placed on it. The woman runs her fingertips up the sides of it until they are vertical. With the left hand on the outside, she digs out the center, pulling the material out to the side, thus building up the rim higher and higher. The sides are then shaped with the two hands, the one inside and the other outside. The bottom of the clay ball is pressed flat against the banana leaf to serve as the base of the finished piece. The sides are thinned down by holding the left hand flat against the outside and by running the fingers of the right hand up the inner side, thus pulling the clay up to the rim. The inner side is smoothed with the first finger, the clay thus removed being placed on the rim. The hands are dipped in water every few minutes to prevent the clay from sticking to them. The final thinning is done with a small scraper made of a piece of gourd or calabash. This has a convex and concave edge, both of which are sharpened, the former used for the interior and the latter, for the exterior. This scraping gives an onion-like appearance to the surface, since it leaves fine lines.

The rim is next smoothed down and rounded off with the side of the forefinger. The upper walls are usually thinner than the lower walls, and are made so by running the thumb and forefinger around the base of the neck until the desired thinness is obtained. Sometimes a small handstone is used for smoothing the outer surface. This is held in the palm and rubbed back and forth until the surface is no longer rough and has a faint polish. A piece of cane is laid across the top in the exact center, and at the points where it crosses the rim a line is drawn downward in the clay with the fingernail. On this line a small cavity is punched in with the finger at the desired distance from the rim, and in this the lugs or handle are placed. For ollas with lugs, the lug is usually placed at a distance below the rim equal to the width of three fingers. The lug or bottom of the handle is inserted in the cavity, and clay added around the sides to strengthen the joint. The top of the handle is attached directly below the rim.

Ollas and bowls are made entirely by molding, since their orifices are not extremely constricted, but pitchers are built up to the neck by molding, and then finished to the orifice by coiling. A piece of clay is rolled in the hand to about the length and diameter of a cigar, and this is pressed into the rim with the thumb and forefinger as it is held with the left hand. The inner and outer surfaces are smoothed down with the fingers and the scraper until the connections cannot be discerned. A spout is formed by pressing in the

two sides of the orifice, thus causing the latter to bulge outward at the point where the spout is desired. The pieces
are left to dry for eight days in the shade, usually in a
corner of the house, again polished inside and out with
the handstone, and the slip applied. A lump of red clay
is ground on the metate to a powder, dissolved in water
to make a thick liquid, and applied first with the forefinger and then with the palm of the hand. Only red is
used as a slip. The decoration, if desired, is then painted
on. It is obtained from small black pebbles which are
ground on the metate and soaked for several hours in
water to make a thick paint. The lines are put on with the
wing feather of a chicken or turkey. All the pottery is
either red or yellowish-brown, and the only decorative coloring is black. The brown is produced by adding a red
slip and by firing with cattle dung. The decoration (Fig. 8,
n, *o*, and *p*) consists of alternating straight and wavy lines,
with an occasional series of curved lines. Only bowls are
decorated, and these only on the interior near the rim.
The decorations have no known significance. None of the
pottery is glazed, although the Indians know of this technique, as they buy many glazed coffeepots from the Pokoman.

The pottery can be fired (*p'ut-a*, "to fire") in any fireplace, although the professional potters build special kilns
for this purpose.[15] As many pieces as can be placed in a
single row around the wall of the kiln can be fired at the
same time. They are set upside down, with flat pieces of

[15] The kiln consists of a circular earthen wall about six inches thick, which is
built up from the ground three to five feet high. A break, about six inches wide, is
left in the wall from top to bottom through which firewood is inserted. Around
the inner side of the wall are set up small stones, about eight inches high, upon
which the pottery is set to keep it out of the fire. The kiln is open at the top and
resembles one of the fireboxes of the kitchen fireplace.

cow dung (*u ta' e wakac*) leaned against them. Any dead wood serves as a firewood, although pine bark is the most commonly used. Straw and dry hay are laid thickly on the pottery and stuffed tightly between the pieces. This produces an intense heat. The firing lasts several hours, after which the pieces are lifted out with sticks and allowed to cool.

The "curing" (*puts-r-es*) is done by the potter herself, although every woman cures the pieces she buys in the market to make sure it was done properly. The usual method is to boil lime water in the container for about an hour, so that the lime penetrates the walls and seals them, as well as filling up any cracks which resulted from the firing.[16] A second boiling with pure water is usually done to remove the taste of the curing agent.

WOODWORKING: TOOLS AND MUSICAL INSTRUMENTS

Woodworking includes the building of houses and sheds[17] and sugar presses[18] and the manufacture of household furniture and equipment,[19] agricultural and textile-working implements, musical instruments, and a number of miscellaneous objects.

All the structures are built of unfinished timbers and limbs, although a few of the wooden articles are given a smooth surface with various woodworking tools. Very little decorative carving is done. The average Indian does nearly all his woodworking with the machete, with which he cuts down shrubs and small trees and does all the simple

[16] A handful of ground maize paste can be boiled in it in place of the lime. Another method is to paint the piece inside and out with thick *chilate* while it is still hot from the kiln, using a maize shuck as a brush.

[17] Described in chap. vi.

[18] Described in chap. v.   [19] Described in chap. vi.

cutting and shaping. In lieu of a saw, which few of the Indians own, it is used for cutting through pieces of wood, for splitting timbers, and for smoothing the sides of timbers and boards. The larger trees are cut down usually with the ax, the average Indian being an excellent tree-chopper. A notch with horizontal base is cut on both sides until the two meet, after which the tree is pushed over.

Wood is joined by splicing, forking, notching, holing, pegging, wedging, tying, and gluing. Splicing is done principally with large timbers, as in housebuilding. The spliced ends are each cut half in two, about a foot back from the end, and the cut half split out. The two ends are fitted together and tied with a bark string. The splice is usually placed directly over the supporting timber underneath. The fork is nearly always used for supporting a horizontal timber above a vertical one, the former being laid in the fork without tying. The vertical timbers are cut so as to leave a natural fork at one end, the other end of which is set in the ground. Notching is done in a piece which passes over and at right angles to another, to which it is made fast by tying. The notch prevents the upper piece from sliding down, as in the case of house rafters. Usually, only the upper piece is notched. Holes are usually square and are cut principally in furniture-making. They are cut entirely through the retaining piece, so that the inserted piece comes flush with the outer surface. Pegs are used to hold joints together, as in presses, and as holders to which twine and rope are tied. They are square in cross-section and triangular in shape, with a pointed end. Wedges are used in the false looms to tighten the warp strands, in houses to level the horizontal timbers, and in sugar presses to tighten the rolls. Metal nails are not used. At almost every point where one piece crosses another, as in houses, the intersec-

tions are tied with strings made of the pliable and tough
bark of certain trees and the woody stalks of certain vines
and bindweeds. Knots are not used, the end of the string
being placed under the last round and drawn tight. Rope
is sometimes used for tying and serves as hinges for doors.
Gluing is used in making musical instruments and in attaching the leather straps to tool handles.

The textile-working tools are described above. The agricultural and general-utility tools, and woodworking implements, are made partly of iron and partly of wood.
Since the Indians do no ironworking, they depend upon the
Ladino blacksmiths in the pueblos[20] for their iron tools.
These use forges and anvils of old Spanish type[21] and sell
to the Indians in the market place iron implement points
and the few other iron articles that are used. The Indians,
however, make their own hafts of any hardwood and attach them themselves.

The four important agricultural tools, all of which have
iron points, are the machete, the digging-stick, the hoe,
and the ax (Fig. 2, p. 75). The first two are undoubtedly of
native origin and are used almost exclusively by the Indians, while the third and fourth, probably of Spanish
origin, are used by both Indians and Ladinos.[22]

[20] See pp. 173–74.

[21] Some of the Indians are said to make a practice of stealing spare rails from
the narrow-gauge railroad which runs through Chiquimula. Sixteen men carry
one of these on their shoulders over the mountainous trails to Jocotán and Olopa
and sell it to the Ladino blacksmiths.

[22] The Ladinos, most of whom live in the wider valleys where the land is
level, use the plow, although much of their agricultural work is done with Indian
tools and methods. The plow is made entirely of wood, sometimes with a small
iron point attached, and is drawn by oxen. For plowing, a man holds the point
in the ground while a boy goads the oxen with a long stick. The Indians have
never taken up the plow, however, even though some of them have milpas in the
level river bottoms which could be plowed. Even those who live near the pueblos
still use the planting-stick entirely, although they sometimes hire themselves
out to Ladino neighbors as plowmen and goaders.

The machete, shown at *a*, is the most important of all the implements and is used in innumerable tasks. The point is six to eight inches long, four to five inches in greatest width, and a quarter-inch or less in thickness. The entire cutting edge is sharpened from the point downward and is used for cutting and splitting wood, chopping trees, and cutting plant stalks. The point is especially used in splitting. The top edge is thrust under plant roots to dig them up. The back is not sharpened and is used for pounding, breaking stones, driving pegs, etc. The neck at the bottom, which is of the same thickness, is about six inches long and is tapered to a point. This is inserted into the haft, which is eighteen inches to two feet long and about one and one-half inches in diameter. It is split back from one end for about eight inches, the neck of the iron point forced in, and the entire split portion thoroughly covered with wild bees' honey and wax, which serve as a glue. The split portion is then securely wrapped around with a leather band to hold the point in place.

The handle of the planting-stick is about seven feet long. The point (*b*), which is about five inches long, is inserted and held in place like that of the machete. The hoe (*p'ahn-w-in-ip'*), shown at *d*, is made with a pointed neck which is inserted into the split end of the handle. Its blade is about six inches wide and about five inches long from the neck down. Hoes are used almost altogether in cultivating gardens and in digging and tending irrigation ditches.

The ax (*t'cahk-ip'*), shown at *c*, is made of a single piece the upper end of which is forged into a circle for the retention of the haft which is inserted from the front and usually tightened with small iron wedges made by the blacksmiths. The head is about four inches long and three to four inches wide at the cutting edge; the handle is usually straight and round and rather short. Axes are used principally for felling the larger trees and splitting large logs. The adz (*e*), which is used much like a hoe but which is much less common, is made like the ax, except that the neck is made narrower so that the head can be easily twisted by the smith. The ax and the adz are the only agricultural implements made by the blacksmiths in which the handle is inserted into the head.[23]

The professional woodworkers make great use of the machete and ax, but most of them also use several other woodworking tools of Spanish origin, similar to those used by the Ladino carpenters. Some of the nonprofessionals own one or two of these as well. The iron points of all are made by the Ladino blacksmiths, and the Indians make and attach their own handles. The adz is used for hollowing out logs and timbers in the making of wooden containers and for smoothing timbers and boards. A crude chisel is used for gouging square and circular holes, especially in furniture-making. A hand block of hardwood with no handle is used as a hammer with which to drive the chisel and to insert wedges and pegs. A few of the professionals own crude planes and saws, but these are seldom seen. The sawhorse is used as a vise and workbench.[24]

The musical instruments of European type are the round

[23] The tools are kept sharp with a crude whetstone (Ch. "forehead stone"), usually a flat piece of sandstone set a few inches in the ground in the courtyard. A wooden whetstone, made of zapote wood, is a foot long and two or three inches wide and thick. The wood has a rough grain and is especially used for sharpening knives. Very few of the Indians own files, and the revolving whetstone is unknown.

[24] The horse consists of two small timbers, each about five feet long, one of which has a fork at one of its ends. A square hole is cut through the forked timber, about one-third of the way back from its unforked end, and large enough for the unforked timber to pass through it. This gives the horse the shape of the multiplication sign, with the upper fork smaller than the lower one. A pair of these is made, one for each end of the timber to be worked on.

drum, violins, guitars, and marimbas, and those of native type are the *tun* and *teponagua* drums, gourd rattler, metal rattler, horn trumpet, and flutes. The violins and guitars are well made, with thin and perfectly smoothed walls. The parts are fixed together with native glue, and the strings are of finely twisted agave fiber. The bow is also strung with three or four similar strands. The European-type drum is made of a thin strip of the inner bark of the *cincho* tree, which is bent into a circle and the ends punched and sewed with twine. The drums vary in diameter from six inches to about three feet and in height from six to about eighteen inches. A deerhide or a doghide is stretched over each end and kept taut by means of ropes on the side which pass alternately from one hide to the other all around the drum. Narrower bands of the bark are sometimes fitted over the edge of the hides at each end, in which case the tightening ropes are fastened to these strips instead of to the hides. It is beaten with two sticks, each about a foot long and tipped with a round ball of uncooked rubber. The marimbas seem and are said to be made by Indian woodworkers, but no information was obtained concerning their manufacture.

The *tun* drum is a small log, about twenty inches long and six in diameter, which has been hollowed out, leaving a shell about one-half inch thick all around. The bottom is taken out completely to facilitate the carving, after which it is re-covered with a thin piece which is fitted and glued in with copal gum. On the upper side is the *H* figure (Fig. 6, *r* [p. 135]), extending nearly from one end to the other, the two tongues of which are beaten with the drumsticks. One of the tongues is slightly longer than the other, so that two tones are produced. The base of the drum contains a small round hole in its center. A small rope is tied around each end and passed over the forehead of the boy who carries it on his back in the processions. The player walks behind, beating it with the rubber-tipped sticks. The *teponagua* drum is similarly made, but is about three feet long, eighteen inches in diameter, and has a relatively wider base (Fig. 6, *s*). Its tone is deep and low.

The metal rattler, or *sonanza*, is made by bending two small pieces of flexible wood into circles, about fifteen inches in diameter, and tying the ends of each with twine. The two are stood side by side about an inch apart, a small block of wood placed between them at every two or three inches along their circumference, and the whole tied securely with twine. Twine is then passed from one circle to the other at intervals around the pieces, and on these are strung small bits of iron which jangle against one another when the instrument is shaken.[25] The flute (Sp. *pito*), the most musical of the instruments, is usually made of cane, although occasionally of clay. It is about a foot long, three-fourths of an inch in diameter, and has four holes along the top. The mouth end is partially filled with copal gum, leaving a small aperture, and the opposite end is completely filled with it. The trumpet (Sp. *bosina*, *cacho*) is made by joining two cattle horns together at their bases and fixing them in place with copal gum. The tip of one of the horns contains a small hole through which the air is blown. The instrument is partially filled with *chicha* when used and makes a noise similar to the roaring of a bull. The gourd rattler (Sp. *morro*), made from the round fruit of the gourd tree, is two to four inches in diameter. It is cut from the tree while green and the meat removed through a small hole. Small pebbles are inserted as rattlers, and a small

---

[25] It is possible that shells or pieces of pottery were formerly used in place of the bits of iron.

wooden handle fitted into the hole. It is used as a toy for infants and as a rattler in ceremonial dances.

MISCELLANEOUS MANUFACTURES

Lime is made in the kiln, which is usually dug near the courtyard at some point where the surface of the ground slopes abruptly downward. The large kilns used by the professional lime-makers, of the same general construction as the small ones,[26] are built at the top of a steep stream bank containing much limestone. The stone is gathered and broken into small pieces with the back of the machete. These are stacked in the kiln on the bench which runs around the inner wall, usually up to the rim of the shaft, and leaving the center open to serve as a flue. A fire, built in the horizontal shaft, is kept going for a day and a night. Dry pine is most often used as a firewood. After the baking, the stones are allowed to cool somewhat, placed in a large storage pot, and slaked by being slowly sprinkled with water while still hot. The lime is stored in the kitchen in the same pot. Much of it is sold to the Ladinos, who use it not only to soften maize husks but to whitewash their clay and plaster house walls.

[26] A level spot is found where the bank is high above the water. A circular hole, five to seven feet deep, four to six feet in diameter at the top and tapering to about three at the bottom, is dug in the top of the bank about two feet back from the edge. A circular wall of the same diameter is built up for about three feet above the shaft. It is made of clay and stones and is slightly constricted at the rim. This provides a shaft which is eight to ten feet deep over all. The interior is plastered with clay, which is fired with the first firing of limestone. At a level with the bottom, and facing the stream, a horizontal opening, about two feet square, is dug in to connect with the vertical shaft and is used for the insertion of firewood. At the bottom of the vertical shaft a bench, about one foot high, is built around the wall, and on this the limestone is stacked when being fired. The small kiln is built by the family to make lime for its own use. It is built at the edge of the courtyard, wherever a small bank can be found, and is about two feet deep and two in diameter. A clay rim about five inches high is built around the shaft.

The men of each family make most of the lime it uses and buy a little in the markets. The men of the larger families co-operate in lime-making and store their product in one of the storehouses of the family head, from which it is taken by the households as they need it for boiling maize. Many of the professional lime-makers own a large kiln in common and co-operate in breaking up the stones, baking and slaking the lime, and gathering firewood. They divide their product equally, each carrying his own to market for sale.

Leather articles are made principally from pig, cow, and deer hides, although the average Indian makes articles from the untanned hides of a variety of wild animals. For tanning, the hide is placed for fifteen days in a large olla of limewater and stirred with a stick every four days. It is then placed on the *burro*, a small split log about four feet long which is stood against the house wall. The hide is tied at its top with a rope, hung down over the curved side of the log, and scraped with a two-edged wooden knife which resembles the one used in scraping agave fiber. Its sharp edge cuts off the flesh which still adheres, and the dull edge is used to scrape off the hair. The hide is then soaked for four days in an olla containing water and maize paste, to remove all traces of the lime, after which it is washed in fresh water and wrung out by tying one end of it to a tree and twisting the other. It is soaked for fifteen days in a wooden canoe which contains water and the pounded bark used for curing,[27] sewed up in the form of the living animal, suspended from a rafter, and filled again with the same curing mixture. It is left hanging for twenty-four hours, after which it takes on a reddish-brown color and is then spread out to dry.

[27] Only oak bark is used for cowhides, while that of the nanse and *nacascolote* is used for deerhides.

The leather tumpline is made from both cowhide and deerhide, the former for the headband and the latter, because of its pliability, for the back covering (Fig. 3, p. 117). The leather headband (*a*) is about four inches wide at the center and sixteen inches long, with its ends tapering off to about an inch in width. Each end is split back in three strips, each six or seven inches long, and each of these is split down its center to about an inch from the end. The split strips at each end are then laid on one another, and the straps passed through them and tied (*b*). The back covering is left in its natural shape, with the leg portions cut off (*c*). The straps at each end of the headband are long enough to be wrapped several times around the bundle to be carried. For firewood and sugar cane, two additional straps are used, one wrapped around each end of the bundle, and with the straps which connect with the headband passed around on either side and tied to the lower strap at the back. The back covering is free and is placed between the load and the carrier's back to protect his skin. The headband is worn with the hair side next to the carrier's head, slightly back of the hairline. He walks in a stooped position, dividing the load between his neck and back.

Sandals are mostly made of cured hide, although occasionally uncured hides are used. Each is cut in the shape of the foot, the buyer placing his bare foot on a large piece of leather and the sandal-maker cutting around it with a knife. Each sandal consists merely of the foot piece and a strap for holding it on. The buyer prepares these with a knife for wearing.[28] Leather bags are made by doubling an

[28] He cuts a small hole on each side, about two inches forward from the heel, and another hole under the crotch of the great toe. The strap passes first through the latter hole and is held in place by a knot on the underside. It passes up between the first and second toe, across the outer side of the foot, through the hole on that side, up and across the top of the heel, down through the hole on the other

oblong-shaped hide end to end, with one end projecting
seven or eight inches beyond the other to serve as the flap
for covering the opening. The bag is sewn on the two sides,
and a leather strap attached which passes over the shoulder. It is used by hunters for carrying powder and shot
when on deer-hunting trips. The hair is left on and the
hide usually untanned. Larger bags of similar type are
sometimes made of cured leather. All are sewn with agave
thread and usually with bone needles or punches. The
inner side of all untanned articles from which the hair is
not removed is rubbed with salted water to keep out moths
and other insects and to prevent the hair from falling out.
The *butaca* chair is covered completely on its upper side
with cured leather, usually cowhide, although an uncured
hide is sometimes used for this, with the hairy side up.
Drums of the European type are covered on top and bottom with doghide or deerhide.[29]

For the manufacture of charcoal, a log is cut into pieces
about two feet long, each of which is split into strips about
three inches in diameter. These are stacked directly over
the kiln in rows, each of about a dozen strips which are
placed about two inches apart. The second row is laid at
right angles to the first, the third at right angles to the
second, and so on until eight or ten rows are stacked. A
wall of boards and timbers is leaned horizontally against
the pile to prevent the smoke from the fire underneath from
escaping too quickly. The strips are constantly sprinkled
to prevent their catching fire. If they burn too quickly,

---

side, up and across the top of the heel again, down through the hole on the other
side, and up and across the instep again, where it meets the strap once more
and is tied to it. The sandal is removed merely by slipping the heel strap down
over the heel and is never untied.

[29] Cowhide is said to be too coarse and thick for proper resonance.

they are pulled from the stack, cooled, and replaced. The large lumps of charcoal are beaten into small pieces with the machete and carried in large fiber bags to the markets.[30] All the charcoal is made by professionals, a number of whom usually work together and divide the product equally for marketing.

Pine torches (Sp. *ocote*; Ch. "fire," "pine stick") are made from the central portion of the ocote pine, a type rich with resin. The trunk is cut into two-foot chunks, and each of these split into strips an inch thick and two inches wide. Torches are carried to light the trails at night, sometimes for lighting the houses,[31] and for transferring fire from the fireplace of one house to that of another. Every family keeps a supply to give to visitors and to travelers caught by darkness.

In making soap of hog grease, strips of wood, usually of oak or jocote, are burned and the ashes (*tan*) collected. These are placed to about a foot in depth in an olla which has a small hole in its bottom center. Boiling water is poured over the ashes slowly and caught in another olla underneath. This ashed water, which contains the potash, is the lye used in soap-making. Some half-dozen parts of this, with one part of hog grease, are boiled for about three days, when the liquid has sufficiently thickened to harden into soap when cooled. The quantity is increased by being boiled with the crushed hearts of wild papaya stalks. The soap is of a faded brown color and

[30] Charcoal is seldom used by the Indians but is sold principally to the Ladino blacksmiths, laundresses, tailors, and housewives. Charcoal used for cooking and ironing is made of the oak, quebracho, and *shaguáy* trees, and that for black-smithing, of pine, *tashiste*, and *chaperna*.

[31] An oil made by boiling castor beans is sometimes used for house lighting. It is placed in a gourd or bowl, one end of a cotton wick laid in it, and the free end of the wick burned.

has little lather. It is patted into round pellets of half a pound each and sold principally to the Ladinos. Vegetable soap made from a number of wild and domestic plants[32] is more commonly made and used by the Indians than pig-fat soap. The roots, fruit, or seed of the plants are ground on the metate or pounded in the coffee mortar, boiled with the lye water for about three days, and cooled and shaped into pellets. It is of a black or ash color, usually. Many of the professional soap-makers have a special oven for soap manufacture, placed either in the courtyard or over the kitchen fireplace (Fig. 5, *D* [p. 133]). It is built usually by the husband of the soap-maker.[33]

Glue is secured from the *yupáy* and *cebollín* plants. The fruit of the former is crushed with the hands and the juice, or "honey," used principally to glue the tips of cigars to prevent unrolling. The milk of the *cebollín* is squeezed out of the fruit and used as a glue in making guitars and violins and is sold to the Ladinos for gluing paper and cloth.

Copal is made from the gum of copal trees. The men find the trees in the hills, notch the trunks in about a dozen places, all on the same side, place a gourd underneath, and allow the gum to drip into it for eight days. The gum, together with a great deal of the tree bark, is then dried in the sun for a day, after which it is put to boil with water in

[32] The most important are the *jaboncillo*, castor bean, *güiril*, and aceituna.

[33] The oven is an inverted cone, about four feet high and three feet in diameter at the top. To make it, limbs are set in the ground in the form of a circle, about three inches apart, with their tops slightly constricted and held in place with withes running horizontally around them. Wet clay and pebbles are laid on both sides of this framework from top to bottom, until the wall is about six inches thick. An opening about a foot wide is left in the wall from top to bottom in front. The whole is inverted and a large cone-shaped earthenware vessel holding five or six gallons and especially made for soap-boiling is inserted in the top, its rim coming flush with the oven rim, and is sealed in with wet clay. The fire is maintained directly beneath this. Four small holes are sometimes left in the upper back side through which the smoke escapes.

a large olla. Fresh water is added as the old boils away. The copal gum rises to the surface slowly and is skimmed off with a gourd dipper. After eight or ten hours of boiling, all the gum is extracted, and it is placed in cold water to harden. It is then shaped in the hands into round, elongated pellets, each of about the size and shape of a cigar, and extremely hard and brittle. Each pellet is wrapped in maize shucks and tied at the ends with shuck string. For ceremonial use, the gum is shaped into small disks.[34]

Candles are made of the fruit of the *cera vegetal* tree as well as of the beeswax taken from the hives of wild bees.[35] The fruit is pounded and boiled for several hours, and the black wax skimmed off with a gourd. The beeswax is prepared in the same way. A candle arc is made of a thin strip of wood,[36] eight or ten feet long, the ends of which are tied together to form a circle. This is suspended in horizontal position from a rafter in the sleeping-house. Small wooden pegs are inserted horizontally into the outer side of the strip, and to each of these is tied a strip of cloth or length of cotton, the free end of which hangs down. These serve as the wicks. The hot wax is poured slowly on the upper end of each strip from top to bottom and is continued until each candle is of the desired thickness. After cooling, they are cut off squarely at one end.[37]

Indigo dye is not used in textile manufacture but entirely for dyeing dresses after they have faded. The dye vat, in

[34] Each disk is of the shape and size of a small coin and is called a "peso." In this form it is a ceremonial money and is sacrificed to the deities by being burned in the incensarios. It is offered as a "payment" to them.

[35] See p. 68.

[36] The vinelike branches of the *cagalero blanco* trees are used for this.

[37] The Indian-made candles are mostly black and seem to be preferred by the Indians to the white, red, and yellow ones made by the Ladino candle-makers.

which it is made, consists of two square holes, or tanks, dug in the ground side by side and with a thin wall of earth separating them. Each tank of the vat is about three feet square, one being about three feet deep and the other about two. A small opening, about two inches in diameter, is cut through the dividing wall, at about six inches above the floor of the shallower vat. This is filled with a wooden plug except when the water is being transferred through it from one vat to the other. The sides and bottoms of both vats are plastered with clay, with a rim of the same plastering laid around the tops of the walls. This is dried completely in the sun each time the vats are used. In Jocotán the Ladinos formerly constructed these vats of concrete and stone masonry.

The leaves of the *jiquilite* plant are cut, tied in small bundles, and stacked in the shallower of the two vats up to a height of about two feet. These are covered with water and left to soak for a day and a night, the dye-maker constantly stirring them with a long stick. The leaves are then taken out and the dye in the water allowed to settle to the bottom, after which the plug in the connecting hole is withdrawn, the water run through to the deeper vat, the water below the hole dipped out, and the paste scooped up. It is tied in cloths, squeezed with the hands, and spread out on boards to dry for a day. It is then shaped into cakes, dried again, and brought to market for sale. For use as a dye, it is ground and soaked with the cloth for several days.

A number of years ago the cultivation of these plants and the manufacture of indigo dye was an important industry. Jocotán at that time was one of the richest centers of the industry and was known as "the pearl of the East." The older Ladinos say that the pueblo was much larger and wealthier than now and that all the hills for miles in every direction were covered with indigo plants. In the courtyards of many of the houses are still to be seen the old extraction vats, now used only as pig stys. The introduction of the cheaper synthetic aniline, however, destroyed the industry throughout the department of Chiquimula.

For the preparation of tobacco, drying frames are set up before the leaves are cut. These consist of six- or seven-foot poles set up in the ground fifteen to twenty feet apart. Across the top of these are laid smaller poles, and hanging from these are fiber strings to each of which are attached several dozen green tobacco stalks. After drying in the sun for about two weeks, they are taken down and laid in a press. Flat stones are laid on the ground to form a circular flat surface about three feet in diameter. Over this is laid a layer of banana leaves, and on this the tobacco stalks and leaves are stacked to a height of about four feet. Another layer of banana leaves is laid over the tobacco, and on top of this another layer of heavy stones, like that at the base. The top stones act as the press. The leaves remain thus for five days, after which they are taken out, the stalks cut off and thrown away, and the leaves replaced in the press as before. Every two days they are taken out, allowed to cool, and re-pressed. This is done for about a month, until the leaves no longer become heated in the press. They are then completely cured and are ready to be made into cigars (Sp. *puro;* Ch. "rolled tobacco") and cigarettes (Sp. *cigaro;* Ch. "shucked tobacco").

The cigar-maker sprinkles each leaf with molasses or *aguardiente* mixed with an essence of anise, bought in the pueblo drug store. She cuts out the veins of the leaves and then cuts each leaf into two parts. The fine parts she rolls up as she cuts the leaves, and they are used as the outer covering of the cigars. The other parts are used as the filler, which is first rolled up and then wrapped in a single fine leaf to make the finished cigar. The ends are glued together with the milk of the *yupáy* fruit. The cigars are then tied in bundles and brought to the markets for sale. The Indians smoke cigars in native-made pipes, breaking off a portion about an inch long and stuffing it into the bowl. For cigarette-making the leaves are cut up thoroughly with a sharp machete or a pair of scissors and the tobacco wrapped in small sections of maize shucks. The Indians seldom smoke them but sell them in bundles to the Ladinos.

CHAPTER VIII

DIVISION OF LABOR

THE division of labor is both individual and region-al.[1] The former is based upon sex, age and status, and professionalization. The sexual division seems to be the most important, while that of age and status is the least rigidly observed.

SEXUAL DIVISION

It is generally believed that women should be excluded from public activity, confined to domestic life and to the domestic group, and have little or no social contact, espe-cially with men, outside their family circle. Community activity of every kind properly belongs only to the men. The men are, in general, responsible for ceremonial activ-ity, and it seems to be felt that this is improper for women, although it is actually divided between the sexes. The men perform all ceremonies of a public sort, in which a communi-ty larger than the domestic family is involved, and on such occasions the women merely prepare the food to be eaten. The private ceremonies which the family performs for it-self are the work of both sexes, the men especially perform-ing those connected with agriculture, while many of those connected with the life-crises, which are directed to the family and patron saints, are performed by the women. There is a tendency for the men to perform the ceremonies of native origin, while the women perform those of Catholic

[1] Described in chap. ii.

187

origin, being said to be "better Catholics" than the men.[2] For example, the prayer-makers who recite the novenas are all women. Political activity, also, is restricted to the men, among both the Indians and the Ladinos.

In theory every economic activity, in whole or in part, is relegated to the one sex or the other. The men are generally responsible for the planting, tending, and harvesting of the milpas, gardens, and orchards. The principal designation of the men is "milpa-makers" or "maize-planters." All their other activities are of little importance in comparison to milpa-making.[3] In general, all the work connected with the production and storing of food is said to belong properly to the men. The men handle the larger domestic animals and especially those used industrially; thus they tend and work the oxens and bulls used at the presses, butcher all large animals for food and hides, and tend hunting dogs; it is said that they should tend and milk the cows. The men are the hunters, trappers, wild-honey collectors, and fishermen; they are thought of as the animal-food collectors. Wild fruits and vegetables which are dangerous and difficult to gather, such as coconuts and avocados, and which are carried with the tumpline and carrying crate for a great distance, are collected by men. They also collect and transport all firewood and hay. In household manufacturing the men usually gather and prepare the raw materials: they cultivate or collect, and pre-

[2] This same division of labor in ceremonial activity is reported from Yucatan (Redfield and Villa, 1934, p. 69).

[3] The Indian, when asked what another does, invariably answers that he "makes milpas," or that he is a *milpero*, and he answers of a woman, "she keeps house." The importance of these two activities is further discussed on pp. 196–97. The term *milpero* was used by some of the informants as a generic name for "man," as opposed to animals, although *cristiano* (Christian) and *hombre* (man; Ch. *winik*) are more often used (see p. 228).

pare, those for textiles, soap, starch, dyes, copal, cigars, gourd containers, candles, pottery, etc. They completely manufacture all articles made outside the house, such as sugar, leather, charcoal, indigo, lime, pine torches, and such articles of clay or wood as sugar presses, furniture, musical instruments, houses, ovens, and vats; and they build and repair the roads and trails.[4] They are supposed, in addition, to make those textile articles that are used by men. The most symbolic male manufacturing activity is woodworking, principally housebuilding and furniture-making, and every man is presumed to be more or less skilled at it. Another characteristic male activity is the making of brooms and the braiding of strips which are made into hats. The average man makes these, or once did.[5]

The most important work for women is house work, which includes cooking, grinding, carrying water for the kitchen, sewing, house-cleaning, and tending the children.[6] Woman's primary work is to keep house, and she is not

[4] Although the Indians do no stoneworking or ironworking, they consider these activities as belonging ideally to the men.

[5] It is a common sight on the trails to see men with heavy loads on their backs, busily weaving a hat spiral as they walk along. The finished end is carried in the shoulder bag and kept rolled up as it is made. When the hands are not otherwise occupied, as when visiting with friends or sitting in the plaza, the Indian pulls out the unfinished end of his hat strip and starts weaving, without seeming to give the task the slightest attention. Many of the men say they do most of this weaving merely to pass the time and to relieve the tedium of the trail and that they give most of their strips to others who need hats. The men make brooms because it is said that the women do not have sufficient strength to do it. No reason was known why the men make hat strips.

[6] Several Indian men explained their reason for never carrying children by the joking remark, "Only women carry children" (Sp. *solo las mujeres llevan las criaturas;* Ch. *in-taka e icik u-qutc-i u y ar*). The joke here is on the double meaning of "carry," since a woman is said in both Spanish and Chorti to "carry" her child during the period of pregnancy. Pregnancy is called *qutc-ur u y ar* ("the carrying of her child").

thought of as doing anything else; but certain other activities are regarded merely as an extension of house work, either because they are done in or near the houses or because many of them involve cooking, sewing, or other household techniques. Women feed and care for the chickens, turkeys, and bees and tend the plants which grow in containers. Assisted by boys, they gather wild fruits and vegetables near the houses, bringing them home in gourds and baskets on their heads, and they gather the wild medicinal plants used in the household. They are generally regarded as the plant-food gatherers. In household manufacturing they make the finished products and prepare them for sale. Women are the weavers: they make cotton thread, mats, woven hats, woven fiber bags, and baskets; the manufacture of these is said to be ideal women's work. In the manufacturing field the women's work is especially characterized by pottery-making; it is said of almost any woman that she is or used to be a potter or without doubt has some mastery of the art, probably because pottery-making is the most symbolic of the female manufacturing activities.

The economic sphere of women is inside or near the house, and their work is primarily familial and domestic. The sphere of the men, on the other hand, is outside the house, and their work consists in producing, collecting, and manufacturing the economic goods which are obtained by means of nonhousehold techniques. The men are the tool-users, and their work is said to be the sort which requires tools. The women are said to know nothing about tools and to have no skill with them. They use certain implements habitually, such as needles, spindles, shuttles, and the basket and dam for fishing, but these are not considered tools in the strict sense, as are the machete, ax, hoe, tumpline, and implements used in textile preparation and leather-making. Most women occasionally use all the commoner tools, but never habitually, and they never pretend to be skilled with them, as the men do. In general, the men work at the most arduous tasks, while the least arduous ones belong to the women. The men's work is more active and full of interest and change, while that of the women requires less nervous energy, is often little more than drudgery, and is nearly always monotonous, since it changes very little from day to day.

In practice the division of labor is less strict than it is supposed to be. For example, the women rather than the men usually milk the cows and occasionally tend the pigs; women very occasionally do weed and hoe the vegetable gardens, although only when the men are busy at other work. Although the men are the fishermen, the women normally do the fishing with the dam and basket. Although the manufacture of ropes, fishing nets, and such braided and netted articles as hammocks, headbands, or tumplines, bag straps, food-hangers, and netted bags is said to belong properly to the men, it is actually done by both sexes, and by women more than by men. An exception to the rule that women do the pottery-making and especially the finishing is that the firing of pottery is men's work.

In normal circumstances a temporary crossing is permitted in the case of the less important economic activities. For example, a man could make a gourd canteen for himself, partly to pass the time, or he could prepare an occasional batch of copal for market sale, and a woman could weed one of the gardens, pick a little fruit, or milk a cow, and it would not be noticed, but it would cause some comment if it were done habitually. In the case of those activities which have symbolic sexual value no crossing of the line is permitted, and the offender may receive a derisive nickname. No man would make pottery, wash clothes, or tend children under any circumstances so long as there were females in his house to do such work, since these are perhaps the most characteristically feminine of occupations and to be avoided at all times. A single incident is soon forgotten, but if repeated the offender soon gets a nickname, and it is hurled at him with much laughter every time he appears in the market plaza.[7] Many of the men take pride in the fact that they never make their wives and daughters do milpa work, or any other work which men are supposed to do, and they boastfully state that they are not the sort, as "others" are, to do women's work.[8]

The sexual division is, of course, more flexible in abnormal circumstances, and in cases of poverty, age, and emergency an individual may cross the sex barrier without exciting ridicule from others. Old men and women, and

[7] A Tunucó Indian man is invariably called "male soap-maker" (Sp. *jabonero;* Ch. *ah tcap ca·p'un*), both in direct address and in reference, every time he appears in the Jocotán market. Several Ladinos stated the name had been used for two or three years. Another is called "male clothes-washer" (Sp. *lavandero;* Ch. *ah poht'c*). A woman in Tuticopote is called "female milpa-maker" (Sp. *milpera;* Ch. *ah tcor-w-ar icik*) because she is said to do all her milpa work and to force her husband to tend the household and children. Such names are occasionally used without humor to identify the individual, as if it were his name. The names, when applied to the improper sex, are all the more ludicrous because of the use of the Spanish agentives *-ero* (masculine) and *-era* (feminine), the Chorti suffixes *-winik* (male) and *-icik* (female), and the Chorti agentive *ah* (usually used only for males), thus forming compounds which are never used seriously in ordinary speech. Thus, a clothes-washer is always *lavandera* in Spanish, and never *lavandero*, since only women wash clothes, and a milpa-maker is *milpero*, and never *milpera*, since only men normally make milpas. In Chorti, if applied jokingly to the improper sex, these terms become *ah poht'c winik* and *ah tcor-w-ar icik*. The Indians and Ladinos see as much humor in the unusual term as in the unusual situation to which it refers.

[8] *sup'ahr-a u ut tia' in-w-ir-i·c tua' u w-ick-ar war-ic a-patn-a tama u tcor*, "He was ashamed when I saw that his wife was working in his milpa." *ma-xa·c-en kotca yep-er tin u-tc-o·p' u patn-ar e icik*, "I am not like others, who do the work of women."

others known to be very poor and "backward," constantly work at activities which properly belong to the opposite sex, and this causes no comment from the Indians. A man could prepare a meal or two if his wife were sick, a widow could tend her milpas and do all the male work about her place, and a widower could cook his own food and care for his children, although none would do these any longer than was necessary. Other Indians would think them unfortunate but would not ridicule them. In a case of prolonged sickness, however, the husband would invite a female relative to live at his house and do his house work, and the widow and widower would sooner or later either find mates or go to live with their relatives, where there would be kinsmen of the proper sex to do such work for them.

The differentiation between the work of the sexes has resulted in a division of almost every total activity into two parts—the one performed by the men and the other by the women, the work of each supplementing that of the other. For example, the women are the potters, although the men do the firing for them; the women do most of the household manufacturing, although the men gather the raw materials used and do most of the heavier work; the women do most of the textile-working, although the men gather and prepare the raw materials; the men tend the milpas and gardens, although the women help by occasionally hoeing, weeding, and gathering cultivated fruits and by tending the pot plants; and the men are generally responsible for the domestic animals, although the women feed the fowls, gather eggs, etc. Every activity is said to be the work and responsibility of one of the sexes, but in every case the opposite sex assists either in the same activity or takes over a phase of it as its own work.

Marketing in the pueblo plazas is done by both sexes,

usually by a man and his wife together, she doing most of the selling while he buys necessities to take home for the ensuing week. The general rule, however, is for each sex to sell the articles which it produces, manufactures, or uses. Thus, only women sell soap, mats, native pottery, gourd vessels, copal, candles, cigars, all dyes except indigo, female remedies, wild fruits and vegetables, and such prepared foods as coffee, cacao, *shepes*, cheese, and boiled maize ears. The men sell uncooked maise, beans, and cultivated fruits, native sugar, hay, firewood, netted fiber articles, male remedies, sandals, charcoal, torches, indigo dye, sewed hats and brooms, and wooden household objects.[9] The women sellers are usually accompanied by their husbands or sons in the plaza, as it is felt to be improper for women, unless old, to sell alone.

The women always carry articles in baskets, gourds, or ollas, which rest either on the head or right hip bone, and they carry children astride the right hip, in a large fiber bag, or in a shawl which passes over the forehead like a tumpline. The men never carry as the women do, and they never carry children except in emergencies. Their method of carrying is with the tumpline, and the containers used are cane crates and large fiber bags. The women occasionally use the tumpline for carrying light objects and children, but this is rare and is said to be improper for women.

AGE AND STATUS DIFFERENCES

The division of labor on the basis of age and status is not clear cut, since there are no formalized and sharply de-

[9] The rule does not apply to the selling of baskets, lime, and fish. Baskets are made and used only by women, but only men sell them in Jocotán, as the basket-making *aldeas* are said to be too far away for women to make the trip. Only men make lime and collect fish, but these are sold only by the women. The Indians could give no reason for this.

fined age and status groups. Three age groups may be
noted. The first consists of children and adolescents who
are still unmarried and therefore living in the households of
their parents. They are dependent upon their parents for
support, and they work for them without pay. Their work
is always unskilled and intermittent, since they merely assist the older workers. They are said to be learning how to
perform such important adult tasks as agriculture, food-
collecting, housebuilding, sugar-pressing, etc. By the time
they reach puberty they leave off playing with the younger
children, pass into the adult group, and take up serious
work with the other adults. Upon entering this group, the
individual usually marries, is set up or sets himself up in a
household of his own, and takes his place as an adult male
among the heads of his family's households. Similarly, the
woman marries soon after puberty and becomes the female
head of her household and is thereafter accepted as an
equal by the other adult women.

The adult group range in age from seventeen or eighteen
to perhaps sixty-five. They are responsible for all the highly skilled and economically valuable work, and they include
all the professional workers, as well as all the heads of
households, whether male or female, since it is presumed
that no individual passes into this group until he marries
and thus acquires a household to provide for and to direct.[10]
This group also contains some of the family heads, as well,
since most of these are in no more than later middle life.
As the family head and his wife grow older, however, they
are gradually released from the more difficult work and

---

[10] In actuality, the unmarried individuals who are at least in their twenties
belong with this group, as they usually work with them as equals, but it is felt
that they are not exactly equals and have no right to consider themselves as
members of the second age group, since theoretically no one passes into that
group until he heads his own household.

come to act merely as work leaders among the younger members. The third age group consists of those who are over sixty-five or seventy years old, and who, because of age or sickness, are no longer able to do hard work. Their work, like that of the first age group, is usually intermittent, so that they have about the same economic status as the adolescents.

PROFESSIONALIZATION

Professionalization is highly developed in the religious and semireligious activities,[11] where the required skill is necessarily restricted to relatively few individuals, but it is much less developed in the economic field. The purely economic activities tend to be either professional or nonprofessional, although there is no hard and fast line between the two. Some of the former are engaged in by families merely to satisfy their own household needs, and therefore nonprofessionally, and many of the latter are slightly professionalized by families who produce a small surplus for sale.

Those activities which the Indians consider as primarily nonprofessional are agriculture, the raising, use, and butchering of domestic animals, hunting, trapping, fishing, food-plant collecting, house work, sugar-making, simple woodworking, housebuilding, the manufacture, for family use only, of lime, gourds, torches, soap, and cheese, and the repairing and building of trails. The Indians consider these activities as of basic importance for the maintenance of the life of the individual and his family group, and they are carried on by everyone without exception.

No individual can avoid working at the principal non-

---

[11] The religious professionals are described in chap. xv, and the semireligious ones in chaps. xiii and xiv.

professional occupations, although the small proportion of
those who earn additional income from special occupations work at them less than do others. The individual
who avoids them completely loses status and is considered
an abnormal individual in his *aldea*, as he is believed to be
shirking the work and responsibility which properly belong
to everyone of his sex.[12] Thus, every man should "make
milpa," assist at building the houses and sheds which his
family occupy, make, at least for his own use, lime, torches,
and simple objects of wood, collect the firewood used in
his kitchen, and work to some extent at repairing trails,
hunt, fish, and butcher and care for animals. He is not
expected to work constantly at all these, but he should to
some extent, and he is expected to have some skill at them.
Similarly, every woman should "keep house," mainly cooking and sewing for her household, tending her children,
washing clothes, gathering wild greens and fruits, and making at least some of the soap, gourd vessels, honey, copal,
and remedies which her household uses. She is expected,
as a normal woman, to have some skill at these tasks.
These nonprofessional activities are called "work." For
the average Indian they are the subsistence activities, since
normally they are not engaged in for the production of a
marketable surplus but only for the production of that
which the family needs for itself. Their techniques, which

[12] The Indians often explain poverty in a household by saying that either now
or probably at some time in the past the husband did not "make milpa" or his
wife did not cook and keep house for her family. Avoidance of these activities
is believed to lead to a bad end. One informant, in referring to an Indian who
had lived for many years in Jocotán pueblo as a laborer for Ladinos, and who
was sent to the Chiquimula penitentiary for murder, said, "Thus it turns out
when they don't make milpa" (Sp. *Así resulta cuando no hacen milpa;* Ch. *ic-to
a-lo'k'-oi tia' ma'tcu' q'an-i a-tcor-o*). An Indian girl who had become something of a prostitute among Ladinos in Jocotán was said to have arrived at her
state because "she did not wish to tend her house" (Sp. *no quería cuidar su casa;*
Ch. *ma'tcu' q'an-i u-qohq-o u y otot*).

are learned from childhood as a part of every individual's education, are said not to be difficult to master, as they are meant for everybody, and everybody can learn them if properly taught by parents and elders; no prestige is therefore attached to them. These are the only activities accompanied with religious beliefs, ceremonies, and ritual prohibitions, a fact which indicates their essential importance in Indian life. Because of their social and economic necessity it is in these activities that a temporary crossing of the sex barrier is possible in abnormal circumstances. Most of them are worked at co-operatively, either by the family or by a number of neighboring families in the same *aldea*; individuals sometimes work at them alone if the work of a group is not required, but co-operative performance is always preferred.

Many Indians slightly professionalize some of these activities by producing or collecting a surplus which they regularly sell in the markets. They are called sellers (*ah tcon-m-ar*). Almost every Indian family sells a small amount of goods produced by nonprofessional work throughout the year, partly to acquire a small income from time to time and partly as a justification for attending the market.[13] The average nonprofessional family sells a few products perhaps once in every month. The term "seller," however, is applied to those who habitually sell such goods, who therefore become known as regular sellers, and who sell goods not produced by a manufacturing process. They handle maize, wild and cultivated vegetables and fruits, meat, honey, firewood, hay, pine torches, and such pre-

---

[13] It seems to be felt that an Indian should not attend unless he has something to sell, for which reason he may carry a gourd or two or a few packages of sugar and offer them for sale. He usually spends his money for needed articles on the same day.

pared foods as coffee, *tortillas*, *shepes*, tamales, boiled maize ears, and cacao. Nearly every family produces or collects these for its own use, or produces most of what it uses, and the sellers make up for their lack and also sell to the Ladinos.

The professional activities are manufacturing, trading, and hiring out at labor. Those who work at these are said to have an *oficio*, or profession. The term seems to refer to any nonsubsistence activity which provides income through the sale of surplus goods or services. Manufacturing (Ch. *tce-y-ax*)[14] includes the making of textiles, pottery, leather, indigo dye, torches, articles of wood, soap, candles, copal, gourds, lime, charcoal, sugar, and cheese, all of which are sold in the markets by the makers themselves. The first six are the most highly professionalized, as they are restricted to relatively few individuals, and most require a degree of skill not possessed by everyone. The others are less so, as the articles themselves are made to some extent by almost every family for its own use. Depending upon their degree of professionalization, the manufacturing techniques are said to be difficult to learn, to require great skill for proper performance, and to be worthy of some prestige. They are learned from another professional worker, usually a parent, and from childhood. These activities are not of the subsistence type but merely supplement the more important subsistence ones and provide additional income for the families who engage in them. Thus, they depend entirely upon the market. They are not performed in connection with any religious beliefs and

---

[14] This is the general Chorti term for "profession," as well, since most of the professionals are manufacturers. Each manufacturing profession is also called by the name of the technique used and the product made.

practices, and there is no social necessity to work at them, although the individual who is known to have considerable skill at some *oficio* acquires prestige because of it.[15] No crossing of the sex barrier is permitted in working at the most important of them. They are not usually worked at co-operatively by groups, since each professional does most of his own work and is merely assisted occasionally by members of his household. Nearly all are concerned with a manufacturing process. The makers are sometimes called sellers, as well, although they are primarily known as manufacturers. There is some tendency to specialization in these activities, or what might be called a crude beginning of the factory type of production.[16]

The Indians and Ladinos tend to think of professionalization in terms of the regional division of labor,[17] thinking of professional activities as being allocated primarily among areas and *aldeas*, and only secondarily among professionalized individuals. Every individual of the proper sex and age is presumed to work at all the activities, professional and nonprofessional, which are peculiar to his area and *aldea*, although many, of course, actually do not, so that the occupational area has much more distinction from others of its kind than does the occupational individual. The latter has some distinction from other indi-

---

[15] Three potters in Tunucó are much respected for their skill, and their mothers are remembered by the older Indians as having been even more skilful and well known in their day.

[16] A number of mat-makers in Oquén produce and prepare more raw materials than they can use themselves and turn this surplus over to others who take it to their own homes and weave it into mats. The latter keep half the mats they weave, which they sell in the Jocotán market. Many basket- and hat-weavers provide materials for others to make into the finished products as well. There are no cases in which the specialized workers are paid in money, although maize and beans are sometimes used for payment.

[17] See pp. 19–24.

viduals, since he is known to have an *oficio* which many of
his neighbors either do not work at or work at to a less extent than himself, and this sets him off somewhat, but a
sufficient number of Indians in the same *aldea* work at the
same occupation to prevent its becoming very much indi-
vidualized. Professionalization, then, is primarily of a collective character, thought to belong more or less to all the
inhabitants of an *aldea* or region, and not of an individual character, except in the case of a few potters, weavers, and musical instrument makers in Jocotán and Olopa
municipios who are widely known for their skill, and therefore accorded some individual prestige over and above
the average of professionals. Thus, most of the women of
Tunucó, a pottery-making *aldea*, either make pottery or
formerly did. It is assumed by the Indians and Ladinos
elsewhere that all Tunucó women are potters; and, even
though it is known that two or three of them spend more
time at this work and are slightly more skilled than all the
others, such individual distinction is not felt to be important. The important distinction is that the Tunuqueños
are potters, and that Tunucó is a pottery *aldea*, just as
Matasano is a torch-making *aldea*, and Oquén, one in which
hats, mats, and brooms are made.

The traders are middlemen whose profession consists
merely in buying and selling at a profit. Only the men
work at this occupation. They visit the *aldeas*, often covering three or four *municipios*, and buy all manner of articles from the Indian manufacturers which they carry on
their backs to all the markets for sale. All of them plant
maize, raise animals, and engage in most of the usual nonprofessional work of other Indians, and merely work as
traders during the periods when they are not required to
work at their homes. They travel to the distant pueblos

of Chiquimula, Zacapa, Gualán, and Jilotepeque, selling goods from Jocotán and Olopa and bringing back articles from those areas for sale in the Jocotán and Olopa markets. The Pokoman traders make the same trips, carrying articles from the Jilotepeque area for sale in Jocotán and Olopa, and taking back articles from those pueblos for sale in their own region. But for these traders there would be little sale of Indian manufactures outside the *municipios* in which they are made, since most of the Ladino merchants import and sell only goods from Chiquimula and Zacapa.

The laborers constitute a small group among the Indians and come usually from the poorer families who have little land and who therefore need additional income in order to buy necessities. They are the group with least prestige among the Indians. The men work as hands at the sugar presses, in the fields during planting, cleaning, and harvesting, as fruit-gatherers, and as carriers, being hired usually by the wealthier families. Their pay is from eight to ten pesos a day, although they are often paid in kind with sugar, maize, beans, coffee, and fruits. The carriers transport goods with the tumpline from the milpas to the presses and storehouses and from the *aldeas* to the markets.[18] The professional coconut gatherers, who are expert climbers, charge a certain amount for each tree. The women laborers do house work for other Indian families, especially during childbirth, sickness, or absence of the mother from home. They are sometimes paid four or five pesos a day but are usually given food, such as maize and beans, to take home. Most of the laboring group are to be found in the *aldeas* which are adjacent to the pueblos

[18] The standard pay for carrying around a hundred pounds from Tunucó to Jocotán, a distance of about twelve miles, is ten pesos, the trip to and from requiring most of a day.

and are hired by the Ladino families as cooks, nurses for children, laundresses, water-carriers, muleteers, and hired hands at the presses and in the milpas. Almost every adult Indian in these *aldeas* works at some time or other during the year as a laborer for Ladinos. The small Indian group in Jocotán and Olopa pueblos earn most of their income by hiring out and are known to the Ladinos and *aldea* Indians as a labor group.

CHAPTER IX

COMMUNITIES AND CLASSES

"MUNICIPIO," TOWN, AND "ALDEA"

THE Indians sometimes refer to themselves as Guatemaltecos, as when marketing or visiting in near-by Honduras, but the designation has little meaning for them. Almost none of them have seen parts of the Republic outside their own area, and none were found who had ever traveled to another Central American country, except for rare visits to Copan. The Indians, as well as most of the Ladinos of the Indian area, have no clear notion of what constitutes the Republic of Guatemala. The department is the largest social unit of which the Indians have any conception. Most of them travel to all the *municipios* of Chiquimula department every few years to visit their few friends and relatives who live in many of them. But while most of the Chorti-speaking Indians call themselves Chiquimultecos, as opposed to the inhabitants of Zacapa, Izabál, and other neighboring departments, this term, like Guatemalteco, has little meaning for them.[1] Both Indian and Ladino live out their social and economic

[1] The name "Guatemala" refers primarily to Guatemala City, and the Guatemalteco is primarily an inhabitant of that city. The Republic is usually called *la república* or *el país* ("the country"), and the usual name for the Guatemalteco is "countryman." The vagueness of *el país* is shown by the fact that, when used in Jocotán, for example, it includes the Copan region of Honduras, since Copan is socially and economically tied up with the department of Chiquimula. Even to the more urban and traveled Ladinos of the pueblos, the Chiquimulteco is primarily an inhabitant of the capital city of Chiquimula and, therefore, like the Guatemalteco, a "city dweller."

lives in areas much smaller than the department, their contacts with the department as a single unit consisting only of rare visits to its different parts for marketing, visiting, and celebrating festivals.

The department of Chiquimula, which contains all the Chorti-speaking Indians except those of Copan, is made up of twelve *municipios;* Chiquimula, Jocotán, Camotán, La Unión, Olopa, San Juan Hermita, Quetzaltepeque, Esquipulas, San Jacinto, Ipala, Concepción, and San José la Arada.[2] The large group of Chorti-speaking Indians of Honduras live in the *municipio* of Copan of the department of Santa Rosa. Within each *municipio,* and surrounding its capital pueblo, are the satellite *aldeas* and *caseríos*[3] which make up the rural area of the *municipio.* The pueblos are primarily Ladino habitations, being the centers of Spanish culture, while the *aldeas* are almost wholly inhabited by Indian families.

The *municipio*[4] has the same name as its pueblo. With the exception of Chiquimula, Jocotán *municipio* is the largest with which the Indians have any contact and contains forty-two Indian *aldeas.* The *municipio* of San Juan Hermita is the smallest in the Indian area, containing only fifteen *aldeas.* The *municipios* vary in width and length from about fifteen to thirty miles. Their boundaries have no special markings, except for wooden gates which are set up across the more important trails where they pass

[2] Formed of territory taken from the *municipio* of Chiquimula, September 11, 1924.

[3] Rural settlements less important than *aldeas.* The term *aldea* is used here to cover, as well, settlements officially called *caseríos.*

[4] Equivalent to English "municipality," and called in Chorti, *noh tcinam* ("great pueblo"). This term is generally understood but does not seem to be commonly used. The *municipio* is usually referred to by the Indians as *e municipio* ("the *municipio*"; *e municipi-op'*, "the *municipios*"). Cf. Tax, 1937.

from one *municipio* into another. These are usually of the slide-pole type and in some cases are connected with a fence which extends for several hundred yards away from the trail on both sides. Along the smaller trails, where there are no gates and fences, many Indians can point out the approximate boundary line by such signs as a fallen tree, a slight rise in the trail, a large boulder, or the crossing of the trail by a stream.[5]

The travel routes of the *municipio* are called roads, or trails, and highways. Each pueblo theoretically has four roads running out of it, one in each of the cardinal directions, and these connect with the pueblos of neighboring *municipios*. In Jocotán pueblo the north highway runs to La Unión, the east one to Camotán and Copan, the south one to Olopa and Esquipulas, and the west one to Chiquimula. A fifth runs northwestward to Zacapa, but it branches off from the La Unión road a few miles north of Jocotán. The four roads leading out of Olopa pueblo run north to Jocotán, northeast to Copan, south to Esquipulas, and west to Quetzaltepeque. In every case the roads leave the pueblo at the four cardinal points, even when the pueblos to which they run do not lie in the true cardinal directions.[6] They pass through the more important Indian *aldeas* between the pueblos and are especially used by the

[5] The boundary is as much a social as a physical one. Each Indian who lives near the line knows to which *municipio* he belongs; nearly every Indian and Ladino over a wide area knows this about him, as well, so that the traveler can say that the line is "between this family and the next one farther on," the two families being perhaps a quarter-mile apart.

[6] The roads are named also according to the pueblos with which they connect. In Jocotán the road to Copan is called "the Copan road" or "the Camotán road," and the road to Olopa, "the Olopa road." Directional names are sometimes used, as "the west road," "the east road," "the north road," and "the south road." The last two names have no Chorti equivalents, as there are no terms for north and south.

Indians for their weekly trips to the markets. They are in most places narrow, winding trails, extremely rough and rocky, and are never used by the Ladinos for pack or riding animals if a highway can be used instead, as they are dangerous in spots for loaded mules.[7] They usually follow the line of least resistance, often running directly over a hill in cases where building around the hill would have been difficult. Wherever possible, they run along the summits of low continuous ridges, where drainage during the rainy season is good; if the hill is too high, they run along its side, paralleling the small stream which flows in the gorge beneath.

The highways connect the most important pueblos and are built primarily for Ladino use. They are, no doubt, more recent than the Indian roads, vary from eight or nine to perhaps twenty feet in width, are usually fenced on both sides, have a dirt base, and are rather smooth and level. The steepest grades in them have been leveled down, and dangerous curves avoided wherever possible. They mostly follow the river valleys, where the terrain is fairly level and free of boulders. One runs from Jocotán to Chiquimula, passing through San Juan Hermita, and thus somewhat parallels the older but more direct road. It is passable by automobile during the dry season. Another runs south to Olopa, paralleling the older Olopa road, and both these are used for military purposes and by the Ladinos for their mule-trains and when traveling by muleback. These two highways are completely separate from the older roads; others, built merely to make the old road more passable for mules, largely follow the latter, leaving them

[7] At such spots the rider dismounts, drives his mule ahead if going downhill, or leads it if going uphill, and thus gets by. The roughness and danger are no hindrance to the Indians, however, as they travel and transport only on foot.

at rough spots and rejoining them a mile or two farther on.
The Copan road contains a separate highway from Camotán to a point about midway between that pueblo and
Copan pueblo, where it rejoins the older road. The road
from Chiquimula to Quetzaltepeque is a highway at spots,
and during the dry season a regular bus line carries passengers between these two pueblos. None of the other roads
of the entire Indian area could in 1933 be used for vehicles.

All roads and highways cross the streams at wide spots
where the depth is not too great to make fording possible.
During the rainy months, when the streams are high and
swift, the Indians cross at an oblique angle and in the direction of the current, usually in groups of three or four, all
holding hands to prevent drowning in the swift current.[8]
There are few bridges, except over the Jocotán River,
which is too deep the year round for fording. These are of
the suspension type, supported by wire cables which are
attached on both sides of the stream to large trees, and
with a catwalk covered with small flimsy boards. They are
called "hammocks," which they resemble, and sway dan-
gerously when the passenger is in midstream. The cat-
walks are too weak to support large animals.[9]

The Indians of one *municipio* consider themselves as
somewhat culturally distinct from those of others, and this
belief has some basis in fact, although in most cases it is
more presumed than real. The *municipios* of Jocotán,

[8] Indian men who live near where the important highways cross the larger
streams, and between Jocotán and Chiquimula, earn money by conducting passengers across, either on their shoulders or by leading the mounted passengers'
mules. They also carry goods across on their shoulders, especially salt, sugar,
and flour, for the Ladino mule-trains.

[9] Riding animals are made to swim across, the rider walking over the bridge
with his saddle and retrieving his animal on the other side. Several deaths by
drowning occur at these bridges every rainy season, the passengers losing their
footing on the catwalk and falling through it.

Camotán, San Juan Hermita, and La Unión are culturally almost identical, differing only in such unimportant respects as the number of days of abstention from sex while performing the planting ceremony and the date for the annual celebration of the *municipio* patron saint, and the Indians and Ladinos consider these *municipios* to be something of a culture group. Their economy is mostly that of the lowland type, the native language and phonetics are identical in all of them, their Catholic religious observances are the same, and they maintain constant social and economic interrelations. The Indians of these *municipios* are said to be "similar"[10] in their customs, although not entirely alike, and to get along well together because of this similarity. Although each of these *municipios* has its own market and celebrates its own festivals independently, Jocotán pueblo is to some extent their social, economic, and religious center. The Camotán and San Juan Hermita Indians attend and depend upon the Jocotán market much more than their own, and the Jocotán festivals seem to be equally if not more important than their own. Olopa *municipio* belongs culturally with this group, since it differs from the others only in that it has a highland economy, and it belongs economically because it supplies highland goods for the larger Jocotán market.

Quetzaltepeque and Esquipulas *municipios* form a culture group by themselves and are said to be "very different"[11] from the Jocotán group, although the Indians of both recognize themselves as having fundamentally the same origin, culture, and language. The Chorti of the

---

[10] Sp. *semejante. a-tcek-t-o᾿ p᾿ kotca in-te᾿ in-te᾿*, "They look like one another"; *xa᾿ c-ir-op᾿ u y eror in-te᾿ in-te᾿*, "They are the same every one"; *ma-xa᾿ c yanyan-op᾿*, "They are not different."

[11] Sp. *muy diferente. xa᾿ c-ir-op᾿ yanyan-op᾿*, "They are different"; *ma᾿ tci a-tcek-t-o᾿ p᾿ kotca non*, "They are not like us."

Quetzaltepeque region is perfectly understood in Jocotán; its phonetics and some of its words are slightly different, but there seem to be no differences in linguistic structure. The Quetzaltepeque Indians are much more Catholic, having always had resident priests. Many of their native ceremonies differ greatly in detail, although they are fundamentally similar to those of Jocotán and Olopa. There is not much contact between the two groups. Jocotán Indians are seldom seen in the Quetzaltepeque plaza, and vice versa, and trips to visit friends and to attend festivals are rarely made.

Each *municipio* has its pueblo; that of the *municipio* of Chiquimula is called the city of Chiquimula, and is the capital of the department. It is called in Spanish the *cabecera*, to distinguish it from the other pueblos of the department. All the other pueblos of the department come under its jurisdiction. It is the most important town in the entire department and is the only one which has rail and highway communication with the outside world. The *cabecera* of chiquimula is the fifth largest town of the Republic.[12] The pueblos of the department of Chiquimula are spaced from about three to thirty-five or forty miles apart. Zacapa, the capital of the department of Zacapa, about thirty-five miles north of Chiquimula, lies well outside the Indian country, although Indian merchants visit it occasionally, and the average Indian journeys to it to celebrate a festival once in every four or five years. Chiquimula is at the edge of the Indian country and is visited by the Indians at least

---

[12] The pueblo is called in Chorti *tcinam*, the derivation of which is unknown. The Spanish term is used in eastern Guatemala in reference to a compact town which contains streets and a plaza and is thought of primarily as a place where Ladinos live. The *pueblanos* are usually Ladinos, although the Indians use the term mostly in reference to the few Indians who live in the pueblos, as opposed to *los aldeanos* (the *aldea* Indians).

once or twice every year for trading and visiting. San Juan
Hermita is twenty-five to thirty miles east and slightly
south from Chiquimula, on the principal road which runs
eastward to Copan. San Jacinto is about fifteen miles
southwest from San Juan Hermita. Jocotán is about fifteen
miles east of San Juan Hermita and seems to be considered
the main center of the Indian country. Two miles farther
east is Camotán, an unimportant pueblo, and Copan is
about thirty-five miles east of Jocotán, lying some ten
miles over the border of Honduras. La Unión is nearly
forty miles north of Jocotán, and Olopa is twenty-five
to thirty miles south. Esquipulas is about eighteen miles
south of Olopa, or about forty-three south from Jocotán,
and Quetzaltepeque is about fifteen miles southwest from
Olopa. These pueblo names are of Spanish, Nahuan, and
Chorti origin.[13]

[13] In the full name of most of the pueblos, the name of its patron saint pre-
cedes the name of the pueblo itself, as Santiago Jocotán (St. James Jocotán),
San Juan Camotán (St. John Camotán), and San Francisco Quetzaltepeque
(St. Francis Quetzaltepeque). The saint's name is dropped in ordinary reference,
although the Ladinos insist that only the full name is the "true" or official one.
The pueblo names of Spanish origin are San Esteban (St. Stephen), San Juan
Hermita (St. John the Hermit), San Jacinto (St. James), and La Unión (The
Union). Those of undoubted Nahuan origin are Jocotán (*jocotl tlan*, "place
of jocote fruit"?), Camotán (*camotl tlan*, "place of sweet potatoes"), Quetzaltepeque ("place of the quetzal bird"?), and Copan, called in the older literature
Copantli ("bridge of wood"?). The others may be either Nahuan or Chorti.
Chiquimula may be *tcikimul ha'* (*ha'*, "stream," "water"). The meaning of *tcikimul* is now unknown to the Indians, although *tciki'* is basket, and *mul*, or *mur*,
is mound or pyramid. According to the older literature, the term referred to the
linnet bird. *tcik* is a Chorti term for bird in general, now almost obsolete.
tcik e mur ha' could have meant "bird-of-the-mound stream." Esquipulas,
called in the older literature Esquipula, may have been *es-kip'-ur ha '(kip'-ur*,
"raised," "lifted"). The *es* could have been *ec* (man's drawers), as many Indians
pronounce it almost in that way. *p'ur* means "to burn," "to char," and *p'u·r*,
"beans." The last two syllables of the name could also have been *ora'* (*or*,
"head"; *ha'*, "stream"; thus, "source of a stream"), since in many other cases the
Chorti *o* was changed to Spanish *u*. Zacapa and Olopa are probably Nahuan,
hispanicized from *Zacapan* and *Olopan* (*-pan*, locative). Zacapa, however, could
be Chorti *sak*, "clear," "white"; *q'ap'*, "arm"; *ha'*, "water." *q'ap' ha'* now refers

The pueblos of the area have been taken over almost completely by the Ladinos since the Conquest. The Indians have little by little been pushed out from them and the surrounding level land and up to the *aldeas* of the higher hills, where the land is much less valuable and cultivable. Jocotán, Olopa, Camotán, La Unión, Quetzaltepeque, Esquipulas, and Copan contain a small population of Indians, perhaps 10–20 per cent, but they are predominantly Ladino. Nevertheless, the Indians consider these towns part of their social and economic area. The churches in them are much used throughout the year as centers for Indian festivals and other Catholic religious observances, and they are important centers for Indian marketing on Sundays. They lie within the strictly Indian area, of which Jocotán is roughly the geographical center. San Juan Hermita contains very few Indians, although many families live in the western part of its *municipio*, and it is seldom used by the Indians for marketing and religious purposes. Most of its Indians are drawn to the Jocotán and Olopa markets and festivals. Zacapa, Chiquimula, San Esteban, and San Jacinto are almost wholly Ladino at the present time, particularly the first two, and are visited by the Indians very rarely. These pueblos contain a few families who are probably pure Indian racially, but they have adopted much Ladino culture, consider themselves Ladinos, and are partially accepted by other Ladinos as such.

All the pueblos mentioned above, with the exception of

---

to the branch of a stream ("arm of water"); thus *sak q'ap' ha'*, or *sak q'ap'a'*, "clear branch." Olopa could be *olop ha'*, or *orop ha'* (*or*, "head"). Copan suggests an origin from *q'op*, "to pick up with the hands," "to gather," and *a· n*, "spring maize," especially since the Indians somewhat lengthen the *a* in the name. The final *a* in the pueblo names could be the shortened form of either a Nahuan locative affix or the Chorti term *ha'*, the latter losing its *h* and glottal stop.

INDIANS COMING IN TO THE MARKET PLAZA IN OLOPA EARLY ON SUNDAY MORNING

La Unión and Olopa, were listed by Juan Galindo as being early Indian towns and as having been founded by Indians.[14] According to Ladinos in Jocotán, the pueblo and *municipio* of La Unión were separated from Jocotán *municipio* by the government authorities about fifty years ago, as Jocotán *municipio* was considered too large to have only one market and political center. Olopa is much older, and none of the Ladinos knows anything about its origin. It seems to be as old and native as Jocotán, although it is smaller, and it is surprising that Galindo, who wrote in 1834, did not mention it.[15]

In the center of Jocotán pueblo is the plaza, an open space about three hundred feet square, the sides of which face in the four cardinal directions. The pueblo church stands in about the center of this and faces west. The plaza is the marketing center, where every Sunday and on festival days from a few hundred to a thousand Indians congregate for buying and selling. Facing the plaza are the principal buildings, the *juzgado* and *comandancia* on the west, and the jail and school on the south, with the other two sides occupied by the larger Ladino stores. The plaza is kept free of weeds and rubbish at all times, the work

[14] See p. 3, n. 4.

[15] There is an *aldea* of Chiquimula *municipio*, called Vado Hondo, which is inhabited by Ladinos and is thought of as a pueblo. The population of the pueblos, as given in the 1921 census, are as follows: Chiquimula, 4,860; Zacapa, 5,087; Quetzaltepeque, 1,140; Jocotán, 894; Olopa, 622; Esquipulas, 1,263; San Juan Hermita, 313; Camotán, 408; La Unión, 282; San Esteban, 401; San Jacinto, 730; and Vado Hondo, 211. At the time of the study the census figures were not available, and the estimates made were in some cases far off, for the Ladinos were of little help in making estimates. They think of the sizes of their pueblos only in relative terms, as that Jocotán is twice as populous as Olopa, and never in terms of actual figures. They seem unable to estimate as high as a thousand, or even five hundred, especially in reference to people. The Indians, of course, think even less in terms of population figures, and altogether in terms of a pueblo's importance as a marketing and religious center.

being done by Indian prisoners who thus work out their fines for drunkenness and fighting during the previous Sunday market. The plaza area is not surfaced, although a part of it surrounding the church is paved with tiling and cobblestones. Most of the Camotán and Olopa plazas are kept planted with a thick grass, called grama, which is used for grazing cows. Seven streets radiate in the four cardinal directions from the plaza, three from its corners and four main ones from near the centers of its four sides. These are called the "principal streets," are paved with cobblestones from the plaza to the edge of the pueblo, and have a concave surface, so that rain water runs down their centers, often flooding them during the rainy season. The four main streets continue from Jocotán as the main highways to neighboring pueblos and wind considerably through the pueblo as if built over old trails. Most of the pueblo houses are built along them, so that the pueblo itself spreads outward from its center in the shape of a starfish. The other three streets do not leave the pueblo, are mostly straight, contain fewer houses, have little paving, and seem to have been laid out more recently. Smaller streets connect the principal streets with one another in a few places, but these are usually no more than wide paths.[16]

The upper-class Ladinos have their houses and many of their stores nearest the plaza, usually on the four principal streets, with the lower-class Ladinos and pueblo Indians living farther out, most of them at the edge where the roads and trails enter the pueblo proper. Most of the

[16] The principal streets are called "its important roads the pueblo" or "its four important roads." The Chorti names refer primarily to important highways which run between pueblos, as there is no Chorti term for "street," and are used in reference to the four main streets because they are continuations of such highways. The Ladinos also refer more commonly to these four as roads, or highways, than as streets.

JOCOTAN PUEBLO, SHOWING THE CHURCH OF CAMOTAN IN THE RIGHT DISTANCE

Ladino structures are built of white-plastered adobe or thick clay wattle-work and are rather commodious. Nearly all are roofed with red tiling, locally made, or occasionally sheet iron, and those of the well-to-do have tiling floors. A large front room faces the street, and an open patio directly behind it has rooms on both sides which are used as living quarters. Jocotán, like all the pueblos except Chiquimula, has no separate stores, as every merchant uses the front room of his home for this purpose. The houses of the Indians are mostly like those of the *aldeas*, sometimes of clay but usually of limbs and thatch.

Each of the four principal streets has a large cross standing in its center, at the point where it leaves the pueblo, and these are said to mark the pueblo boundaries as well as to protect the pueblo itself against the entrance of evil spirits. At the pueblo's edge are the *cofradía* and the *chichería*, both of which are important meeting places for the Indians during market days and festivals. The latter, run by a Ladino, dispenses *chicha* to the men at a peso a gourdful— about the only alcoholic drink the Indians can afford.

Outside Jocotán are the milpas and gardens of the Ladinos, occupying the level lands of Jocotán Valley for several miles in every direction. No Indian could afford to buy land so near the pueblo. This valley is perhaps two miles wide north and south, with the Jocotán River on the northern side, about half a mile from the pueblo.

Olopa pueblo is about one-half the size of Jocotán and is of less importance as a trading center, although it is the most important marketing pueblo of the highland Indians. Its church stands completely outside the plaza and is probably more recent than that of Jocotán. The four principal streets lead outward from the corners of the plaza and continue to neighboring pueblos. Olopa sits on the crest of a small hill, the sides of which are too steep in places for ascent, and all the surrounding region is extremely mountainous.

Each *aldea*[17] occupies a single geographical area, and it considers all the land and resources within that area as its own. The land is made up of house sites, milpa and garden land, orchards, unused milpa land which may or may not be lying fallow at any given time, and land which is too rough or rocky to be used for any purpose except grazing. There are no actual boundary marks which separate one *aldea* from another, and yet any Indian knows with some accuracy where his own *aldea* ends and the others which surround it begin. Trails sometimes divide them, but not usually. To this area the Indian feels a strong emotional attachment, since he was born within it, most of his friends and relatives live there, and he himself has probably lived there all his life. It is his neighborhood, the habitat of his family and kin, and the area in which his domestic life and productive work go on throughout the year. Those Indians who have lived for many years in a pueblo, and have perhaps become much Ladinoized, are felt by the *aldea* Indians to be living unnaturally and almost in a foreign area, principally because they are for the most part laborers with little time or opportunity to cultivate their own milpas. It is said to be "bad" for an Indian to live in a pueblo, and many pueblo Indians seem to feel this way themselves.[18]

[17] The *aldea* is called in Chorti *sian otot* ("many houses"). Another Spanish name, used only by the Indians, is *valle* ("valley"), probably used because the typical *aldea* is located on both sides of a stream. An *aldea* Indian is *ah sian otot;* a small and unimportant *aldea*, or a *caserío*, *ut sian otot* or *im-p'ihk e otot tar* ("few houses place"); a large *aldea*, *noh sian otot;* and the *aldea* area, *ta sian otot*, or *sian otot tar* ("many houses place"). The Indian refers to his own *aldea* as *ni sian otot* ("my *aldea*"), or as *ni tur-tar* ("my place, locality, or neighborhood").

[18] *ma-xa`c p'amp'an xai tur-u in-te' Indio tame`tcinam*, "It is bad if an Indian lives in the pueblo."

The *aldea* Indians seldom remove from the *aldea* of birth, except in cases of marriage into another *aldea*.

Each *aldea* has a proper name which in most cases has been taken from such outstanding and unusual natural features as mountains, cliffs, streams, clay deposits, a species of wild or cultivated plant, or the slope of the terrain, and the name often refers to the feature as well as to the *aldea*. Many of the names contain the locative *ta* initially, and the suffix *ha'* ("water," "stream") is common.[19] In many cases the names have no observable relation to any of the characteristics of the *aldeas* to which they refer, although they may have had in the past.[20]

A few of the names are partly or wholly untranslatable, as they contain stems no longer used. Most of the Chorti names have been hispanicized, as Guaraquiche and Tunucó.[21] A few of the *aldeas* have only Spanish or Nahuan names, but these may all be of recent origin, since the first

[19] As in *ta pohp'* (*pohp'*, "sedge," "mat"; Sp. *Tapóp*), which is a center for mat-making and sedge-growing, and *ta naranjó* (*naranjo*, "orange tree"), in which *aldea* many oranges are grown for the Jocotán market. Similarly, *ta noh ha'* (*noh ha'*, "much water," "lake") and *war a·n ha'* (*war a·n*, "growing maize"). An inhabitant of Tapóp, for example, is called *ah ta pohp'* (Sp. *Tapopero*), while *e ta pohp'-op'* (the Tapoperos) denotes all the Indians of that *aldea*.

[20] The translation of many is not at all certain, especially because of the fact that the Indian informants themselves could not be made to realize that the polysyllabic names were really combinations of stems, having always considered them to be single words. Although they knew that *ha'* meant water or stream, they never seemed to be certain that the last syllable of *war a·n ha'* (pronounced *wara·na'*), for example, was the same stem. Similarly for *war* and *a·n*. They usually refused, or were unable, to consider possible meanings for the parts of names and could never get beyond saying that *war*, by itself, meant "standing," and that *war a·n ha'* was merely the name of a place (*xa·c u q'apa' taka*, "it's a mere name"; Sp. *es mero nombre*). They were always amused at literal translations.

[21] Guaraquiche is from *u arak itc* ("its domestic chili"), and Tunucó, from *tun u qohn* (*tun*, "rock"; *u*, possessive; *qohn*, "stream").

settling of many of them is still remembered by the older Ladinos of Jocotán and Olopa.[22]

Since marriage is most usual among the families of a single *aldea*, most of the people are interrelated by blood or marriage or both. But there are cases of marriages outside, so that each *aldea* has a few individuals brought up in other *aldeas*.

Some of the *aldeas* have been completely deserted within the memory of Indians now living, the families having joined their relatives in other *aldeas*, usually where land was better or more available. The names of these continue to be used, however, referring now to the mere localities where the families once lived.

The *aldeas* are located always near one or more streams, since water is needed throughout the year for irrigation and household uses. Most of the streams of the area are small and swift, and usually two or three of them meander through a single *aldea* to join another and larger stream below. *Aldeas* are often located on the side of a hill which has a large stream, varying in width through the year from a few inches to eight or ten feet, running through the narrow valley below it. On both sides of it are the family sites, each from a hundred yards to a half-mile from its nearest neighbor, the former distance being the more usual. The land between the family milpas is usually rough and precipitous and often too rocky for cultivation. Trails connect the family groups with one another and with the main pueblo

[22] The most important *aldeas* of Jocotán *municipio* are *Oquén* (pronounced *okéng*, derivation unknown), Amatillo ("little amate tree"; Ch. *ut xun te'*, although the Spanish name is more commonly used), Tunucó, Guaraquiche, Tapuán (probably *t'ap' u a· n*, "his maize going upward"), Morral, and Pajcó (probably *pax q'o'*, "sour gourd"). The most important of Olopa *municipio* are Tuticopote (lit. *ta u ti' q'opot*, "at the mouth of the forest"), Piedra de Amolar, El Rodeo, Chancó (*tcan qohn*, "winding stream"), and Nochán (*noh tcan* "great snake").

trails. Jocotán and Olopa *municipios* are extremely mountainous and, because of excessive erosion, very rough, and
travel is often impossible except along the narrow trails
which connect the *aldeas*. Irrigation canals tap the stream
at the upper end of the *aldea*, pass by all the plots of those
families who irrigate, and join the same or another stream
at the lower end. Orchards of fruit trees spread out from
both sides of the stream, planted in the low sandy soil so
that irrigation is not required. Other family orchards are
scattered about the *aldeas*, usually irrigated from convenient springs.

The average *aldea* of Jocotán and Olopa *municipios* contains around twenty-five family groups, made up of sixty
to eighty households, although some are three or four
times larger than others. The average population seems to
be between two and three hundred individuals. The geographical size varies considerably, depending both upon
the number of *aldea* inhabitants and upon the compactness
of the family units. It averages two to three miles across
in any direction, the shape largely determined by the topography and the location of the natural resources. Those
built along the banks of a stream which runs through a
narrow valley are usually long and narrow, while those
built on fairly level land and in wider valleys are more or
less circular. Within the *aldea*, the families often cluster
together in small groups, thus leaving large spaces nearly
unoccupied. There is no plan in the *aldea* layout—nothing
that could be called streets or a central plaza. The trails
connecting the households and families simply wind
through them on their way to other *aldeas*, and the families
are located as near these trails as possible.

The *aldea*, as well as the *caserío*, is a much less important
and clearly defined area than is the *municipio*. It is little

more than a rural district in the Indian's mind. Its boundaries, although more or less known to everyone, are not
marked and are of little significance, since political and
economic control for all the *aldeas* of a *municipio* emanates
principally from its pueblo, and very little from within the
aldea itself. Thus, one *aldea* has little physical distinction
from another and is more a region, or rural locality, than a
clearly delimited village. It is a social group, in that its
families co-operate among themselves in agriculture, hunting, fishing, and celebrating the family ceremonies and festivals, but family co-operation is not totally confined to
the *aldea*. It has no important cultural distinction from
any other *aldea* within the same *municipio*. Certain *aldeas*
are distinguished from others on the basis of their occupations or the presumed character of their families, but
such differences are unimportant and are not thought of as
constituting real cultural differentiation.

The *municipio*, on the other hand, is a significant community unit and the only one with which affiliation has
much meaning.[23] Its boundaries are well known and
marked; it is in every respect a social, economic, political,
and religious unit, as opposed to other *municipios;* and it
has some cultural distinction from other *municipios*. All
the important activity of the Indian's life takes place within it, and he is never required to leave it except for rare, and
unnecessary, visits to the markets, festivals, and homes of
friends and relatives outside it. Any Indian or Ladino,
whether he lives in an *aldea* or in the pueblo, usually identifies himself by the name of his *municipio*. Thus, a Ladino
or Indian of Jocotán pueblo is a Jocoteco, and so is an Indian who lives in any *aldea* of Jocotán *municipio*. Similar-

---

[23] As is the case in western Guatemala as well (see Tax, 1937, p. 432).

ly, any Olopa Indian is an Olopeño.[24] This is his primary
identification, especially to the world at large, as when
traveling in another *municipio*. Outside his own *municipio*
he never identifies himself by the name of his *aldea*. To
other Jocotecos, the Tunucó Indian calls himself a Tunu-
queño, as when he reports to the Jocotán officials for military or road service, but when in Chiquimula or Copan, he
is a Jocoteco, or says he comes from Jocotán.

He speaks of "those" Quetzaltepequeños and of "we"
Jocotecos, considering all the Jocoteco Indians to be the
same people and like himself. Those of other *municipios*
are called "outsiders" or "other people," while those of his
own *municipio* are "my people."[25] Most of his friends and
relatives live in his *municipio*, and he visits them often but
seldom visits outside it. Thus, the Jocoteco's social relations are much more constant and intimate with other
Jocotecos than with most Camotecos or Olopeños. When
visiting in other *municipios*, even with friends, the Indians
act somewhat as strangers, treat everyone with politeness,
speak only when spoken to, and are careful to call no undue
attention to themselves, as by getting drunk and disorderly. This behavior is not noticeable when they visit the
pueblo and other *aldeas* of their own *municipios*, where

[24] The Spanish names of the inhabitants of the other *municipios* are: Camotán, *Camotecos;* Copan, *Copanecos;* San Juan Hermita (usually shortened to
San Juan), *San Juanecos;* La Unión, *Unionecos;* Quetzaltepeque, *Quetzaltepequeños;* Chiquimula, *Chiquimultecos;* Zacapa, *Zacapeños;* San Esteban, *Estebane-
cos;* San Jacinto, *Jacintecos,* and Esquipulas, *Esquipultecos.* The Chorti equivalents are formed by adding the pluralizer *-op'* to the same Spanish names, as *e
Jocotec-op'* ("the Jocotecos"), *e Olopeñ-op'* ("the Olopeños"), and *e Camotec-op'*
("the Camotecos").

[25] *ne'n xa'c in-te' Jocoteco,* "I am a Jocoteco" (Sp. *soy Jocoteco*); *non e
Jocotec-op',* "we Jocotecos" (Sp. *nosotros los Jocotecos*); *xa'c-ir-op' tu' pat-er*
("those of outside"), "outsiders" (Sp. *los de afuera*); *yep'-er winik-op',* "other
people" (Sp. *otra gente*); *ni winik-op',* "my people."

they feel they are among their own people and are not afraid of getting into trouble with Ladino officials or other Indians.

The handling of nearly all the goods which the Indians grow, manufacture, market, and consume takes place within the *municipio;* its *aldeas* are the areas of production and its pueblo the point of distribution, as well as the area of Ladino manufacturing. No part of it is economically independent, although the whole *municipio* is more or less economically independent of other *municipios.* Its pueblo contains all the offices of its political and military officials, and these exercise political control over all the *municipio* inhabitants. They maintain order in his *aldea* and try all complaints in the pueblo court. The Indian does unpaid military service and road work only within his *municipio,* and it is these officials who exact penalties if he fails to report. Nearly all the important calendric festivals and ceremonies are celebrated by the *municipio* as a unit; each *municipio* has its one church and its one set of *mayordomos* and *padrinos* in charge of all community religious observances; Indians who come from other *municipios* attend festivals merely as guests. Each has its one important rain-making ceremony which is meant to bring rain primarily to the *municipio,* and each celebrates its annual festival as a separate group. The patron saints are the patrons of entire *municipios* and not merely of the pueblos in the churches of which they are usually kept, and the protective power of each is spread over his *municipio* to the complete exclusion of other *municipios.*

RACES AND CLASSES

In Jocotán and Olopa *municipios* the whites and mixed whites, or Ladinos, form the dominant population of the pueblos, and the Indians, most of whom seem to be full blood, occupy the rural *aldeas*. There is an extreme cultural and social distinction between the two peoples. The Ladinos consider themselves an urban people, like those of Chiquimula and other cities, principally because they are of Spanish speech and culture and are largely white racially, although a small proportion of them have some Indian blood, and all make some use of many Indian techniques, such as maize-grinding on the metate, tillage farming, and native cooking. Every Ladino man raises maize and beans to some extent, regardless of his wealth or other occupation, and those of the lower class make their living by farming their own milpas and working for wages in the milpas of the wealthier Ladinos. Their costume is predominantly European; they build large adobe houses and make use of riding and pack animals and some machinery. They are definitely the upper class of the *municipio* and exercise political and economic control over it. The Indians, with the exception of the few who live at the edges of the pueblos, are entirely rural, use Chorti as their preferred language, are of predominantly Indian race and culture, wear typically Indian costume, build clay and thatched houses, use no machinery, travel only on foot, and carry loads on their backs with the tumpline. Nearly all the *aldea* Indians own their land and work it as independent farmers, each family being an almost completely self-sufficient unit, but they have very little political voice and are the only group from whom free public labor is exacted.

The distinction between the Indian and Ladino groups is based more upon cultural than upon racial differences.[26] A number of Ladinos of prestige in Jocotán are of half or more Indian blood but are completely accepted as Ladinos

[26] The distinction is much like that in western Guatemala (see Tax, 1937).

because they are culturally and psychologically non-Indian in every respect. Any individual tends to be adopted by the opposite group after having lived with it for a number of years and having taken over its culture traits. One very important cultural distinction rests on the type of footgear, the Ladinos wearing shoes usually, and the Indians, sandals. If an Indian decides that he would be better off as a Ladino, he moves to the pueblo, wears shoes and as much European clothing as he can afford, pretends to be able to speak only Spanish, refers to the *aldea* Indians as "they" instead of as "we," pretends not to understand the Indian customs, learns a Ladino trade, marries a Ladino woman if he can, and keeps his children in the public school, with the result that over a period of years he comes gradually to be looked upon as a Ladino by everybody, although a lower-class one. His origin is not forgotten by others during his lifetime, and he is secretly considered inferior, especially if he retains, as he usually does, a single Indian trait which can be pointed out as a mark of inferiority. The conversion is usually not complete until the second generation.[27]

The same process goes on in the case of a Ladino, usually of mixed blood, who has lived for many years in an *aldea*, has become somewhat Indianized, and possibly has taken an Indian wife. He continues to consider himself a Ladino, although those in the pueblo usually do not, and they try as much as possible to behave toward him as they do to-

[27] One of these converted Ladinos was elected alcalde of Jocotán in 1932. He was racially pure Indian but had lived as a Ladino in Jocotán for about thirty years. Many Ladinos thought it disgraceful that he should have been elected. They enumerated his faults and then stated why they actually disliked his being alcalde by saying with great disgust, *Es hombre de caites* ("He is a man of sandals"). In 1933 there were six former Indians in Jocotán trying to convert themselves into Ladinos. The Indian women are said never to attempt it. When asked if such individuals are Ladinos, the Ladinos answer, with humor or disgust, *asi dice él* ("so he says").

ward any Indian. He jokingly refers to himself as *muy Indio* ("very Indian"), but considers himself a superior individual among his Indian friends and married relatives. The conservative Indians definitely prefer their own kind, marry Indian women, cling to Indian ways of life, and express a great deal of contempt for the Ladinos as a group. They realize that the latter look down upon them, and so adopt as much as they can the same attitude in return.[28]

The Indians of those *aldeas* which are remotest from the pueblos are more conservative in every respect and make greater use of the Indian culture and language than do those who live near the pueblos and for whom the pueblo is accessible almost every day. The former are all Chorti-speaking, faithfully perform the native religious ceremonies during the year, have almost no intimate social contacts with Ladinos, and use many Indian techniques which show little European influence. The majority of the Indians are of this group and are known to the Ladinos and progressive Indians as backward mountaineers. Their Spanish is limited and ungrammatical, they have little or no use for formal schooling, and nearly all are illiterate. These are the self-sufficient Indian group, who depend upon the Ladinos only for maintaining order in the *aldeas* and for such foreign commodities as salt, matches, iron, and cloth. The progressive Indians are somewhat Ladinoized and usu-

---

[28] Several texts were taken down in Chorti in which the informants expounded on the fact that the Indians were considered inferior by the Ladinos, and listed the reasons, apparently standardized, why they considered the Ladinos the inferior group. The two main reasons were that the Ladinos were not good milpa-makers and that many of their women were prostitutes or nearly so, or at least would not stay at home and keep house as women should, but were continually gossiping and visiting. Usually they were not specific, merely repeating over and over that the Ladinos were "no good" (*ma-p'amp'an e Ladin-op'*, "no good the Ladinos"). The conservative Indians genuinely feel that much of their culture is preferable to that of the Ladinos, but it is obvious that a great deal of their expressed dislike is mere retaliation.

ally pride themselves upon it. They are partially literate, more Catholic, maintain friendly relations with Ladinos as much as they can, usually wear one or two articles of Ladino-type clothing, eat many Ladino foods, and have adopted many non-Indian techniques. The Ladinos exploit this group, hiring them at low wages as domestics, field hands, and general laborers. A few of the Ladino men have casual sex relations with these women, although it does not seem to be common, and marriage with them almost never occurs. Only a small portion of the Indians are of this group, and they are not much respected by the conservatives.

There are no distinct social classes among the Indians, although there are social and economic differences among individuals. Certain ones have prestige, in the eyes of both Indians and Ladinos, based upon the possession of land, wealth, influence with Ladino merchants and officials, professional knowledge and ability, and aptitude for leadership. Juliano Cervantes, who is perhaps the most respected man in Tunucó, owns many milpas, implements, and houses, votes in local and national elections, and is much respected by the important Ladinos in Jocotán.[29] Skilled potters and mat-weavers enjoy prestige and are known for their ability in their own and near-by *aldeas*. The *padrinos*, curers, and other esoteric professionals have perhaps the greatest prestige among the Indians and are known to the Ladinos as "wise men" (Sp. *sabios*) who must be accorded some respect. Such individuals are often chosen as leaders in community activity, as when a group of families plant, harvest, fish, or repair trails co-operatively, and they are often used by the alcalde as unofficial representatives in

[29] The Jocotán Ladinos speak of three or four Indians in each *aldea* as being worthy of respect and point them out as examples which all the Indians should follow.

their *aldeas*. No *aldea* contains many of them, however, and none of their community behavior indicates that they feel themselves to be a common-interest group.

Most of the Indians are industrious, hardworking, and regular in their habits. The lazy individual is much despised, while the man who raises maize and beans and the woman who looks after her household are liked and socially accepted. Those who follow the esoteric professions are often shiftless but, being somewhat outside the pale of social intercourse, are rather expected to have bad qualities. Drunkenness and fighting are the only common vices, though fights over flirtations with married women are often reported. The Indians seem dependable and reliable in situations within their own society. Stealing, which is never condoned by the Indians, is rare except for an occasional theft of maize or a few feet of land, and thefts are usually reported speedily to the alcalde for punishment.[30] They are extremely clean physically, bathing several times weekly, and usually the clothes are kept neatly washed and starched.

The term "Chorti" is primarily the name of the language, and only secondarily the name of the Indians who speak it.[31] It is not much used, as the Indians commonly refer to themselves and their language by a number of Spanish terms, which are generally used by the Ladinos

[30] The Ladinos insist that the Indians continually steal, but this is probably no more than a crystallized and traditional belief concerning a poor and somewhat despised people. The Ladino usually cannot cite actual cases of such stealing, although he is certain that they are thieves in general.

[31] The informants agreed that a Chorti-speaking Indian, and especially a male, could be denoted as *ah tcor ti'* (*ah tcor ti-op'*, "the Chorti-speaking people"), or as *tcor ti' winik* ("Chorti man"), to distinguish him from the Ladinos and from non-Chorti-speaking Indians, such as the Pokoman. Similarly, a woman could be referred to as *tcor ti' icik* ("Chorti woman"). In Spanish, as well, the language is sometimes called *el Chorti*, and the Indians who speak it, *los Chortis*, but very rarely. None of these Indian or Spanish terms is generally used.

as well. The language is *lenguaje*, which means "idiom," and is used by everyone as a proper noun, referring to Chorti only. A *lenguajero* is an Indian who speaks Chorti, as opposed to one who speaks it very little or who speaks only Spanish.[32] The most common term for "Indian," used principally by the Ladinos, is *indio*. They also use *indito* ("little Indian"), *natural* ("native"), and *los indígenes* ("the indigenes"). *Indito* has the least connotation of inferiority and is used affectionately, in direct address, and when the speaker wishes to avoid giving offense. A great degree of inferiority is expressed in the term "mountaineer," and especially in the terms "sandal-wearer," "man of sandals," and "woman of sandals."[33] The Indians refer to themselves as *indios*, or *inditos* (Ch. *e indi-op'*, "the Indians"), and often as *cristianos* (Christians) and *católicos* (Catholics), although the last two seem to refer primarily to man, as opposed to animals and supernatural beings.[34] The Indians refer to the Ladinos commonly as *in-te' ladino* ("a Ladino") and as *e ladin-op'* ("the Ladinos"), as well as *ah tsuk* ("bearded one"), *e tsuk-op'* ("the bearded ones"), and *e tsuk ladin-op'* ("the beard Ladinos"). Their contemptuous term for the Ladinos is *sambos*.[35]

[32] *Lenguaje* is pronounced as *lenguaja*, the last syllable very gutteral and barely heard. *Bien, habla lenguaje*, "Yes, indeed, he speaks Chorti" (Ch. *p'an u-y-ar-e e tcor ti'*); *Hay lenguajeros allí*, "There are Chorti-speaking Indians there" (Ch. *ayan e ah tcor ti-op' yexa'*). The Pokoman are said not to speak *lenguaje*, although they speak "their" *lenguaje*.

[33] The Sp. *de la montaña* ("of the mountain") has the special meaning of "backwoodsy" or "countrified," and also means "Indian-like." The Ladinos use *de caites* in reference to Ladino men and women who are so Indian-like and "degraded" as to wear sandals instead of shoes, and it indicates great disgust.

[34] As in the statement, "He is not a man, he is an apparition" (Sp. *No es cristiano, es espanto;* Ch. *ma-xa˙c in-te' cristiano, xa˙c in-te' p'ahq' ut*).

[35] This may be a corruption of the Spanish *ambos*, meaning "both" (referring possibly to their dual race).

CHAPTER X

POLITICAL ORGANIZATION

OFFICIAL GOVERNMENT

THE Indians have no native political organization, although the government of the Republic, under the control of the Ladino population, has imposed one upon them for the last three centuries or more. This government is almost entirely Spanish and has existed in Guatemala since colonial days. The Republic is divided into twenty-two departments, each with its capital city. The city of Chiquimula is the seat of government for the department of Chiquimula, and located in it are the two departmental governing bodies: the civil and the military. This dual division is maintained throughout the entire departmental government. The department is divided into *municipios*, the principal pueblo of each being the governing seat in which are located the offices of the subordinate *municipio* officials. The civil and military head of the department is the *jefe político* ("political chief") who is appointed by the president and who is the superior of all the officials of the *municipios*. He is also the *comandante*, in charge of the military establishment of the department, as well as the departmental prison. He is in every way the chief departmental official.[1]

[1] This official is the most feared and respected in the whole departmental government, as the Ladinos believe his power to be almost unlimited. He is said to be responsible only to the president of Guatemala and to have ample opportunity to play the tyrant in his area. The *jefe político* of Chiquimula from 1931 to 1933 was generally admitted, however, to be capable and well liked.

Jocotán pueblo, like all other pueblos of the department, contains the offices of the two governing bodies, the *juzgado* ("city hall") and the *comandancia* ("military office"), both of which are located on the plaza, facing the church. The *juzgado* is the civil and judicial branch of the *municipio* government, and its head is the *alcalde mayor* ("principal mayor").[2] He is elected for one year by the voting population of the *municipio*, nearly all of whom are the pueblo Ladinos. He has two assistants, the principal one of whom is the *alcalde segundo* ("second alcalde"), also called *el segundo* ("the second"), who is elected by the voters. He has no duties except when the first alcalde is ill or absent from the pueblo, in which cases he acts temporarily as first alcalde. The second assistant, known variously as *el tercer alcalde* ("the third alcalde"), *el tercero* ("the third"), and *el regidor*, is always an Indian, who acts as interpreter when Indians are brought in for questioning and trial, runs errands for the alcalde and other officials, and conveys information and orders from the alcalde's office to the Indians in all the *aldeas*. He is supposed to serve for one year, after which time another Indian is "appointed" by the first alcalde; but, when a willing and capable one is found, he is usually persuaded by the alcalde and other Ladinos to serve indefinitely.[3] None of the alcaldes receives pay, although they command considerable prestige. The *regidor* is especially respected by all the Indians of the *municipio*.

[2] In 1936 the municipal system was changed by act of the central government. The offices of alcalde and second alcalde were abolished; substituted were *intendentes* appointed by the president, responsible to him and to the *jefe político*, and paid from municipal funds. The description here is of the old system as it existed in 1931–33; the new laws have probably not changed the *aldea* political organization.

[3] The *regidor* in Jocotán in 1932 had been serving for six years and would, no doubt, have continued for many years more but for his death in the summer of 1933.

The *juzgado* collects fees from Indian families who borrow the patron saint from the church to celebrate it in the *aldeas*, and every Sunday it collects a fee, of from two to about ten pesos, from each Indian who sells goods in the plaza. It collects fines from Indians who get drunk and disorderly on market and festival days, who fail to report for community labor, and who fail to keep their children in the *aldea* schools, but income from this source is small due to the fact that most of the Indians either work out or lie out their fines in the pueblo jail, being allowed five pesos a day for this. Jailing costs the *juzgado* nothing, as the prisoners must feed themselves. It collects a little in taxes from most of the Ladinos, and from a few of the wealthier Indians, and beyond this it seems to have no source of income.[4] It tries all civil cases, varying from drunkenness and fighting to fairly serious crimes, and imposes fines and imprisonment up to several months.[5] The first alcalde acts as judge in trying cases. One of the most important tasks of the *juzgado* is that of keeping the public buildings and roads of the *municipio* in repair. New buildings and roads are seldom constructed, but the old ones need constant repair during and after the rainy season. The first alcalde requisitions the Indian men from the *aldeas*, who usually do this work without pay, and he appoints citizens and soldiers to direct them. The *juzgado* reads all the proclamations which come from Chiquimula. The alcaldes, accompanied by several Indians who beat drums, march slowly around the plaza until a crowd gathers, whereupon the second alcalde reads the message in a loud voice. It is usually read twice,

[4] A head tax (*ornato*) of a quetzal a year, payable by men between the ages of eighteen and sixty, has recently been levied. Half of the proceeds goes for public works in the township, the other half to the central government.

[5] Most murder trials are held in Chiquimula, where murderers are either shot or imprisoned.

so that everyone may hear, and is seldom translated into Chorti unless read on market or festival days, when there are many Indians in the plaza.

The *comandancia* is directed by the *comandante* ("commandant"), who is appointed by the president through the *jefe político* in Chiquimula, and he seems to hold his position as long as his work is satisfactory. In time of war the *comandancia* serves as a military post, and at all times it is the equivalent of a police department. Associated with it is a detachment of soldiers, nearly all Indians, who act as civil police. The Jocotán detachment usually numbers about ten men, who are stationed in Jocotán as regular soldiers. They receive no pay. The *comandancia* is the executive branch of the *municipio* government, its principal duty being that of enforcing the orders and decisions of the *juzgado* and of carrying out instructions from the *jefe político*. This dual government extends over the pueblo and all the *aldeas* which belong to the *municipio*. The *comandante* is the only pueblo official who is paid.[6]

The *comandancia* acts as the police force, especially on Sundays and festival days, when there is much marketing, drinking, and fighting. The soldiers, armed with rifles, go out in groups to make all arrests, search the *aldeas* for Indians charged with crimes, work the prisoners on the roads and public buildings, and escort prisoners to and from Chiquimula for trial.[7] They maintain the jail and guard the prisoners. Street-cleaning and the cleaning of

[6] He seems to command more respect as an official, especially from the Indians, than does the alcalde, no doubt because he is not easily subject to recall, is not intimately known in the pueblo and *municipio*, and is presumed to have real authority, being the representative of the all-powerful *jefe político*.

[7] They were kept especially busy in 1933 escorting the mule-trains which carried loads of the outlawed silver pesos to the Chiquimula railroad for shipment to Guatemala City.

the plaza after the Sunday market are regularly done by the few Indian prisoners who are jailed every Sunday for drunkenness and fighting, and who thus work out their fines. Each works with a long rope tied around his waist, the other end of which is tied to the wrist of an Indian guard. Prisoners are neither fed nor paid. The *comandancia* enforces the free labor of the Indian men, sending soldiers to the *aldeas* to arrest them if they fail to report. The soldiers carry all official messages to and from Chiquimula, and from one pueblo to another, and they are sent to any part of the *municipio* to bring in Indians who are wanted for any reason by the alcalde or *comandante*.[8]

Each *aldea* has its local officials, of whom the *auxiliar* ("assistant") is the chief. He is appointed by the pueblo alcalde and is a resident of the *aldea* he governs. All the *auxiliars* seem to be Indians of more or less pure blood, as the alcaldes say they make a point of selecting individuals for this work who will without doubt be accepted by the mass of Indians. The *auxiliar* is assisted by a civil commissioner, also appointed by the alcalde. The two work together, selecting men from the *aldea* who are to go to the pueblo to do public work from time to time, persuading defaulters to pay their debts owing in other places, especially in the Ladino stores of the pueblos, and collecting property taxes when the *juzgado* is in need of finances. The *auxiliar*'s assistant spends three or four days every three months in the pueblo to receive special orders from the alcalde, which he reports to his chief at home. A third official, the military commissioner, represents the *comandancia* in his *aldea*. He is appointed by the *comandante* and acts as

[8] The Ladinos say the chief purpose of the *comandancia* is to guard the country against "invasion" from Honduras, although of course no such danger has existed for a long time.

a policeman in making arrests and in forcing the men to go to the pueblos to do public work. The *caseríos*, since they contain few families, have no local government. Each is governed by the three officials of the nearest *aldea*.

The duties of these three *aldea* officials are not well differentiated, and all three seem to work together on every occasion. Each has a group of assistants who can be called on in cases of necessity or in times of danger. The *auxiliar* has three; the civil commissioner, six; and the military commissioner, one. Their services are said to be required especially in time of war. At other times they are called on to assist in making difficult arrests.[9] Every Saturday three of the assistants from each *aldea*, one from the group of each official, go to the pueblo to receive orders from the alcalde and *comandante* to be carried out during the following week, thus enabling the latter to keep in constant touch with all the *aldeas* under their jurisdiction. The *aldea* officials receive no pay.

Each of the three *aldea* officials, although usually only the *auxiliar*, carries a small black cane, about eighteen inches long, which is the symbol of his office and authority. He carries it during his stay in the pueblo, so that everyone may know who is he, and always when carrying out official business in his *aldea*. The canes are provided by the *juzgado* and are used in most parts of Middle America in the same way. The officials are always men, and usually elderly, since women are completely debarred from political activity. Political service is an *aldea* activity, as the officers confine their activities to a single *aldea*. They secure free labor for the *juzgado*, see that roads and trails

---

[9] It is not uncommon for all the officials and assistants, together with twenty or thirty men, to gather in a certain part of the *aldea* and from there proceed in a body to a house to arrest one man.

are repaired, deliver mail to the families of their *aldeas*, and call out the men for community action. The activity tends to be professionalized, since certain men in each *aldea*, because of education, native ability, and willingness to serve, are almost invariably appointed year after year by the Ladino authorities to serve as officials. Each *aldea* has three, and perhaps twice as many men who take turns in occupying the positions, so that the six or seven possible appointees are generally looked upon as professional politicians, whether they are in or out of office. They have great prestige in their own *aldeas*, and their authority to enforce labor or make arrests is seldom questioned.

The presence of a Ladino government in the *municipios* has had no great effect upon the native Indian life, since nearly all political activity is confined to the cities and pueblos, where few Indians live, and because of the fact that the Indians still settle many of their disputes among themselves through the use of sorcery and feuding on the part of independent families, consequently having recourse to the Ladino authorities usually as a last resort. This is especially true of the more conservative Indians who live farthest from the pueblos. The alcaldes constantly have difficulty in persuading these families to bring their disputes to the *juzgado*, where they can be settled legally.[10] The progressive Indians and Ladinos, however, turn to the *juzgado* in every difficulty and are constantly reporting trivial and imaginary complaints. The majority of the Indians seem to avoid contact with pueblo officials as much as possible and are content to take no part in the political life of their *municipio*. Only a few of the wealthier ones

[10] Often the alcalde does not hear of a dispute until the families involved have been fighting and casting black magic upon one another for some time, upon which he requests the *comandante* to send several soldiers to the *aldea* to bring in the family heads for consultation.

vote and take great pride in doing so, but most care nothing about it and consider politics a Ladino concern.

Every adult Indian male, except the very old, is required to put in ten days of unpaid labor on the roads of his *municipio* every year.[11] This work is usually done on the important routes which connect the pueblos with one another and with Chiquimula, since these are used for animal traffic and by everybody. Work on the unimportant *aldea* trails is not required, since these are used only by Indians, who have no transport animals, and never require more than an occasional weeding. The latter is done constantly by the men, partly as diversion, as they walk along them. Road work is mostly done at the close of the rainy season, after the trails have dried up. No pay is given, and each man supplies his own food. In lieu of this work, an Indian may pay the alcalde five pesos for each of ten days, and this is usually given to another Indian who works in his place. Every Indian male is also subject to call by the alcalde at any time of crisis, as to repair washouts and bridges after floods, and damage to the church and other public buildings from storms and rain. This is almost never paid for, although at times the alcalde furnishes the men with *tortillas* and beans while they are at work.[12]

Every able-bodied Indian man is supposed to serve at the *comandancia* as a soldier for two weeks of each year, for which he receives no pay, but those who are forced to

[11] The central government has now reorganized the system of road work. Every man between the ages of eighteen and sixty (regardless of race) must give two weeks' service on the roads each year or pay the sum of two quetzales; the money goes for equipment and materials.

[12] In the summer of 1932, when the Motagua River rose forty feet and flooded a wide area, the rail line from Zacapa to El Salvador was washed out in many places, so that Chiquimula and near-by towns were isolated. Hundreds of Indians from all over the department were called to Chiquimula to help in repairing it. They were said to have received some food for this, but no money.

serve are usually only younger men of large families who
are not needed at home for milpa work. A few serve continuously, being glad of the chance to live in the pueblo, and
are paid about seven pesos a day. The soldiers wear blue-
denim uniforms, usually well worn, with Indian sandals
and straw hats. Most of the Indians dislike military service and put it off as long as possible by claiming to have
sickness or milpa work to do at home. The latter excuse
carries more weight than any other, unless repeated too
often, after which the Indian reports for duty or is fined.
The Ladinos never serve as soldiers.

"ALDEA" CO-OPERATION

But if the formal political institutions are primarily foreign, community co-operation, especially in economic activities, but also in certain ceremonies and festivals and the
burial of the dead, is an integral part of rural Indian life.
Every family performs its own ceremonies individually,
such as those connected with birth, marriage, death, and
the protection of its milpas, but the more important community ceremonies and festivals are celebrated co-operatively. These are conducted by the professional *padrinos*,
but all the families who attend them share the expense and
labor required.[13] Neighboring families always bury their
dead co-operatively, as in digging the grave, carrying the
corpse, and covering it over. Grave-digging is difficult, as
the Indians do not have shovels, and often requires a whole
day for a group of men, who take turns at the work until
the hole is sufficiently deep. The family of the deceased

---

[13] For the celebration of the patron saint in Jocotán on July 24, for example,
every family of the entire *municipio* is expected to contribute as many pesos and
as much maize, beans, and other foods as it can afford, and the women co-operate
in cooking the *chilate*, *tortillas*, and cacao which everyone consumes during the
celebration.

have the right to call upon anyone in the *aldea* for help during this crisis.

The trails which run between the closely grouped households of a large family are kept clean and new ones opened up by the men of the family who use them, but such work on trails which connect the family groups with one another throughout the *aldea* is done by all the men of the families concerned. They seldom work together, except in building a new trail from a group of houses to the large trail which leads to the pueblo or other *aldeas*. The families agree on apportioning the work, and each man does his share, or cleans his portion of the trail, in his spare time. As many as twenty-five or thirty men co-operate in their annual work on the large *aldea* and pueblo roads, usually directed by the appointed *aldea* officials.

Nearly all the important activities are worked at with some degree of co-operation, especially those of the subsistence type which are concerned with acquiring food and the important material objects needed for family life, which require the simultaneous labor of a group of workers, and which are not professionalized.[14] The important economic activities usually co-operatively done, in whole or in part, are agriculture, butchering, hunting, fishing, food-plant collecting, house work, sugar-making, housebuilding, lime- and charcoal-making, and the transport of goods to the market for sale. House work is normally done by the women of each household, the wife being helped by her older daughters, but during times of family crisis, as when there is advanced pregnancy, birth, sickness, or death, the

[14] Most professional labor, like pottery-making, is engaged in by a single worker who is partially assisted by one or two members of his household, but the Indians do not consider this as co-operative. A few of the professionals sometimes band together to make their product, dividing it equally to be marketed later, but this does not seem to be a common practice.

female relatives and neighbors gather at the stricken household to do this work. Perhaps two or three come each day, returning home at night if they live near by, and the relatives often live with the household until the crisis is over. In many cases the husband's work also, in his milpas and elsewhere, is done by his male relatives and neighbors. These decide among themselves as to what and how much work each shall do and take turns until the husband is well again.

The co-operative units are the individual families and the groups of neighboring families, all of whom usually live near one another in the same aldea. The single-household family co-operates in everything it does, the husband doing the male work, the wife the female work, and both assisted by all their unmarried children over the age of five or six. In the multiple-household family all the households co-operate in the family's nonprofessional and subsistence activities, the family male head being in charge of such work, directing it, deciding when and how it shall be done, apportioning it among all the adults, and dividing the proceeds among his family's households when it is finished. He is in every way the head of his family group and is therefore responsible for its co-operative work. Each dependent household does its professional work without assistance from the other households, since this type of work has no value beyond yielding additional income and is not considered necessary for maintaining the life and economic independence of the family group.

Interfamily co-operation occurs in the most important phases of the activities listed above, although each family works at the less important parts usually by itself.[15] The

[15] The smaller families, which usually contain only one household, co-operate much more with other families than do those containing several households.

entire *aldea* is presumed by the Indians to be a co-operating group, since throughout a given year almost every family in it helps and is helped to some extent by every other. The Indian feels that he should help every family in his *aldea* at some time or other, if only by way of being a good neighbor, and so calls on them when he has spare time to take a turn in their milpas or to help in case of sickness, death, or other crisis. Formal co-operation, however, is principally found among the small groups of neighboring families who, by agreement, pool their work every year in planting, harvesting, storing the maize and beans, and repairing the families' trails, and among the intermarrying families. The latter especially help one another on all important occasions, sometimes working together as closely as a single family. Every family returns the help given it as soon as possible, either during the same working season or during the following year.[16]

In most of the co-operative activities there are no special tasks which require more skill than any others, and all the Indians possess skill at working at them about equally. In agriculture, for example, every man knows how to do every phase of the work, and all the members of the co-operating group either do the same tasks simultaneously or take turns at the different tasks during the course of the work. Certain phases of sugar-making, housebuilding, hunting, and butchering, however, are somewhat difficult and require a skill which most of the Indians do not have. Every *aldea* contains a few men who are known to be more

Many of the latter have enough adults of the proper sex to carry out their co-operative work among themselves and so are fairly independent of other families, while the former are forced to work with other families in almost all but the purely professional activities.

[16] Co-operation is called *tak-ar* (*tak-r-e*, "to help"). The co-operating group is *tak-ar-op'* or *tak-r-en-op'* ("they help one another").

skilled than others at these tasks, and they are usually invited by the family or group of families when they have such work to do. They do not set themselves up as professionals and are not said to have an *oficio*, as does a potter or weaver. They are given food while working and usually food and other articles to take home, but these are said to be gifts and not payment. They are called upon for help only within their own *aldeas*, since the *aldea* is the interfamily co-operative area, and, like all co-operative workers, they help only their friends and neighbors. Thus, there is only a personal relationship between themselves and those who "hire" them, although they vehemently deny that they are either hired or paid.[17] They have some prestige in their *aldeas* because of their special skills and are pointed out by other Indians as "very fine workers." Although they receive more in the way of gifts for their help in co-operative work than do the unskilled Indians, their income from this source is relatively much less than that which the potter or basket-maker derives from his purely professional work.[18]

The skilled sugar-makers are those who have learned to boil the cane juice properly and evenly and to pour it properly into the molds. No skill is required in the other phases of sugar-making. In housebuilding the skilled worker is the one who can join and notch the important timbers, using only the machete for this purpose since only the professional carpenters have woodworking tools. The skilled hunter who is asked to go on all hunting parties is one who

[17] The skilled worker says he is "merely helping" (Ch. *in-taka in-tak-r-e*, "I am only helping him") his friend or neighbor, as any Indian should, and is not being hired, since if he were hired he would be no more than a laborer, or *mozo*.

[18] They have no *oficio*, strictly speaking, but it is admitted they might have an *oficito* ("little profession"), meaning possibly that their work is on the verge of becoming an oficio and looks somewhat like one.

owns a gun and knows how to load and fire it. Some of these men are called professional hunters, since they hunt considerably and acquire a fair income from the sale of meat, furs, and hides, although hunting is normally considered a nonprofessional activity. The skilled butcher, of whom there are few among the *aldea* Indians, owns one or two sharp knives and is adept at slashing a pig's throat, drawing out all the blood to make into the much-liked *moronga*, scraping the hide, and carving the meat into the usual long wavy strips. Most of them learned this work from a Ladino butcher in Jocotán or Olopa. The Indians are not accustomed to killing large animals and seem to be afraid to attempt it unless a man with some skill at it is around while the work is going on.

In all co-operative labor the workers are given food, and sometimes feasts, by the family in whose interest they are working, and for the duration of the work itself. During the days when a group of neighbors are building a house, the owner's wife and daughters keep a large supply of boiled beans, *tortillas*, *atol*, vegetables, and fruits always available for the workers to eat when they like, and at the conclusion of the work they are treated to something of a feast. If the working group passes from one family to another, as in planting and harvesting, each family supplies food while its milpas are being worked on. If a neighbor merely drops in to assist a family for a few hours at some task, he is given a meal before going home, and possibly a few boiled maize ears or *tortillas* to take with him. All co-operative labor is thus paid for in food and by returning the same assistance at a future time. Those who have a special skill are given more food than are others, as their help is more valuable. The butcher, for example, gets two or three choice cuts, the skilled hunter gets first choice of the venison, and the sugar-maker gets a large load of both sugar and fresh cane juice to make into *chicha*.

The co-operative activities are necessary to maintain physical life, being mostly of the subsistence type and concerned with providing food and shelter, for which reason the Indians feel that responsibility for them should be assumed by the community, or neighborhood of families. Everybody in a neighborhood or *aldea* must be taken care of, so far as these activities are concerned, and the Indians state that, if a man cannot take care of them by himself, his neighbors and relatives must do them for him. There is no escaping this. The Indian says it is his duty to call fairly often on his neighbors to inquire if he can help them in any way and to help them at least a little every year. One must be neighborly, and the only way to be so is to help one's neighbors in their work.

The economic co-operative activities can be best done, or only done, by groups. Housebuilding requires a number of workers for dragging the heavy timbers to the house site and for lifting them into place, and in butchering, deer-hunting, and sugar-making many phases of the work must be carried on simultaneously. In sugar-making the cane juice would not remain fresh long enough for one man to do all the work, and the press itself requires several men to operate. In planting, harvesting, and storing, the work must be done quickly and only at given times, since it is attuned to the seasons and weather. If weevils get into the storehouse, the maize must be quickly shelled, cured, and restored to a granary, or it is lost, and this is usually done with the help of as many families as can be rounded up. The cost of buying and maintaining implements forces many families to co-operate, especially at sugar-making, since bulls are expensive and even the smaller presses cost too much for the poorer families to build. As a result, perhaps a third of the families in Tunucó, for example, own presses and bulls; the other families form into pressing groups when their cane is ready and either hire presses and bulls outright from the owners, each paying his share of the rental in sugar, or co-operate with the owners themselves. Very few of the Indians can afford to buy shotguns, so that most of those who hunt must accompany the man who has one and assist usually in rounding up the animals.

Those activities which require a special skill must necessarily be co-operative, as most of the Indians prefer not to attempt them without the help of skilled workers. These are invited to co-operate, and very often the work is put off until one or two such workers can come. In housebuilding, the family gathers all the materials and makes them ready, and then lays them aside until a skilled builder in the *aldea* finds time to join the group to prepare and lay the heavy timbers.

Much co-operation seems to be done merely because it provides fun and excitement and turns otherwise drab and monotonous work into something of a social occasion. Most of the co-operating groups carry on almost as much play as work, stop frequently for smoking, talking, and horseplay, and exchange much news and gossip. The planting of the milpas in May is the only co-operative activity which has little or none of the social element, since it must be done quickly and is too serious a task to be worked at in a playful mood. The average Indian constantly visits his neighbors throughout the year, and especially when he has no important milpa work to do, to join with them in almost every kind of work they do. They are often seen working together at small tasks, in which co-operation is not at all required. The callers are said to be merely "visiting" the man whom they are helping, since visiting usually takes the form of helping the family at whatever work they are doing when the visitor calls. To be willing to co-operate at all times whenever possible is perhaps the best reputation an Indian can have in his community, and an unwillingness to do this marks him as thoroughly mean and anti-social.[19]

[19] The main reason why one Indian is fond of another and considers him fine in every way is because "he helps me," and most of those he does not like and with whom he has no social contacts are those who do not exchange help with him.

CHAPTER XI

SOCIAL ORGANIZATION

THE FAMILY AND MARRIAGE

THE family group is either of the single-household type, consisting of a man, his wife, and their dependent children, all of whom live together in their own houses and who independently cultivate their own land, or of the multiple-household type, consisting of a number of related and mutually dependent households, all of whom live either together or in the same neighborhood, and who act as a co-operating group in performing all their important social, economic, and religious activity. The latter is a lineage group, all the members of which are related through descent from its oldest surviving parents or through marriage into the family.[1] The members of the multiple-household family are usually of three generation levels, which correspond roughly to the three status groups within the family. The upper generation are the oldest man and his wife, who are the family male and female heads. The man is referred to by all the family members, of whatever generation level, as "our father," and his wife is referred to as "our mother."[2] The middle generation in-

[1] Both types of family are called *mactak* (from *tak-ar*, "help," "assistance"; *tak-r-e*, "to help," "to co-operate"; meaning of *mac* in this compound unknown). The multiple-household family is sometimes called *noh mactak* ("large family") to differentiate it from the single-household type. The family group has no Spanish name, except possibly *rancho* and *ranchería*, which are sometimes used, although these terms refer more to the family's land and houses than to its members.

[2] He is called *u tata' e mactak*, "the family's father," or *u yum-ar e mactak*, "the family's master," "headman." *ka tata'*, "our father" (this is also the

clude their married sons and daughters who, with their
mates, are the heads of the various dependent households
which comprise the family.[3] The lower generation are the
unmarried children of both the family head and of his
sons and daughters, most of whom are under the usual marriage age and who therefore live in their respective households with their parents and are supported by them. Included in this generation are the great-grandchildren of the
family head, who also live in the households of their parents and grandparents. All these are called "grandchildren."[4]

The multiple-household family is composed of one chief
household, that of the family head, and from one or two to
seven or eight dependent households. Each of the latter
is made up of the husband, who is either the son or son-in-
law of the family head, his wife, and their dependent children who are living with them, all of whom usually occupy
one sleeping-house and one kitchen. Not all the children
are the offspring of the parents, since the adoption of
orphaned children is a general practice.[5] The chief household consists of the family male head, his wife, his unmar-

---

native name for God). His wife is called *u tu' e mactak*, "the family's mother."
ka tu', "our mother" (this is also the native name for the moon deity and
the Virgin Mary).

[3] Such a son or son-in-law is called *u tata' e otot*, "the household's father," or
u yum-ar e otot, "the household's headman." His wife is *u tu' e otot*, "the household's mother."

[4] See below, pp. 265, 270, 272.

[5] Many households are said to have as many children dead as alive, as infant
mortality is high. The Indian seems to expect that a third or a fourth of his
children will die before they reach the age of two years; but, once the child
reaches that age, its chances of survival are said to be good.

Some households have as many adopted children as they have of their own.
The adopted child seems to be as much loved and cared for as is the biological
child, and he has the same inheritance rights. The parents make little distinction in behavior between their own and their adopted children.

ried children, and those of his married children and their mates who are continuing as members of his family and who are still serving their four-year period of marriage service.[6]

New households within the family are set up only after the marriage of any of its members. The latter may be the children, the grandchildren, or the great-grandchildren of the family head. If the first, they are members of his household; if the second, they are members of the households of his sons and daughters; and, if the third, they are members of the households of his grandsons and granddaughters. In every case the children of the family are members of their parents' household until marriage. The family head is theoretically responsible for arranging their marriage with the children of the intermarrying family. If they become members of the latter group, he has no further responsibility for them; but, if they remain as members of his own family, they live in his household and work for him, just as do his unmarried children, during their four-year period of marriage service. At the end of that time he calls upon his sons and sons-in-law, who are the heads of his family's households, and with their aid he builds a new house on the family house site which the couple will henceforth occupy. As the owner of most of his family's property, he turns over to the couple a certain amount of the family land, a few domestic animals, and household and agricultural equipment. The couple function from then on

---

[6] The household is called *otot* ("house"), and the chief household, *noh y otot* ("chief house"). The term refers primarily to a house, and, secondarily, or in a social sense, to its occupants (man, wife, and children, usually) and their possessions. The nearest local Spanish term to "household" is *familia* ("family"), although this refers primarily to one's children and other direct descendants. Thus, an unmarried person may be said in Spanish to have no *familia*, though of course he is a member of a family group.

as a distinct household. When his grandchildren and great-grandchildren marry, if he is still living, he calls upon their parents and grandparents to aid him in setting them up as new and separate households.

If the marrying member is the family head's own child or grandchild, the couple always perform their marriage service in his household and under his direction; but, if it is his great-grandchild, the couple may perform the service in the household of his son or son-in-law, who is the grandfather of the couple. This son or son-in-law assumes most of the responsibility for the marriage and the subsequent setting-up of the couple as a household, although the family head is felt to be really in charge of all marriage matters, and his consent is obtained for everything done. Thus, although the family head continues throughout his life to be looked upon as the head of his lineage group in every respect, in actuality his headship and responsibility extend only to those members who are two generations below himself, since the sons and sons-in-law, once they have grandchildren, take over much of the role of family head within their own households. By this time the family head is usually very old, and the households of his sons and sons-in-law have already begun to function somewhat as distinct family groups, each with its own set of households. In such cases the son or son-in-law actually arranges his grandchild's marriage, exacts marriage service from him, and sets him up later in a separate household.

Upon the death of the male head of the family, his wife theoretically becomes its head, but in actual practice her sons and sons-in-law control family affairs. Upon her death, the last link which binds the family together is lost, and the family as a unit breaks up. Each household inherits equally of the family property, and each household head becomes the head of his new family group. The multiple-household type of family seems to be the more common, although it is said to be fast giving way to the single-household type, as many of the younger Indians prefer to move away from their immediate families after marriage to set up independent households on their own. Even in such cases, however, they usually continue to co-operate to some extent with their family groups throughout the year, especially in the more important agricultural and ceremonial activity. The older Indians believe it proper for married children to live in households dependent upon and cooperating with the family of either the husband or the wife. In very few cases do the married children separate themselves completely from their family groups.[7]

The family has proper names for its members and households and a single proper name for its entire group. The individual given names are all Spanish. The household name, or surname (Ch. *q'apa'*),[8] is always the name of the household father, and, since descent is reckoned in the male line, the surname of the family head remains in his

[7] These two family types are found at Chan Kom (Redfield and Villa, 1934, pp. 87–91).

[8] The most common translatable native names are *apsum* (*ap*, "hammock"; *sum*, "to net"), *p'orha'* (*p'or*, "to abound"; *ha'*, "water"), *mus* ("the breath"?), *aris* (*ar*, "to yield"; *is*, "sweet potato"), *asmen* (*as*, "to play"; *men*, "to make"?), *puk'ir* ("hospitality"), *q'ana·n* (*q'an*, "yellow"; *a·n*, "spring maize"), *q'u·m pa'* (*q'u·m*, "maize paste"; *pa'*, "tortilla"), *sara·n* (*sar*, "spotted"), *matcor* (*ma*, "negative"; *tcor*, "milpa"; thus, infertile, barren), *cerin* ("snail"?), *wa·ncin* (*wa·n*, "standing"; *cin*, "to go"), *mantcame* (*man*, "to buy"), *mantca·r* (*tca·r*, "stepchild"?), *mantar* (*tar*, "locality," "place"), *mertcor* (meaning of *mer* unknown), *munec* (*ec*, "man's drawers"), *p'ahna'* (*p'ahn*, "to boil"; *ha'*, "water"), and *to·par* ("a hop," "a skip"). The common untranslatable native names are *mo·s*, *arotc*, *asmun*, *ausum*, *carcente'*, *ternerax*, *centex*, *ceron*, *tcakon*, *tcasmarai*, *tco*, *watcin*, *ki·sar*, and *teas*. The most common which are derived from Spanish and Nahuan are *antón*, *siramáwa*, *klimak'ó*, *sirawa*, *morói* (possibly from Sp. *moráy*, "oak tree"), *sinkwír*, *solís*, *ardón*, *kasteyón*, *walís*, *oromán*, and *sútcite* (N. *xóchitl*, "flower"?).

family in the cases of sons who remain as members of his family group, but it goes to the intermarrying family in the cases of sons who become members of the other family. It makes no difference whether the daughters remain in the family or not, since they take the household names of their husbands in every case. Most of the household names are native, although some are of Spanish and Nahuan origin.

The family name, called in Spanish *apodo*[9] ("nick-name"), is applied to all the members of a family group, whether they are biological members of it or have entered it through marriage. It is not used by a family in reference to themselves, as they consider it uncomplimentary,[10] and it is never used in direct address, except when the speaker wishes to show his anger or disgust. All other families, however, refer to the family by it and so are able to differentiate that family from all others.[11] The biological family members begin to have this name applied to them very early in life, and the member who enters the family through marriage comes to be known by it soon after his marriage. The latter thereupon loses the *apodo* of his biological family, which he had formerly, and for the rest of his life he is known by the new one. His children receive the same family *apodo* which he has adopted, since they are born into the family and so receive it by right of birth. If the child's father is a biological member of his family, he receives his *apodo* through his father; but, if his father has

[9] Ch. *q'apa' mactak*, "family name," or *tca' q'apa'*, "second name."

[10] In many cases a family has both a Spanish and an Indian *apodo*; it readily admits having the former, which has little uncomplimentary meaning and some-times identifies itself by it, but the latter, which is considered very uncompli-mentary, is used only in reference to it by others.

[11] The Lacandones have animal names to designate families, transmitted from father to son (Tozzer, 1907, pp. 40–43). These, without doubt, are family names and not nicknames.

come into his family through marriage, he receives his
apodo through his mother, who is a biological member of
his family. Thus, the *apodo* is the only name the family
has which remains forever in it, regardless of whether its
members stay in it or marry out of it.[12]

The *apodos* are generally taken from the names of plants,
animals, minerals, and environmental phenomena. Most
are of native origin, but many Spanish and Nahuan terms
are used.[13] The *apodos* are referred to in Spanish as nicknames, and it is possible that a few of them are merely
nicknames of comparatively recent origin, especially those
which are considered the least uncomplimentary, as well
as the few which have no Chorti equivalents.[14] No informant could say, however, when his family had received its
apodo, all of them assuming that they had always had
them. The Ladinos in Jocotán, Camotán, and Olopa
pueblos have true nicknames, the origins of which are
known and joked about by almost everybody.[15] Some of
these go back three or four generations, and all are uncom-

[12] Rabbit (Sp. *conejo*; Ch. *t'ur*) is the *apodo* of the largest family in Jocotán
pueblo; *t'ur-op'* (plural) refers to the family members collectively or as a group,
and *ah t'ur* or *in-te' t'ur* ("one of the rabbits"), to any member of that family.

[13] The most common translatable *apodos* are *tcap t'cit'c* ("boiled animal
blood"; Sp. *moronga*), *ah wara˙ m* ("visitor"), *cirun* ("courageous"?), *tcuhp'up'*
(a type of squirrel; Sp. *agouti, cotuza*), *ehmatc* ("raccoon"), *qurqur* ("small
penis"?), *pohp'* ("sedge"), *kakau'* ("cacao"), *koko'* ("coconut"), *hahpin* (from
hahp, "to seize"?), *p'ut'sin* (from *p'ut's*, "to incense"?), *t'ur* ("rabbit"; Sp.
conejo),*t'ca˙ n qohn* ("winding stream"; Sp.*Chancó*),*p'a˙ cna* ("evil-speaking"; Sp.
desdicho), *we˙ rin* (from *we˙ r*, "meat"?), *q'omoc* ("sunflower"), *queso* ("cheese"),
and *yux* ("necklace"). The most common which cannot be translated are
mariax, pulul, and *temsiax*. The most common of Spanish and Nahuan origin
are *tcatat* (N. *tcatatl?* a type of greens), *sárkos, túrno, angelines*, and *kantc* (from
Spanich *canche*, "blond"?).

[14] Starr (pp. 73–74) reported the use of "nicknames" among the Chol and
believed many of them to be old family names still preserved.

[15] At Mitla nicknames are given, but only to individuals, especially children,
and never to domestic groups (Parsons, 1936, p. 82).

plimentary.[16] Since not more than a dozen or so of Span-
ish-given names seem to be used for each sex by the Indians, and very few more than that by the Ladinos, it is
impossible to identify any individual, even in the same
aldea or pueblo, merely by his given name. Twenty Manuel's were discovered in Jocotán pueblo and eight in Tunucó, and several Ladinos stated that there were probably
twice as many. Identification is made occasionally by reference to the Spanish or Chorti name of the household to
which the individual belongs, but more often by reference
to his family's *apodo*.[17]

It has been stated that the family is the unit which arranges the marriage of its members to the members of another family in its *aldea*. Usually, only two families intermarry, the children of the one tending to marry the children of the same generation level in the other, but there
are many exceptions to the rule. The Indians merely feel
that this is the ideal arrangement, but usually they do not
seem to object strongly if a family member should marry

[16] A family in Camotán is said to have an ancestor of four generations ago
who would eat nothing but soft-boiled eggs. He became known as *huevo
tibio* ("tepid egg"), and the name was applied to his family. This became
shortened to *el tibio* ("the tepid one"), and the family are still known in all the
pueblos as *los tibios*. About sixty years ago a man in Jocotán would get drunk
and jokingly call everybody he met *chucha maisera* ("maize-stealing bitch"),
and his descendants are referred to in the whole region as *las chuchas maiseras*,
or simply as *las maiseras*. A few years ago a half-witted girl in Jocotán, after
attending a wedding, shouted all over the pueblo that she wanted a beautiful
dress with seven colors in it. She is still known as *la siete colores* ("the seven
colors"). The *tintininica* family, calles *los tintininicas*, are descended from a
woman who used to sing "tintininica, tintininica" for hours at a time while rock-
ing her children to sleep.

[17] Thus, in conversation, a speaker refers to Santiago, and his listener immediately asks, "Which Santiago?" as this is a very common name in Jocotán.
The speaker then says, "Santiago of the Rabbits" (Sp. *Santiago de los Conejos;*
Ch. *Santiago e t'ur-op'*) or "Santiago de los Tibios." This formula is invariably
gone through with in conversation when reference is made to a third person.

into a third family.[18] There is a feeling that intermarrying families should have different *apodos*, although many Indians said that they knew of exceptions; in all the cases known where the pairs of families married most or all their children between themselves this rule was observed. Further, even those individuals who "elope" and marry whom they choose prefer a mate with a different *apodo*.

When a young man or woman is ready or wishes to marry, his or her father or grandfather goes to the parents of the intermarrying family and asks that a marriage be consummated. If both parents are dead, his godfather acts as his parent, requesting the marriage or acceding to it. The parents usually do not force a son or daughter into an undesired marriage, although in most cases the children are easily persuaded to accept the parents' choice. The Middle-American custom of using matchmakers is unknown.[19]

The head of a family where there is a son or grandson of marriageable age consults with his adult sons and sons-in-law to decide upon a suitable mate in the other family and to determine whether they can afford a marriage feast and the best time for holding the ceremony. He then confers with the head of the other family, allowing the other a reasonable time to discuss the matter with his sons and sons-in-law. Some of the offspring of the two families may be already intermarried. They meet again, and it is then decided which family shall assume complete responsibility

[18] A man in Tunucó did this in 1926, and there has been ill-feeling between him and his father ever since, but the rest of his family have attached little importance to it and seem to have accepted his wife. The younger Indians say that the old man is merely "old fashioned" and that his attitude is what is to be expected from old people, although most of these younger Indians themselves have married "properly."

[19] See Gann and Thompson, 1935, p. 171.

for arranging and paying for the marriage. Usually it is the family that is more desirous of the marriage which assumes the expense. After the marriage the father who paid for the marriage builds a house for the couple near his own house group. They leave only when he gives them permission to do so, which is usually at the end of four years. During this time the young man is performing bride service for his father or father-in-law, for which he receives only his keep. This applies as well to the young wife, although her period of marriage service is said to be three years. The family status of both is similar to that of son and daughter in every way. When their period of service is over, the parents or parents-in-law give a part of their land to the man to cultivate, together with a few pigs, turkeys, and chickens, and certain household equipment.

The adopted child-in-law thus accepted remains a member of his mate's family thereafter, as do all his or her descendants who do not pass out of it through marriage to other families. The two intermarrying families maintain close personal relations among themselves, often play and work together, and constantly exchange visits and gifts of maize. They help each other in planting, harvesting, performing ceremonies, and in time of family crisis, such as sickness, death, and extreme poverty. As a result of this, the adopted member of a family does not lose complete touch with his biological family, since his regular visits and aid to them are considered his interfamilial duty.

Separation or abandonment is common on the part of both sexes. Separations result either because the woman persists in talking with other men[20] or because one of the couple does not properly perform his part of the household work. Very often a woman, to avoid punishment, runs off

[20] See p. 302.

with her lover. If the husband does not want his wife, he may use this offense as an excuse for abandoning her in order to take another woman. Adultery is the cause of only a few separations, since the wife is carefully guarded by her husband, and he is usually informed by his relatives and friends of any love affair which might develop in his absence. In cases of abandonment it is said to be the rule that the husband retain his land and field equipment while the wife retains the house and its equipment. For a serious offense a man can eject his wife and retain all his property, while she may go home to her kinspeople or take up with another man. She usually takes the latter course. Where there is very little property to be considered, the husband may simply abandon his wife, children, and property and merely take up with another woman in a distant *aldea*. It is also the rule that the husband keep all the older male children, and the wife the older female children and all children under ten or eleven years old. She often prefers, however, that the husband keep all the young children, since she would have difficulty in supporting them. Her usual course is to find another man as quickly as possible and have children by him.

The external relations of the family with other families in its own and other *aldeas* are both formal and informal, the latter consisting of frequent visits and exchange of gossip at one another's houses. On such occasions the visitor from another family is made very much at home, given food and a hammock to lie in, and assisted in whatever work he may be doing in that locality. It is incumbent upon every family to treat every visitor in this way, and one of the worst reputations a family can have is that it is not hospitable to any visitor, whether he be friend or stranger, Indian or Ladino.[21] The formal social relations are maintained by gift-making and feuding.

In July, when the first maize in the lowlands is ready to be eaten, the family head sends loads of ears to many of the families in his *aldea*, and especially to his friends in the highlands, where the first maize does not ripen until about two weeks later, both as a token of friendship to these families and as a way of celebrating the first eating of fresh maize for the year. This month is one of general rejoicing and of thanksgiving to the family saints for having made the maize plants grow and ripen, and so gifts of it are exchanged by all families to strengthen old family bonds and to make friends with new families. The lowland families return the gifts very soon afterward, and those in the highlands return them as soon as their maize ripens. Fresh maize, as well as vegetables and venison, is often sent to a family with which an old feud has been going on to indicate a desire to make peace.

Most of the feuds between families have their origin in disputes over land, although fights between a husband and his wife's lover are fairly common. Feuds may be kept alive for many years before being finally settled, either by physical violence or by sorcery. In either case the contending families act as units, the aggrieved family attempting to cause physical or magical harm to the other in its most vulnerable spot. It makes no difference whether the final victims were the cause of the feud in the first place, which

[21] The visitor or traveler has the right to demand, at least for a night, to be treated as a member of the family, and, if he is not so treated, he reports the fact to everyone he knows. The Indians of Naranjo, in Camotán *municipio*, are characterized by other Indians as being "merely pigs" (Sp. *puros coches*; Ch. *in-taka e tcitam-op'*) because they are said to be surly and inhospitable to strangers.

may have started many years before; if they are members
of the offending family, any harm done to them by the
offended family helps to settle the score. Very often a
child or sick member of the family is singled out for retaliation, especially if sorcery is used, since these are much
more vulnerable to black magic than are adults and persons in good health. The harmed family then often retali-
ates in the same way, and the feud goes on.[22] Sorcery is
more common and much more feared than physical violence. Individual fighting among the men is a common
practice, usually over disputes which the Ladinos consider trivial, and nearly always on market and festival
days, when many of the Indians drink heavily.[23]

The average Indian seems strongly attached to his family, to its land and possessions, and to the neighborhood
and region in which it has always lived. He feels himself

[22] In the summer of 1932 seven men and boys of a Tunucó family, while pressing cane, were attacked with machetes by eight men of an aggrieved family and
chopped to pieces. The mutilated bodies were carried on stretchers over nine miles
of muddy trails and swollen streams to Jocotán for burial in the cemetery. The
killers escaped to Honduras but were captured next year when they ventured
back and were given five-year terms in the prison at Chiquimula. This feud,
according to many of the Indians, had been going on for about fifteen years, and
everyone in the whole region knew the history of it. The father of the family to
whom the dead belonged had moved his fence a few feet onto the land of the
offended family, and the latter had harbored its grudge all that time until it
decided to act. They got drunk—a customary prelude—and settled the score,
Most of the Indians seemed not to consider that murder had been committed.
since the killing had not been done without cause and so refused to aid the Ladino
authorities in Jocotán in capturing the killers. These feuds are more temporary
than permanent and always have a definite cause which is generally known.
They thus differ from the more formal feuds found among other peoples, which
go on for generations and the initial cause of which is no longer remembered.

[23] Fighting is seldom done openly unless the men are extremely drunk. The
usual custom is for the aggrieved Indian to harbor his grudge, perhaps over a
period of years, until a day when he finds his enemy drunk in the pueblo.
He follows him home, waits until he goes to sleep under a tree along the trail,
and then hacks him with his machete. Usually only wounds are given, but
deaths are occasionally reported. Many Indian men have long deep scars
across their faces and heads which they claim were given them by their enemies
in this way.

an inalienable part of his family group and speaks proudly of the excellent maize it produces, its hospitality to
friends and strangers, the fact that none of its members is
lazy and unwilling to plant milpas, the fine houses in which
it lives, and the superior climate and soil of its neighborhood. The average family head never tires of pointing out
the superior qualities of his family establishment, referring
to it as "my home" or "my ranch," even though he may
own only three or four huts and perhaps a couple of acres
of rocky land. He considers most of the Ladinos and pueblo Indians as unfortunate because they cannot or do not
"make milpa," and thus lead unnatural lives. His primary
attachment is to his family; his real home, the locale of
greatest emotional attachment, is the small area upon
which are laid out his family's houses, milpas, gardens, and
orchards.

THE KINSHIP SYSTEM

The system of kinship terminology (Fig. 12) shows no
evidence of Spanish influence. A few terms of possibly
Nahuan origin have supplanted their Chorti equivalents
in common usage, but the latter are still understood. In
addition to the Indian terms, Spanish terms are also used
by all except a few of the older Indians, whose Spanish is
limited. The Spanish terms as used by the Indians are included in the list below. The basic Chorti terms number
twenty-two; in addition, many compounds referring to
various kin are formed. The terms and their applications
follow:

1. *iht'sin*[24] (recip. *sak'un*), younger sibling (Sp. *hermano menor*);
   younger cousin of any remove who is of ego's generation level (Sp.
   primo hermano menor).

[24] Possibly *wiht'sin*, as the possessive form in the third person appears both as
u wiht'sin and *u y iht'sin*. The *w* may be merely a euphonic semivowel, although
y is nearly always used in such cases. Derivation unknown.

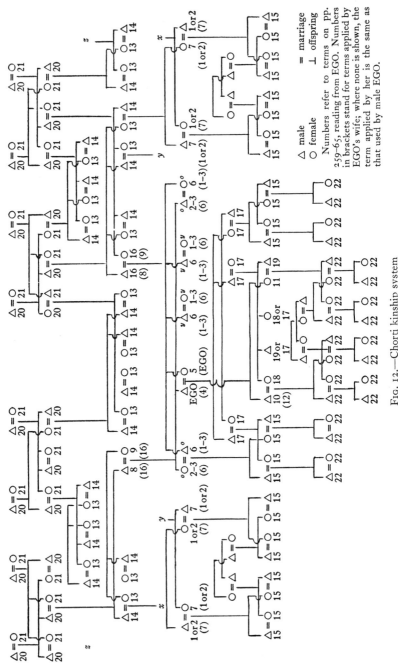

FIG. 12.—Chorti kinship system

Numbers refer to terms on pp. 259–65, reading from EGO. Numbers in brackets stand for terms applied by EGO's wife; where none is shown, the term applied by her is the same as that used by male EGO.

△ male   = marriage
○ female ⊥ offspring

2. *sak'un*[25] (recip. *iht'sin*), elder sibling (Sp. *hermano mayor*); elder cousin of any remove who is of ego's generation level (Sp. *primo hermano mayor*).

3. *ihta·n*[26] (recip. *ihta·n*), any sibling; mate of a sibling of ego's mate (Sp. *hermano, hermana*). *tca' u w ihta·n*, step-sibling, half-sibling (Sp. *hermanastro, hermanastra*).

   brother, wife's sister's husband, husband's sister's husband
   sister, wife's brother's wife, husband's brother's wife

4. *nocip'*[27] (recip. *ickar*), husband (Sp. *esposo, hombre*).

5. *ickar*[28] (recip. *nocip'*), wife (Sp. *esposa, mujer*).

6. *mu'* (recip. *mu'*), sibling's mate; mate's sibling; sibling of sibling's mate (Sp. *cuñado*).

   brother's wife, brother's wife's sister, sister's husband's sister, husband's sister
   sister's husband, sister's husband's brother, brother's wife's brother, husband's brother

7. *awan*[29] (recip. *awan*), mate of cousin of the same generation level as ego (i.e., the mate of any collateral *sak'un* or *iht'sin*); cousin's mate's sibling; mate's cousin.

8. *tata'*[30] (recip. *u'nen, iht'cok*), father (Sp. *padre, táta*); title of respect for older men, usually prefixed to the personal name;[31] affectionate term for an older man; term used in direct address to older men.[32] *tca' tata'* (recip. *tca·r*), stepfather (Sp. *padrastro*).

[25] No doubt a compound, but derivation unknown.

[26] This also may be *wihta·n*, as the third person possessive form is both *u wihta·n* and *u y ihta·n*. Derivation unknown.

[27] *cip*, or *cib*, means "husband" in many related languages. The meaning of *no* (or *noc*) in this term is unknown, unless it is a form of *noh*, "great."

[28] This may be *wick-ar*, as the third person possessive form is *u wick-ar*. The term, however, is probably a compound of *icik*, "woman," and *-ar*, particularizing suffix.

[29] Derivation unknown.

[30] *Tata'* is probably of Nahuan origin (from *tatatl?*), although many of the languages of Guatemala contain very similar terms meaning "father." The Maya *yum* is seldom used in Chorti in this sense, as it refers principally to deity and family head and to "father" only in the sense that he is a family head. *Tca' yum* is also understood as stepfather, though it is seldom used.

[31] This is equivalent to the Sp. *don* or *señor*, as *tata' Juan* ("Don Juan").

[32] As *eya tata'*, "Look here, father!" "Oh, father!" *tin a-yo·p-a tata'*, "Where do you come from, father?" An older man is affectionately referred to as *ni tata'* ("my father") or *in-te' tata'* ("a father"). The older men of a community are called *e tat-o·p'* ("the fathers").

9. *tu'*[33] (recip. *ar*, *iht'cok*), mother (Sp. *madre*, *nána*); title of respect for older women, prefixed to the personal name;[34] affectionate term for an older woman; term used in direct address to older women.[35] *tca' tu'* (recip. *tca·r*), stepmother (Sp. *madrastra*).

10. *u'nen*[36] (recip. *tata'*), son of male ego (Sp. *hijo*). *u y u'nen-op'*, his sons; *ni u'nen*, my son; *u'nen sit's*, young son, infant boy; *tca' u'nen* (recip. *tca' tata'*), stepson.

11. *iht'cok*[37] (recip. *tata'*), daughter (Sp. *hija*). *u w iht'cok-tak-op'*,[38] his daughters (Sp. *sus hijas*); *tca' iht'cok* (recip. *tca' tata'*), stepdaughter. The term also denotes a female child (Sp. *niña*), an older girl (Sp. *muchacha*), and an unmarried woman under twenty or twenty-five years old (Sp. *soltera*), but without reference to kinship;[39] it is suffixed to certain kinship terms which do not indicate sex to denote a young female[40] (Sp. *hembra*) and is used in direct address to girls and young women.[41]

[33] *Tu'*, likewise, seems to be of Nahuan origin. The Maya *na'*, "mother," is not used but appears in compounds in which it seems to have that meaning (see *q'ohna'*). It was understood by many of the older Indians as meaning "mother." *tca' na'* was undersood as stepmother, as well.

[34] Equivalent to the Sp. *doña* or *señora*, as *tu' María* ("Doña María"). The Spanish terms, whether in addressing males or females (see n. 30), are more commonly used. At Mitla, *dat* ("father") and *nana* ("mother") are the respectful titles prefixed to personal names (Parsons, 1936, p. 83).

[35] As *tuq'a a-tcon-i tu'*, "What are you selling, mother?" The older women of a community are affectionately referred to as *e to·p'* ("the mothers"), and an older woman, as *ni tu'* ("my mother") or *in-te' tu'* ("a mother").

[36] This term may be derived from Chorti *u* (third person possessive adjective) and Sp. *nene* ("child"), or it may be *ut nen* (pronounced *u'nen*), from *ut* ("small," "diminutive") and Sp. *nen* ("child").

[37] *t'cok*, "young," "fresh," "green" (as plants). Meaning of *ih*, which appears also in *iht'sin* and *ihta· n*, is unknown.

[38] *-op'* is the plural suffix for nearly all stems in the language. *tak-op'* is used, however, for pluralizing *iht'cok* and *icik* ("woman") and with no others. Meaning of *tak* in this sense is unknown.

[39] As *in-te' iht'cok u-y-ar-en-ic*, "a girl said to me." This is the nearest term the Indians have to "virgin," although it is rarely used in this sense, as they seem to think of young women more in terms of marital status than of virginity. "Virgin" to them usually refers to the Virgin Mary only.

[40] See n. 70 below.

[41] As *tuq'a a-q'an-i iht'cok*, "What do you want, girl?"

12. *ar*[42] (recip. *tu'*, *tata'*), son of female ego; any child of male or female ego. *u y ar-op'*, his or her children; *u y ar sit's*, her male child; *u y ar iht'cok*, her female child; *tuno·r u y ar-op'*, all his or her children; *tca·r*[43] (recip. *tca' tata'*, *tca' tu'*), stepchild of either sex; *u tca·r-op'*, his or her stepchildren (Sp. *sus hijastros*); *tca·r sit's*, male stepchild (Sp. *hijastro*); *tca:r iht'cok*, female stepchild (Sp. *hijastra*); *tcohp'-a-p'ir u y ar*, *t'oc-p'ir u y ar*,[44] adopted child; *tcatca·r*,[45] twin (Sp. *gemelo*); *tcatca·r-op'*, twins.

13. *q'ohna'*[46] (recip. *k'war*), female kin one generation above ego but excluding the mother of both ego and ego's mate (Sp. *tía*). *tca' q'ohna'* (recip. *tca' k'war*), sister or female cousin of stepfather or stepmother of the same generation as the latter.

> father's sister, mother's brother's wife
> mother's sister, father's brother's wife
> wife's father's sister, wife's mother's brother's wife
> wife's mother's sister, wife's father's brother's wife
> husband's father's sister, husband's mother's brother's wife
> husband's mother's sister, husband's father's brother's wife
> father's female cousin, mother's male cousin's wife
> mother's female cousin, father's male cousin's wife

14. *mama'*[47] (recip. *k'war*), equivalent to *q'ohna'*, but denoting males only (Sp. *tío*). *tca' mama'* (recip. *tca' k'war*), brother or male cousin of ego's stepfather or stepmother of the same generation level as the latter.

> father's brother, mother's sister's husband
> mother's brother, father's sister's husband
> wife's father's brother, wife's mother's sister's husband
> wife's mother's brother, wife's father's sister's husband
> husband's father's brother, husband's mother's sister's husband
> husband's mother's brother, husband's father's sister's husband
> father's male cousin, mother's female cousin's husband
> mother's male cousin, father's female cousin's husband

[42] *ar-i*, "to give birth to," "to exude," "to give forth."

[43] From *tca'*, "second," "twice," and *ar*, "son," "child."

[44] *tcohp'-a*, or *tcoh-p'a*, "to grow up," "to be raised"; *tcohp'-es*, *t'oc-i*, "to raise children or animals."

[45] From *tcatca'* (*tca'*, "two"), "double," "twinned," "paired," and *ar*, "child." *tcatca' sak'un*, elder brother or cousin who is one of twins; *tcatca' ni w ihta:n*, "my twin sibling."

[46] Meaning of *q'oh* unknown, but it may be related to *qohr* (small part of anything, diminutive). It also appears in *q'oh yum* (see *mama'*). *na'* in this compound may have once meant "mother."

[47] Derivation unknown.

15. *k'war*[48] (recip. *mama'*, *q'ohna'*), kin of the first descending generation, excepting ego's own children (Sp. *sobrino*, *sobrina*). The term
includes any child of siblings or cousins of the same generation level
as ego (i.e., the child of any *sak'un* or *iht'sin*), as well as any similar
kin of his mate. *k'war sit's*, young "nephew"; *k'war iht'cok*, young
"niece."

16. *p'icam*[49] (recip. *nyar*, *arip'*), mate's parent. *p'icam winik*, father-
in-law (Sp. *suegro*); *p'icam icik*, mother-in-law (Sp. *suegra*).

17. *p'icmar*[50] (recip. *p'icmar*), parent of son's wife or daughter's husband. *p'icmar winik*, child's mate's father; *p'icmar icik*, child's
mate's mother.

18. *arip'*[51] (recip. *p'icam*), son's wife (Sp. *nuera*); son's wife's sister.
u y arip', his son's wife; *u y arip'-op'*, his sons' wives, his son's
wives' sisters; *arip' icik*, grown daughter-in-law; *arip' iht'cok*, young
daughter-in-law, young sister of daughter-in-law.

19. *nyar*, *nyart'sir*[52] (recip. *p'icam*), daughter's husband (Sp. *yerno*);
daughter's husband's brother. *u nyar-op'*, *u nyart'sir-op'*, his daughters' husbands, his daughters' husbands' brothers; *nyar winik*,
grown son-in-law; *nyar sit's*, young son-in-law, young brother of
son-in-law.

20. *tata'noy* (recip. *sit's*), male kin two or more ascending generations
above ego and his mate (Sp. *abuelo*); any aged man; term used in
direct address to aged men.
    grandfather
    grandfather's brother, grandmother's sister's husband
    grandmother's brother, grandfather's sister's husband

21. *na'noy*[53] (recip. *sit's*), equivalent to *tata'noy*, but denoting females
only (Sp. *abuela*); any aged woman; term used in direct address to
aged women.[54]

[48] Meaning of *k'w* unknown; *ar*, "child."

[49] Derivation unknown.

[50] Possibly a contraction of *p'icam* and -*ar*, particularizing suffix. *ar*, of
course, could also mean "son," "child."

[51] This term contains *ar*, "son," "child." *ip'* may be the instrumental suffix
-*ip'*.

[52] Both these contain *ar*, "son," but the meaning of *ny* and *t'sir* is unknown.

[53] Meaning of *noy* in this, and in *tata'noy*, is unknown. It may be related to
noh, "great," "important," or to *oi* (or *oix*), "corner post," "support."

[54] An aged man is affectionately called *in-te' tata'noy* ("a grandfather"; Sp.
abuelito), and an aged woman, *in-te' na'noy* ("a grandmother"; Sp. *abuelita*).
The aged men of a community are *e tata'noy-op'* ("the grandfathers"), and the
aged women, *e na'noy-op'* ("the grandmothers").

    grandmother
    grandfather's sister, grandmother's brother's wife
    grandmother's sister, grandfather's brother's wife

22. *sit's* (recip. *tata'noy, na'noy*), grandchild (Sp. *nieto, nieta*); kin two or more descending generations below ego. The term also denotes a male child (Sp. *niño*) or young boy[55] (Sp. *muchacho*); it is suffixed to certain kinship terms which do not indicate sex to denote a young male[56] (Sp. *macho*) and is used in direct address to children of either sex.[57] *sit's iht'cok*, any young female two or more generations below ego.

    p'ia˙r,[58] any kin, but primarily a blood kin (Sp. *familia*). *u p'ia˙r-op'*, his kin group (Sp. *su familia*); *in-te' ni p'ia˙r*, one of my kin (Sp. *un mi familia*); *tuno˙r u p'ia˙r*, all his kin; *tca' p'ia˙r*, any step-kin.

    nuhp' p'ia˙r, nuhp'-p'ir p'ia˙r,[59] any affinal kin.

Of the twenty-two terms, nine refer, with few exceptions, to all the kin of a given generation, ten to a restricted group of a generation level, and three to single kin. In twelve of the terms the sex of the kin referred to is implicit; in the other ten it is indicated, if at all, by suffixes denoting both age and sex. Sex distinctions are more frequently made in terms for kin of ascending than of descending generations. Relative age is implicit in one set of sibling terms, but in no others. Generation level is implicit in all terms used between relatives of one and successive generations; relatives beyond the grandparent and grandchild generations are not distinguished terminologically from those of the grandparents and grandchildren, respectively.

The system of kin classification is consistent with and

[55] As *in-te' sit's*, "a boy." A similar term, *tehrom* ("boy," "youth"), refers to a male slightly older than a *sit's* but does not denote kinship.

[56] See n. 70 below.

[57] As in *lar ta˙ra sit's*, "Come here, child!" *kotca a-q'apa' sit's*, "What is your name, boy?"

[58] From *p'ia'*, "to accompany," "to work with." *p'ia˙r* (lit. *p'ia'-ar*), "friend," "companion," "relative," "co-worker."

[59] From *nuhp'-i*, "to marry," and *nuhp'-p'ir*, "married."

can best be understood in connection with the Chorti preferential marriage system. Whether or not it may have been based upon a cross-cousin marriage institution of the past,[60] now prohibited as incest, the kinship system today fits the preferred marriage based on sibling and cousin exchange better than it would one based on cousin marriage.[61] The chart (Fig. 12) is arranged to include as many of the preferred marriages as possible and is to that extent of course idealized; but it shows clearly the consonance of the kinship terminology with the ideal marriage system.

The siblings of Households A and B of extended Family I are expected to marry siblings of Households A and B, respectively, of extended Family II. Families I and II are not related by blood, but the siblings of A are usually first cousins of the siblings of B. Ego denotes all his elder siblings and his elder cousins of any remove who are of the same generation level, regardless of sex, as *sak'un*, and his younger siblings and cousins, regardless of sex, as *iht'sin*.[62] He denotes his own siblings, regardless of either sex or age, as *ihta·n;* this term refers to all the siblings (*u w ihta·n-op'*, "his siblings") of his household (I A) and differentiates them from collateral first cousins (of I B); it denotes the group of siblings who are to intermarry with his mate's siblings (of II A). He differentiates his mate from the lat-

[60] Studies of the kinship terms given in the Motul dictionary and of Conquest writers lead to the conclusion that the Maya of Yucatan may have practiced cross-cousin marriage at the time of the Conquest (see Eggan, 1934).

[61] Thus, in a typical cross-cousin marriage system the mother-in-law is called by the same term as the father's sister, and the father-in-law by the same term as the mother's brother, while cross-cousins are merged terminologically with spouses or siblings-in-law and distinguished from parallel cousins.

[62] Ego's elder first cousin is sometimes denoted as *tca' sak'un* (second elder sibling), and his younger first cousin, as *tca' iht'sin* (second younger sibling), and his second cousins of his generation level, as *uc sak'un* and *uc iht'sin* (*uc*, "three," "third"), but these terms are rarely used.

ter's siblings by *nocip'* ("husband") or *ickar* ("wife"), and refers to any of his mate's siblings as *mu'*. Thus, ego's mate's sibling is *mu'*, and the mate of this sibling is *ihta·n*, that is, the sibling of ego. Likewise, ego's sibling's mate is *mu'*; this mate's sibling is *mu'*, and the latter's mate is *ihta·n*, or ego's own sibling. Ego's siblings refer to his mate and his mate's siblings as *mu'*, as well, and his mate's siblings refer to himself and his siblings as *mu'*. The group of his mate's siblings is *u mo·p'* ("his mate's siblings"; lit. *u mu'-op'*), each of whom is an *ihta·n* of his mate and a potential sibling-in-law of one of his own siblings.

The mate of any first cousin (of I B), as well as any sibling of such a mate, is called *awan*, and after marriage ego extends the term to include any cousin (of II B) of his mate, since ego's first cousins' mates and their siblings are theoretically his own mate's first cousins. Thus, the mates of the siblings of I B are ego's cousins-in-law (*awan*) and, being of Household II B, are often his mate's first cousins (*sak'un* or *iht'sin*), and the mates of the siblings of D, who are ego's cousins-in-law, are often ego's own first cousins, of I B. Ego calls a sibling of II B and the mate of a sibling of I B, *awan*, whether or not they are the same individual, since they theoretically and often are the same. The *awan-op'* (cousins' mates, mate's cousins), therefore, are the group of siblings who are ego's mate's cousins, and with whom ego's cousins theoretically are intermarrying, just as the *mo·p'* are the group of siblings with whom ego's siblings are intermarrying.

In the first ascending generation, ego's own parents are *tata'* and *tu'* (or *yum* and *na'*), and all his other blood and affinal kin at this level are called *q'ohna'* for the females and *mama'* for the males. Ego thus differentiates his own parents from the latter's siblings and siblings' mates. Most of the siblings of the father are married to the siblings of the mother, so that nearly every *q'ohna'* and *mama'* of ego through his parents is related by blood to him. For example, every mate of the mother's siblings is usually a sibling of the father, and every mate of the father's siblings is usually a sibling of the mother. Similarly, every mate of a father's first cousin is theoretically a mother's first cousin, and every mate of a mother's first cousin is a father's first cousin. The same terms are applied to any cousin and cousin's mate of the father or mother. Ego applies these terms to all the similar kin of his mate, but only after marriage, since before his marriage they were the heads of the households of his mate's family and therefore not related to him at all. Nearly every *q'ohna'* and *mama'* of ego's mate are, of course, similarly intermarried among themselves, but none of ego's kin of this generation is related by blood to those of his mate of the same generation level. Ego denotes his mate's parents as *p'icam*, these being the parents of the group of siblings (Household II A), or *mo᛫ p'*, with whom ego and his siblings are intermarrying, and thus distinguishes his mate's parents from their siblings and cousins, just as he does for his own kin.

All the blood and affinal kin of two or more ascending generations above ego are called *tata'noy* (males) and *na'noy* (females).[63] These include ego's grandparents and greatparents, their siblings and cousins of the same generation level, and the mates of all these. All are lumped together and called "grandparents" (*tata'noy-op'*), denoting all ego's blood and affinal kin who are at least one generation above his own parents. Ego applies these same names to all the similar kin of his mate as well. The sib-

---

[63] Any sister of a grandmother is sometimes called *tu' ilama* (*tu'*, "mother," *ilama*, "old woman"), but this term is seldom used.

lings of the paternal grandfather are theoretically intermarried with those of the paternal grandmother, as are
those of the maternal grandfather and grandmother. Thus,
on the side of either parent of ego, the grandfather's
brother is usually the grandmother's sister's husband, the
grandfather's sister is the grandmother's brother's wife,
and the grandmother's sister is the grandfather's brother's
wife.

In the first descending generation the male ego calls his
son *u'nen*, the female ego calls hers *ar*, and both call a
daughter *iht'cok*. The children of either ego are called
u y ar-op' ("his or their children"). Ego denotes every collateral blood and affinal kin who is of the same generation
level as his children as *k'war*, thus distinguishing the former
from his direct offspring. The term includes the children
both of ego's siblings and of his cousins of the same generation level as himself and is extended to include the mates of
these. Every blood *k'war* of ego is theoretically a blood
k'war of his mate, since it is presumed that ego and his siblings and cousins are intermarried with ego's mate's siblings and cousins, so that even before ego's marriage he
denoted all or most of the *k'war* group of his subsequent
mate by that name, just as the latter denoted all or most of
ego's *k'war* group. Although the mate of any *k'war* is also
called by that name, none is related by blood to either ego
or his mate, since each *k'war* and his siblings and cousins
are intermarried with families of no blood relation to themselves, just as ego and his siblings and cousins had previously intermarried with an unrelated family or families.

Ego's daughter's husband is *nyar*, and his son's wife,
arip', and he denotes the parents of either of these as
p'icmar, which term seems to signify the *p'icam* ("father-
in-law") of ego through his own child (*ar*). Ego's *p'icmar*,

who is of the same generation level as himself, is the head of the household or family with whom his own children are intermarrying, and every sibling and sibling's mate of the *p'icmar* is denoted by the same term. Ego refers to every child of his *p'icmar*, whether unmarried or married into a family other than that of ego, as his son-in-law or daughter-in-law, since at least one of these children is already married to one of his own children, and theoretically the other children of the *p'icmar* will marry those of ego. In practice, however, ego sometimes denotes those siblings of his child's mate who are not married to his own children as *p'icmar*, or as *u y ar-op' ni p'icmar* ("my *p'icmar*'s children"), thus extending the term to include every member of his *p'icmar*'s family who is not married into his own. All the blood and affinal kin of the second descending generation downward from ego are called by one term, *sit's* ("grandchildren"), just as all his kin of the same generation levels above himself are lumped together as "grandparents." The grandchild is *sit's*, as are all ego's direct and collateral descendants two or more generations below, their mates, and the siblings and cousins of these mates, and after marriage ego applies the term to all the similar kin of his mate.[64]

The kin of each generation level have one or more group names, which are formed by pluralizing the kin names. On ego's generation level his siblings of both sexes are called *ni w ihta᾽ n-op'* (Sp. *mis hermanos*). All the blood kin of his generation who are older than he are *ni sak'un-op'* ("my elder siblings and cousins"), and his younger blood kin, *ni w iht'sin-op'* ("my younger siblings and cousins").

[64] As *ni sit's*, "my 'grandchildren' "; *u sit's*, "his 'grandchildren' "; *p'amp'an tua' ayan-on im-p'on* (or *diálma*) *ka sit's*, "It is good that we have many 'grandchildren.' "

The Spanish *hermanos* ("brothers") seems to refer loosely to all ego's blood kin of his generation. All ego's mate's siblings and siblings' mates are *ni mo'p'* ("my siblings-in-law"), and his mate's cousins and cousins' mates are *ni awan-op'* ("my cousins-in-law"). The general Chorti term for both these groups is *ni mo'p'*, and the Spanish, *mis cuñados* ("my brothers-in-law"), which terms seem to denote any "in-law" of ego's generation. Ego denotes his children's mates' parents and the latter's siblings and cousins as *ni p'icmar-op'*, which group is theoretically the parents of all the children with whom his own children and those of his siblings and cousins are intermarrying.[65]

In the first ascending generation all collateral kin, blood and affinal, are *ni mam-o'p'* ("my 'uncles'"; Sp. *mis tíos*), and *ni q'ohn-o'p'* ("my 'aunts'"; Sp. *mis tías*). The former term loosely denotes all the collateral male and female kin one generation above ego. Ego's parents are *ni tat-o'p'* ("my 'fathers'"; Sp. *mis padres*), and his mate's parents, *ni p'icam-op'* ("my parents-in-law"; Sp. *mis suegros*), who are of the same generation level as his parents. *ni tat-o'p'* sometimes denotes all ego's kin one generation above him. All ego's lineal and collateral kin, blood and affinal, of the second ascending generation upward are *ni tata'noy-op'* ("my 'grandfathers'"; Sp. *mis abuelos*), and *ni na'noy-op'* ("my 'grandmothers'"; Sp. *mis abuelas*), and the former term loosely designates all the kin of two or more generations above ego. Ego's children are *ni w ar-op'* ("my children"; Sp. *mis hijos*, "my sons"); his sons-in-law are *ni nyar-op'*, and his daughters-in-law, *ni w arip'-op'*. All the mates of his children, regardless of sex, are loosely designated as *ni nyar-op'* ("my 'sons-in-law'"; Sp. *mis yernos*).

[65] The Spanish term, *consuegro*, is not known to the Chorti.

All ego's collateral blood and affinal kin of his children's generation, regardless of sex, are *ni k'war-op'* ("my 'nephews and nieces' "; Sp. *mis sobrinos*). *ni w ar-op'*, however, refers loosely to all ego's kin one generation below him. Ego's grandchildren and great grandchildren are *ni sit's-op'* ("my grandchildren"; Sp. *mis nietos*), and the collective form of the same term (*ni sit's*) denotes all ego's blood and affinal kin two or more generations below himself. *ni sit's* is sometimes loosely used to denote any kin of ego who is at least one generation below himself, all being referred to, especially if they are young and he is old, as "my children."

The lineage group cuts vertically through the generation groups and differentiates ego's siblings and his direct ascendants and descendants from all his collateral kin. It is denoted over three generations, including ego's own and one above and below him. A wider vertical group, that of the sociological family, includes both ego's lineage kin and certain of his nearest collateral kin, and these family kin, related to ego by both blood and marriage, are sometimes differentiated from the collateral kin outside his family by suffixing *ni mactak* ("my family") or *u mactak* ("his family") to the kin name. Thus, *k'war ni mactak* ("my family 'nephew or niece' "), or *q'ohna' ni mactak* ("my family 'aunt' ").[66] Ego's grandfather is distinguished from all his collateral male kin of the grandfather's generation, who are the heads of other families, as *ni tata'noy ni mactak*, or as *u yum-ar ni mactak* ("my family's head"). Every other

[66] The family membership changes, of course, when new families are formed. If the head of ego's family is his father, every child of his own siblings, for example, is a member of ego's family and is called *k'war ni mactak*, but once ego himself, through the death of his father, becomes a family head, his siblings' children become members of other family groups, since normally each of ego's siblings is then the head of his own family. In such a case the sibling's child is called merely *k'war*.

"grandfather" is merely *ni tata'noy*. Ego's "grandchildren" who are members of his family are *ni sit's ni mactak*, distinguishing them from similar kin (*ni sit's*) who are members of other family groups. *ni mama' ni mactak* ("my family 'uncle'") differentiates the males of his parents' generation who are members of his family from those who belong to other families.[67]

Blood kin are differentiated from affinal by suffixing *mactak* ("family," "blood kinship") to any of the terms. Thus, ego's sister's child is his *k'war mactak*, and his son's child is *sit's mactak*, while any mate of his *k'war*'s is called merely *k'war*, and his son's child's mate, *sit's*. *ni tata'noy mactak* denotes any of ego's male kin of the second ascending generation who is related to him by blood, thus differentiated from any of his affinal "grandfathers." *ni q'ohna' mactak* denotes a blood "aunt," such as ego's mother's sister or father's sister, and excludes a mother's brother's wife who came from an outside family and who is therefore not a father's sister. She is called merely *q'ohna'*.[68] The blood kin as a group are called *ni p'ia˙r-op'* ("my blood kin"), or *ni p'ia˙r-op' mactak*, and the affinal kin, *ni nuhp'-p'ir p'ia˙r-op'* ("my married kin"). Ego's half-blood kin, such as step-brother or half-brother, are denoted by prefixing *tca'* ("two," "second") to the kin name.[69] Age and sex are indicated in those kin names which include all ages and both sexes by suffixing *winik* ("man," "male") and

[67] Nonfamily kin are sometimes denoted by descriptive terms, as *in-te' ni sit's u mactak ni w ihta'n* ("a *sit's* of my sibling's family"), or *in-te' ni k'war u mactak ni sak'un* ("a 'nephew' of my cousin's family").

[68] The Sp. *de familia* is much used to denote blood kinship, as *ni k'war de familia* ("my blood *k'war*"), or *ni q'ohna' de familia* ("my blood aunt").

[69] As in *tca' iht'sin*, younger step-sibling or step-cousin; *tca' sak'un*, elder step-sibling or step-cousin; *tca' mu'*, step-sibling-in-law, half-sibling-in-law; *tca' p'icam*, mate's step-parent; *tca' k'war*, step-nephew, step-niece; *tca' sit's*, step-"grandchild."

icik ("woman," "female") to terms referring to adults, and *sit's* ("boy," "male child") and *iht'cok* ("girl," "female child") to terms referring to infants and to individuals under or near the age of puberty.[70] For such kin, however, the kinship distinction seems to be more important than that of age or sex. Individual kin are referred to by *in-te'* ("a," "one").[71]

As soon as he marries, ego classifies his mate's kin in much the same way as he does his own. The horizontal generation groups are extended to include every similar collateral kin of the mate. Ego refers to his mate's family as *ni tca' mactak* ("my second family"), as this is the family with whom his own co-operates most closely in all its social, religious, and economic activity.[72]

It is considered ideal for two family groups to intermarry all their members of the same generation levels among their respective households, as previously described, and most

[70] The most important examples of these have been given in the list of kinship terms. Others with *winik* suffixed are *iht'sin winik*, younger man sibling or cousin; *sak'un winik*, elder man sibling or cousin; *ihta' n winik*, man sibling; *mu' winik*, man sibling-in-law; *awan winik*, man cousin-in-law; *tca' r winik*, grown stepson; *k'war winik*, grown "nephew"; and *sit's winik*, grown "grandson." Others with *icik* suffixed are *iht'sin icik*, younger woman sibling or cousin; *sak'un icik*, elder woman sibling or cousin; *ihta' n icik*, woman sibling; *mu' icik*, woman sibling-in-law; *awan icik*, woman cousin-in-law; *tca' r icik*, grown stepdaughter; *k'war icik*, grown "niece"; *sit's icik*, grown "granddaughter." Others with *sit's* suffixed are *iht'sin sit's*, younger boy sibling or cousin; *sak'un sit's*, elder boy sibling or cousin; *ihta' n sit's*, boy sibling; *mu' sit's*, boy sibling-in-law. Others with *iht'cok* suffixed are *iht'sin iht'cok*, younger girl sibling or cousin; *sak'un iht'cok*, elder girl sibling or cousin; *ihta' n iht'cok*, girl sibling; *mu' iht'cok*, girl sibling-in-law.

[71] As *in-te' ni sit's*, "one of my 'grandchildren,'" "a 'grandchild' of mine" (lit. "one my grandchild"); *in-te' ni w ihta' n*, "a sibling of mine"; *in-te' u mu'*, "a sibling-in-law of his"; *in-te' ni p'ia'r mactak*, "a blood kinsman of mine"; *in-te' ni nuhp'-p'ir p'ia' r*, "an affinal kinsman of mine."

[72] For clarity, ego sometimes distinguishes a kin through his mate from a similar kin of his own by such expressions as *in-te' u k'war ni w ick-ar*, "a k'war of my wife"; *u awan ni nocip'*, "my husband's cousin-in-law"; *in-te' ni sit's u mactak ni w ick-ar*, "a sit's of my wife's family."

marriages are said by the older Indians to be still of this type. A great many younger Indians, however, "elope" and find mates outside the family groups with whom they are supposed to intermarry, thus refusing to permit their elders to make their choices for them. Some families were observed in which the elders themselves ignored the family-marriage arrangement and seemed content to let their children marry whomever they wished. It is possible that these individual marriages are now more common than those between dual families, and the older Indians complain that the custom is breaking down in favor of the more attractive Ladino custom of romantic marriage.[73] In all cases, however, the affinal kin are named as if the siblings of one family were intermarrying only with those of one other unrelated family, regardless of whether or not this arrangement is observed in practice. Thus, ego calls his mate's sibling's mate *ihta'n* ("sibling"), even though this kin may come from a family other than that of ego and be of no blood relation to him. In such a case, ego may explain that his mate's sibling's mate is not "really" his own sibling, but he merely calls him that,[74] since he is married to a *mu'* of ego and has thus taken the place of one of ego's siblings.[75]

[73] *xai ma'tci in-tcox-p'e tuq'ot u-q'an-i tua' in-nuhp'-i takar*, "If I do not love her, why should I marry her?" *ma'tci u-q'an-i u-nuhp'-i takar-en xai ma'tci u-tcox-p'-e'n*, "She does not want to marry me if she does not love me." *e ladin-op' u-nuhp'-i-op' tin u-q'an-i-op' in-q'an-i in-tce kotce'ra up'an*, "The Ladinos marry whom they wish; I like to do it that way also." *ma'tci in-q'an-i a-nuhm-se-n-en u-men ni mactak*, "I do not wish to be married off by my family."

[74] *ni w ihta'n in-taka u q'apa' pero ma-xa'c ni w ihta'n*, "My sibling he is merely called, but he is not my sibling." *xa'c ni w ihta'n pero ma-xa'c in-te' ni mactak*, "He is my brother, but he is not one of my blood kin."

[75] A mate's sibling's mate who is actually ego's sibling may be called, as previously stated, *ni w ihta'n mactak* ("my blood sibling"), and one who is not of blood relation, *ni w ihta'n nuhp'-i-ar* ("my marriage sibling"), *in-te' ni w ihta'n nuhp'-p'ir takar ni mu'* ("a 'sibling' of mine married to my sibling-in-law"), or *u nocip' ni mu'* ("my sibling-in-law's husband").

Property is owned by individuals, families, groups of families, and the community. Any Indian over the marriage age, usually fifteen to eighteen, is said to own certain property, personal belongings like clothes, tobacco pipes, jewelry, charms, and a variety of objects which he has collected and considers of some value, and he keeps most of these in his chest in the sleeping-house. Each man and youth individually owns his machete, as this implement is as much a part of his costume as a working tool, and he carries it with him every time he leaves the house. He owns his tumpline, which he uses every day in a variety of ways, and two or three small netted shoulder bags, all of which are also more or less a part of his costume. Women and girls own their sewing equipment, colored religious pictures, newspaper photographs, and odds and ends which they proudly exhibit to friends as being *muy bonito* ("very pretty"). Theoretically, any adult may do with such property as he wishes, although in practice he usually consults the male head of his family before disposing of anything which might have economic value for his family group. Those under the marriage age, being considered children, are said to own nothing, since the personal property they use was mostly acquired by the male head of their family and so is owned by him.

The family property consists of land, domestic animals, houses and household furnishings, certain implements, and ceremonial objects. The right to land is established by cultivating a plot continuously for two or three years and especially by building a fence around it. If a plot is left to lie fallow for several years, the owning family, if it suspects that another family may take it, often maintains its right to it by partially burning the vegetation on it every spring and thus announcing to other families in the *aldea* that the milpa has not been given up. If this is not done, it may revert to common property. A few of the Indians have titles to their land, which are registered in the alcalde's office, but this seems to be true only of the wealthier ones. If the poorer families wish new milpas, they make them out of the best unused land they can find and as near their houses as possible.

Land is the most valuable property which the Indians have, as is shown by the fact that they constantly refer to it, use it as the measure of the individual's or family's wealth, and most of the arguments and fights between families have their origin in disputes over it. The Indian's *hogar* ("place"), or *rancho* ("farm"), which includes both his land and his houses, is the one possession he is proud of, constantly improves and beautifies, and considers inalienable. Other possessions are more or less inalienable, but not to the same degree. He rates the wealth and economic position of his neighbors on the basis of the amount of land they own, its productivity, the number and size of their houses, their fruit trees, and how *bonito*[76] their places are. A typical land squabble is caused by the fact that a family moves one of its fences a few feet over on the adjoining land of a neighbor; the latter moves it back, the two families claim the maize grown on the disputed spot, and the dispute may go on for many years.[77]

[76] This is an adjective of all work in Guatemalan Spanish. Its Chorti equivalent is *qalan*, which may be a corruption of Sp. *galán*, equivalent to *bonito*. If applied to a simple personal object it means simply "pretty," but if to more valuable things, it means also valuable, productive, useful, desirable, etc.

[77] The more progressive Indians take such disputes to the *aldea* officials, who in turn report them to the pueblo alcalde. The latter calls the disputing families in for consultation and tries to settle the problem amicably but does not always succeed. The families often continue to fight in spite of the alcalde's threats of imposing fines and jail sentences on both of them. The more conservative

In the multiple-household family, which consists of the chief household of the family head, together with the dependent households of his married sons and daughters who are members of his family group, property is owned and controlled both by the dependent households and by the larger family. The family owns all the land which the various households use, the family head parceling it out to his households as he sees fit. He is considered the owner of it, since he acquired most of it before any of his sons and daughters had married, and since any land acquired afterward was got only with his permission and help. If he wishes, he may take land from one of his households and give it to another to cultivate, as when a son or son-in-law drinks excessively and neglects his milpa work. Although the entire family group works co-operatively on all its land in planting and harvesting, and under the direction of the family head, each household owns the produce of the land it cultivates and may dispose of it as it wishes. The family head also owns the larger and more expensive domestic animals, such as cows and bulls. If he owns several of the former, he often gives one to a newly married son or son-in-law to milk for his household, although the cow always remains family property so far as disposal is concerned. Each household, however, owns its pigs, chickens, and turkeys.

The family owns all the houses its households occupy, since they were built by co-operative family labor and under the direction of the family head. He is the owner of all the implements which the family group uses in co-operative labor, since, like the houses, they were made by the

families usually settle their land disputes by feuding and by hiring sorcerers to work black magic upon their enemies, without recourse to the authorities. Their disputes often get to the alcalde's attention only after their progressive neighbors report them.

family working co-operatively. For example, the family works co-operatively at sugar-making, lime-making, fish-trapping and fish-seining, deer-hunting, and tobacco-pressing, and so the family, in the person of its male head, is said to own all the implements and animals used in these activities.

The family head also owns such implements as hoes, axes, carpentry tools, planting-sticks, and others which are expensive to buy. He is said to own the fish traps, since they were built under his direction and by his family working as a group, and for the same reason he owns the sugar press, bulls, oxen, cows, lime kilns, and tobacco press. Only he can dispose of these and acquire new ones. Each household usually owns the implements it uses in its professional work, since in most cases it does such work without the help of other households.

The family head is also the owner of his family's ceremonial objects, which consist of the effigies of the saints, the altar, incense burners, the saints' drums, candles burned on the altar before the saints, other sacred objects which are usually kept on the altar table, and the family yard crosses. These are used co-operatively. A few families have a separate altar-house for its ceremonial property, and he is the owner of this. His ownership of these objects rests upon the fact that he acquired them in the first place, probably before any of his children had married and become heads of households within his family group, and on the fact that he is in charge of all ceremonies which his family performs in its milpas and to its patron saints, being in every respect his family's religious and economic head. If one of the households wishes to make use of family property for itself, it must ask permission to do so from the family head.

In the single-household family the ownership and control of family property is vested in the male head. Such property is said to belong to him, and only he can dispose of it or acquire new property.

Small groups of families sometimes own property collectively, especially where the manufacture and use of such property requires the co-operative work of a number of families. In the lime-making *aldeas* it is common for four or five neighboring families to build a single large lime kiln at the bank of a stream near their houses. If one of the professionals wishes to make lime by himself, he speaks for the kiln a few days in advance, so that the others can plan accordingly. Some of the poorer sugar-making families own sugar presses, bulls, and other paraphernalia in common, partly because such equipment is expensive to build and maintain. Although each family owns the irrigation ditches which run over its land, neighboring families are said to own those which run from the main ditch to their adjoining milpas and orchards. This group of families dug the latter co-operatively, and they usually work together in repairing them.

The most important communal property is the unused land, which is of economic value not only because it contains such natural resources as clays, water for household and irrigation purposes, wild animals, fruits and greens, fish, uncut firewood, timber used in woodworking, and wild plants used in the manufacturing processes but also because it can be made into new milpas, gardens, and orchards. Some of the unused land in Jocotán and Olopa *municipios* is too rocky, steep, or covered with dense natural vegetation ever to be easily made into agricultural plots, but most of it is considered by the less wealthy Indians in times of crisis to be barely worth clearing and cultivating and so constitutes the marginal land of the area. A family with poor land may cultivate, along with its one or two good milpas, eight or ten tiny plots on such land, planting each only once in every four or five years. Cultivated plots which have been abandoned for two or three years revert to the reserve class and can be appropriated by any family. Abandoned houses may also be taken over, although new owners usually burn them down and build their own. The unused land, natural resources, and houses are property of the reserve class, since they are said not to be owned exclusively by any family, and can be taken over by any family whenever it wishes.

The larger irrigation ditches which tap a stream and run through the *aldea* are said to be owned by everybody, since they serve the entire *aldea*. The *aldea* ceremonial house is owned by the *aldea*, as well as all the trails which run through the *aldea* to connect with the pueblo trails. The *aldea* school is called *aldea* property, although it is actually owned and controlled by the pueblo government. All these were built in the first place by the co-operative work of all the *aldea* men, under the direction usually of one of the *aldea* officials, and the latter calls upon them when there is any repair work to be done. When asked who owns the communal property, the Indians say, "We own it,"[78] and the pronoun seems to exclude the Indians of other *aldeas*. Actually, of course, the final control of it is vested in the pueblo alcalde and *comandante*.

In the single-household family inheritance is usually a simple matter. If the husband dies, his wife theoretically inherits all his property. If she is still young and her children are small, she may find another man to take her husband's place as soon as possible and thus continue to live

[78] *non ka-qet-e* (*qet-e*, "to own," "to keep").

on her property as before, or she may return with her children to her father's house and become a dependent in his household just as she was before her marriage. In such a case, her father takes charge of her property, either using it himself or dividing it among his sons and sons-in-law who are members of his family group. It is said that the wife still owns this property and may reclaim it when she remarries, but her family make use of it until that time. If her father is dead, she may go to live with a married brother or sister. If she has a son who is near adulthood, she usually continues living on her property, her son assuming the economic role of her husband until she remarries.

Upon her death, if there are older children, the latter continue living in her houses and working her land as before. Married sons and daughters who have set up their households elsewhere theoretically inherit from her, as well, although in most cases the older children who were living with her at the time of her death, if they are able, use all the property as if it were their own. If all her children are small, they may go to her father's house to live, or each may go to live with his godparent, who is expected to act as the parent of the child in every way until the latter grows up or marries. In either case the father or godparent assumes control of the property and is supposed to return it to the children when they become adults. If the wife's parents and her children's godparents are dead, the children are adopted by neighboring families. Adoption of completely orphaned children is said to be common.

In the multiple-household family, in which most of the property used by the households is owned by the family male head, and in which every family member has inheritance rights, inheritance is more complicated and is usually attended by much quarreling over the division of property. If the family male head dies, his wife theoretically becomes the family head and inherits his property. Her oldest son who is living as a member of her family group takes his father's place in most matters, so that the family continues to function as a unit. Upon her death, the family as a unit breaks up, and her sons and daughters inherit all her property. Those who continued as members of her family group after their marriage, and who did not move away to set up independent households of their own, meet and decide how the property is to be divided. Those who moved away and became independent families are considered to have lost their inheritance rights by thus separating themselves from their parents and siblings. The parent may request on his deathbed that such children be given certain of his property, but those who have remained in his family often ignore this if possible and try to keep the property among themselves, thus causing lengthy quarrels and complaints to the alcalde's office.

The principle of equal inheritance applies, although the older sons and those with the greatest number of children usually receive larger shares than do the younger unmarried children. The sons and daughters who, upon marriage, become members of their mates' families are supposed to inherit equally with those who remained at home after marriage, although, as was mentioned above, those who had set up households independently of either family group are felt to have no inheritance rights. Those who have become members of other families, however, usually inherit only movable property, such as household and personal effects and domestic animals, while nonmovable property, such as land and houses, is inherited by the sons and daughters who have remained in the father's family, and who will therefore continue to live on his land. The division of property is partly based upon sex, as well, each sex receiving property which it can best use or with which it is usually associated. The men inherit sugar presses, most of the land, implements used in agriculture, hunting, and fishing, the religious paraphernalia, and the father's personal possessions. The women are said to inherit houses, although each son actually inherits the houses in which his household lives, and they inherit the parents' household furniture, pottery, the mother's personal possessions, and all manufactured products with which women usually work. If there is enough land to go round, each of the unmarried sons and daughters inherits a portion of it, the former to cultivate it for himself when he grows up and the latter to transfer it to her husband when she marries.

CHAPTER XII

INDIVIDUAL LIFE-CYCLE

CHILDBIRTH

PREGNANCY is known to have no supernatural cause. It is believed that the father, by means of sexual intercourse, places a tiny child in the mother's womb, and there it grows during maternity to the size of an infant, at which time it is ready to be born. Pregnancy, however, is believed to be a ritually unclean condition, for which reason certain acts on the part of the pregnant woman are forbidden or frowned upon, as liable to cause harm to herself, her child, or another person or thing. Her body contains a harmful *aigre*[1] with which she can infect other persons and objects at close range, and so contact with her is avoided as much as possible. She is worried if an eclipse of the sun or moon occurs during her pregnancy, as this is said to cause great danger that her child will be born without one of its external body parts, such as a part of one of the extremities or a portion of the face or head.[2] At such a time she is careful not to leave the houses.[3] During pregnancy she is said to be especially "weak" and therefore unable to resist black magic and magical illness, and so is careful to avoid sorcerers, persons with evil eye and strong blood, and persons suffering from any kind of magical illness.[4] Her principal cleansing rem-

[1] See chap. xiii, esp. pp. 328 and 330 (n. 17).

[2] There is the same belief at Mitla (Parsons, 1936, p. 72).

[3] As also in Yucatan (Saville, 1921, p. 186).

[4] See chap. xiii, esp. p. 312.

edy after contact with such persons is a body bath in the fumes of burning copal. She and her family pray at intervals to the family saints, asking that all turn out well.

A great variety of remedies are used both to induce and to avoid pregnancy. For the first, "increasing" remedies are taken, and for the second, "closing-up" remedies. The most important is made from the roots of the *guapito* herb. The female roots are chopped up, soaked in water, and the potion drunk to induce pregnancy and to relieve menstrual pains, while the same potion made of the male roots is taken to avoid it. After pregnancy, the potion of the female roots is taken to insure a daughter, and that of the male roots, to insure a son. The fruit of the *chilillo* tree, which resembles the penis, is boiled and the potion drunk to insure a male child.[5] Most of the remedies taken to avoid pregnancy are also used to produce abortions and are called "expelling" remedies. Peppermint leaves are eaten in the food for the first three days after menstruation to prevent conception from that time until the next menstrual period. They are eaten by the men "to weaken themselves" so they will not impregnate their wives.[6] The root of the guaco is boiled and the potion drunk to prevent pregnancy and to induce abortions. Abortive remedies are usually taken over nine-day periods.[7] Menstruation, when

[5] Other inducing remedies are made from the coyol palm, the heart of the trunk being boiled and the potion drunk; the inner bark of the mango tree, the boiled potion of which is used as a vaginal douche; and the *subín* tree.

[6] The men sometimes drink a mixture of weak vanilla extract and alcohol to increase their sexual virility.

[7] Other abortive remedies are made from quina bark, vanilla pods, *manzanilla* flowers, the *shaguáy* tree, and the leaves of the *tinta de monte*. Great quantities of thick black bean soup, without salt, is a favorite abortive remedy. Many Indian and Ladino men and women claimed that abortives were fairly commonly used and that there was no great community objection to the practice. The Ladino women are inclined to look upon abortion as a sin, although the ones

late, is induced by taking a boiled potion of rue or *apacina* leaves. These are called "opening-up" remedies.

The mother usually does most of her work up to a day or two before delivery, and on the day of birth the husband leaves the house and whiles away the time at the houses of friends or works in his milpas. The rest of the family retreat to the kitchen, leaving the woman alone in the sleeping-house. It is said to be her privilege, if she wishes, to give birth to her child alone and without assistance.[8] A midwife is usually employed, however, and is paid either in money or in food. She prepares or buys native remedies, usually herbs, which the mother takes to predetermine the sex of her child, to relieve labor pains, to induce quick delivery, to stop hemorrhages, and to restore her health afterward. The midwife sometimes massages her patient, although a professional massager is called in for difficult cases.

Just before delivery the midwife spreads a mat on the floor of the sleeping-house, lays a cotton blanket over this, and places her patient on it in a kneeling position. After much massaging, the child is born and is wrapped in a cloth and placed in a twine basket. The midwife cuts the umbilical cord with a sharpened machete and cauterizes the wound. The principal remedies used for this are rose-

---

talked with admitted that Ladino women use abortive remedies as generally as do the Indians, buying them secretly from the Indian herbalists on market days. The Indians do not seem to have this moral attitude toward it. Many Indian women asked privately for some of the superior remedies which they assumed were made in the United States, admitting that the native remedies could not always be depended upon.

[8] The husband is expected to remain at home and assist at the delivery in Chan Kom (Redfield and Villa, 1934, p. 181). Among the Socotz Maya of British Honduras, the mother may go unaccompanied into the near by bush and there deliver her child, although the general Socotz custom is that of employing midwives and of giving birth in the house (Thompson, 1930, p. 78).

mary and sedge. The rosemary shoots are toasted, ground to a powder, the powder sifted through a cloth, and applied as a poultice to the cut. The sedge stalks are toasted, ground, mixed with "oil of amibar," and applied also as a poultice. Remedies are previously taken to expel the placenta, a common one being deer-horn powder. The horn is toasted in the fireplace, ground to a powder, mixed with water, and drunk. A boiled potion of quina bark, rosemary leaves, agave roots, the *flor de piedra*, or nutmeg is also taken for this purpose. The midwife places the placenta in a gourd, and the father wraps it securely, gourd and all, in a banana leaf and buries it in a secret and shaded spot somewhere on the family land, since it is believed that, if a sorcerer or personal enemy should find it, he could work black magic on the child.[9] The infant is immediately bathed in the fumes of copal or in remedial plant potions to protect it against black magic and *aigres*. The mother takes remedies for a month or so after the birth for the same purpose, since she is especially liable to sorcery and evil eye during that time.

The principal remedy taken for all pains connected with menstruation, pregnancy, and childbirth is the cake of kaolin, made in Esquipulas, which is usually mixed with other remedies to make it more palatable. A boiled potion of the leaves of the *hoja del aire* weed, which are believed to contain air, is drunk by first mothers during the last months of pregnancy to remove *aigre* from their stomachs, since they "do not know how to give birth to a child." A boiled potion of the *grama colorada* or of *tecomasuche* shoots and flowers is drunk to hasten delivery and to expel the placenta. A boiled potion of rue leaves is used as a

[9] Oil of amibar is bought from the pueblo druggist. The deer-horn remedy is used at Mitla when labor is prolonged (Parsons, 1936, p. 75). Cf. the Mitla custom of placenta burial in the corner of a house (*ibid.*, p. 76).

body wash to relieve labor and delivery pains and to stop after-delivery hemorrhages.[10] A boiled potion of the *agenciana* root is taken to quiet the nerves. In cases of delayed or difficult delivery, a boiled potion of quina bark is drunk to "avoid gangrene."[11]

Many plant remedies are taken to avoid and relieve hemorrhages at birth. Boiled potions of *zarza dormilona* leaves, achiote seeds, the fruit peel of the passionflower, maize and sedge flowers, malva leaves, and the leaves and flowers of the *orégano montés* are the most important.[12] Many of these remedies are taken in large doses to induce the menstrual flow, and in light doses to stop it when excessive, the same remedy being used in both cases. They are often drunk by older women to induce the flow after the menopause.

For eight days after delivery, which is the period of the birth festival, the mother does no work and eats only maize preparations. If she has not sufficient milk, or is too sick to suckle her child, a wet nurse is employed. A variety of remedies are taken to restore her to normal health, to increase her breast milk and reduce it when it is believed to be excessive, and to relieve breast pains. *Santa María* leaves are boiled with *jute* shellfish and eaten to increase the milk. *Hipericón* leaves are boiled with other remedial plants and the potion drunk to restore her health. This is also taken during pregnancy to relieve morning sickness and after delivery to expel the placenta. It is a standard remedy among the Indians. The most important

[10] The *orejuela de ratón*, *chalchupa*, and *chichimora* are also thus used.

[11] *tua' ma˙ tci u-mor-i e yac-ar*, "in order that she not get the 'greenness'" (gangrene).

[12] Others are made from *apasina*, the leaves of which are soaked in salt water; from wild rue leaves, from which an unboiled potion is made; and from the *esquinsuche*. All are drunk.

remedy for restoring the health is the boiled tea made from three different plants. The first, made from *epazote* leaves, is taken for three days after delivery; the second, from *ciguapacte* leaves, for a week or two after the first; and the third, from the *culantrillo negro* herb, for a month or so thereafter. The mother also drinks a hot beverage made of unripe plantains, which remedy is drunk by all convalescents.

During the last few months of pregnancy the expectant mother and her family pray at intervals to the saints, and especially to the Virgin, asking that no harm come to the mother or child. Candles are burned on the family altar when the pregnant woman has been exposed to any danger. The birth festival begins with the day of birth and continues theoretically for eight days, although it is often celebrated for only two or three days in practice. Relatives and freinds who live at some distance arrive a few days before, and the women prepare the festival foods, especially turkeys, tamales, *chilate*, *tortillas*, and coffee. Anyone in the *aldea* may participate, and everyone is expected at least to come and pay his respects to the child's parents. In some cases the eight-day period is given over merely to venerating the family saints, burning candles on the altar, and praying for all manner of good fortune for the mother and child, to be followed on the ninth day with the feasting and merrymaking, as is done during the funeral festival. In either case the mother observes the occasion by doing no work during the eight days and by eating nothing but maize preparations.

The father goes to the pueblo soon after the birth of his child and asks a Ladino friend who has an almanac, or the priest if he is available, the name of the saint who is associated with his child's birthday, which name is usually given to the child. In many cases the name of the patron saint is given or a name is chosen at random, one the sound of which appeals to the parents, and in a few cases the name of the parent of the same sex is given. The first names are, of course, all Spanish, although the household and family names are both Spanish and Chorti.

BAPTISM

The expectant mother chooses the *padrino* whom she wishes to act as her child's godparent. A few days before the birth of her child, she sends to him and his wife a chicken, roasted on the spit, by one of the members of her family. This is her request that they serve as godparents. No *padrino* refuses when asked unless he has an urgent reason, as it is considered his duty to accept and to aid in the subsequent rearing of the child. Immediately after birth, another chicken is roasted on the spit and sent to the godparents, as before, as a sign to them that the child is born. They serve thereafter in this capacity, and responsibility ends only after the child has grown up or married.

Forty days after the birth the mother, child, and godparents journey to the pueblo and meet at the church for the baptism. The child is held during this ceremony by the *padrino*, who also pays the priest. Immediately afterward, a dinner is given in honor of the godparents, usually in the pueblo and in the house of one of the mother's friends, and is paid for by the child's parents. Before going home, the godfather buys gifts and ornaments in the pueblo for the infant; these he gives to its mother. The baptismal festival[13] begins with the day of baptism and continues

---

[13] *tcui-m-ar*, "baptism" (from *tcuy-i*, "to sew," referring to the sewing of the first clothes of the newborn infant); *tcui-m-ar q'in*, "baptismal festival." The forty-day period preceding baptism may be a vestige of the use of the ancient

for eight days. It is celebrated in the *aldea* home of the family, with drinking and the eating of festival foods, but it is not considered as important an occasion as the birth and marriage festivals except by the more Ladinoized Indians. The family saints are venerated during the eight days and asked to send good health to the child. The god-parents may be present during this time, especially if they live near by and can go home each night, but otherwise they return home after the baptism. On the ninth day the mother gives to the godparents, or sends to them, cooked male and female turkeys, a large jug of unsweetened *atol*, and a gourdful of *tortillas*. The godparents send back a gift of sixteen pesos to be used in buying necessities for the child, together with other articles, such as a child's shirt, a quantity of food, soap, etc. After about six months the mother and child go to visit the godparents for a day, taking with them a cooked chicken. The godmother cooks a feast for them, and the godfather sometimes gives a tiny chicken to the child as a parting gift.[14]

The godfather often acts in every way as the actual father in the event of the latter's death. He gives his ward advice, gets him out of difficulties, sometimes trains him in a man's work, and may act as his parent when he marries. The same is done by the godmother for her fe-

---

Maya calendar, intended to represent two months, each of twenty days; it may be the Pentecostal period which precedes Easter; or it may be the forty-day period which must elapse in Catholic countries between birth and churching.

[14] In Quetzaltepeque the mother sends to the godparents one peso's worth of wheat bread and four pesos' worth of chocolate, both before and immediately after birth. The *padrino*, before baptism, furnishes for the child a long cotton dress and cap, which it wears during the ceremony at the church. After the baptism the mother sends to the godparents five pesos' worth of wheat bread and twelve pesos' worth of chocolate. In return, the godparents send a tiny shirt for the child. The visit six months later is not made.

male godchild. If both parents die, and the godchild is young, the godparent may receive that portion of the property which the child inherited and put it to his own use, in return for which he must bring up the child as one of his own family. As soon as the young man or woman becomes eighteen years of age, his inheritance is made up to him by his godfather. Where there is more than one minor child, each godfather receives his ward's share out of the total property, each child going to live in the home of its own godfather, leaving the adult children in their own home. If the children are more than eighteen years old at the time of the parents' death, the godparents take no hand in the matter, as each son and daughter receives his own inheritance. Matters relating to the wardship of orphaned children by godparents are arranged by agreement between the latter and the children's relatives.

GROWING UP

Infants are usually kept in a large twined basket made for this purpose. Tiny hammocks are sometimes used, especially for day sleeping. This is hung in the kitchen, the mother keeping it swinging as she goes about her work. Sleep is induced by washing infants in a boiled potion of the leaves of *zarza dormilona*, sometimes called *sensitiva*. Raw coral leaves, which are believed to have sleep-inducing effects, are placed under an infant's pillow for the same purpose. Mothers take especial care to protect their infants from evil eye, strong blood, the magic of sorcerers, and the contamination of pregnant women and persons sick with magical disease, especially when at markets and festivals. Rue is commonly used for this purpose. Infants are also carried with a red cloth over their faces and heads, or with necklaces of red beads, and they usually wear small pendant crosses around their necks.[15]

Children nurse at the breast for two years. It is believed that, if a child nurses longer, blood will begin to run out his nose and he will become pale and die. For this reason most mothers are said to try to force the child, if he is not too anemic, to eat ordinary food as soon as he is two years old; nevertheless, a number of cases in which children three or four years old were still taking the breast along with adult food were observed. Forced weaning is done by rubbing distasteful remedies on the nipples, the principal of which is the sap taken from the yellow-flowered aloe leaves. Food for infant children usually consists of crushed beans and *tortillas* which have been soaked in water. During the teething stage, children are given a boiled potion of anise seeds to drink as a sedative.[16]

When a child is from three to six months old, the mother, or one of her daughters, begins carrying it astride her hip in typical Indian fashion. This continues for about a year and a half, after which the child is allowed to walk, which it can usually do by the time it is two years old. Before reaching this age it is left to crawl around over the earth floor or courtyard when not being carried. Mothers carry their infants over the trails, especially to market, either in a large fiber bag with shoulder strap or in a long wide shawl, the ends of which are tied together. In both cases the container is supported on the left shoulder, the child

[15] At Chan Kom mothers paint crosses on their children's foreheads and breasts with indigo to protect them from sickness (Redfield and Villa, 1934, p. 111). At Jacaltenango a necklace of beads is put around the neck of a new-born infant (La Farge and Byers, 1931, p. 86).

[16] One mother said she had seen children still nursing for a month or so after the two-year period who were extremely pale and thin, losing blood through the nose every day. Aloe is used also at Mitla (Parsons, 1936, p. 85).

resting in it in a sitting position on the right side of the mother's back, just above her hip.[17] Until about five years old the boys usually wear no clothing when at home, except in the higher altitudes and during the cold season. From this time on they wear merely a shirt until the age of eleven or twelve, when they dress as men do. They seldom wear sandals, however, until fifteen or sixteen. The girls wear little or nothing at home for the first three or four years, after which they are dressed in miniature women's clothing. They never wear sandals, since these belong solely to the men.

At the age of six or seven the son begins to accompany his father at work, and for the ensuing two or three years he is learning to perform the labor he must subsequently do as a grown man: building houses, carrying loads with the tumpline, securing firewood, and, above all, tending the milpas and gardens. When twelve or thirteen, he can usually do all of a man's work and is ready, after two or three years more, to marry or take a woman and set up a house for himself. The girls, at five or six, are instructed by their mothers in cooking, sewing by hand, and carrying water and other things on the head and hip. If the mother is a potter, basket-maker, or fiber-worker, the girl begins by watching her mother as these objects are being made and later makes them herself. At this age the girl begins to take care of her younger brother or sister, carrying the child on her hip, as her mother does, wherever she goes, and watching it when at home. At the age of eleven or twelve she is sharing the house work with her mother and continues to do so for a few years more, until she takes a man or marries.

[17] In a few cases women were seen carrying their children in containers supported with the tumpline, although this is not a common practice, as women make little use of the tumpline.

The Indians have no children's or adults' games. When children come together and are in a playful mood, they merely chase one another and pretend to fight with the hands. They are lively, but never organize in games. A favorite pastime for boys is that in which one grabs another's hat and is chased by the group until caught, with much shouting and laughter. The girls play very little and almost never with boys. Older girls are expected by adults to be demure and shy, "like their mothers." They talk very little and in a low tone among themselves, even when alone, and show no excitement in one another's company.[18]

Children's toys include dolls, bows and arrows, tops, accordions, bull-roarers, and miniature objects. Dolls, which are uncommon, are merely sticks with crude faces carved at the upper end and dressed roughly in cloth. Bows and arrows are made of any available wood. A small branch is cut while green, seasoned, made into a bow, and strung with a heavy agave cord. The arrow is merely a stick sharpened at the point, with turkey feathers attached to the other end. Bows are used only by boys at play, who set up a pole in the ground and practice shooting at it; they sometimes hunt birds with them. Adult hunters never use the bow and seem to have no skill with it. A top is commonly made of a small fruit of the gourd tree. A small stick, about six inches long, is passed through the center of the dried gourd, and sharpened at the spinning point. An agave twine is wrapped around the upper end of the stick, the latter held with the left forefinger against the outer side of a stick which is grasped in the left palm, and the free end of the twine jerked with the right hand.

---

[18] The boys are much given to practical jokes, such as throwing the ground-up beans of the velvet bean vine into the air near groups of adults, thus causing their skin to irritate.

The top spins as it falls to the ground. Tops of European origin are carved from oak or *guayaba* wood and spun on a nail which has been driven into the bottom and filed to a point. These are the favorites among the Ladino children.

An imitation accordion is made of palm frond strands which are woven in an oblong shape, about half an inch thick and wide and a foot long. Children stretch it back and forth in imitation of the accordion player. The bull-roarer, which consists of a light piece of wood attached to the end of an agave cord, four or five feet long, is known to the Indians, but they seldom make it. The most common of the toys are the miniature pottery and wooden objects which are made in imitation of those used by adults. With these, children play at the work of their parents: the young girls make tiny pottery vessels and play house with them, while boys pretend to clean and plant milpas with their small machetes and planting-sticks. Miniature pottery made by the young daughters of professional potters, properly fired and decorated, is much sold in the Jocotán market for use both as toys and kitchen containers.

All the larger *aldeas* of Jocotán and Olopa *municipios* have schools, which are kept open only a few months of the year. The school is a large, two-room thatched house, one room being used for classes and the other as temporary living quarters for the Ladino teacher, who comes from the pueblo. Most of the entering children are seven or eight years old, and they attend only once or twice a week for two or three years, after which they cease coming altogether. The attitude of the Indian parents toward formal education varies from mere toleration to absolute rejection. The average parent definitely states that milpa work is the one really important thing for a boy to learn, and house work, the important thing for a girl.[19]

No notice is taken of puberty in boys, but the girls fast for eight days following their first menses,[20] eating only maize foods, and taking various remedies to induce menstruation if retarded. A number of women stated that the young girls very often had their first menses at the age of twelve or thirteen and that the period should last for only three days of each month. During this time the girl does only light work. At the time of first menstruation the mother instructs her daughter in the matter. For the rest of her life she eats only maize for three days of each month while menstruating, whether the period lasts for a longer time or not. There is no segregation of the girl except that she usually keeps to the kitchen. The Ladino women say that the flow in Indian women is slight and that usually no cloth is worn. The older women recognize that they are unclean during menstruation and at least pretend to avoid close contact with infants and ailing adults during the three-day period.

Menstruation is said to be the monthly escape of air from the body through the vagina, and the blood is explained by the fact that the air, being violent, rips open blood vessels on its way out. No explanation could be obtained

[19] The progressive parent, especially if he is somewhat Ladinoized, admits that a little knowledge of reading and writing will do his children no harm. Most of the conservative parents refuse to send their children to the school until the teachers reports them to the alcalde, who then threatens them with a fine. This gets all the truant children back for a while, but every month or so the Tunucó teacher has to report the conservative families in order to keep any attendance at all.

[20] This eight-day period is sometimes referred to as a "girl's festival," although it is observed as such only by the girl herself. She is said at this time to "become a woman" (*a-puhn-a tama' n-te' icik*, "she changes into a woman"; *kone' r u-tcek-t-es u ut e icik*, "now she takes on the appearance of a woman").

for its monthly occurrence. A few informants believed vaguely that it was associated with the changes of the moon, the woman being "full" when the moon was full, and therefore menstruating, and "dry" for the rest of the month. Menstruation theoretically lasts only three days, which is the women's period of ritual uncleanliness, and she becomes "clean" immediately afterward, even though the flow may continue.[21] No explanation was found for menstruation occurring when the moon was not full.

MARRIAGE

Girls usually marry for the first time between the ages of sixteen and twenty, and boys when about two years older. There are many unmarried girls of twelve and thirteen who are living with men, but in nearly every case they are daughters of poor parents who are glad to be rid of them as soon as a man will take them. If the parents intend, however, that their children be married, they keep them at home until they reach the ages given above. First-cousin marriage is occasionally found, although it is frowned upon by the church. The alcaldes try to prevent cousin marriage by doubling or tripling the license fee, and the priests refuse to marry first cousins under any circumstances.[22] Marriages are legalized by the alcaldes, who sell the license to the couple. The marriage *padrino* sometimes pays for this. The less Ladinoized Indians dispense with the church ceremony, feeling that the purchase of a license is sufficient, and solemnize their marriages with the native marriage festival which is celebrated for the following eight days at the home of the parents

[21] This is another example of the ritual use of "three" by women.

[22] Cf. the restriction on first-cousin marriage in Chan Kom, Yucatan (Redfield and Villa, 1934, p. 96).

who are paying the expenses. The Catholic priest is seldom available to perform the ceremony, which may be the main reason why most of the Indian couples are not "married."

The marriage ceremony, usually performed fourteen days after the marriage agreement has been made, is entirely Catholic and is held in the pueblo church,[23] after which all go home to prepare for the marriage festival. This begins the next day, as a marrying couple are forbidden to eat on the day of their marriage, and continues for eight days. The couple eat nothing during the eight-day period except maize preparations, especially *tortillas* and coffee. On the first day a feast is held, at which the godparents, both sets of parents, the married couple, and friends and relatives of both families are present. In the afternoon a table is set in the house of the parents who are paying for the marriage. These parents furnish everything; they set the table with *atol*, *chilate*, *tortillas*, coffee, meats, and other foods, and then retire. Eating at the table are only the godparents, the parents who are not paying for the marriage, and the married couple, the latter confining themselves to coffee and *tortillas*. The parents who are paying for the marriage, and with whom the couple will live, eat in the kitchen. Friends and relatives come to the house but merely to dance later in the evening.

After dark the entire group dance to accordion music and drink *chicha;* the godparents usually drink *aguardiente*. At first the floor is given over to those involved in the marriage. The godfather dances with the bride, the god-

---

[23] For the marriage ceremony the couple kneel in front of the altar, and the marriage godparents appear in front of them, each holding a lighted yellow candle in the right hand. The godfather, taking a cord in his hand, places the center of its length around the man's neck and hands over the candle to him. The godmother takes the two ends of the cord, twists them once, and places them around the woman's neck, giving the woman her candle. The priest, if present, repeats mass at the church altar. At the conclusion of the mass the priest gives the benediction and places a ring on the woman's finger.

mother with the groom, and the two visiting parents with each other. After a time everyone joins in, although at no time during the dance does anyone else dance with these six principals. While the godparents are dancing with the newlyweds, a group of men outside the house shoot off skyrockets at intervals. At four or five in the morning the godparents leave; this is a signal that the dance is over. Shortly afterward, three friends of the family carry to the godparents' house a large olla of *atol*, a basket of *tortillas*, and a gourd of meat, which is provided by the parents who furnished the feast. After delivering it, the messengers shoot off a skyrocket as a signal to the parents that the offering has been accepted, and the parents fire a rocket acknowleding the signal. This ends the first day. The festival theoretically continues for seven days more, and the wealthier families sometimes give a feast on the ninth day.

Strict monogamy is the rule, although there are three known cases in which a man keeps a concubine in the same house with his wife and has children by both of them. Concubinage on the part of married individuals is, however, generally frowned upon, especially when the relationship is not kept from general knowledge. Nearly all the unmarried and many of the married men have secret sex relations with unmarried girls who live with their own families, and this seems to be looked upon, like drunkenness, as an amiable weakness rather than as a vice. An unmarried couple who live together in their own house and who function in the community as a family usually receive from the community the status accorded to properly married families.[24] The husband acts as spokesman on

[24] Since the church refuses to sanction an unmarried union, some unmarried parents become married as soon after the birth of their children as they can, after which the children are baptized. Children of unmarried parents, according

every occasion. Unmarried women may have any sort of intercourse with outsiders, but married women are prohibited from having personal contact with men outside the family. The woman is freed from this prohibition only when her husband dies. Even deserted wives are bound by it, whether the husband is living with another woman or not, since, because divorce is unknown, a woman is considered by the church as married until the death of her husband. The prohibition operates equally in the case of women who are living with men but are not married to them. If the rule is broken, the wronged husband is expected to inflict the standard penalty. He is considered justified in killing the offending man and in whipping his wife with a leather quirt. If she persists, it is said that he may kill her.[25]

DEATH AND BURIAL

All the family's dead are buried somewhere on its own land, usually not far from the chief household and in a rocky spot which is unfit for cultivation and well shaded with trees and undergrowth.[26] The graves are placed fairly close together. A few of the *aldeas*, especially those nearest

to Ladino custom, take the name of the mother. Some fathers acknowledge their children by registering their names with the alcalde's office, after which they take his surname. Most of the *aldea* Indians, however, do not bother with this procedure.

[25] The husband meets the offending man, usually on a festival day in the pueblo, and attacks him with his machete. If the husband kills him, the Indians do not consider it a crime but hide him from the authorities, or furnish him with provisions to get away to Honduras until the affair has blown over. If the husband is killed, the Indians hunt out the offender and turn him over to the *comandante* for punishment. Whipping for infidelity was done in Yucatan (Saville, 1921, p. 184).

[26] Starr (1900) reported that the Chol buried dead children under the floor of the house, although none of the informants had ever heard of such a custom.

the pueblos, use communal cemeteries which have been set aside by the church, and in a few cases the dead are carried on stretchers from the *aldeas* to the pueblos to be buried in the church's cemetery. The family's households co-operate in burying their dead, in paying the cost of the funeral feast, and in performing the funeral ceremony, although they are usually assisted by many other families of the *aldea*. The members of the family who entered it through marriage are buried on that family's land rather than on the land of their biological families, although the latter take a greater part in the funeral than do any other families in the *aldea*.

At death the relatives of the deceased gather at his house and remain with the family until the occasion is celebrated. The corpse is laid out on a bed in the sleeping-house, the hands crossed at the wrists, and the feet tied with liana or banana-leaf string. A white cotton mantle, eight or ten feet square, the material for which is bought in the pueblo, is draped over the body, and it remains thus for twenty-four hours. This period is increased to three days by the pueblo Indians. The corpses of children who die during the *florescencia* (the period between October 1 and December 31) are adorned with *flor amarilla* flowers during the funeral ceremony. The friends of the family in the *aldea* bring large candles, about two feet long, which are kept lighted for a day and a night, one at the head of the corpse, one at the feet, and one on each side. This is no doubt a Catholic custom. Several lighted candles are placed on the altar, as well, usually one at each corner. No ceremony is performed during the twenty-four hours. Before burial, a litter is made for carrying the corpse, and the men friends of the family dig a grave to a depth of about four feet, or five "hands" (spans).

After the twenty-four-hour period, the corpse is placed on the litter. The hands and feet are untied, the hands are clasped, and between them is placed a small wooden cross. The body is dressed in its usual clothes, although barefoot, and is wrapped in the cotton mantle with which it was covered since death. It is finally wrapped in and tied around with a string. Four men, two at each end, carry the litter. They march in front, while members of the family and friends follow, most of whom carry lighted candles and pray in audible voices. No ceremony is performed at the grave. Six men lower the body. It is deposited in a sleeping position and oriented in an east-west direction, with the head at the east end. A hat and pair of sandals which the dead man had lately worn are laid on the mat at about the center of the body. For women, a shawl is laid on the mat. The four pallbearers then pull in the loose earth with hoes and tamp it down with the back of the hoes, as no Indian would step into a half-filled grave to tamp with his feet. Immediately afterward, all those present, and especially the pallbearers, incense their bodies and hands with copal.

The litter is taken apart and is chopped into small sticks which are laid in a heap on top of the grave where they remain until, months later, they have been carried away to be used as firewood. The purpose of this may be to destroy the last object with which the corpse came in contact. Usually a small cross is set in one end of the grave. A *tecomate* gourd filled with river water is always set at the head end and tied with its cord to the cross. It is said that the water is for the dead to drink. No food is offered either within or above the grave. Some months later, when friends come to the spot to pay their respects, they bring a gourd of river water which they pour on the soil directly above the body. After the burial, the group return to the family's house, the candles are put out, and each person claims what remains of the one he contributed.

The funeral festival begins immediately following burial and continues for eight days, during which time the family of the deceased, and especially his immediate household, eat only maize preparations, principally *atol* and *tortillas*. The women of the households prepare food in the kitchen, which is served to friends who come to pay their respects to the deceased. On the first day of the festival the men of the family set up a temporary funeral altar in the center of the floor of the sleeping-house, directly in front of the permanent altar, and orient it, like the grave, in an east-west direction, with the head at the east end.[27] During the eight days a novena is recited at this altar by a prayer-maker, who is usually a friend of the deceased. This is usually done at sunset, although sometimes at sunrise, and lasts for about an hour. While it is being said, the family and friends pray for the dead member. On the morning of the ninth day a table is set in the kitchen with a great variety of foods, among them those of which the deceased was especially fond. The food is left untouched until about ten in the evening, during which time it is be-

[27] Six stalks of carrizo are set up in the ground, three on each side, to inclose an oblong space about three feet wide and five or six long. The pair of stalks at the head of the altar are set about five feet apart, while the other two pairs are equidistant from each other, about three feet. The tops of these are bent and tied together to form three arches. Between the central and widest arch, and in the center of the altar, are set up two crosses on the floor, each about two feet high, and entwined with *conte* leaves. A third cross is set up in the house in which the rest of the family sleep. At the other end of the altar, and in the center, is set a large candle about three inches in diameter and two feet long. On either side of this a bamboo stick is set up in the ground, to contain a small candle in its upper end. Thus, there are three crosses, three candles, and three arches. Near the altar are placed certain of the dead person's belongings, such as a tumpline, clothing, a rope or two, and a machete.

lieved the spirit of the deceased returns to partake of the feast set out for him. A rosary is then said, after which the prayer-maker takes the food from the table and divides it among all the people present. Most of it is eaten immediately, and some taken home. This festival is celebrated three times in all: immediately after death, after the lapse of six months, and after the lapse of a year. After each occasion the temporary altar is torn down, and a new one set up prior to the next celebration.

CHAPTER XIII

SICKNESS

GENERAL CAUSES

THE anatomical knowledge of the Indians is extremely limited, caused partly, no doubt, by their fear of corpses and their belief that many illnesses can result from any contact with death. But owing to the presence of the Ladino druggists in the pueblos, all of whom are familiar with medicine, disease, and anatomy, those Indians nearer the pueblos who have many Ladino contacts seem to be slowly quitting their old beliefs concerning these subjects. The more conservative Indians of the remoter *aldeas*, however, still hold to most of their former notions concerning both the causation and nature of illness and the structure of the body. The little they have learned from the druggists has merely been made to fit into the framework of their own ideology and interpreted solely from the Indian point of view.

The stomach, womb, and intestines are considered a single organ, containing all the matter which the body throws off. Thus the unborn child is in the mother's stomach, and the placenta is said to come out of it. This collective organ is located in the intestinal region, while the heart is said to be where the stomach actually is and in the center of the body. The Indian places his hand on his stomach and complains of a heart pain. The lungs are believed to be in the upper back; lung ailments are indicated by placing the hand over the opposite shoulder and laying it on the scapulas. The kidneys are said to be located over the hips, even though kidney pains are known to be in the lower back. The brain is said to be a cloudy liquid or paste, resembling jellied *atol*, and nasal mucus is a little of this paste escaping through the nose due to the presence of air in the head. Blood is the agent which keeps the body warm and which carries strength to all parts of it. Many remedies are taken to "warm" and "strengthen" it. One is said to be born with a supply of it, which his body keeps for the rest of his life. There seems to be no notion of the replenishing of the blood, which may account for the great fear the Indians have of flesh cuts.

Body excrement is said to be the "bad part" of the food eaten, for which the body has no use. Food is taken into the stomach, which is known to be the digestive organ, and "used," the stomach throwing off the useless part. Digestion is said to be similar to the boiling of sugar-cane juice: the boiling separates the juice, which is the same as food, from the scum and bits of stalk, which are the same as excrement, and which are thrown away.[1] The Indians have Chorti and Spanish names for the vital organs, although the Chorti names for several are no longer known, and for all the inner and outer parts of the body.

Illness is said to be caused by "fright," *aigre*, and magical seizure by sorcery, and any given illness is ascribed to one or a combination of these. The first refers to any kind of mental and physical upset in the body's functioning and is only partly equivalent to the term as we use it; the second refers to the various types of air or wind which enter the body and cause pain and illness; and the third

[1] The term for excrement, *ta'*, which means "excretion" in general, refers also to any useless part of a thing, as the meat of gourds, the useless sap and milk of plants, and the useless scum on boiled liquids.

refers to the magical sending of harmful substances into the body and the harming of the body by sympathetic magic. The Indians do not consistently make any clear distinction among these causes:"[2] all three so merge into one another that they almost represent the same thing, namely, an outside agency or force which has entered the body or with which the body has come in contact. Illness is never thought to be a condition arising from causes within the body itself but always from contact with something harmful from the outside.[3] The curers and diviners, of course, make clear distinctions as to the nature and cause of illness, but the average Indian does not pretend to be able to do this in every case. There are remedies and magical procedures both to protect one's self in advance of such contact and to cleanse the body after it has taken place.

Susceptibility to illness in persons, animals, or plants is determined by physical and mental condition. The "weak" person is very susceptible to frights, *aigres*, and sorcery, while the "strong" one is comparatively safe. Strength and weakness vary with each individual and vary

[2] At one time they may all be said to be merely different forms of *aigre*, at another they are all frights or both frights and *aigres*, and at another they are all sympathetic magic. Different Indians will ascribe the same illness to any of the three, or to a combination of them, and the same individual often admits that the illness could be caused by the presence of any of them.

[3] There is no notion of the germ theory of disease among the Indians or among the less literate of the Ladinos. Don Manuel Vasquez, the Ladino druggist at Jocotán, has explained the theory to many of them, but it seems they either reject it outright as being only a Ladino belief or accept it and fit it into their own beliefs, in which case they consider germs to be "little animals" (Sp. *animalitos*) which are sent upon the victim by sorcery, either in their own form, as are toads, snakes, and insects, or in the form of evil wind. Thus, Don Manuel has merely supplied the sorcerers with one more agency for causing illness. Germs are called "increase of the body," which term denotes any abnormal body substance or growth.

from time to time in the same individual. Strength refers
to great resistive powers to illness, while weakness signifies
that the body is upset in some way, its functioning abnormal, and its resistive powers so low that a harmful
outside agency is enabled during the time to come in
contact with it or get into it. The two conditions may be
either inherent or acquired. Inherent strength or weakness is more or less permanent, is a natural and normal
condition, and is determined by the possession of physical
and personal qualities. The physical qualities are those of
age, body strength, and health. For example, infants and
aged persons are especially weak, while youths and those
in middle life are strong. A puny individual is weak, and
one of great strength and robust health is strong. Any sick
person is weak until he becomes well again. Among the
personal qualities, those which are desirable make for
weakness, while those which are undesirable make for
strength. An attractive woman is weaker than a plain one,
and a much-liked man is weaker than one who is generally
disliked. A modest and retiring individual is weaker than
one who is aggressive and offensive. Parents often refer
to their children as having bad personal qualities in order
not to call undue attention to their good ones. If a stranger
exclaims over a child's prettiness, especially in public, its
parents hastily deny that it is prettier than the average.
A plant is weak in proportion to the beauty of its flowers
and leaves, an ugly, thorny weed being one of the strongest
of plants. Similarly, a plant of nauseating odor is stronger
than one of pleasing odor. Cute animals are weaker than
those which lack or have outgrown this quality. Domestic
animals and plants, probably because of their association
with people and their identification with family life, are
weaker than wild ones. Also, a tame animal is weaker than

one which shies away or which threatens when approached. Desirable personal qualities further make for susceptibility to illness because they may arouse the jealousy of sorcerers and personal enemies, who then work black magic against those who have them out of pure spite and envy. Pretty children and pets are especially liable to attack by magic, while plain ones may escape the sorcerer's notice.

Acquired weakness, which is temporary, is not considered normal, since it is induced in an individual who does not normally have it. It is caused by any maladjustment of the normal physical and emotional condition, and the individual remains weak, and therefore liable to illness, until he makes himself strong again. The physical maladjustment is caused by any sudden body blow, jerk, strain, or pain, and by excessive exposure. Men become weakened by carrying too heavy a load over rough trails and thus straining their backs and legs, by working in the milpas until overfatigued, or by excessive fighting when drunk. Overwork, lack of sleep, and loss of appetite often lead to weakening. The body is especially weak during excessive sweating and flushing of the face. When very hungry or drunk, the resistive powers are low, as many frights and *aigres* are said to be contracted during such times. Any sudden blow, as from a falling object or the kick of an animal, causes weakening. Extreme wounds, bruises, and burns are very weakening, especially to the body parts affected, and blows to the head are worst of all. Exposure to water and cold, especially when perspiring, is said to be dangerous and weakening during the cold season. When carrying heavy loads, the Indians are careful in crossing streams, usually resting and cooling off before taking to the water. Any weakening is said to be greater if the individual is drunk at the time he receives the blow or exposure. Women are especially weak during menstruation,[4] pregnancy, the menopause, childbirth, and for several months after delivery. A period of any emotional upset such as anger, excitement, hysteria, and jealousy is weakening. The wife calms her angry husband and crying child for fear they may receive a fright or an evil wind get into them at such a time.

The general term for sickness is *mok*, or *mwak*. To get sick from a natural cause is *mor*, which means "to gather up" or "to collect." Thus, one "collects" a cold or a fever. To become sick as a result of sorcery, malediction, or contact with a ritually unclean agent is *hahp'*, which means "to seize" or "to capture." Thus, one is "seized" with *hijillo* or sickness by magic. To get well is *t'sa·k*, and to get better, *us-ta* ("to improve"). All sickness accompanied by any kind of pain is commonly referred to as a pain or ache in the body or in the part affected or as an *aigre* in that part, since nearly all illness is accompanied with pain or caused by *aigre*. Thus, "head pain" loosely denotes any head discomfort or illness, and "stomach pain," any stomach discomfort or illness. Similarly, "head *aigre*" and "stomach *aigre*" have the same general meanings. These are general terms used in reference to any sickness, and many of the commoner diseases and ailments have no other names, but usually an ailment has also a specific name which is more descriptive of the actual condition and which differentiates it from others in the same part of the body. Thus, a head cold is commonly referred to by saying, "My head hurts," or "There is an *aigre* in my head," although it is specifically described by saying, "My nasal passages are closed up." Asthma might also be called "pain in the head" or "*aigre* of the head." Similarly,

---

[4] Beliefs about menstruation are mentioned on pp. 298–99.

dysentery is commonly called "*aigre* of the rectum" but is differentiated from diarrhea and other bowel and rectal ailments by the term "blood in the bowels." Another general term is "soreness," which is caused by a weaker *aigre* and is often used instead of pain or *aigre*.

FRIGHT

The fright, as a form of illness, is any emotional shock caused by the encounter, or the fear of an encounter, with anything which frightens or terrorizes. It ranges from slight fear to extreme terror, depending upon the thing encountered, but in every case the individual is said to have been "frightened" or to have been "seized with a fright" as a result of the encounter.[5] The fright itself is a definite illness, but it is more important because it produces general body weakening and so may lead to other and more serious illness. The agencies which cause it are natural situations in which the individual fears for his bodily safety or natural objects the sight of which is shocking, ritually unclean persons or objects, and supernatural beings. The first usually causes only slight fear, while the second and third may be extremely terrifying, and great precautions are taken to avoid encounters and contact with them.

Thunder and electric storms cause many frights, especially to women and children. Any dangerous animal, like a poisonous snake, an angry bull, or a large wild animal, frightens persons on lonely trails and at night. Women get frights when witnessing a drunken fight among men with machetes, fearing they will kill each other or harm

---

[5] *p'a·q'-ar*, "fright" (*p'a·q'-i*, "to frighten," "to terrify"); Sp. *espanto*. *p'a·q'-p'ir*, "frightened" (Sp. *espantado*); *hahp'-p'ir u-men e p'a·q'-ar*, "seized with a fright" (Sp. *agarrado por un espanto*).

her, especially if she sees flowing blood and wounds. Since most of the Indians do not swim, they get frights from falling into deep water or whirlpools and from stumbling when fording swift and flooded streams. A fright will result if the individual greatly fears that any body blow or exposure may so weaken him as to permit an *aigre* to enter his body.

The ritually unclean persons and objects are dangerous because they not only infect one with *aigre* but also cause one to contract it after being frightened by them. It is the fear of the resulting *aigre* which causes fright when they are encountered. At a funeral an individual may become so frightened from looking at a corpse as to become completely unnerved, and he is said to have a death fright. Persons with "evil eye" cause fright, if the encounter is sudden and without warning, merely by looking at another, especially at a young child or a sick adult. Individuals who are said to have "strong blood" can, when emotionally agitated, cause fright in others who are susceptible by looking at them or coming near them. Pregnant and menstruating women, especially the former, are ritually unclean and cause many frights. Sorcerers cause frights because they are assumed to have the evil eye, are ritually unclean, and are known to be able to work black magic on anyone who excites their anger or envy. In general, anyone who has received a fright from these agents can give it to another person through contact; having become ritually unclean, they can infect others at close range. Other frights are not considered so dangerous, but it is vaguely believed that all are transmissible.

The supernatural beings which cause fright are apparitions and spirits of the dead. Apparitions appear to people, especially to those of immoral conduct, on lonely trails at night; such encounters are said to frighten people out of their senses, causing idiocy and insanity. This is called an apparition fright. A spirit of the dead appears to a person in a dream, presumably to harm him, particularly if he was a former enemy, and on awakening he has a fright for several days, called a spirit fright. Such spirits are also said to appear occasionally, like apparitions, to people on trails at night. An Indian may believe that a spirit or apparition is constantly pursuing him, especially if he can see no other cause for his general ill health, and he sees evidence of such pursuit in noises at night, the falling of stones across his trail, etc.

An encounter with the agencies which cause fright may come about either accidentally or deliberately. In the first case there is no human agency at work, and the meeting is said merely to have "happened." In the second, a sorcerer or person who sent a malediction is responsible, and a deliberately sent fright is more feared than an accidental one, as it is more terrifying and weakening to the body. A sorcerer, out of pure spite or because he was paid to do so, is believed to be able to send any of the frightening agencies to the locality where his victim lives, thus arranging a terrifying encounter. A slight fright is usually thought to have been accidental, and the more terrifying ones are suspected to have been arranged by a sorcerer. Persons who send maledictions upon their enemies, and who are not professional sorcerers, are vaguely believed to be able to send agencies which cause minor frights.

The condition of fright is said to develop into a state of general nervousness, lack of energy, anemia, loss of appetite, dull and persistent headache, and lack of blood and color in the face. Most frights are said to be spread over the entire body, thus weakening the body and rendering it liable to general illness, but most accidents, such as broken bones and wounds, cause weakness only in the body area affected and lead to illness only in that area. A general fright is called "fright of the body," and an extreme one, "fright of the heart," since the more serious ones are said to be located in the heart. The frights are classified on the basis of the person or animal who has them, their cause, and their locality in the body.[6] Slight frights are usually cured by the patient himself, the principal remedies being tobacco, sage, artemisia, *guarumo*, and copal, but for serious cases, especially when the fright was caused by a sorcerer or contact with a corpse or apparition, a professional curer may be called in.

The Indians are inclined to consider all causes of body weakness as frights, whether the shock is mental or physical, so that it is difficult to say whether fright is a definite illness in itself or is merely another name for body weakening, in which case it would be no more than a precondition for real illness. The latter may be correct, since the principal effect of fright is that of weakening the body's resistance to the entrance of *aigre* and other foreign matter, which are the cause of nearly all serious illness and disease. The usual diagnosis of serious illness and pain is that the body was first weakened, nearly always by a fright which may or may not be remembered, and its resistive power so lowered that it was unable at the time to prevent a harmful agency from entering it. The mental and emo-

---

[6] Examples of the first type are frights common to men, frights common to women, frights common to children, and frights common to animals, as cows, dogs, etc. Names of the second type are formed by adding *u-men e* ("because of the") and the name of the agent, as *p'a·q'-ar u-men e tcan*, "fright caused by a snake," and *p'a·q'-ar u-men e q'ahq'*, "fright caused by a burn." Names of the third type are formed merely by adding the possessive adjective and the part of the body which has been frightened, as *p'a·q'-ar u p'ahn*, "fright of the body," or *p'a·q'-ar u ut u ta*,' "fright in the rectum."

tional shock caused by any bodily harm seems to be as important, if not more so, than the physical upset in rendering the body or a part of it temporarily weak and susceptible, and often they seem in the Indian mind to be the same thing, called fright in either case.[7] For this reason the term "fright" may be interpreted to mean any kind of shock or weakness which the individual may sustain, ranging from any temporary loss of mental and physical equilibrium up to fear and extreme terror.

NATURAL "AIGRES"

The *aigres* are the principal substance which enter the body to cause illness, pains, aches, and malfunctioning. They are said to be somewhat like ordinary air or wind; the Indians are certain that *aigre* is not quite the same as ordinary air but have difficulty in explaining the difference. The beneficial aspect of air or wind is that which gives life to infants at birth, which people breathe, and which carries rain. *Aigre* seems to be the harmful aspect, since it creates an abnormal condition by seeping into the solid parts of human, animal, and plant bodies instead of performing, as beneficial air does, the function of maintaining life. An *aigre* is any air or wind which causes sickness to human beings and animals by getting into their weakened bodies, or which, by blowing too fiercely or by carrying no moisture, causes plants to produce little or no fruit and to wither and die. *Aigre* is said to exist in the form of drops and to get into the body a drop at a time. It also spreads from one part of the body to another in the form

[7] E.g., a crushed hand is known to be weakened because of the crushing and so liable to *aigre*, but the weakness seems to be as much attributed to the "frightening" which the crushing is said to cause. Not only is the hand crushed but the sufferer, and even the hand itself, have been "frightened."

of drops, which are said to be able to pass through the
skin, flesh, and other solid substances.

Susceptibility to *aigre*, as to fright, is determined by
physical and emotional condition. Before it can enter, the
body must usually be weakened from some cause, the
most common of which is fright, although if it is strong
enough it may enter the body of a strong and healthy
person. Body weakness merely renders the individual more
susceptible than otherwise. Persons, like infants and the
aged, with inherent weakness, are especially vulnerable
at all times, while those with acquired weakness are in
danger until they take remedies to cure the weakness. The
wind-gods are the bearers of all *aigres*, especially those
sent by sorcery, and they act as impersonal agents in
bringing them to sufferers and in taking them away once
they are expelled from the body. *Aigre* acquired by contact is said to "jump" from one person to another.[8]

Aigre is of three principal classes, each of which has a
different source. The first is considered of natural origin
and enters the body in an accidental way, apparently from
the surrounding air. The usual *aigre* is of this class and
varies from slight discomfort to minor disease and illness.
It is not greatly feared unless, as not often happens, it
develops into extreme illness, since there are many remedies which will expel it. The second class, acquired from
contact with ritually unclean persons and objects, is more
feared because it is of nonnatural origin and because such
an *aigre* is believed to be more malignant and difficult to
expel than a natural one. It is much less similar to ordinary air than is natural *aigre* and is described later with

[8] *Aigre* is an early Spanish term meaning "air," or "atmosphere." Air is
now called by the modern term, *aire*, and the Indians and Ladinos reserve *aigre*
to refer in a specific sense to the evil air or wind which is the cause of most sickness. The Chorti term for both is *ikar*.

its coincident *hijillo*. The third class, which is sent upon
the victim by black magic, is the most feared of all, since
it is deliberate and malicious and can be made by the
sender to last over a long period and even cause death.
Much mysteriousness surrounds the *aigre* of the sorcerer
or personal enemy, the victim usually not knowing from
where it comes, what kind of *aigre* it is, or how serious
the unknown sender intends it to be. The Indians differentiate this *aigre* from the first class mainly by the fact
that it is deliberately sent by magical ceremony. It is
extremely tenacious, in spite of most remedies taken to
expel it. It will be described below under "Sorcery."

The natural *aigres* are named for (1) the agent or source
which caused them to enter the body, (2) the part of the
body in which they are localized, and (3) their inherent
characteristics and the bodily condition they cause.[9]

Of the *aigres* named for their source, fright *aigre*, which
comes as a result of any fright, is the most dangerous of all.
When caused by an encounter with an apparition or spirit
of the dead on lonely trails at night,[10] it is said to cause
idiocy and insanity. It is usually located in the heart and
so is sometimes called heart *aigre*. Water *aigre* is caused
by falling in midstream and getting soaked or by a sudden
fear of drowning. Fire *aigre* is caused by extreme burning
of the flesh and by fear of any large fire. Women are said
to get this *aigre* when their houses burn down and they
lose their possessions. Lightning *aigre* is caused by the fear
of lightning, as during an electric storm. During a thun-
derstorm the Indians are subject to thunder *aigre*. Death

[9] At Chan Kom the *aigres*, or winds, have different forms and so are named
on the basis of their form, their source, and the kind of ailment they cause (Redfield and Villa, 1934, pp. 165–66).

[10] When it is associated with *hijillo;* see pp. 326, 328.

aigre is caused by looking at and being frightened by a corpse. Snake *aigre* is caused by an encounter with or by the bite of a poisonous snake. Bull *aigre* and tiger *aigre* are caused by unexpected encounters with angry bulls or jaguars on lonely trails, especially at night. Evil-eye *aigre* is caused, usually in children and young animals only, by being looked at and frightened by a person who has the evil eye.

The following are examples of the second group. Body *aigre* is suffused all over the body and results in anemia, nervousness, loss of appetite, and weakness. The patient is said to have "pain all over his body." Woman's *aigre* is in the stomach and bowels and causes pain during menstruation and childbirth. Head *aigre* causes headache, neuralgia, and dizziness and, if not cured, is said to descend in time to the heart and cause death. Headaches are also caused by the supposed presence of the placenta in the mother's stomach, the *aigre* having ascended to her head. Forehead *aigre* causes sinus pains and headaches. Jaw *aigre* causes lockjaw, mumps, etc. Stomach *aigre* causes stomach-ache, stomach colics, indigestion, peritonitis, and intestinal pains. Labor pains are sometimes said to be caused by stomach *aigre* which enters through the mouth and is swallowed. Heart *aigre* causes heart pains, palpitation, and heart failure. Chest *aigre* causes pleurisy and other chest pains. Bone *aigre* causes rheumatic pains, neuralgia, and all bone pains caused by bruises, blows, and strains. Joint *aigre* causes arthritis and all joint pains. Eye *aigre* causes eye pains, eye-watering, conjunctivitis, and sometimes blindness. Tooth *aigre* causes toothache, sore gums, and decay in teeth. Scapula *aigre* causes pain in the scapula bone and is sometimes said to be the cause of tuberculosis and other lung pains and ailments. Ear *aigre* causes earache and sometimes deafness. Throat *aigre* causes sore throat, coughing, and general throat pains. Knee *aigre* causes knee and leg pains. Back *aigre* causes most forms of backache, and arm or leg *aigre* causes general pains and soreness in these extremities. Liver *aigre* causes liver pains, constipation, and pains in the lower back. Rectum *aigre* causes rectal soreness, diarrhea, piles, and dysentery. Penis *aigre* causes soreness in the penis, venereal disease, and sometimes sexual impotence.

Aigres named for the bodily conditions they cause, each such condition comprising a number of specific ailments, are windiness, coldness, warmth, burning, fire, swelling, dryness, wetness, congestion, excess of body function and weight, excess of growth in the body, rotting, stiffness, weakening, acidity, and body-spotting. Each condition and ailment has a native name.

Windiness, or "wind," is caused by wind; it results in sour stomach, dizziness, nausea, morning sickness, idiocy, insanity, hydrophobia, excessive menstruation, and many other ailments. It also causes a very common ailment called colic, which refers to any shooting pain in the body, resulting usually in a cramp. It is usually localized in the trunk and is considered very serious. The Indians call almost any sudden pain a colic and take dozens of remedies to relieve it. Windiness or wind is a moving *aigre* and, because of its movement, causes most of the violent and sudden upsets in the body. It is also called violent *aigre*, being said to turn round and round inside the body. Other names are whirlwind, whirlwind of the stomach, and whirlwind of the head.

Coldness, caused by a cold *aigre*, is said to be a condition which destroys the body heat; it causes chills especially. Numbness is an advanced stage of coldness and indicates that the cold *aigre* has reached the body surface in its attempt to get out. Coldness refers to any lowering of the body temperature, whether real or imaginary, and is relieved by remedies which "warm up the body." It is usually associated in the body with other *aigres* to produce given conditions.

Warmth refers in general to any excessive body temperature and is relieved by taking remedies to "cool the body." Hot *aigre* is the cause of all excessive body warmth, inflammation, surface eruptions, skin chapping, etc. These conditions are caused by the attempt of the hot *aigre* to get out of the body through the skin, rectum, nose, and mouth, or extremeties. Warmth also includes "burning," "fire," and swelling. A slight burning results in flushing of the face and light fevers, and, associated with other conditions, it causes coughs, whooping cough, sore throat, and tuberculosis. An extreme burning is a fever and is usually a general condition with other symptoms. Malarial fever is said to be caused by a hot *aigre* in the head and a cold one in the rest of the body. The Indians speak of having fever in all the organs, the eyes and nose, the arms and legs, and even the toes.

Fire, one of the most common of the causes of illness, is equivalent when spread over the body to very extreme fever, but the term specifically refers to local inflammations and surface eruptions of every kind. A slight fire causes pimples, small sores, and itching conditions, while an extreme one causes boils, ulcers, abscesses, cancer, and all large sores. The inflammation and redness are said to indicate that the fire has reached the surface of the body, and eruptions are the openings it has made through the flesh and skin.[11] "Fire in the head" is accompanied by

[11] The conditions of coldness and warmth may or may not refer to actual coldness or warmth as we define the terms. Warmth, which includes fever and fire, is

fever in the brow, headache caused by the fire, eruptions on the head and face, and causes such ailments as hay fever, catarrh, and bronchitis. "Fire in the mouth" is caused by a fire in the stomach which is sending its heat up the throat and into the mouth, where it results in mouth sores, tender gums, burning tongue, and sore, dry lips. "Fire in the body" causes venereal disease, pneumonia, and many others. Fever is distinguished from fire by the fact that it causes no inflammation or eruptions; but, once inflammation is present, the fever is said to have changed into a fire and to be working its way to the surface of the body. Interior fever accompanied with inflammation is called "fire fever." Both fire and fever are relieved by cooling the body and by inducing perspiration.

Any swelling without inflammation is said to be caused by a hot air which raises the flesh through expanding in the body; but, if inflammation is present, it is called a fire which is doing the same thing, as in cases of diphtheria, elephantiasis, tumors, bruises, erysipelas, and other ailments. Swelling is relieved by "diminishing the body."

Dryness, caused by a dry *aigre*, refers to any drying-up of a body liquid or secretion, to emaciation in persons and animals, and to withering and death in plants. It is similar to congestion, and many of the conditions are called by

---

in many cases a real condition of excess body heat, as in the case of fevers, but in many cases of inflammation and swelling there is little excess warmth present, and in others it is purely imaginary. Warmth seems to be associated with good health, vigor, sufficient weight, and proper body functioning in general, whereas coldness is associated with the opposites of these, and these conditions may be present either in the entire body or in merely a part of it—even a foot, an eye, the scalp, or a pimple. Any Indian, in diagnosing a real or imaginary illness, is inclined to base his decision upon these associations and to say that he has a "cold" or a "fire" in some part of his body, although when asked he admits he feels neither actual cold nor warmth. Perfectly healthy adults complain of a "cold" in the hand or arm or of a "fire" at the base of the stomach or in the liver.

both names. It includes lack of urine, breast milk, saliva, perspiration, and menstrual flow; dryness of skin, body emaciation or thinness, anemia, tuberculosis, the menopause, sexual impotence, and many others. It is relieved by "dampening the body." It is the principal cause of withering and death in plants. In the wind-god ceremony the deities are asked not to allow any malicious person to send a dry *aigre* upon the young maize sprouts. Dampness is a condition of excessive moisture, water, or damp *aigre* in any body part and is relieved by "drying up the body" or by drying the affected part. It refers to excessive perspiration, open sores, patches of skin covered with a fungus, and any imaginary dampness in one of the vital organs.

Congestion is any closing-up of a body passage or stoppage of a body function and is caused by a "closing-up" *aigre*. It includes such conditions as menopause and lack of menstruation, retention of placenta after delivery, constipation of bowels, lack of urine, cold in the head or throat, nasal congestion, asthma, deafness, blindness, loss of speech or taste, lack of perspiration, lockjaw, and many others, and is relieved by taking purgatives or laxatives to "open up the body." These remedies are especially taken to expel the placenta, induce menstruation, and produce abortions. To contract any congestion is to "become closed up." Congestion of the body is induced in cases where body excretion is excessive, as in diarrhea, dysentery, hemorrhages, excess of breast milk, etc.

Excess of body function, caused by the "opening-up" *aigre*, refers to any excess of excretion and is the opposite of congestion and dryness. It includes such conditions as diarrhea, dysentery, excessive urine, excessive menstrual flow, hemorrhage, wound bleeding, excessive emission of pus from sores, excessive emission from the penis and vagina, and excess of nasal mucus, of saliva, of tears, of perspiration, of ear wax, of breast milk, of body odor, of vomiting, and of falling hair. Excess of body function also includes any excess of body size or weight, such as pregnancy, obesity, and any kind of swelling not associated with illness. It is relieved by "closing up" or "drying up" the body or the affected part and is sometimes called "lessening" the body function. Thus, "closing up" is done to induce pregnancy, relieve diarrhea and dysentery, stop vomiting, avoid miscarriage, close and heal open sores, and stop falling hair.

Excess of growth in the body, which is the cause of much sickness, is called "increase," or "excess," and refers to any abnormal body growth or substance. The placenta is called "body increase," and the term refers also to tumors, goiter, gallstones, lumps under the skin, and any foreign matter sent by the sorcerer into his victim's stomach and head. It is vaguely thought to be caused by *aigre*, or to be equivalent to some kind of *aigre*, since it is difficult for the Indians to conceive of any cause for sickness other than air and wind, and is cured by "drawing out" the substance.

Shaking, caused by the shaking *aigre*, primarily refers to any nervous condition, but also to fits and convulsions, and is caused by a vibrating *aigre* in the body. Chills are called by this name, although they are said to be caused by both vibrating and cold *aigres*. The chill is an advanced stage of coldness and, if accompanied by fever, is called "chill fever." It is relieved by "calming the body."

Rotting is not important. Several informants stated they knew of Indians whose stomachs or other body parts were slowly rotting, caused by *aigre* or body "filth," and that the condition was relieved by professional curers. Stiffening, caused by a stiffening *aigre*, is a condition in which the muscles, and sometimes the vital organs, are said to become stiff; stiffening *aigres* cause most muscle cramps. Superficial stiffness, as a crick in the neck, is relieved with body washes, and "stomach stiffness," with a stomach wash, although for serious cases the Indians go to professional massagers. The condition is relieved by "loosening" the body. Stiffness is sometimes called a "tying up" and is similar to congestion.

Weakness, or weakening, an illness of which the Indians often complain, seems to refer to the loss of strength resulting from anemia, although many who do not look anemic claim to have it. The organs are sometimes said to be weakening and slowly dying, and remedies are taken to strengthen them. The Ladino druggists say that this organic weakness is imaginary. Acidity is a real sickness when used in reference to the stomach, in which case it is usually said to be caused by windiness, but is otherwise imaginary. One Indian complained that his whole body was turning acid. It is relieved by taking remedies to "sweeten the body" or to "sweeten the stomach." Spots on the body, or body coloring, is one of the names given to any illness in which there is skin discoloration of any kind. It includes loss of pigmentation, measles, scarlet fever, jaundice, freckles, and other conditions.

"HIJILLO"

Ritually unclean persons and objects, which include those with evil eye and strong blood, pregnant and menstruating women, corpses, sorcerers, apparitions and spirits of the dead, and all individuals who have been infected by these, cause natural *aigre* to enter the body as a result of fright when encountering them. But they also carry a special kind of *aigre* within themselves, which is the cause

of their being ritually unclean, and infect others with it
at close range. It is called in Spanish, *hijillo*, and sometimes *gas* ("gas"); it is merely called *aigre* in Chorti but
is differentiated from the natural *aigres* by reference to
the agent which carries it.[12] *Hijillo* is said to be very different from ordinary air, although fundamentally like it, and
is so murky and unclean as to be almost visible, like a dirty
vapor. It gets into the body through any opening and,
especially *hijillo* from a corpse, saturates the clothes. It is
much more dangerous and tenacious than natural *aigre*
and is more liable to result in extreme illness and death.
It does not enter the body from the surrounding air, as
do natural *aigres*, since it is spread only by contact with
the agents who have it. One may contract *hijillo* merely
by looking at the agents, unless at a safe distance, and it
seems to be unavoidable if one comes too close or touches
them. Any normal person infected with *hijillo* is believed
to be a carrier and therefore able to infect others until he
has cleansed himself of it. During his sickness his friends
visit him; but, if they are even slightly ill, they do not enter
his sleeping-house but talk to him from the outside.

The evil eye is possessed mostly by those Indians,
nearly all of whom are men, who have one or both eyes of
a glassy or hypnotic appearance, or who have an abnormal
eye which attracts the attention; but some whose eyes
seem perfectly normal are said to have evil eye. They are
said not to inflict harm or sickness deliberately and mali-
ciously, as they are born with the evil eye and so cannot
help it, and this is proved by the fact that they are both
willing to cure it when they have infected another and to
avoid such infection whenever possible. All sorcerers have
the evil eye and are said to infect others with it out of mere

[12] As "*aigre* of the evil eye," "*aigre* of an apparition."

spite or jealousy. Infants and pretty children and animals are especially liable to evil eye, since they have little resistance to it and arouse the envy of sorcerers because of their beauty. Adults are seldom affected by it. Strong blood is a condition in which the blood contains *hijillo*, which can be given to others upon sight or close contact.[13] The most dangerous *hijillo* is that exuded by a corpse, called death *aigre*, which remains in the corpse until complete dissolution. Some of it escapes through the mouth before burial. It is feared that some may escape even after burial, and this is given as one of the reasons why the dead are buried at some distance from the houses, milpas, and gardens. A menstruating woman exudes *hijillo*, which is especially avoided by men, and that of a pregnant woman is much more harmful.

All sorcerers are believed to possess *hijillo*, although the Indians are not certain whether the sorcerer's *aigre* is a form of *hijillo* or merely a natural *aigre* which he sends deliberately upon his victim by magic. Both are believed possible for the sorcerer, since he is so evil and dangerous a person as to be able to cause harm in every conceivable way. Spirits of the dead, especially by appearing to persons in dreams, infect them with *hijillo*, and its ill effects increase if the spirit continues to hound its victim over a long period. Many Indians complain of being pursued by a spirit of the dead, which is often but not always the spirit of a former enemy, and in this way account for their breaking out with sores and rash. Apparitions[14] infect their victims with *hijillo* by pursuing them, meeting them on lone trails at night, and embracing them.

[13] *ut*, "evil eye" ("eye"); *e ut*, "the eye" (Sp. *ojo, mal ojo*). *e ikar u ut*, "the *hijillo* of evil eye"; *t'cit'c-er*, "strong blood" ("blood"); Sp. *sangre, sangre fuerte*.

[14] See pp. 404-9.

Persons, animals, plants, and objects are susceptible to *hijillo* according to their degree of weakness at the time of contact. Those with open sores or wounds are the most susceptible of all, since it is very liable to enter the body through such openings, though it may also enter through the natural openings, especially the nose and mouth. Infants, the aged, the sick, young animal pets, and small plants like peppermint and others which require much care and grow only in containers are said to be "delicate" and are more susceptible to *hijillo* than are adults of normal age and health, adult and wild animals, and large hardy plants, which are said to be stronger.[15] Any object is delicate while it is being manufactured; it is said, like young maize, to be "growing" at that time, and susceptible until the process is finished. The agents can give *hijillo* at all times, but especially when they are angered, emotionally agitated in any way, excited, or physically exhausted. At such times it seems to increase in strength and to come to the surface of their bodies, where it is easily contracted by others. Any normal person, when extremely angered, seems to possess a weak form of *hijillo* at the time, but it is not especially dangerous except to ailing children.

Hijillo may result in any illness, and even death, but it usually causes pimples, sores, and rash to break out all over the body, especially on the face and neck, and it produces high fever and "fire in the body." Infants break out in this way after being looked at or touched by a person with evil eye or strong blood. Adults sometimes get fever and fire, the latter causing internal inflammations and extreme soreness in the mouth and throat. *Hijillo* is most feared, however, because it aggravates any sickness already present, interferes with any growing, healing, or

[15] *in-q'un*, "weak," "delicate" (Sp. *delicado*).

manufacturing process, aggravates all malfunctioning conditions, and is harmful to sacred objects, such as effigies of saints and crosses. Those sick with catarrh and other nasal troubles, or with sores and wounds, are especially careful at funerals and usually do not attend,[16] and they avoid meeting pregnant women. After contact with *hijillo*, one's sores and flesh cuts become swollen and pussy and refuse to heal, one's slight fever rises, and every pain increases.[17]

Remedies used to cleanse the body of *hijillo* are used as well to safeguard the body from it. The most common is copal. It is usually mixed with the dried leaves of garlic and sweet basil and placed in a pot of burning charcoal. The Indian holds his unclean clothes in the fumes and then stands naked over the pot for about a half-hour. This removes the *hijillo* and protects him against it for some time after. If copal cannot be obtained immediately, the clothes may be thrown away. This cleansing is always done after attending a funeral, especially by the pallbearers and those sick in any way. The former particularly cleanse their hands, as these had come in contact with the corpse. Many Indians take such a bath before attending a funeral,

[16] At Mitla a sick person does not attend a wake for fear his sickness will become worse (Parsons, 1936, p. 142).

[17] If a pregnant or menstruating woman looks at an olla of soap while it is boiling, it might fall and spill on the ground, or the soap will not harden properly; and, if she comes too near pottery while it is being made, the pieces may crack, lose their shape, and not "cure" properly. Similarly, agave fiber may lose its strength if she touches it while it is being prepared. Her presence in a milpa may retard the growth of young maize and other plants; and pot plants, especially peppermint, are said to wither and die instantly if she touches them. Sores and wounds on another individual become inflamed and refuse to heal if she looks at them. It is said that she is not to touch the food of others or to come in contact with the family and wayside crosses. Her near presence nullifies a religious ceremony, and she is forbidden from entering any of the ceremonial houses. Any of the other carriers of *hijillo* may cause these same effects.

and it is given infants suspected to have been exposed to evil eye. The most common preventive and cure for evil eye is wild rue. If the mother suspects a certain individual of having caused it in her child, as at a market or festival, she takes her child to him and asks him to cure it. Unless he is a sorcerer, he is always willing to do so. He chews the leaves and spits his saliva all over the face and head, and sometimes the body, of the child, often finishing by spitting a cross on its chest.[18] If the mother does not know who caused it, she goes to a professional curer. Anyone who has the evil eye can avoid any harm he may cause by spitting immediately after looking at or touching an infant. Those who infect others with strong blood are also willing to cure, unless they are sorcerers. They chew the leaves of sage, tobacco, or artemisia and spit their saliva over the face, head, and body of an infant or young animal to cure it, and, in extreme cases, spit the form of a cross on the front of the body.

Red is much used as a preventive against *hijillo*, and in some cases it seems to remove it. It is especially used for evil eye. Infants are carried, when at markets or festivals, with a red cloth either around their heads or close by so that the mother can instantly cover the child's face with it if an individual with evil eye approaches. In many cases a necklace or bracelet of the bright red seeds of the coral tree is placed around the infant's neck as a protection. The mother, if her child is suckling, often covers each of her breasts with a small square of red cloth, sewn into her shirt on the outer side, as it is believed that *hijillo* could pass to her child by way of her breasts if these were looked at or touched by any of the contaminating agents. Deli-

[18] Rue is used to protect a child from evil wind at Chan Kom. The mother chews it and rubs it on the child's eyelids (Redfield and Villa, 1934, p. 169).

cate plants, like peppermint, as well as those growing in special beds before transplanting, like tomatoes and tobacco, wither and die after contracting *hijillo* unless protected immediately by a red cloth which is thrown over them. Ashes are thrown over small plants, and against the trunks of valuable fruit trees for the same purpose. A small cross, hung on an agave twine around the neck, protects one from *hijillo* and is often worn by children, especially when sick and in public places.

SORCERY

Sickness caused by sorcery includes frights and *aigres* magically sent or arranged, "filth" sent into the body, and pain sent by sympathetic magic. Sorcerers are said to cause frights that may result in natural *aigres;* to infect others with or to send to their victims a harmful *aigre*, or *hijillo;* and to arrange for their victims to encounter any of the agents which cause fright. The most dangerous and feared of magically sent sickness is that of filth, which includes frogs, snakes, worms, flies, maggots, and various sticky and slimy substances. All are extremely revolting to the senses and are said to cause sickness because of this quality. They are sent principally into the head and stomach, although the sorcerers can cause them to enter any part of the body, and usually result in death unless removed by the curers, who pretend to extract the substances in various ways. Pain sent by sympathetic magic is not a common form of sickness, although it seems to be much feared. In this case no foreign substance enters the body, the pain being merely transferred to the victim from the object upon which the sorcerer is inflicting harm.

All illness, misfortune, and death which has its source in black magic is believed to be caused by personal enemies and sorcerers. The sending of maledictions upon one's enemies, without the aid of a professional sorcerer, is said to be done especially by the women. Curses are brought to the victim by the wind-gods and may take any form ranging from slight sickness to death. Any individual is believed to be able to do this to his enemy, and to his enemy's family and domestic animals, if he wishes such misfortune often enough. Usually he goes to a secluded spot and speaks his malediction in a loud voice. Many slight ailments are attributed to this cause. If the mere wishing of harm does not suffice, the Indian may burn a candle on the doorstep of the pueblo church at midnight, either on a Thursday or a Friday. It is stood upside down with the wick end pointing toward the Devil, who is asked to send the harm to the victim. The sender lights the bottom end, spends a few minutes in thrusting cactus needles through the candle, all the while saying in an audible voice that such thrusts are meant for the victim, and leaves the candle to burn for the rest of the night. If the performer of this ceremony is wishing good for himself or others, he sets the candle right side up, with the wick end pointing toward God, and recites his prayer.[19]

Magical poisoning is a common method of causing harm to an enemy. Five or six plants, all of which have an extremely disgusting taste or odor, and which produce nausea if eaten, are used. The *camotillo* herb is the most common. Sorcerers sometimes are paid to cause sickness and death by poisoning, but usually it is done by nonsorcerers. The Indians are said to poison their enemies magically for reasons varying from the theft of a handful of maize up to

[19] At Mitla one who is robbed burns the bottom end of a candle on a Friday noon to San Antonio, asking the saint to send misfortune upon the thief (Parsons, 1936, p. 141).

the murder of a member of one's family. Some part of the plant, usually the root, is ground up and a small portion surreptitiously placed in the enemy's food. It is said that he can be made to die on a given number of days after he has eaten the poison: the poisoner prepares the concoction and stores it away for as many days as he wishes, and when the victim eats it he will die an equal number of days afterward.[20]

The sorcerers[21] are greatly feared, even those who are only suspected of having some ability for black magic. Many individuals seem to have been forced into the practice of sorcery as a result of social pressure. The possession of mental and emotional peculiarities stamps an individual as a possible sorcerer, and, according to the Ladinos, he is often convinced by the community attitude toward him that he is one. From early life he is marked off because of such peculiarities, and the possession of them causes others to ascribe occult powers and knowledge to him. If a man has an eye with abnormal appearance, for example, people gossip that he has the power of the evil eye; in time he comes to believe it himself and begins inflicting others with sickness. If a man or woman is antisocial and given to doing strange things which the community neither approves nor understands, it is gossiped that he is perhaps a sorcerer; in time this individual believes himself to have

[20] No Indian was found who admitted having administered poison in this way, but every Indian claims to know of many instances of it. It is said that the Ladinos make great use of it in doing away with their enemies, especially in Honduras, where even politicians are believed to use it for removing their competitors for public office. The Jocotán druggist says that the *camotillo* root contains strychnine. The roots are chewed and the saliva swallowed to relieve cough and to improve the singing qualities of the voice.

[21] *pos-i*, "to work black magic" (Sp. *echizar, brujear*); *pos-on, pos-on-er*, "black magic" (Sp. *echicería, brujería*); *ah pos-on-er*, "sorcerer" (Sp. *echicero, brujo*).

such powers and accepts payment indirectly for performing black magic upon others. The sorcerers are never dangerous but appear to be slightly unbalanced; they do strange things, such as visiting graves at night, meeting evil spirits in secluded spots, and talking to themselves, and they are popularly supposed to do many other abnormal things which they probably do not do. There are other individuals who are supposed to practice sorcery who actually do not, and they deplore their unfortunate reputations. Usually, the sorcerers practice only black magic, causing disease and misfortune to others, but it is said they have the ability to cure magically as well. It is believed that he who can cause harm can also divine and cure it, since all esoteric knowledge comes from *ah q'in*, the sun-god.[22]

No Indian seems to know actually who is a sorcerer and who is not, since no suspected sorcerer would under any circumstances admit being one. In hiring a sorcerer, the Indian goes to the person whom he suspects of being a sorcerer and in whose powers he has great faith and asks how he can bring harm to his enemy. The suspect strongly denies that he is a sorcerer but states that he knows a sorcerer in some other locality and promises to make contact with him. He asks for all the needed information concerning the victim and accepts the fee which the sorcerer will charge, which he promises to turn over to the sorcerer himself. Any individual who is known to have entered into this sort of bargain with a great many people is assumed to be a sorcerer himself, even though no one is able to prove it.[23] Because of the mystery which surrounds

[22] See p. 399.

[23] Much of the information concerning the activities of sorcerers given in this paper is, therefore, secondhand, consisting principally of what the average Indian

the identity and work of the sorcerer, it is impossible to
know how many there are in any *aldea*, although each
aldea is known to contain a few. There are both male and
female sorcerers, the proponderance male, and each is said
to train a son or daughter to follow in his work. Their work
is usually for others, for money, but in many cases they
are believed to cause magical harm out of spite or jealousy.
The sorcerer is initiated by making a pact with the Devil,
who is the chief of the evil supernaturals and the patron
of sorcerers, and from him he receives his knowledge and
power. In return for this, he agrees to give his soul to the
Devil when he dies.[24]

Before practicing black magic, the sorcerer warns his
victim anonymously that he is to be harmed, and this is
done by leaving a candle in the victim's house, the wick
end pointing downward. A common method of warning is
made possible by gossip; the enemy who has hired the
sorcerer hints to a friend that he has heard that so-and-so
is being attacked by sorcery. This friend mentions it to
others, etc., until after some time the victim receives the

---

and Ladino either knows or suspects concerning them. A number of suspected
sorcerers, all of whom claimed to know nothing firsthand about sorcery, volun-
teered what they called hearsay information about sorcerers whom they had
known. Many of them seemed to speak as actual sorcerers, since they were able
to give much more information than other Indians.

[24] The initiate fasts on Thursdays for seven weeks, eating nothing on these
seven days but a small piece of *tortilla* three times a day. As he eats each piece,
he recites the credo backward to the Devil. After the seven weeks he goes at
eleven o'clock at night to the front door of the pueblo church and there meets
the Devil. He recites the credo backward three times, knocks three times on the
door, and says in a loud voice, "Get up, Doña María, get up, Don Juan; give me
a cup of chocolate!" (Ch. *hatc-p'-en tu' María, hatc-p'-en tata' Juan, a-w-ahq'-u-
en in-te' ta' s e kakau'*). It is said that the Devil appears and that the two go to the
cemetery to meet María and Juan. The latter give him the chocolate, which he
drinks, and he makes the agreement with the Devil to give up his soul (*u-y-ahq'-u
u p'ic-an*) when he dies. From then on the man or woman is said to have the
knowledge and power of a sorcerer. The identity of Juan and María is not
known.

information. It is said that none of the intermediaries ever knows who actually started the rumor. Before the sorcerer performs any ceremony, he first asks his *sahurin*[25] which method should be practiced upon his victim. Since he is an evil person, he has the spirit in the calf of his left leg. He crosses his left leg over his knee, raises his trousers, rubs the calf with the palm, and in some cases spits tobacco on it. He then puts yes-or-no questions in an audible voice to the spirit: Should he bury the image of his victim and, if so, should it be of wax or cloth? Should he send worms up his nose or frogs into his stomach?[26] The spirit answers him as it does the curer and diviner.

The sorcerers have four methods of inflicting harm: they (1) maltreat a specially prepared image of the victim; (2) appear before him in the guise of a familiar and harmless animal, such as a pig or vulture, and throw the sickness upon him at close range; (3) bury candles and copal; and (4) send sickness and death by prayer alone. The third method is the most often used.

For the first, some article, such as a piece of his clothing, his nail parings, or his excrement, with which the victim has had intimate association, is obtained. A placenta or umbilical cord is said to be the best of all. If the sorcerer is asked to destroy the victim's crop, he will attempt to steal the cobs from which the victim took the seed he planted. If he is to dry up a cow, he steals some of her milk. If a piece of clothing is obtained, this is sewed and stuffed with banana leaves in the form of a man. If the other things are secured, they are either placed inside the

[25] The patron of the diviner (see p. 399).

[26] "Is it necessary that I bury an image of so-and-so? Perhaps it should be of wax, perhaps of a piece of cloth? Is it necessary that I send worms up his nose to kill him, to make him suffer? Will it be best to send a frog into his stomach, an earthworm into his intestines?" etc.

effigy or used alone. An image resembling the victim is often made of beeswax and wrapped with a piece of his clothing if possible. In any case, the image or other object is maltreated by burying it in the ground, thrusting spines through it, or burning, boiling, and scorching it. All three are sometimes used together.[27]

The sorcerer takes his image or other object to a secluded spot in the hills, on either a Thursday or a Friday, at 11:00 A.M. or 11:00 P.M., and buries it about a foot underground. He must be observed by no one, or the magic will not work. Squatting over the spot, he recites a prayer to the Devil, asking him to take the victim as his own.[28] The image or other object may be stood up on the ground, supported with the right hand, and long spines run through it with the left. As he jabs the image, he repeats that the wounds are meant for his victim, addressing the latter and calling him by name. If the spine is pushed clean through, a mortal wound is said to be given, but slight pains can be caused by merely pricking the image. The pain can also be localized in the victim, since wherever the image is stabbed the victim is said to feel the pain in the same part of his body.[29] If death is desired, the performance is concluded with a heart stab.[30]

[27] *tcek*, "image," "doll" (*Sp. muñeca*).

[28] "O King Lucifer of Hell, I come to hand over so-and-so to you. I come to sell him to you according to my agreement (made with my employer). Already I am not yours, since I have brought a substitute to take my place. I hand him over to you, you of the seven states of Hell."

[29] Thus, the sorcerer can control the intensity of his harm and its localization upon the victim. An act repeated once or twice will result in slight sickness, but, if repeated many times, the victim dies. If the buried image is left in the ground for only a few minutes, the victim has a few body pains, but, if left indefinitely, he suffocates. The prayers, also, are repeated according to the degree of harm desired.

[30] "O so-and-so, I am stabbing this image. It is you. I stab it to hurt you, to pain you. You offended me, you offended my friend, and so I am stabbing you. I am making you sick. Now I am going to kill you."

The burning of an image takes many forms. If the image
is of wax, it may be stood up on a hot *comal*, and, as it
slowly melts, the sorcerer, who is squatting before it, calls
it by name and tells it how much it is suffering.[31] The
melting wax, as it runs down the image's body, is said to
be the tears and perspiration of the suffering victim.
Images and other objects are sometimes thrown into the
fire or on live coals and similar imprecations pronounced.
Burning or scorching is also done with the seed-maize
cobs, which are placed on a *comal* or in the fire and told
directly how they are drying up and dying.[32] An umbilical
cord or the excrement of an individual is sometimes treated
in this way to cause bodily harm to the former owner.
Milk taken from the cow of the victim is boiled in order
to dry up the animal, the heat and dryness being thus
magically transferred to the cow's bag.[33]

The inflicting of harm by appearing in the guise of a
harmless animal is said to be often done. The owl is a bird
of ill omen; it is believed usually to be a sorceress in dis-
guise, especially if it is tame and seems desirous of human
company, and its constant presence near a home for several days and nights portends the death of a member of the
family. Mustard seed are sometimes sprinkled before the
doors of the houses to protect the inmates. The bird, when
flying over the seed, is said to fall helpless to the ground,
whereupon it can be caught and killed, and any harm

[31] "O so-and-so, you are burning up, you are in pain, all your body is burning.
Now you are dying, you are dying. You are perspiring, your perspiration runs
down over your body."

[32] "O maize of so-and-so, you are dying, you are drying up, your body is
drying little by little; right now you are burning; you will never sprout. So-and-
so will have no maize in his milpas when it is time for him to harvest, and he will
be working with hunger. Of what use will you be to him, since you will never
be able to sprout and grow?"

[33] Some of the Indians stated that most milk is made into cheese before selling
so that others, especially one's enemies, cannot boil it.

thereby avoided.[34] A vulture which hangs around the house and is unusually tame is feared to be a sorcerer who has taken this form in order to approach his victim unrecognized.

If the three candles and copal wax are buried, no prayers are used. The candles are usually black and very small, and the copal has been shaped into a hard round ball of about the size of a man's fist. The significance of these is not known, except that black candles and copal are both sacred substances, and the latter is much used as a sacrifice in religious ceremonies and as a curative for certain magical ills. It is probable that the sorcerer offers them as a payment to the evil deity whose aid he expects. If the curer suspects that this method of sorcery is used upon his patient, he buries twice as many candles and twice as much copal as he thinks the sorcerer used, thus working superior magic.

If prayer only is used, the sorcerer performs no other ceremony. He may send any kind of harm this way: crop failure, personal misfortune, etc.; but he usually attempts to send worms to his victim's nose. This is one of the most common forms of black magic and is considered one of the most deadly. It is believed that the worms will in time eat into the brain and so produce death.[35] Other diseases, usually grave ones which the Indians know little about and therefore are least able to cure with ordinary herbs, such

[34] Mustard seed are used at Mitla to catch a witch which is hanging around the house (Parsons, 1936, p. 134).

[35] Don Manuel Vasquez, the Jocotán druggist, explains this sickness by the fact that in that part of Guatemala there is a dipterous fly (*Caliphora vomitora?*) which deposits its eggs in decomposed meat and sometimes in living flesh, in which they thrive until reaching the adult stage. Often an Indian, especially when drunk, will sleep during the day on the trail or in his milpas, and this fly deposits her eggs in his nasal passages. Soon his nose and throat are filled with small worms which are extremely difficult to expel.

as venereal disease, insanity, epileptic fits, tuberculosis, and paralysis, are sent in this way. Frogs, snakes, and insects are sent into a victim's stomach and other organs to produce vomiting, anemia, cancer, tumors, and gangrenous growths. When the sorcerer wishes to send worms to his victim's nose, he repeats a prayer which is directed to one of the aspects of the Devil, the evil spirit of flies, who is asked by the sorcerer to lend his aid.[36]

Because associative magic is much used by the sorcerers, the Indians usually bury their excrement and nail pairings, the father buries the umbilical cord of his newborn child in a secret spot, and, after the maize-planting, the seed cobs are secretly buried. Likewise, a charm when once used, and no longer needed, is buried or destroyed. In the use of sympathetic magic the image of a victim is often made to resemble the latter as much as possible, usually containing one or two of his most prominent characteristics, such as a goiter, a short leg, the custom of wearing a certain piece of clothing, or the lack of a finger or hand. The use of suggestion, the sorcerer repeating over and over what is being done to the victim and how terrible and agonizing it must be, and telling him that he is dying or is already dead, is said to hasten the magic as well as to increase its effect. The very wise sorcerers can throw magic a great distance, while those who are less wise must get nearer their victims. The messengers of the sorcerers and of all malicious persons are the wind-gods,[37] who carry prayers to the deities addressed and spoken imprecations to the victims. Every individual is said to have a degree

[36] This devil is asked to come on one of the evil days and at the "most silent" hour to seize the victim, to place worms in his nose, and to kill him. He is asked to prevent the victim from sending the same worms back upon the sorcerer.

[37] See p. 397.

of resistance to black magic, depending upon his health, age, and general condition. Adults have more resistance than children, infants and the aged have very little, and a healthy individual has much more than an ailing one. A sick infant is said to have none. For this reason an enemy often employs a sorcerer to work magic on a very young child or sick member of his victim's family, thereby hitting his victim in an indirect but much easier way. Fathers of newborn children implore their family saints to protect the infants and sick mothers from all possible enemies and sorcerers. Sorcery is said always to be performed on either Thursday or Friday, and at 11:00 A.M. or 11:00 P.M., at which times its effect is believed to be assured.[38] Similarly, a wild and secluded spot in the forest or high in the hills, where nobody lives or comes, is said to be the best locality for carrying out an act of magic.

[38] These are called the hours and days of the sorcerers. The hours are said to be the most "silent" (*tsus taka*) of the twenty-four, especially 11:00 P.M., and therefore most suitable for secret acts of sorcery. It is said that sorcerers do not send black magic at any other time.

CHAPTER XIV

MEDICINE

P ROFESSIONAL services enlisted in curing sickness include those of midwives, diviners, curers, herbalists, massagers, and surgeons. (The midwives have been discussed in chap. xii.) Although the Indians speak of a given practitioner as employing only one curative technique, in most cases he or she works at several of them. For example, nearly all diviners are also curers, most massagers are also surgeons and herbalists, and the female herbalists do most of the massaging in childbirth cases. The Indians distinguish two general types of curing professionals: the diviners and curers who work by means of supernatural power and the midwives, massagers, herbalists, and surgeons who lack this power and so "merely cure with their hands."

The diviners,[1] who are mostly men, principally divine the causes of sickness, determine whether it is of natural or of magical origin, and decide who would be the best curer for the patient to see. They also locate lost objects and give general information concerning the future. Some of them are also curers and sorcerers. Like the sorcerers and curers, they receive their information from the sun-god and so devote themselves principally to diagnosing sickness which the patient believes to be of magical origin. Most of them are considered good people, are much re-

[1] *ah q'in* (*q'in-i*, "to divine," "to predict"); Sp. *adivinador*.

spected, and are usually paid in money for their services. Diviners are often called upon to point out sorcerers and drought-makers,[2] to locate runaway lovers and domestic animals, to find lost money, and to predict any kind of future occurrence. They divine whether it will rain and how much, whether the crops will be good, etc. They often tell the patient just what method the sorcerer has used to bewitch him, and the patient passes this information along to his curer.

The diviner gets his information by asking questions of the spirit *sahurín*,[3] who is in the calf of his right leg, by examining the contents of an egg in a gourd container, by feeling the pulse, and by looking into a "crystal." The first method is most often used. He goes to the house of his patient and darkens the interior, since diviners say they cannot work well in strong light. He sits next to the bed, chews tobacco, rubs the saliva on his right leg, and in a few minutes begins his diagnosis. This consists in asking direct questions of the spirit concerning the probable cause of the sickness.[4] The spirit in his calf twitches the calf muscles if the answer is "Yes," while no twitching signifies "No." The whole procedure is carried out with great dignity and in dramatic manner. Each time the diviner gets an affirmative answer he turns to the gathered family and triumphantly announces his find.[5] The second method is

[2] See p. 377.

[3] See p. 399.

[4] The questions often run: "What caused the sickness? Was it an evil wind? Was it a sorcerer? Did he appear in the guise of an animal? Did he work black magic? Did he stab a candle? Was it the *hijillo* of an apparition or of a spirit of the dead? Was it a lightning fright?" etc.

[5] He often says: "Ha! Didn't I tell you so! It is as I thought it was. I knew it at once. Soon I will tell you what is ailing this man here, what he has in his body," etc.

not much used, and it was impossible to find out what the
diviner pretends to see in the egg. The latter is broken in
a gourd, with the yolk kept intact, and examined in a
darkened room. He does not ask questions but repeats
his findings slowly to the family as he inspects the egg.[6]
The feeling of the pulse[7] is sometimes done. If the pulse
beats fast, the illness is said to be grave and probably
caused by magic, and if slow, to be probably of natural
origin and therefore easy to cure. The pulse, however, does
not seem to indicate how the curing is to be done. The
fourth method, that of examining a crystal, is the least
often used. Every diviner carries in his shoulder bag a few
small pieces of broken glass, usually colored, as well as
pieces of quartz, and he pretends to see future happenings
take place within them. A diviner in Tunucó claimed to be
able to see within the stone or glass the exact locality
where any lost person or object was.[8]

The four methods of divining are often used together,
especially in cases of extreme illness. The diviner's fee
varies from five cents to a half-dollar (American equivalent), and he is often given a great quantity of food to take
home. Some of the diviners claim to be helped in their
work if they eat only maize for four days preceding their
divination and refrain from sexual intercourse during the
same period. These prohibitions, observed also by the
rain-making *padrinos*,[9] do not seem to be absolutely necessary for divination. After the visit of the diviner, a boy

[6] Called *t'cuhk qu'm* (*t'cuhk-u*, "to inspect"; *qu'm*, "egg").

[7] *p'ic-an*, "the pulse" (see p. 402, n. 38). *piht'c-i u p'ic-an*, "to feel his
pulse."

[8] Crystal divining is called *t'cuhk sas tun* (*sas tun*, "clear stone," "transparent
stone").

[9] Described in chap. xv.

of the family is sent to get the curer, who usually lives in the same *aldea*, or the patient goes himself to the curer's house for treatment.

Nearly all sickness of the natural kind, such as slight malaria, colds, coughs, chills, and fever, are usually cured by the Indian himself. For each ailment there are dozens of native herbs with curative properties, and much herbal knowledge is possessed by everyone, every family continually making use of it. If the ailment is severe, the Indian may go to his professional curer rather than attempt to cure himself. Of all the specialists who deal with sickness, the curers are the most important, since their treatment is concerned principally with sickness caused by black magic.

The curers are much respected and feared because of their ability to work with magic, but they are considered good people since their magic is used only in the treatment of ailments and as a protection against black magic. Their relations to others are never very friendly since they are believed to lead strange lives and to be in contact with supernatural beings. Like all the other "wise men," they exhibit a slight strain of insanity, which peculiarity is considered by the Indians to be natural and proper for those who engage in an occult profession. Although they work at the usual activities of other Indians, most of them make their living principally from curing. There are curers of both sexes, but most are males. Each *aldea* has from one to three or four who are called upon to cure the more serious ailments where black magic is suspected. Since each curer trains a son or daughter, and usually no other, to follow in his work, the profession is confined to certain families. The curer is paid usually in money and occasionally in food, clothing, or firewood. The best known of them have standard charges for each cure, ranging from a few cents to a dollar or more.

The curers[10] treat principally frights, *aigres*, and the presence in the body of poisonous foreign matter, most of which is caused by sorcery, the malediction of an enemy, pursuit by an evil spirit, or contact with a ritual object. They also protect possible victims against all forms of illness and misfortune, though many Indians do this for themselves, and they manufacture charms and heart balms. They insist upon working in semidarkness, as light is said to prevent their establishing contact with the agents which cause illness, and so usually close all openings in the patients' houses during their visits. They employ any of five treatments and sometimes all five in serious cases, which may be called "seizing," spitting, incensing, "pulling," and the magical injection of food into the patient's body. Two special techniques, often used in connection with the first three treatments, are exhortation and the use of the sacred form of the cross. As most curers are also diviners, they often begin treatment by chewing tobacco, spitting the saliva on the calf of their right leg, and asking the sun deity which cure is best.

The seizing treatment is the most important and makes use of live black turkeys and chickens, turkey eggs, and tobacco and artemisia leaves. The curer slowly passes these, one after another, over the patient's body, all the while calling upon the saints and especially upon San Antonio de Monte, the patron of medicine, to drive out the fright, *aigre*, or foreign matter, and calling upon the latter to come out and to enter that which he holds in his hands.

---

[10] They are called by several names, the most important of which are *ah nir-om* (*nir-i*, "to cure"; *nir-om*, "a cure") and *ah puha'-y-ax* (*puha'*, "to cure"; *puha'-y-ax*, "a cure"). The Spanish term is *curandero*.

He calls all the saints by name, asking each to help him, and calls by name every type of sickness he knows of, telling each to come out.[11] Tobacco leaves are especially used in this way to cure frights. The curative objects are usually passed thoroughly over the body four times, requiring about a half-hour, after which the objects themselves, which then contain the sickness, are destroyed and thrown away. In cases of serious illness, especially *hijillo*, they are buried to prevent "contamination." They are said usually to turn red, as evidence that they contain the "fire" or fever of the patient. Before he leaves, the curer is often asked to cleanse the chicken or turkey so that it will not have to be destroyed. This is done by passing a live frog, or any small and useless animal, over the fowl's body. The sickness is thus transferred to the frog, which is killed and buried. If the patient is not well in eight days, the curer comes again and repeats the treatment, giving it four times in all, if necessary.[12]

Two beliefs are held with regard to this treatment. In the first place, it is said that the curative objects, with the help of the saints, "seize" the sickness from the patient's body and transfer it to themselves, thus being active agents in removing the sickness. No curer was found who could explain the manner of the seizing, beyond saying that "it merely seizes it." In the second place, the curative objects are passive and are presented to the disease-causing

[11] His exhortation runs: "*Aigre*, come out of the body of So-and-so; Fright, come out of the body of So-and-so; Fire, come out, come out. See, here is a new place for you, a better place for you; come into this, quit the body of So-and-so, pass into the turkey; Saint So-and-so [here he calls several saints by name], make the man's sickness leave, drive it into that which I hold in my hand."

[12] The seizing treatment is called in local Spanish, *chucur*, which is a corruption of Ch. *tcuk-ur* (*tcuk-i*, "to seize," "to capture"; *tcuk-ur*, "a seizing"). The curer who specializes in it is called *ah tcuk-ur* (Sp. *chucurero*).

agents as an offering. This offering, however, differs from that in the religious ceremony in that it is presented to the agents not for them to consume as food or as a propitiation but rather as a new and better substance for them to occupy. Here, also, is expressed the idea of substitution, the turkey or other object being offered to the sickness as an abode in exchange for the patient, after which the new abode is destroyed and buried and the sickness buried with it.[13]

The spitting treatment[14] makes use of tobacco, rue, sage, and artemisia, of which the first is the most important.[15] The curer chews one or several of these and spits his saliva all over the body of his patient, blowing or spraying it with a hissing sound through his teeth. The patient is spit on from head to foot, especially on the face, and in serious cases the curer spits the form of a cross on the body, running from the head to the crotch, and from shoulder to shoulder. This is usually done four times and is repeated after a lapse of eight days if the patient does not improve. Spitting is often done in connection with seizing, the two together, especially if repeated four times over a period of thirty-two days, being said to be extremely curative. Spitting is the standard treatment for curing and warding off evil eye and strong blood, especially in children's cases.

[13] This has some resemblance to a treatment in Dzitas, Yucatan, called *kex* ("exchange"), in which a ceremonial offering of a chicken is made to the sickness in return for a successful termination of the illness. This is primarily a propitiation, or "payment," however (Redfield and Park, 1940, pp. 69–71).

[14] Called *huht* (*huht-a*, to spray spittle through the teeth), and sometimes *t'uhp* (*t'uhp-a*, "to spit"). Curers who specialize in this are called *ah huht* or *ah t'uhp*.

[15] Indian women are often seen in the pueblo streets and plaza picking up the butts of cigars and cigarettes which they sell to the curers, since partially smoked tobacco is believed to be especially efficacious in curing.

Incensing with the fumes of copal is regarded by the Indians as a similar treatment, since it is believed to affect the patient in the same way. The curer stands his patient naked over a censer of burning copal, so that the fumes completely envelop his body for a few minutes.[16] The clothes are often similarly incensed. In both spitting and incensing, the remedies used, and especially the form of the cross, are considered extremely powerful and cleansing, so that the illness is said to be forced off or out of the body by them. Since these treatments cleanse the body, they therefore render it impervious for a time to future illness, accidents, and misfortune. This is especially true in the case of copal, which protects persons, animals, and plants from sorcery, *aigres*, frights, and the *hijillo* of evil eye, strong blood, and corpses.

The pulling treatment[17] is used to extract any foreign substance, called "filth," which has been sent by sorcery into the patient's body. This usually takes the form of worms in the nose but includes frogs, insects, and nauseating substances which are said to be sent into the stomach and other organs. The curer passes his hands over his patient, who is lying on a bed, and imitates a pulling movement in the air, the purpose of which is to pull the worms out. He calls upon the worms to come out and also asks the saints, calling them by name, to drive out the worms. He tells the worms they are dying and that, if they do not instantly leave, he will kill them all. He then takes a gourd vessel in one hand and with the other performs a pulling

[16] Incensing is called *p'u't's* (*p'u't's-a*, "to incense"). In Dzitas, Yucatan, there is a treatment called *santiguar*, in which curative objects which are considered "pure" are placed in contact with the body to coerce sickness out of it (Redfield and Park, 1940, pp. 70–71).

[17] Called *p'ac* (*p'ac-i*, "to pull out"), and the curer who specializes in it, *ah p'ac*.

motion just above the patient's head and nose. This means he has forced all the worms out of the rest of the body and into the head. By a little more pulling, he forces them through the nose and into the gourd, and then holds the gourd up for everyone to see.[18] The treatment is performed dramatically, and the family of the patient, who are ranged around the bed, are deeply impressed. According to the Jocotán druggist, the curer, aided by the semidarkness, slips a slimy substance of some kind into the gourd, often the young of wild bees which he finds in the mountains,[19] and exhibits this as the worms. Some of the Indians suspect this but seem to believe nonetheless in the efficacy of the treatment. Sometimes the patient, if very sick, vomits into the gourd, or the curer induces vomiting with nauseating remedies, and the curer exhibits this as the worms he was supposed to expel.[20]

The curer often gives sustenance in a magical way to the individuals who, because of extreme sickness, weakness, or nausea, cannot eat. Eggs and maize preparations usually serve as foods in this treatment and are used as poultices to be placed on the patient's body.[21] Almost any hot food can be used in this way, being applied while still

[18] One curer always triumphantly exclaimed: "Here they are, I told you! I knew the worms were there, and that I would draw them out," etc.

[19] According to Parsons (1939, p. 466), the Pueblo curers of the Southwest "extract" an unidentified substance resembling a headless centipede. The Chorti curers claim to remove an insect-like object, and call it a giant insect sent by a sorcerer.

[20] Worms are also expelled from the nose with the leaves of *apacina*, aloe, sweet basil, and wild sweet basil, all of which are of nauseating odor. The leaves are pounded to a paste, stuffed into the patient's nostrils, and the latter made to inhale deeply. The odor is said to expel the worms by causing the body to "vomit" them through the nose.

[21] Called *p'aʼk weʼ*, or *tʼas weʼ* (*p'aʼk, tʼas*, "to bind," "to lay on"; *weʼ*, "food"; thus, "food-poulticing").

warm from the fire. It is believed that the strength of the
food, through contact with the patient, is transferred to
his body, just as a patient's sickness is transferred, by
means of contact, to a turkey or an egg. Foods used in this
way are thrown away after the treatment, as all their
strength is supposed to have passed into the sick person,
and since they have acquired any *aigre* which he may have
at the time.[22] The poultices are changed every eight days,
each time fresh food being used, and if necessary the treatment is applied four times.

The curers manufacture charms and heart balms for sale
and give information as to their preparation and use. For
an ailment in which the skin loses its pigmentation and
becomes spotted,[23] said to be caused by a sorcerer, the
curers recommend the victim to find a rue vine and to go to
it secretly at night. He is to embrace it three times, each
time rubbing the vine over the skin spots where the color
was lost, and to repeat the cure on four consecutive nights.
After effecting a cure, the vine is said to wither and die. A
species of green fly, called in Spanish *cantárida*, is said
to produce in a woman acquiescence to sexual intercourse.
The wings are pulled off, cut into pieces, mixed with
aguardiente, and given to a woman to drink. She must not
know of what is being done, or the charm will not work.
It is said that in a few minutes after drinking she becomes
dispuesta ("willing"). Tobacco leaves are pounded up,
mixed with *aguardiente*, and given to a woman to drink.

[22] The eggs are boiled until hard and cut in half. Coriander seed are ground to
a powder, mixed with *aguardiente*, and this soaked into the yolks. The latter
are then placed in a poultice and applied, with the yolks against the flesh, at the
nape of the neck, on the inner side of each wrist, and on each ankle. Warm *tortillas* are applied in the same way.

[23] *sar-in u p'ahn, sar-in u ut* ("spotted body," "spotted face"); Sp. *mal de
anda.*

She is said to become unconscious, so that the man is able to have intercourse with her. The *siguamonte* bird is much used as a means of inducing a person of the opposite sex to sexual relations. The curers cut out the heart, bake it over a fire, grind it to a powder, and sell it in this form. The buyer mixes it with a drink or with food and gives it to another to eat or drink. The decoction, like most charms, causes the victim to lose his will power and to do whatever is suggested to him. This particular charm is an aphrodisiac as well. If the giver of a charm should accidentally swallow any portion of it, he is said to become temporarily insane or to suffer from vertigo for several days.

The flower of the amate tree is a talisman and assures its owner of lifelong happiness, good health, success in love- and money-making, and safety from the harm of sorcerers and evil spirits. He will also possess bravery and boldness, will be invulnerable to all harm, and will be able to dominate all wild animals, even poisonous snakes. The tree is said not to produce visible flowers, being reproduced by spores, but the curers insist that it produces a single flower each year. It becomes visible and falls to the ground on a Friday at midnight, at which time an evil spirit, usually the Devil, suddenly appears and seizes it for himself. The tree from which it is to be taken must be deep in the forest, far from any habitation, and it can be obtained only when it falls to the ground. It is said that many men have tried to get one of these flowers but have failed, owing to their being stricken with terror upon seeing the evil spirit. They immediately sickened from the fright, and some are believed to have died.[24]

[24] An informant related how an Indian, on the advice of a curer, tried to get one of these flowers. On Holy Friday he stationed himself beneath an amate tree,

In order to learn to hate an individual who no longer returns one's love, the Indian is advised to find a sage plant growing far from any habitation, deep in the forest. No one is to know what he intends to do, or the spell will not work. An informant said he found the plant and for nine consecutive days went to it, each day passing in front of it nine times, and each time repeating a set phrase. With each repetition he pulled off several leaves and shoots of the plant and threw them into the air. According to the curer, each day the man's love for the woman (or vice versa) will decrease until finally, on the ninth, he loathes and despises her.[25]

The herbalists[26] are mostly old people, usually women who are versed in preparing and applying medicinal herbs, and many of them are midwives as well. They search for herbs in the mountains and sometimes grow them in gardens near their houses. When ready for use, they prepare the desired parts of the plants in various ways, tie them in

---

far from any habitation and deep in the forest, and waited. At midnight a strong wind suddenly blew up, and he heard a loud flapping of wings. The flower, at all other times invisible but now visible, fell to the ground, and he was on the point of seizing it when the Devil appeared and disputed its possession. The latter had eyes of fire and showed a hairy black hand, terrible to look at. The man fled, leaving behind the flower, and was sick for a long time after.

[25] A commonly used expression is, "I hate you, so-and-so (Sp. *te aborrezco, fulano de tal;* Ch. *im-p'a˙c-i,* or *ma˙tci in-q'an-i-et*). Many of the Ladinos use these charms and heart balms, usually buying them secretly from the Indian curers and herbalists. Several elderly Ladino women warned that one should be careful of what he ate and drank in the Indian and Ladino houses where girls of marriageable age lived, as they might give him something which contained a love charm. Such information is given somewhat in a joking manner, but it is obvious that it is believed to a certain extent. The Ladinos insist they do not believe in charms, but after relating seriously how such and such a person was "subdued," they always ask how it could have happened unless something like a charm were used. The Indians believe entirely in charms and heart balms.

[26] *ah t'sak,* "herbalist" (*t'sak-i,* "to cure"; *t'sak, t'sak-ar,* "remedy"); Sp. *yerbero* (*yerba,* "herb.")

bundles, and carry them to all the Sunday and festival markets for sale. The herbalists cure only natural ailments. They are said not to be able to cure those of magical origin, since they do not possess the spirit of the sun-god, *sahurin*, in the calf of their right leg. They are usually paid in money for their services and remedies.

The massagers[27] are usually men who are supposed to be versed in human anatomy and are employed to relieve pains which cannot be cured by medicines. The massager cures only natural ailments, since, like the herbalist, he usually uses no prayers and does not have the *sahurin* in his leg. His work consists of massaging the body for the purpose of forcing out the ailments through an extremity. The patient is laid on the bed in the sleeping-house, and the massager rubs the pain area with both hands and sometimes beats the spot with his fists. He rubs toward the nearest extremity, the purpose being to force the fright or *aigre* out through that extremity. For example, if the aigre is thought to be in the arm, he rubs toward the hands until the *aigre* is forced out through the fingers. An *aigre* in the leg is forced out through the toes, and one in the lower back, out through the penis or leg. He pulls an *aigre* out also by drawing his hands through the air in a pulling motion directly above the patient's body and toward the extremities. If done properly, this imitative magic is said to be more effective than the rubbing.

The massagers often pinch the patient's flesh violently, pulling it out from the body as far as possible and letting it snap back. This causes a loud, popping noise and is said by the massagers to be the breaking-loose, or "unfastening," of the *aigre* from the body. The massager calls upon the *aigre* or other sickness to break loose or unfasten

[27] *ah lahp' p'ahn*, "massager" (*lahp'*, "to rub with the hands"); Sp. *masajista*.

itself. An important sickness treated by the massagers is sour stomach, or dyspepsia. The patient is covered with warm hog grease and massaged in the abdominal and dorsal regions in the manner described above. Much suggestion is used, until finally the stomach *aigre* "unfastens" itself. For nine days thereafter the patient drinks a boiled tea made of the *hierba del toro* plant.[28]

The surgeons[29] are principally employed in binding broken bones, but they also treat wounds, staunch bleeding, cure gangrene, sores, ulcers, and cancer, and open the flesh to permit an *aigre* to escape. In general, they treat all flesh conditions which require external treatment and for which no ritual cure is needed. They are often called upon after fights between families and after accidents at the sugar presses. Wounds are bound with plasters made from herbs, tied on with banana leaves and agave string. Broken bones are bound with a splint consisting of several lengths of split carrizo stalks. A plaster is made of crushed boiled beans, the leaves and sap of the *suelda Consuelda*, or the leaves of the white annona, and laid on thickly all around the break. Over this is wrapped several layers of leaves, usually of the same plant, and laid on this, running lengthwise, are the carrizo splints, tied securely around with agave string. These materials are changed every eight days and a new plaster applied, as the old one is said to have lost its strength by that time. Skin erup-

---

[28] The massager says, "*Aigre*, of a snake, *Aigre* of a bull, Fright of thunder, make yourself crack, unfasten yourself," etc.

[29] *ah qatc t'cak-on-er* (*qatc-i*, "to bind"; *t'cak-on-er*, "wound"), surgeon; *ah qatc p'ak*, "bone-setter." The bone-setter at Chan Kom is called *kax baac* ("bone-tier"). These two stems seem to be equivalent to the Chorti *qatc p'ak* (Redfield and Villa, 1934, p. 172). The *kax baac*, as a massager, rubs downward along the limbs, as does the Chorti massager.

tions are cured usually with small plasters made from various herbs. The surgeon opens the flesh, sometimes a half-inch deep over the pain area, to permit the *aigre* within, which is causing the pain, to escape. He uses a small sharp flint knife for this purpose.

For medicinal purposes the Indians use plants, animals, and minerals, of which the first are of greatest importance. Hundreds of native wild and domestic plants are used in some medicinal way by individuals in general and by the professional curers and herbalists. Every adult knows something about them, and especially do the women, who are able to prepare remedies from them to cure most of the minor sickness in their families. For major sickness, however, as at childbirth or in the case of serious disease, the curer or herbalist is called in, both because they are known to possess a great deal of special knowledge and because their presence and treatment are reassuring. The plant parts used are roots, bark, milk and sap, leaves, shoots, flowers, buds, fruit juice, fruit meat and seed, and entire plants. *Tortillas* and wheat bread are often used medicinally as well.

Plant remedies are prepared in many ways. The plant may be used in its crude or raw state without preparation, and many minor ailments, such as slight colds or colic, are treated with them. It may be placed in a cloth, as in the case of seeds, and beaten with a stone, or in a small bowl, as in the case of leaves and bark, and crushed with a pestle. It may be ground on the metate, as in the case of hard seeds, shells, roots, and baked materials. It may be toasted, baked in a kiln, or dried in the sun, after which it is reduced to a powder and usually applied locally. It may be reduced to ashes and applied locally as a poultice. The plant part may be soaked in water, with or without salt, or in fruit juice, *chicha*, *aguardiente*, or hog grease, usually for several hours until the liquid becomes thoroughly flavored with the plant, after which the liquid is strained out. These cold "teas" are much taken medicinally. Medicinal plants or parts are often left in the open air, outside the house, to soak overnight, and the potion drunk early the next morning. The dew thus collected is said to have great medicinal value. The plant part may be boiled in water to make a tea or soup, usually to be taken either internally through the mouth, rectum, or vagina, or to be applied externally as a body wash.

Plant remedies are applied raw as a poultice or plaster to relieve swellings, boils, ulcers, aches, affected teeth and gums, flesh wounds, body blows, and fevers. Various foods are also applied as poultices as a means of magically injecting food into the body. Remedies are rubbed on the affected area with the hand to kill external body parasites, remove *aigre* from the limbs, relieve sore eyes, etc. They are chewed, usually in the raw state, and the saliva swallowed, as in the case of throat troubles. The saliva is spit on the body of the patient to cure his sickness as well. The fruit of the medicinal plant is eaten, especially for throat conditions. The ground parts of the plant are mixed with foods and eaten, as in the case of medicines taken regularly as preventives. A potion is made of the plants and drunk, used as a gargle, or held in the mouth, boiled or unboiled, for stomach and intestinal troubles, female disorders, throat troubles, aching teeth, "fire in the mouth," and other ailments. The potion may be injected as a douche, either rectal or vaginal, for which purpose a native douche bag is used.[30]

The use of animals and animal parts is not so important as is the use of plants, but almost every available wild and domestic animal is used in some medicinal way. The use of eggs and fowls in curing and divining sickness has already been described. The milk of a black cow is used to wash the head to cure dizziness and is drunk in the mornings by pregnant women to relieve morning sickness. Deer horns are baked in a fire, ground on the metate, and the powder taken in a potion to relieve *aigre* of the stomach and to expel the placenta. The flesh of the *taltuza*, a small brown animal, is fried, the grease soaked in cotton, and the wad stuffed in the ear to relieve deafness. The flesh of the opossum is fried and the grease used as a plaster to relieve swellings. The spines of the porcupine are used to open inflamed gums and thus remove pus; smallpox sores are treated in this way. A young dog, usually a week or so old, is killed, cut into pieces, and a piece of the flesh attached as a poultice to each of the wrists and ankles, and to the nape of the neck to relieve fevers. A grown dog is cut open in the abdominal region and the feet of the patient placed inside the opening, also to relieve fevers. The grease taken from a dog's breast is applied as a poultice to the pain area to relieve rheumatic pains.

The head and tail of the rattlesnake or coral snake are cut off, each to a length of a span, the skin taken off, the

[30] The douche bag is made by tying up the two ends of a cow's intestine and is two or three feet long. A piece of reed, usually of the type used in making handles for skyrockets, is stuck into one end. This is injected into either the rectum or the vagina, and the liquid forced out of the bag by pressure with the hands. The douche liquids are made of various herbs, used for serious sickness, and salt, used for minor inflammations.

meat toasted until dry and hard, ground, and sprinkled over foods to be eaten to cure venereal disease. It is taken every day for four days. The *jute*, a type of water snail, is boiled with *Santa María* leaves and the potion drunk by mothers to increase their milk. Soap made from hog lard is mixed with tallow and used as a poultice to relieve reddening, watering, and pain in the eye; it is placed behind the ear of the same side. The honey of the wild *talnete* bees, which are black, is both rubbed on the pain area and drunk to relieve pain and swelling resulting from a body blow. The heart of the sparrow is cut out, toasted, ground, and made into a potion which is drunk to remove a heart *aigre*. A live black frog is rubbed on the calf of the leg or any other part of the body to reduce swelling; the frog is said to turn red, since it has drawn the fire, or swelling, out of the patient and into its own body. Frogs are said to be able to do this because they are "cold" animals. A piece of the frog's hide is laid as a plaster on the flesh directly over a splinter, and the latter is said to come to the surface in a day or two. Cobweb and spider web are taken from a wall or ceiling and held against a flesh cut to cure it and to free the blood from poisons.

The principal mineral remedies are clays, earth, and salt. Kaolin, much used medicinally, is secured in the mountains near Esquipulas, cleaned, and pressed into small cakes, each about two inches long, an inch wide, and a quarter-inch thick. A raised figure of the Virgin, the patroness of childbirth, is molded on one side. These are blessed by the Catholic priests in the temple at Esquipulas and sold to the Indian and Ladino women throughout eastern Guatemala. The cakes are ground on the metate, mixed with water, and drunk to stop excessive flow during menstruation and to relieve all childbirth pains. Lime, a "hot" substance, is mixed with hog soap and placed on an aching tooth. It is said to produce heat which breaks the tooth into pieces, causing it to fall out. A small amount of adobe mud is taken from a house wall, dampened, held to the nose, and inhaled to stop nosebleed. A weak solution of salt and water is used as a vaginal and rectal douche to relieve minor inflammations and frictions.[31]

The dosage varies with the type and intensity of the ailment. For most conditions it is believed that, the stronger and the larger the dose, the better, with the result that many Indians seem to aggravate rather than to relieve their sickness. For body functions which require regulating, a strong dose is taken or applied to induce the function, and a light dose of the same remedy, to stop it when excessive. Thus, a heavy dose induces late menstruation, bowel movement, and the passage of urine, while a light one reduces excessive flow and hemorrhage, relieves diarrhea and dysentery, and reduces excessive urine. The same dosages are taken to regulate the flow of saliva and eye water, to regulate perspiration, and to increase or lessen the flow of blood through the body.

For most minor ailments the remedy is taken continuously until relieved or cured. For serious sickness, however, the time of taking is important, since remedies taken at the proper time are more efficacious than they would otherwise be. For example, the remedy may be repeated several times, each time after the lapse of three, four, or eight days, or it may be taken for three, four, or eight days continuously, and then repeated after the lapse of the

[31] A type of salt, called in Spanish, *sal villana* ("native salt"), and in Chorti, "mountain salt," is much used, especially in remedies. It resembles the imported salt but is not so clean and white. The Indians and Ladinos refer to it as "local" salt, and it is probably found somewhere in the Republic, but I did not discover where.

same number of days it was taken. The number "4" is especially used by men,[32] as it is in many ways their ritual number, and the number "3" by women, as 3 is the ritual number for females. These numbers are used by the proper sexes even when treating the same sickness. The number "8" is used by both sexes. Some remedies are taken over nine-day periods, especially by the women in treating purely female conditions. The early morning, before eating, is a favorite time for taking remedies, as the body is said to be weak at that time and therefore susceptible to the effect of medicines. Fasting is often done during the period of treatment, the patient eating only maize preparations, as this keeps the body in proper condition for any type of curing.

Most of the remedies no doubt have real curative value, as in many cases they are the same as those used the world over in treating similar conditions. The use of quina bark to prevent and cure malaria is an example. This value has, of course, been discovered over a long period of time by trial and error, and many stories are told of how certain plants or preparations were discovered in the distant past to be of value in the treatment and prevention of sickness.[33] Such discovery constantly goes on, as almost any

[32] The importance of the number "4" is especially shown in the taking of remedies believed to be ordinarily poisonous. Any poisonous plant is considered extremely curative if taken properly, since it has "power," and the use of this number apparently prevents its being fatal. If the remedy is made from four seeds or from four leaves of the plant, or is taken continuously for four days or four days apart, etc., it will be curative, but otherwise it may result in death. Thus, the *camotillo* herb is said to be fatal if taken indiscriminately and is given secretly to poison one's enemies, but it is curative if taken as described above. Many poisonous plants are thus rendered of medicinal value.

[33] A professional curer related how the curative properties of the conacaste tree were discovered. Long ago a mad dog bit a youth, and in a few days the symptoms now known to be those of hydrophobia appeared. He went mad and attempted to bite other people. His attacks became more frequent and violent,

Indian can tell of an illness he once had which could not be cured until he stumbled on a remedy hitherto unknown, or at least unknown to him.[34] Every curer claims to have special remedies, unknown to other curers, which he discovered in this accidental way in treating himself and his patients.

A great many remedies are used both because they are believed to have curative qualities, either inherent or acquired because of association or resemblance to some sacred personage or object, and because in some way they resemble the part of the body for which they are used, the manner in which they are to affect the body, the cause of the sickness, or the condition caused by the sickness. The notion that like produces like, or that like affects like, seems to apply. Most such remedies probably have little actual medicinal value, although their psychological value is often great. Almost all plants appealing strongly to the

---

but the curers were at a loss for a treatment. It was decided to take him to Jocotán. Four men were selected to carry him by force, but, as he showed superhuman strength, a messenger was sent to another *aldea* to bring more men. In the meantime the youth was tied to a tree to prevent his escape. He attacked the tree, biting and chewing the bark, and, when the men returned, they observed that his condition had improved, and by the time the party reached Jocotán he had regained his senses and was docile. He was given more of the bark to chew and ultimately was cured. The tree was a conacaste, and, after further experimenting, it was finally established that this bark was the proper remedy. Subsequently, it was found to be effective in other cases of poisoning.

[34] These stories all follow the same pattern: the man once had a serious illness, usually one which could not be diagnosed, since it was different from any illness ever seen before; the remedies and treatment of the curers did not help and the sickness became worse (*ma·tc-i·c u-y-up-i-op' u-t'sa·k-t-es-en*, "They could not cure me"); the man, by the most improbable accident, came into some sort of contact with the remedy, not knowing, of course, that it had any curative value; he noticed that his condition improved and suspected the remedy had something to do with it; he tried it several times and got well; and he told others about it, so that before long everybody was using it. Or perhaps others laughed at his remedy and refused to accept it until he had successfully demonstrated its value in several cases of the same sickness.

senses are believed to have curative power. An herb is said to be efficacious in proportion to the degree of dislike which people have for its odor or taste and to the degree of nausea which it produces. Thus, many nauseating plants are used to dispel foreign matter from the body, especially that sent by sorcery, and are also taken to strengthen the body and blood. The foreign matter is said to be "vomited" from the body, even though it may not be actually vomited. Other plants, like copal and rue, are used as medicines probably because of the pungency of their odor, and so are especially used for cleansing the body of nonnatural *aigres*. Plants which are merely pleasing, like most flowers, are not often used medicinally, although all such flowers are used in a religious way to adorn sacred places and objects. Many poisonous plants, already referred to, are curative if taken in small quantities and with the proper ritual safeguard. The stubs of candles burned before the images of the Virgin or the patron saint in the church, and sold to the Indians by the *mayordomos*, are of great medicinal value,[35] and the kaolin cakes with the raised image of the Virgin are the most important remedy used by the women for all female troubles. The form of the cross, spit on the patient's body, is especially curative. *Conte* leaves, which have the shape of the cross, are prepared and taken with many other remedies, as the leaves are said to give added power to the remedies.

[35] When the candle has burned down to three or four inches of the bottom, and is therefore completely blessed, it is blown out and the stub taken home. It is cut into small pieces, mixed with lemon juice, the whole pressed with the hands into a flat cake, the cake wrapped in a cloth, and the whole applied to the forehead to relieve a headache resulting from fever. Without the lemon juice, it is applied to pain areas to relieve and cure swellings, pain resulting from a blow, internal inflammations, and serious burns. Candles blessed before the patron saint are the most efficacious of all, he being the most powerful of the saints in his *municipio*.

The leaves of the *chipilín* plant and others are held upward when cut, if to be used as a vomitory, and downward, if to be used as a purgative. The *guapito* herb is of two varieties, "male" and "female," the former resembling the penis and the latter the vagina. The male roots are taken to avoid pregnancy and to insure a son, and the female roots, to induce pregnancy and to insure a daughter. Some of the curers reverse this belief, recommending the male roots to induce pregnancy and the female roots to avoid it. This type of belief is held with regard to many plants whose parts resemble the penis or vagina. The roots of the *chilillo* tree, which resemble the penis, are prepared and rubbed on the penis to relieve soreness and venereal disease, and a potion of them is drunk to induce pregnancy and insure a male child. Remedies made from snakes, which are said to resemble the penis, are taken for venereal disease and penis pains. The *ciguapacte* shrub, believed to contain air in its leaves, is prepared and applied to the soles of the feet to draw out fever caused by a hot *aigre*. Many "air-containing" plants are used to remove *aigre* from the body. Coconut milk[36] is drunk to increase the urine. Very juicy limes are cut in half and the open side laid against the penis for this purpose. Several plants with fruit of the shape of the female breast are used to increase the urine as well. Plants with a great deal of milky sap are used to increase the breast milk and are fed to cows to increase their yield.

The seed of the *ojo de venado* and *zarza de venado* vines, which resemble deer's eyes, are used to cure evil eye, and their leaves are used to remove eye cataracts. The *calzoncillo* vine, the leaves of which have the shape of an Indian's drawers, are used to remove inflammation of the prostate

[36] Called "the coconut's urine."

gland. Plants with yellow parts, as the yellow-flowered aloe, *flor amarilla*, and *escobilla negra*, all of which have yellow flowers, are made into remedies for jaundice. Yellow remedies also remove pus from sores. Red plants are used for many blood conditions as well as to draw out "fire," which is said to be red. The red sauce made from achiote seeds and the red sap of the *sangre de drago* are taken to stop excessive menstrual flow and bleeding from wounds and hemorrhages, to remove fire from the stomach, and to reduce all swellings caused by fire in the body. The bark of the caulote tree is soaked in water until the latter is red and the potion drunk to remove fire from any body part. Yellow is associated with strength, and yellow plants are used to strengthen the body, improve the blood, and cure anemia. Yellow maize is fed to roosters and male turkeys to give them virility and to fighting cocks by the Ladinos, who seem to have this same belief concerning yellow. Several plants and plant parts are believed to contain opiates and thus induce sleep, and many of the native names of these contain the stem *wai*, "to sleep." Potions made of them are drunk and used as a body wash, or their leaves placed under the pillow at night, in cases of insomnia and for putting crying infants to sleep. They are used, like the lignum vitae, to relieve aching teeth and to stop excessive body excretion, in which cases the ache or the body part affected is said to be put to sleep, and are used for all nervous conditions to "calm" or "quiet" the body. They are also thrown into still streams during the dry season to poison fish, although the fish are said to be put to sleep and not poisoned. Many of these plants merely imitate sleep in some way, such as the *sensitiva* and a small wild herb called *way-n-em t'ic*, the leaves of which fold up, or "sleep," upon being touched. Those who do not need a sleep-inducing remedy avoid these plants, for fear they will sleep continuously for days without waking. The leaves and shoots of the coral tree, much eaten as greens, are made fit for eating by being boiled twice, as the second boiling is said to destroy their toxic effects.

Many remedies which cure a given illness, if taken by a person who does not suffer from it, are said to cause him to contract the same illness immediately. For example, the rattlesnake remedy cures venereal disease, but it will give the disease to a well person who takes it. The charms are especially retroactive, causing insanity and other sickness to the giver if he should accidentally swallow them.[37] The Indians are therefore wary of taking medicines until they are certain they have diagnosed their sickness properly and are taking the right remedy for it. Although the curers and many of the older Indians insist that certain ailments, especially those sent by sorcery, can be cured only by ceremonial cures, the Indians in general believe that medicines bought from the pueblo druggist are of greater curative value than those which they themselves prepare from native ingredients. They seem to ascribe a special power to medicines put up in bottles and in the form of capsules and pills which are sold to them in paper boxes. The pictures and writing on the labels seem to give such medicines added power and genuineness.[38] Every Indian has two or

[37] See p. 353. This double effect is shown in the belief concerning the rosebud charm in Yucatan. This charm attracts a man to the giver, usually a woman, if placed under his pillow; but, if she accidentally smells it, she temporarily loses her mind (Saville, 1921, p. 207).

[38] The Jocotán druggist says that the Indians, when buying medicines, often ask him to attach labels which contain a picture and printed instructions. Most of the Indians cannot read but seem to feel that the medicine is all the more potent if the instructions go with it. Many of them spoke of the superior value of their store medicines by exhibiting the bottles or boxes they came in and by pointing out that the directions were all there in great detail, for anybody to see.

three small bottles which he calls his "medicine bottles," each with an agave cord tied around its neck, the other end of which he carries looped around his wrist when he brings it into the pueblo to be refilled. The Indians also believe that drugstore remedies are much more concentrated than their own, that is, more "powerful," probably because they come in smaller quantities, and this is no doubt true in most cases, though not in all. Many remedies are prepared in Guatemala City from the same plants which the Indians use to cure a given illness, and often they prefer the prepared product, which they buy properly packaged, to their own.[39]

[39] The former is said to be *mas fuerte* ("stronger") than the latter, which strength seems to be something more than a mere concentration of ingredients. The Indians are fascinated by the fact that a small pill, tablet, or capsule, which they of course cannot make, is of equal or greater curative power than a large bundle of remedial leaves and roots. Drugstore remedies are also said to be *mas bonito* ("prettier"), especially if made in attractive colors which the Indians cannot duplicate.

CHAPTER XV

RELIGIOUS ORGANIZATION AND PARAPHERNALIA

IT IS impossible to state for how long the Chorti-speaking Indians have been subjected to Christianity. Catholicism was first introduced to them in 1524 and was continued with apparently little success until 1530, at which time the priests abandoned the region, probably because of the Indian revolt.[1] The histories of the province contain no information as to when missionary work was resumed. It is probable, however, that a few churches had been built and were actively at work among these Indians at least by the end of the sixteenth century, since the image of the Black Christ of Esquipulas was sculptured in Antigua Guatemala for the Esquipulas church in 1595.[2] Churches were built in the principal Indian pueblos of Chiquimula: Jocotán, Olopa, Camotán, San Juan Hermita, Quetzaltepeque, and Esquipulas.[3] The Ladinos in Copan and Jocotán claim that Copan had no early church, although they are probably mistaken in this. Stephens, who traveled from Chiquimula to Copan in 1841, described

[1] See p. 4.

[2] The earliest recorded date in the extant baptismal records of the present church in Jocotán is 1680, but this date is probably that of the founding of the present structure, since, according to the Jocotán Ladinos, the original church and its records were destroyed by fire shortly before that time. The ruins of this church still remain. Its burning seems to coincide with the last revolt of the Chol (see p. 5, n. 7), although the two events probably are not related.

[3] The ruins of the original church of Chiquimula still stand at the edge of the city.

the ruins of many small churches which he passed,[4] and from this it may be concluded that mission establishments were founded in or near many of the Indian *aldeas*. Only the pueblo churches, however, have remained intact and in use.

The religion of the Indians today contains both Catholic and native elements. These do not exist separately but have been more or less fused into a single religious system, and in most cases the Indians seem unaware that any historic fusion has taken place or that their religious beliefs and practices have more than a single origin. They have adapted two religions to each other, thereby producing a third which they consider as native to themselves.[5] Catholic elements seem to have been accepted or ignored on the basis of their degree of similarity to corresponding native elements. In many cases there has been complete fusion, as between certain native deities and the Catholic patron saints. The Indians refer to these by their Chorti and Spanish names without seeming to feel that they may have a dual character.[6] Each is considered a single deity with a single character and role and not as having both a native and a Catholic character and role. In cases of semifusion the Catholic element, being somewhat similar to a native one, is allowed to exist side by side with the latter. Each is considered an equally important and integral part of the native religion but performs only a part of the original function it presumably had before fusion took place. For example, the Catholic priests are said to belong primarily

[4] Stephens, 1841, Vol. I, chaps. iv and v.

[5] Cf. La Farge, 1927, pp. 4–5.

[6] It is felt that the deities should have double names if only because the Indians themselves are bilingual, speaking both Spanish and *lenguaje* (Chorti), and must therefore have two names for everything.

to the pueblos and the Ladinos and to "have permission" from God to perform only those religious duties connected with the church, while the native rain priests, or *padrinos*, belong primarily to the *aldeas* and the Indians, and only they have permission to perform the native ceremonies. There is some fusion even of the priestly role, since Catholic priests sometimes perform the new-house ceremony, but in general this role is divided between the two types of specialists and the two fields of religion.

In some cases a Catholic element having no native counterpart is merely accepted into the native structure as a new element. Examples are God, Christ, certain saints whose festival days do not correspond with any native festivals or ceremonies, and much of the church's doctrine and history. These, if known at all, are accepted as religious elements, but they have very little significance, as compared with the patron saints, for example, in the religious life of most of the Indians. Such elements are said to be universal and to belong to all peoples, while the other two types, which the Indians believe in varying degree to be their own, are said to belong primarily to Indians and Indian life. The Catholic priests complain that the Indians have distorted and therefore destroyed the efficacy of the Catholic rituals, an attitude which the Indians fail to understand, since they consider themselves as religious and as *católico* as is the priest himself. They do not look objectively upon their Catholic forms of worship as they do in the case of Protestantism,[7] since they make little or no distinction between the Catholic and native elements in

---

[7] The Society of Friends (Quaker) of California has operated its mission and school in Chiquimula since around 1906 and has set up more or less permanent missions in the other pueblos of the department. Until 1933 they had made no converts among the Indians and had about decided to concentrate thereafter on the Ladinos, with whom they had had some success.

the religious system which they believe they have always had.[8]

The average Indian is much more religious-minded and proclerical than is the average Ladino. The latter, except in Quetzaltepeque, seem to be anticlerical and refuse to support local priests in their *municipios*. They believe religion to be good in the abstract but fear the church organization and refuse to turn their children over to it. The priests are disliked by many of the Ladinos as being money-grabbers, immoral perons, and economically useless members of society. This dislike is accompanied by many stories which seem to be known to everyone.[9] Quetzaltepeque *municipio* is extremely Catholic; there every day all the school children march in a procession from school to the church for an hour or so of religious instruction from the priest, much to the disgust of the Ladinos of neighboring *municipios*. The Quetzaltepeque Ladinos seem to have none of the antichurch attitude and dislike of priests which is so marked in Jocotán and Olopa.[10] This antichurch attitude, however, does not extend to the Indians. They accept the little church organization which eastern Guatemala offers them and are not critical of it. They are said by the Jocotán and Olopa Ladinos, who consider it a sign of backwardness, to be the only real Catholics in the region. The Jocotán church seems to be used almost entire-

[8] Cf. Thompson, 1930, p. 56.

[9] These are told with a mixture of disgust and relish. The priests are said to persuade rich widows and dying persons to leave their property to the church (meaning to the priests), to seduce young girls, and to have affairs with married women; they are said to have houses full of wines and valuables, to be extremely rich, and to wax fat as parasites while everyone else has to work.

[10] In each of the pueblos there are one or two families known to be strongly Catholic, referred to slightingly as being *muy católico*. The Quetzaltepeque priest is forced to put up at their houses during his infrequent visits to these pueblo churches.

ly by the Indians and is thought of by the Ladinos as primarily an Indian place of worship.

The religious life of the Indians centers around the Catholic churches and *cofradías* in the pueblos and around the ceremonial houses and sacred spots in the *aldeas*. Only the Quetzaltepeque and Esquipulas churches have permanent Catholic priests. The Quetzaltepeque priest travels by muleback to Jocotán and neighboring pueblos for all the important festivals and performs services in his own church regularly. The other pueblo churches have had priests stationed at them from time to time, but they soon had to leave, as too few of the Ladinos would contribute to the priests' upkeep and the Indians were too poor to contribute much. Each of these churches is therefore placed in the charge of local Indian *mayordomos*, who keep the building in some repair, collect contributions to the saints, and toll the bells.

The most important native religious specialist is the *padrino*. Almost any old man who is much respected in his community and whose moral life is acceptable can consider himself and be considered a *padrino*. The *padrinos*, including the rain-makers, the "captain," and the *mayordomos* are the leaders of all the community religious activity, as only they know how to recite the prayers and perform the ceremonies. They are distinct from the sorcerers, curers, and diviners, who are endowed with a knowledge and power all their own, although the Indians are inclined to consider any person with esoteric knowledge and power as a *padrino*. In a strict sense, therefore, the *padrino* is the religious specialist, and in a loose sense he is what the Indians call a "wise man" (Sp. *sabio*). Other religious specialists are the prayer-makers, dancers, and musicians.

There are several types of *padrinos*. Those in charge of

the rain-making ceremonies are the most important.[11]   It is their principal duty to bring on the rain at the end of the dry season in April as well as to check it during the year when there is too much.   These *padrinos* are the only individuals who "have permission" from God and the native deities to perform the rain-making ceremonies, the agricultural ceremonies, and the transition rites, and only they know how to conduct them.   The Catholic priest is said not to have this permission and must confine himself to purely church matters.   They are considered good people, since without their services the rainy season could not be brought on or cloudbursts stopped, and individuals could not properly and safely pass through their transition periods.   They have great influence and prestige, which sometimes spreads over a wide area.   One of the *padrinos* of Tunucó, for example, is known even to the Ladinos in the city of Chiquimula.   They seem to be more respected and feared than loved, since most exhibit signs of slight insanity and many suffer from delusions of grandeur.   Each seems certain that only he knows how to produce the rain or check it and that most of the other *padrinos* are sheer frauds and liars.   If he is old, he usually has worked out for himself a secret formula and procedure and believes that his variation is the vital part of the ceremony.   There does not seem to be any important difference, however, among these formulas.   Their wives[12] assist them in some of their

[11] These are called *hor tca˙n*, or *ah hor tca˙n*, and in Indian-Spanish, *horchán* (*los horchanes*, "the wise men").   The derivation of the Chorti name is not certain.   It may be *hor*, "head chief," and *tca'n*, "ceremony," or *ha'*, "water," "rain," *or*, "head," "chief," and *tca˙n*, "ceremony."   *hor tca˙n* usually refers to the rain-making ceremony ("chief ceremony"), and *ah hor tca˙n*, to the *padrino* who directs it.   The Spanish name is *padrino de agua* ("*padrino* of water," "rain").

[12] "The *padrino*'s wife" (Sp. *la horchana, la padrina de agua*).

work, although no women take any actual part in the ceremonies.

The most important individual *padrino* in the *municipio* is one known as the captain,[13] whose duty it is to care for the pueblo saint throughout the year of his captaincy. He is either elected or appointed each year on the saint's day and serves for the year following. In Jocotán and Olopa *municipios* he is appointed by either the Catholic priest or the alcalde and is merely the chief of the church *mayordomos*, described below. In Quetzaltepeque he is elected at a meeting of the local *padrinos* from among their own number and is in every respect the chief *padrino* of his *municipio*. In that pueblo on December 19, which is the saint's day, all the Indians meet at the *cofradía* to elect their captain. They feast for a day and a night on *chilate*, cacao, and *tortillas* and drink a great deal of *chicha*. These foods are prepared by the women at the fireplace and in the large boiling ovens in the courtyard. During the day the *padrinos* meet in the sleeping-house to choose a captain. The man chosen is one who is greatly respected by everyone, and his position is considered the highest the Indians can bestow. The captain has his own houses and milpas as other Indians do, but other Indians do most of his work for him. They come in groups to plant, tend, and harvest his crops, and after the harvest they bring him quantities of maize, beans, vegetables, and other foods. His house is said to be always filled with food and other gifts, so that he and his wife maintain the highest Indian standard of living. If no *padrino* wishes to accept the office on the saint's day, the old one continues as captain for the year following. In some cases the same captain continues for five or six consecutive years.

[13] *u wink-ir e santo*, "the guardian of the saint" (Sp. *el capitán*).

In Quetzaltepeque the captain is required to set up an effigy of the patron saint in his altar-house during his year in office, to decorate his altar with flowers, maize, beans, many varieties of vegetables, and colored crepe paper, and in general to venerate the saint throughout the year. Indians come from all over the *municipio* to his house to offer their prayers to the saint and to make requests of him. The captain accepts contributions from these pilgrims, a peso or two from each, and directs them in any of his milpa work they are willing to do. He saves the contributions to pay the expenses of the festival at the end of his term.[14] He is supposed not to have sexual intercourse with his wife (Sp. *la capitana*) during his year in office, as this is considered harmful to any rain-making ceremonies he may perform. During the year his wife must not go out beyond her husband's houses and milpas, although this rule is not always observed. One of her chief duties is to sprinkle the floors of her houses with water every day during the year, and especially when rain is desired, as this is believed to bring on the rain and to keep it coming.

The *padrinos* who serve as keepers of the churches are called *mayordomos*[15] and are nominally in charge of the church between the rare visits of the priest. There are four of them, presumably appointed by the priest, although the alcaldes seem to make the final choices. Each serves one week of each month and holds his position for life, or as long as he wishes. Most of them are versed in the Catholic

[14] The Ladinos and many of the Indians say that captains are placed in charge of the saint because of the fact that the priest and *mayordomos* would steal the contributions. The captains are considered honest people who might not steal, although it is agreed that they probably steal a little. The captains put the money out at interest, thus offsetting somewhat the expense incurred by their position.

[15] *u wink-ir e tekpan*, "guardian of the church."

prayers and are considered wise men by the Indians. Their pay consists of what they can earn from the sale of candle stubs which have been blessed by being burned before the patron saint and the Virgin, to be used medicinally by the Indians, and, according to the Ladinos, also of as much of the Indian contributions to the saints as they can withhold from the priest. They never conduct mass, although they assist the priest when he is present, and at all other times they have charge of the church building, keep in their possession the masks, costumes, and other paraphernalia used in the festival dances, and repair them. Each *mayordomo* during his week's stay at the church lives in the *cofradía* building.

A class of *padrinos*, called drought-makers,[16] are considered bad and malicious and are extremely feared and hated. It is believed that they deliberately prevent the advent of the rainy season in May, produce droughts at various times during the year, and cause the crops to wither and die. Sorcerers sometimes do these things, but the drought-makers are said to do nothing else and are looked upon as being *padrinos* with antisocial tendencies. They live to themselves and, like the sorcerers, are given to queer and abnormal practices, such as visiting graves, wandering around at night, muttering to themselves, etc. Although many *padrinos*, especially the older and more eccentric ones, are known or suspected to be drought-makers, without exception they strongly deny it.[17] In the rain-making ceremony in April, God and the native deities are especially requested to permit no drought-makers to destroy the cere-

[16] Called in Chorti *ah hor q'in* (*q'in*, "sun," "drought," "dry season"), and in Indian-Spanish, *horquín* (*los horquines*, "the drought-makers"). The Spanish name is *padrino de verano* (*verano*, "summer," "drought").

[17] For this reason it was impossible to get any but hearsay information concerning them.

mony and thus stop the rains. They are often said to be hired by a number of families of one *aldea* to produce a drought in another, so that late in the year the families of the latter will have to buy maize from the former when the price is high.[18] The drought-makers seem to have no other function in the social life of the Indians than to act as convenient scapegoats when the ceremonies of the rain-making *padrinos* are unsuccessful.

The prayer-makers[19] are usually women who have learned the Catholic prayers from a priest or other prayer-maker and are employed to recite them during novenas. They are usually paid in food, receiving a greater share of the feast than any of the invited guests. Many of the prayer-makers are the wives of *padrinos* and are thought to possess a certain power and knowledge because of association with their husbands.

The dancers[20] are employed in the pueblos during the patron-saint festivals. They are all men and work in groups, since each dance requires a team. Each pueblo has its own dancing group who live in *aldeas* near by. There are about ten men who regularly perform the dances at

[18] A drought-maker's work was suspected in the latter part of May, 1932, in Tunucó. The rain was already a month late, and the planting seemed to be destroyed. The Indians suspected an old *padrino* living in Camotán as being the drought-maker responsible. They petitioned the alcalde of Jocotán to arrest him, but the alcalde scoffed at their beliefs. Finally, he had to arrest the man to prevent the Indians from killing him. He was brought to the Jocotán jail, where he denied that he had been making drought, but named two other *padrinos* as suspects. In his shoulder bag was found a quantity of copal gum, candle stubs, long vegetable spines, and other objects ordinarily used in black magic, and the Indians considered this as proof of the old man's guilt. The Ladino alcalde, not entirely emancipated from Indian ways of thinking, at last agreed with them, and threatened the Indian with punishment if he continued to make drought. His employers, if any, were never found out.

[19] *ah q'aht* (*q'aht-i*, "to ask," "to beg," "to pray for"); Sp. *rogador*.

[20] *ah akut* (pronounced *ah kut; akut*, "a dance"; *akt-a*, "to dance"); Sp. *bailador*.

Jocotán, and about five others who are trained to serve as substitutes. This number includes the trainer, the man who acts as director, and the musician who plays the marimba and *tun*. They are paid only in food, which is given them for the duration of the festival. The trainer sometimes acts as prompter during the dances. The place is held on the team for life, and each man trains one or two of his sons who will some day take his place. The musicians, all men, are hired to play during many religious ceremonies and often play for secular dances. They usually play in groups of three or four, although for secular dances only one may be asked by the family to come because of the expense. They are usually given large quantities of food to take home. The best known of the musicians are those who play the flute, *tun*, and marimba, and these are especially desired at festivals, saints' vigils, and transition rites. Each *municipio* has a band of musicians who are regularly called upon to play during the four-day celebration of the festival.

The religious paraphernalia seem to have a degree of sacredness and are mostly treated as sacred objects, although some of them are also put to secular use. The ceremonial musical instruments are the *tun*, *teponagua*, marimba, trumpet, rattler, and *sonanza*. Each church owns its set of these instruments, and they are used for all important ceremonies and festivals. Only the professional musicians are allowed to use them, and they are kept at all times in the *cofradía* by the *mayordomos*. The *tuns* are very scarce, as only the Jocotán and Quetzaltepeque churches have them, but it is said that formerly they were owned by every church. A great deal of mystery surrounds them, and stories are told of the miraculous appearance of each instrument in the past. They are said to be so old that no one knows who carved them or of what wood they are made. The *teponagua*, resembling the *tun* but much larger, is not considered so necessary for ceremonies, receives less care, and has no sacred origin. Each church has one dilapidated marimba which is brought out during festivals and played by a single musician in front of the church, usually in accompaniment to the dances.[21] The other ceremonial instruments are much less used. The Indians use violins, guitars, and accordions, but only for secular occasions.

The masks used in the festival dances are used only by the professional dancers. They are never lent to anyone, and it is said that they must not go outside the *municipio*. All are carved from wood, and most are painted a pasty white. They are all old, no one knowing their age, and the Indians say they have always had them. It is said that new ones could not be made, as no one knows how to carve them, and, further, new masks would not be suitable for the dances. Both the crowns and the masks are considered nonduplicable. The former are tall hats elaborately built, containing much colored crepe paper and a small bell in the center. The saint-carrier is a long raftlike litter[22] made of limbs and boards and is used only for transporting the patron saints in processions around the plaza and through the pueblo streets. It is carried by four men, one at each

[21] It is about four feet long and three high, and its tone is bad and distinctly unmusical. It is inferior in every way to the fine marimbas used in Jocotán and Chiquimula by the Ladino marimba players.

[22] Made of two long limbs, each nine or ten feet long, and six or seven smaller limbs which serve as the crosspieces. The former are about two feet apart, with the latter tied on at right angles to them, and about a foot apart. The ends of the long limbs extend outward from the carrier about three feet at each end and are used as handles by the four men who carry it. Some of these carriers are covered on the upper side with cedar boards. The same type of litter is used for transporting the corpse from the house to the grave at burial (see p. 304).

corner, with the images stood up on its center. Jocotán has
two of these, usually stored in one corner of the church.

Candles are used for all ceremonies; black and gray ones
for native ceremonies and white ones for all transition rites
and ceremonies connected with the church. They vary
from a few inches to about two feet in length, the largest
being two inches in diameter. The women candle-makers
group themselves at the church door on market and festival days and do a thriving business with Indians who enter
to burn candles before the saints. It is said that the saints
are pleased to have candles burned before them and that
candles are a form of sacrifice, corresponding to the copal
"money" which is sacrificed in many ceremonies. The
stubs of candles burned in the church are used medicinally
and in family religious ceremonies. The Indians steal these
or burn their own for such purposes. In the latter case the
candle is burned for a few moments before the patron saint
or Virgin, snuffed out, and carefully wrapped in a cloth.
These are considered of greater power than unblessed candles and are especially used in ceremonies to the family
saints. The *mayordomos* make a business of selling candle
stubs thus sacralized. Water, taken from a sacred spring
or river, and from the church font by the pueblo Indians,
is used in most of the agricultural ceremonies, in the dedication of new houses, and in some of the transition rites.
Sacred water[23] is believed to drive out evil spirits and
sickness and to protect a person, object, or place from all
harm.

Incense burners may be used only by the *padrinos* or
the male head of the family who owns them. They are
seldom taken out of the altar-house, and, when one is
dropped or broken, it is mended carefully with copal gum,

[23] *uh ha'* (Sp. *agua bendita*).

since a new one would require a long time to become as sacred as the old one. The new ones sold in the markets are not sacred but become so only after many months of use on an altar. Copal is burned in them as an incense during all ceremonies, and when used they are not swung in the hands but merely rest on the altar table or floor. Most are without decoration, but a few have human heads molded to their crowns. These seem to have no significance, however.

Stone axes are often kept on altars because they are believed to have some sacred value. They are about three inches long and two wide, with a sharp edge and blunt head but contain no performation for a handle. The Indians claim them to be ancient, and they appear to be. They are said to be the same as those used by the Working Men for beating the clouds into rain and to have been thrown by them at a Chicchan to punish the latter for some misdeed.[24] Flint has some of the sacred quality, as it is associated with the rain-making deities, who strike lightning from it, and pieces of it are kept on altars. These are usually unshaped, but a few are crude arrow points, probably ancient.[25]

The altar is set up in the family houses, in the *aldea* ceremonial houses, and in the pueblo *cofradías*. Each family, if not too poor, has its ceremonial altar, usually in

[24] See p. 396.

[25] These axes are called "cloud stone." Flint is also called "cloud stone," as well as "fire stone." Wherever lightning strikes, a stone ax is believed to be buried in the ground, as the lightning was caused by the swift passage of the ax through the air. A number of Indians own such polished axes, all said to have been found where lightning had struck. Juan Hernandez, an informant of Tunucó, has one which he says he found in the courtyard of the Jocotán church a few years ago, just after lightning had struck and demolished the bell tower.

one of the sleeping-houses, set up always at the end opposite the door.[26] Four stalks of large cane, each seven or eight feet high and with leaves attached, are set up permanently in the floor in a square or rectangle, about four by six feet in area. Their tops are tied together to form two arches which spread across from the sides of the altar. The four stalks are said to represent and to inclose a milpa, or the world, while the arches are the overspreading sky. Sometimes six stalks are used, three on each side.[27] A table, sometimes movable but usually built in like a bed, is placed in the center under the arches and is used as a repository for the saints and their cases, the offerings of *atol, chilate*, maize, beans, and other foods offered to the saints and native deities during ceremonies, and the incense burners. A lighted candle stands at each corner of it. The altar framework is built somewhat like a house and is sometimes referred to as a house.[28] Its two crosses usually stand behind it, tied with liana to the altar framework. It usually has four drums hanging on a wall near by, a large and small one for St. Manuel and a large and small one for the Virgin. The altar is used only by the family who owns it. The altar of the *aldea* ceremonial house is similar to the family one, except that it has no saint and is used only by the *padrinos* for the rain-making and Day of the Dead ceremonies. The altars in the *cofradías* do not differ fundamentally but are much more elaborate and are kept decorated by the *mayordomos*

[26] See La Farge, 1927, p. 12.

[27] This much of the altar is similar to the temporary one set up in the sleeping-house after death for the funeral ceremony (see p. 305). The altar is called "saint's table."

[28] The altar in Yucatan resembles a house and contains the same arches above it (Redfield and Villa, 1934, p. 131).

through the year. That at Quetzaltepeque is the best example in the entire region.[29]

The wealthier Indians have special altar-houses, in which only the altar and saints are kept. These are built like any sleeping-house and are kept closed and darkened at all times. During ceremonies it is supposed to be entered only by the men, although at other times it is used by everybody and seems to have little more sacredness than any other house. The women usually do not work in it, however. Sick persons, and especially menstruating women, must avoid entering it. Most of the larger *aldeas* have a ceremonial house, the construction of which is like that of any house, consisting usually of a sleeping-house and kitchen. The former is the actual ceremonial house, while the latter is used by the women for cooking food during ceremonies. Like any altar-house, it is somewhat sacred during ceremonies but does not seem to be so at other times. Women and individuals sick with magical disease, however, are not supposed to enter it at any time. It is kept locked when not being used.

[29] Its table is set up in the ground like that of the family altar and covered with a bed covering of thin reeds. A sedge mat is laid over this to provide a smooth surface. A mat made of carrizo bark hangs behind it as a backdrop. Along the ceiling, and extending to five or six feet in front of the altar table, carrizo stalks are tied horizontally to one another to form a lattice work, which covers the whole structure. It is usually covered over with a sedge mat. On the floor stand four large wooden candle-holders, one at each corner of the altar, in which large candles are burned during ceremonies. In the center of the table stand the black image of St. Francis, the Conqueror, and a doll representing the Virgin. The whole altar is entwined and covered with flowers, pine needles, *conte*, maize, and banana leaves, and many species of vines. The saints can hardly be seen for the plants around them. Ears of maize, fruits, and vegetables are suspended from the covering above and laid on the floor in front of the altar at all times, and especially during any ceremony. Beneath the altar, on the floor, is a small wooden canoe filled with water, in which four frogs are kept alive the year round by being fed a plant called *parpar*. One candle burns on the table, just in front of the saints, and is said to be kept burning day and night throughout the year. Between ceremonies the room is kept closed and darkened.

The *cofradía* is found only in the pueblos and is used in connection with festivals. The *mayordomos* live in it during their period of service at the church and use it as a storage-house for the festival paraphernalia. On festival days the Indians bring their contributions of maize to this house, and the women grind it and cook it into foods, especially *chilate* and *tortillas*, which are often given gratis to those who attend the festival.[30] The house is usually built at the edge of the pueblo, near some important trail which leads to large outlying *aldeas*. It is built like any other house but is much larger and has a large courtyard, since on important festivals many hundreds of Indians congregate around it. In the courtyard stands a clay oven, used for boiling the *chilate* served to the Indians on festival days.[31] The *cofradías* usually contain an altar, and those at Jocotán and Quetzaltepeque have separate images of the patron saints. The Quetzaltepeque *cofradía* is the most elaborate among the Indians. In the rear stands the altar with the saint, and around it, on the floor, are four large candle-holders made of wood or pottery, each with three sprawling legs. Directly in front of the altar is a large table with four chairs set up to it, and in front of each chair, lying on the table, is a gourd filled with *chilate* and covered over with a cloth. A fifth gourd of *chilate* is in the center of the table. The *chilate* is never touched but serves as a food for the saint and the four rain deities,[32] the center gourd being that of the saint. The room remains thus

[30] During the years when the crops are poor, however, only the dancers and musicians are fed gratis.

[31] It has solid walls all around, except for a small opening in front for the insertion of firewood, and contains a large flat-bottomed olla (Fig. 5, E [p. 133]).

[32] See below, pp. 392–95.

throughout the year and is kept darkened between ceremonies.

Each of the seven pueblos of the Chorti-speaking area[33]
contains its one church[34] which serves as the religious center for the *municipio* in which it is located and as the seat
of the *municipio* patron saint. Most seem to be of about
the same age, having probably been built during the seventeenth century. The Camotán church may be of eight-
eenth-century style of construction, and those of Olopa
and Copan seem even later. Only the Quetzaltepeque and
Esquipulas churches are kept in any semblance of repair
and used for regular mass, since only these two churches
have permanent priests. The churches of the other pueblos
are used as little more than storehouses for saints' images
and certain religious equipment. Each church faces west,
with the altar at the east end. Its side walls are divided
into areas, each ten to fifteen feet long, and in each stands
a saint's image upon a high foundation. These areas are
said to belong to the saints who occupy them. The patron
saint and his consort, the Virgin, occupy the principal and
largest area, usually near the altar. A few benches are at
the east end, in front of the altar, while the west or front
end is empty except for stored articles which the *mayordomos*, the alcalde, or the military *comandante* have
brought in to keep out of the rain.[35]

The sacred food plants are used as a sacrifice to a deity,
either as a food for him to eat or as a "payment" to him

[33] Jocotán, Camotán, La Unión, San Juan Hermita, Olopa, Quetzaltepeque,
Esquipulas, and Copan. The Chiquimula church is the largest in the department.

[34] Ch. *tekpan* (derivation unknown).

[35] The churches are nominally owned and controlled by the Catholic church
of Guatemala, but each pueblo considers its church and religious equipment to
be pueblo property, so that the alcaldes actually control them.

THE CHURCH DOOR IN JOCOTAN ON SUNDAY MORNING

The beggar with the stick is praying for alms as the man at the right reaches in his money bag for a peso to give him. The seated women are candle-sellers.

for his favors, and as a special food to be eaten by the participants at any ceremony or festival. Maize is eaten ceremonially and offered as a sacrificial food. *Chilate* and *atol*, gruels made from maize, are both eaten and sacrificed. Cacao, another sacred food, is often mixed with *chilate* and frothed with a chocolate beater to be drunk. It is also mixed with maize, frothed, and drunk ceremonially, although it is never offered as a ceremonial food. Coffee seems to have taken on some of this sacredness but not to a great extent. Beans are mixed with ground maize and made into *tortillas*, which are eaten on most ceremonial occasions. Pumpkins and pumpkin seed are especially eaten on the Day of the Dead.

The principal sacred nonfood plants are used as sacrifices and for manufacturing and adorning sacred objects. Pine needles are used during festivals to adorn altars, ceremonial houses, and sacred objects of every kind and are sprinkled over the floors of houses and scattered on the ground around crosses. Graves are often covered with them on religious days. Carrizo cane is much used in making altars. Copal gum is one of the most sacred of substances. Its fumes cure any form of sickness and serve, because of their odor, as a sacrifice to the deities. Copal is often made in the form of another sacred object, especially maize ears, and thus used as a sacrifice; made into round pellets called "pesos," it is offered as a ceremonial payment for the favors asked of the deities.[36] The *jiote* tree is used as the

[36] It is possible that copal pellets, along with cacao beans, served as an actual medium of exchange in the past, its use and value as a money being preserved only ceremonially at the present time. None of the Indians had any knowledge or opinions about this, but the informants stated that, while the silver pesos were the money used "for paying people" (*tua' u-t'oy-i e winik-op'*), the copal "pesos" were the money used "for paying God and his helpers" (*tua' u-t'oy-i e ka tata' up'-an u tak-r-en-op'*).

upright piece in many crosses, and the *conte* vine, the leaves of which are roughly in the shape of the cross, are used to adorn all sacred objects, especially crosses and altars. Almost every flowering plant is used by the Indians for decorating sacred objects and places. These are laid on in great profusion, as each Indian leaves his bundle of flowers as a votive offering.[37]

Of the sacred animals, turkeys, chickens, and the eggs of both are most used ceremonially. Cooked fowls are exchanged as gifts at transition rites, and the flesh and blood of uncooked ones are offered as a sacrifice in the rain-making and agricultural ceremonies. Many of the Indians say that only turkeys should be used for the latter purpose and that they should not be eaten secularly. Turkeys and chickens are used by the specialists in divining and curing disease. Deer are considered especially important animals and are never hunted without first making sacrificial payment to the deer-god. The snake has great symbolic value, since actual snakes are somewhat equivalent to the snake deity of rain, Chicchan.[38] It is said that after a rain more snakes than usual are to be seen, being Chicchans who have come out of the earth to produce the rain, while during the dry season they are scarcely seen at all, since during that time the Chicchans are living inside the hills. The Indians greatly fear all snakes, especially poisonous ones.[39]

[37] Important plants thus used are the *platanillo, flor de muerto, flor de la cruz, rosa de Santa María, chiche, chilmecate, peine de mico,* virgin bud, *palo de Mayo, flor de Mayo, hierba del pollo,* orchid, *cundeamor, hoja colorada, hoja verde,* and the *chichicuilote* palm.

[38] See p. 394.

[39] Women are afraid to defecate at night without a torch to light up the spot, since they believe a snake may enter the rectum and cause violent illness. This is similar to the belief concerning the salamander in Mexico.

The frog also is vaguely associated with water and rain, although it is not personified. The owl is associated with death and certain forms of sorcery. Oxen and bulls are not sacred animals, although their economic importance seems to be recognized.[40]

[40] It is said that on Ascension Thursday (forty days after Easter) one must not work oxen or bulls for the reason that in ancient times a man worked his ox on this day, and the ox said to him, "Let us not work today, but tomorrow; this day is a festival," (*iri ka-patn-a sahmi pero ehk'ar ce q'in ira xa' c in-te' noh q'in*).

CHAPTER XVI

THE SUPERNATURAL AND SACRED

SUPERNATURAL BEINGS

THE sacra in Chorti religious life and ideology consist of supernatural beings, including saints and associated crosses, and of sacred places and concepts. The sacred places, including topographical features and places where rituals are performed, etc., and the sacred concepts such as directions, numbers, animals, etc., are associated in many cases with supernatural beings. These will be discussed separately.

The supernatural beings are classified into six groups, the first of which is the Christian God, the chief of all. The second group are all the beneficial native deities (*yum*), now referred to as God's helpers, who take orders from him. These native deities still perform their original duties but are now directed by God, who is their overlord. The third group are the patrons (*tcur, yum*). These are the patron saints of the pueblos and families, as well as the patron deities of esoteric professionals, and are referred to as the "helpers" of the social groups they represent. The fourth group may be called guardians (*wink-ir*). They are the protectors of the various natural phenomena with which they are associated and seem to differ from the patrons mostly in that they are not helpful to man. The saints and crosses, of course, are powers falling into the third and fourth classes, but not all patrons and guardians are saints. The fifth group are the apparitions (Sp. *espanto;* Ch. *p'ahq' ut*), who are primarily evil beings who frighten evildoers into good behavior. The sixth group are the spirits (Sp. *espíritu;* Ch. *mein*). These are passive beings and seem to represent the essence of the persons, animals, plants, and natural phenomena with which they are associated.

The beings associated with agriculture and its attendant earth and sky phenomena are by far the most important. Field and garden culture, and especially the cultivation of maize, is the one important occupation at which every Indian must work,[1] so that the group of deities who are responsible for the fertilization of plant life, the enrichment of the soil, and the coming of rain are the most thought of and propitiated.

The Indians believe that each supernatural being belongs primarily to only one of the six groups but that any of them might assume at times any of the other five roles. Thus, the apparitions not only frighten people at night but also are spirits in that they represent natural phenomena. Similarly, the passive maize spirit is closely identified with the active earth-god, and even the rain deities are said at times to assume the role of apparitions.

The following list of supernaturals includes all except the saints and crosses, which are described in the following chapters.

The Christian God[2] has no definite character or function, except that he is nominally the head of the pantheon. He is mentioned in all the prayers and is said to be the cause of all good in the world but is very little thought of as a personal agent who can directly influence man's affairs.[3]

---

[1] This was true for the ancient Maya as well (Gann and Thompson, 1935, p. 120; Thompson, 1927, p. 41).

[2] Ch. *ka tata'*, "Our Father" (Sp. *Dios, Nuestro Padre*). God is referred to as *e ka tata'* ("the Our Father"). The native name is no doubt a translation of the Spanish.

[3] Cf. La Farge, 1927, pp. 7–8; Sapper, 1925; and Thompson, 1930, p. 56.

He is addressed as the chief of all the deities, and all the
other deities, both native and Catholic, are referred to as
his "ministers" or his assistants. Christ,[4] as apart from
God, is an anthropomorphic being and is spoken of in
personal terms. He is mentioned in all the prayers and is
sometimes referred to as the creator of the world and,
therefore, as the chief of all the deities. He seems never to
be thought of, however, as a redeemer or savior of man-
kind, and the crucifixion story, although known, seems to
have little significance.[5] He is especially honored by the
Easter festival, which lasts for four days preceding Easter
Sunday, and during which time all the families protect
him from the "Jews," who are out to kill him at that time.[6]
Neither God nor Christ seems to have native counterparts.

The native deities include the Chicchans, the Working
Men, *ah katiyon*, the wind-gods, the gods of death and of
sleep, the native patron guardians, and the spirits of natural phenomena.

Chicchan[7] is the most important of the native deities

[4] *u y u'nen e ka tata'* (*u y u'nen*, "his son").

[5] A story is told of how Christ was pursued by the Jews, who intended to kill
him. He came to a stream where a woman was washing clothes. As he passed, he
cautioned her not to tell the Jews which direction he took. She betrayed him,
with the result that he was captured and killed. Afterward, Christ came back to
earth and punished her by changing her into a magpie, "because she talked all
the time." The present magpie is the descendant of this woman, and gossipy old
women are called magpies in both languages.

[6] To the Indians, the Jews are no more than a mythical people who are believed long ago to have killed Christ. Although some of them know vaguely that
there are "Judíos" living today, they do not seem to feel that the ancient and
modern Jews are the same people, and many seemed surprised that a Jewish
people still existed. The mythical Jews are, of course, considered by the Indians
to be the most evil of people.

[7] Sp. "King Serpent"; Ch. *ah tcix tcan* (*tcan*, "snake"). The meaning of *tcix*
is not clear. It can mean fiber, or fibrous, in which case the notion of "feathered"

and is generally thought of as a giant snake, although this form has many modifications. He may have the giant form of an ordinary snake; or his upper body may be that of a man while his lower body is that of a feathered snake; or he may be a gigantic man appearing like a snake to people. He is sometimes said to have four horns on his head, two small ones in front and two large ones at the back, the former having the luster of gold. The female[8] is said to be a fish in the lower body and a woman in the upper. All the Chicchans, however, are primarily thought of as giant snakes, resembling actual snakes. They are sometimes males with female consorts, at other times male or female only, depending upon the particular phenomenon of the earth or sky which they embody or represent. They are both one and innumerable, being said to exist not only singly in certain localities but everywhere at once.[9]

The sky Chicchans, who produce most of the sky phenomena, are four in number, each living in one of the four world-directions at the bottom of a large lake.[10] The one at the north is the chief (*noh tcix tcan*), who gives orders to the other three, his assistants. According to another belief, a pair of both sexes is said to occupy each of the four directions, with a fifth pair, the chiefs, at the north. The

may be expressed, or it can be the stem which now means horse, but which may formerly have meant deer. Deer is now denoted solely as *masa'* (from the Nahuan) and never as *tcix*. Förstemann (p. 561) says *chic* (the first stem of *tcix tcan*) means great, and that it may be *chii*, "to sting," "to bite." If *tcix* ever meant "great" in Chorti, it would account for the term being applied to the horse, the largest animal the Indians ever saw. *tcix* might be related to *t'cix* or *t'ci'x* (from *t'ci'*, "to grow," "to increase"), thus meaning "abundance," "greatness."

[8] Usually called "Chicchan of the Great Water."

[9] Chicchan may be the equivalent of the ancient Maya *kukul can*.

[10] One lives in the Golfo Dulce near the northern town of Puerto Barrios, another in Lake Nonojá near Camotán, another in Lake Tuticopote near Olopa, and a fourth in Lake Guijá near El Salvador.

sky Chicchans are fused with four or five saints, Balthazar
being in the north, and Gabriel, Raphael, Michael, Peter,
Paul, and the Angel of Hope occupying the other directions. With the exception of Balthazar, the informants
could not agree on the saints' locations. The north Chicchan is the only one who has a native name, and he is
usually referred to by that name. Cloudbursts and violent
rainstorms are caused by the swift passage of a female
Chicchan across the sky, the impact of her body against
the clouds causing the water to fall. The rainbow is the
body of a Chicchan stretched across the sky. Thunder is
the shout of a Chicchan to his companions on the other
side of the horizon; the answers of the others cause continuous thunder.[11]

The earth Chicchans,[12] who produce earth phenomena,
are innumerable. One or many of them live in every body
of water, being its spirit or essence.[13] They live in streams
during the rainy season and in hills during the dry season
and are believed to inhabit the sea and all lakes the year
round. They also live in the ground under trees. Although
invisible, they are said to have some relation to actual
snakes. A dead snake found near a tree where lightning
has struck is said to be an earth Chicchan which had been
killed by a sky Chicchan. The earth Chicchans especially

[11] For this reason the deity is sometimes called *ah kirik-n-ar* (*kirik*, "thunder";
kirik-na, "to thunder").

[12] These are called merely *tcix tcan*, without the agentive prefix.

[13] Snakes are not killed if found near a stream or other body of water, since it
is feared that the actual snake may be the Chicchan who inhabits that body of
water, and if killed the latter would dry up, having lost its spirit. This rule is
said to be observed especially during the dry season, when all the streams and
small lakes are low. At Mitla is a belief that a two-horned snake, which lives in a
spring and falls out of the sky, sends flood, and that to kill the snake spirit of a
body of water will cause the latter to dry up (Parsons, 1936, pp. 223 and 333–34).

live at the bottom of lakes high in the mountains.[14] Since
springs are the sources of most of the streams, Chicchan
recedes up the streams as the dry season approaches, enters the springs, and lives during the dry season in the
hills from which the streams issue. As the rainy season
nears, he comes out of his hill and enters the streams, the
size of his body causing them to swell. If too many Chicchans swim down the streams at the same time, the latter
rise above their banks and floods result. If a Chicchan
crosses the land to get to another stream his long body,
winding around the sides of the hills, pushes down rocks
and earth, thus causing landslides. In his passage from
one stream to another, Chicchan destroys everything in his
path, and this is the cause of hurricanes.[15] As the rainy
season comes to an end, the streams gradually diminish,
which is a sign that Chicchan is leaving them, until finally
he enters the spring sources. Earthquakes are caused by
the movements of the Chicchans within the hills.[16] Thus,
the Chicchans are responsible for both the beneficial and
the harmful conditions of the earth and sky.

The Working Men[17] are a group of deities who are closely associated with the Chicchans in producing sky phenomena and are sometimes confused with them. They
belong only to the sky and are said to be giant men, but

[14] A principal locality is Lake Tuticopote, near the *aldea* of the same name. It
is said that this Chicchan has been seen by Indians, on clear days, swimming in
the lake. This is the only instance known in which a Chicchan, or any other
deity, has been claimed to be actually seen.

[15] After a hurricane the Indians say, "A Chicchan has passed."

[16] The shaking at the earth's surface indicates that the Chicchan is turning
in his sleep. If he turns completely over to lie on his other side, a violent earthquake results.

[17] Sp. *Angeles Trabajadores* ("Working Angels"); Ch. *ah patn-ar winik-op'*
(*patn-a*, "to work"; *winik-op'*, "men," "people").

there is no other description of them. They are four in number, one at each world-direction who acts as the "companion" of a Chicchan. Several informants thought them to be superior to the Chicchans, the latter acting as their assistants. The one at the north is the chief of the four. In producing rain, the earth Chicchans churn up the water of the streams, lakes, and sea, causing it to ascend to the sky in the form of clouds, and the Working Men then beat the water out of the clouds so that it will fall as rain. It is principally they who are called upon in the rain-making ceremony in April. The Working Men produce other phenomena as well. Lightning is sent by one of them to punish or kill an earth Chicchan.[18] They carry stone axes with which they kill Chicchans, and lightning is caused by the passage of one of their axes through the air. A spot struck by lightning, especially a tree, is said to have been hit by an ax to kill an earth Chicchan under it.[19] They also use their axes for beating the clouds into rain. They are responsible for the rain which comes in May and continues until about November; but, if rain is desired during the dry season, from November to May, a different group of four deities, the Younger Working Men,[20] are addressed in the ceremonies. These are said to resemble the Working Men but are subservient to them and are far less powerful. When rain is needed for the dry-season crops of beans and lowland maize, the regular rain-making ceremony is re-

[18] Since they cause lightning, the Working Men are sometimes called "Lightning-makers."

[19] Near such spots it is said that a dead snake can always be found, together with one of the axes, buried in the ground.

[20] Ch. *ah qu˙ m-ic winik-op'* (from *qu˙ m*, "egg"); Sp. *Angeles Menores* ("Minor Angels"). *qu˙ m-ic* refers to the smallest or last of a series of things, as the little finger, the youngest child of a family, etc.

peated and directed to these deities. *ah katiyon*[21] is closely associated with the Working Men and the Chicchans.
His identity and role is not clear, but he is sometimes dual
sexed, although usually a male only; he is both one and innumerable in number, lives in each of the four directions,
and assists in producing rain by beating the clouds.[22]

The wind-gods[23] are present in every movement of air
and so have no fixed locality. Their counterparts among
the saints are Peter, the chief, and Lawrence and Francis.
They ride on horseback, as their Spanish name indicates,
but this is of course a Spanish innovation. They are either
three in number or innumerable and are always male.
They are both beneficial and destructive. After the rain-
making ceremony, when the Working Men have beaten
the clouds into rain, the wind-gods carry the rain over the
world so that the maize can be planted, but after the planting they may, unless propitiated by the wind-god ceremony, destroy the young plants by bringing an *aigre* to
them which will cause them to wither and die. They blow
the first breath into newborn children, without which the
latter would die, and they reclaim the breath at death.
They are the bearers of sickness, since it is they who place
the *aigres* in the victim's body; but they also carry away
evil wind after the curer has extracted it from his patient.
They are actively propitiated to protect the young maize
plants from destruction, but in all their other relations
with man they seem to be completely impersonal.

[21] Derivation unknown; Sp. *Angel Príncito*.

[22] Some of the informants stated that each direction contained one of these
deities, one Working Man, one sky Chicchan, and a single Chicchan in the north
superior to all, thus making a total of thirteen sky deities.

[23] Sp. *Hombres de Caballo* ("Horsemen"); Ch. *ah yum ikar* (*yum*, "lord,"
"master"; *ikar*, "air," "wind").

Chamer,[24] the god of death, is both a giant male dressed in female's clothes and a male with a female consort, each dressed according to his sex, the male causing death to women, and the female, to men. Chamer is a skeleton, dressed in a white robe like that used to cover the corpse during the funeral ceremony; he carries a long weapon resembling a scythe, made of a wooden handle with a bone knife tied at one end. He is invisible to all except his intended victim; if the latter sees the deity very near, he may soon die, but if at a great distance, there is no immediate harm. During sickness Chamer stands watching at one end of the bed; if at the patient's head, the latter can be cured, but if at the feet, he is doomed to die, and no curer can save him.[25] The curer always asks of his patron deity where Chamer is standing in order to determine the possibility of a cure. At the moment of death Chamer strikes his victim in the heart with his knife, and this is the immediate cause of death. He is said to live wherever there is a grave and also to inhabit Catholic cemeteries. Since every individual is believed to have his appointed day to die, he is safe from Chamer during a sickness if that day has not arrived, and the deity must stand at his head; but if the day has arrived, the deity stands at his feet and strikes him at the last moment.

The god of sleep[26] is of dual sex, the male sending sleep to women, and the female, to men. He is innumerable and has no visible form. He sends normal sleep at night but plays an evil role as the assistant and companion of the

[24] *ah tcam-er* (*tcam-ai*, "to die"; *tcam-er*, "death"); Sp. *el dueño de los muertos, El Muerto.* The Maya equivalent is *Cimi* ("death"), which was an ancient day name.

[25] This may be a Spanish belief.

[26] *ah way-n-ix* (*way-an*, "to sleep"; *way-n-ix*, "sleep").

death-god. Since Chamer cannot bring death to an individual until the latter is asleep or in a coma, his companion puts the individual to sleep for him. Extreme day drowsiness is considered a sign that the sleep-god is trying to put his victim to sleep for this purpose. As long as an individual is awake, he is in no danger of death, except by accident or violence. Night drowsiness causes no fear, as the god of sleep is then performing his proper duty.

Besides the saints, the important patrons and guardians are the god of sun and light, the moon deity, the deer-god, and the god of remedies and *mer tcor*.

ah q'in[27] is the god of the sun and light, of knowledge, and of magical power and so is the patron of sorcerers, curers, and diviners. He has no known form and is both good and bad, depending upon whom he aids at any given time. The supernatural power which he confers upon the esoteric professionals is called *sahorin*,[28] and they possess it in the calves of their legs. They address their questions to the calf of the leg, and the sun-god answers them by a twitching of the calf muscles. It is said that the twitching is done by the *sahorin*, which is often referred to as if it were a spirit, and possibly the representative of the sun-god. The esoteric professionals are often referred to by this name, as well, and it is said that they "have *sahorin*." Another deity, *ah kilis*, is associated vaguely with the sun

[27] *q'in*, "to divine," "to predict"; Sp. *Padre Eterno, San Gregorio, Espíritu Santo*. The name *ah kin* was applied to both native and Catholic priests in Yucatan. Gann quotes Landa to the effect that *kin* was derived from Yuc. *kinyah*, "to divine" (Sp. *echar suertes*; Gann, 1916, p. 48).

[28] Derivation unknown, although *sa'*, or *sasa'* (probably *sas ha'*), is the brain, and *hor* is the head, or intelligence. It is called in local Spanish, *sahurín*, and the word may come from the Castillian *zahorí*. In Jacaltenango the diviner is called *zahorín* (La Farge and Byers, 1931, p. 153).

and is said to eat the latter when angry, thus causing the sun's eclipse.[29]

The moon deity[30] is the patroness of childbirth and also has some connection with plant growth. She is said to lose partially her powers of fecundity during an eclipse, for which reason women fear an elipse during pregnancy. All planting, except that of the first maize at the beginning of the rainy season, is started either four days before or four days after one of the moon's phases, preferably when it is waxing, so that the seeds will have the best chance of germination. All useful trees, especially fruit trees, are said to belong to her and to receive their productivity from her. In a vague way she is considered the female consort of the sun-god, and she lights the world at night "while her companion sleeps."

The deer-god[31] is the protector of wild animals, especially deer, and is the patron of deer-hunters. He is said to live in certain hills, a number of which are scattered over Jocotán and Olopa *municipios*.[32] He is dual sexed, the male being the protector of female deer, and the female, of male deer. Deer-hunters, before going out, always secure permission from him to take one of his animals, and

[29] Derivation of *kilis* is unknown. This deity is also called "Sun-eater." Several informants thought that this deity ate the moon also, thus causing its eclipse, but were not certain.

[30] *ka tu'*, "Our Mother"; *e ka tu'*, "the moon," "the moon-goddess." The original Chorti name for the moon, *ux*, or *uh*, which appears in Juan Galindo's Chorti list, is not known or used. The moon deity is sometimes referred to as *Nuestra Señora*, and as the "Queen of the World," being identified with the Virgin.

[31] *ah wink-ir masa'* (*wink-ir*, "headman," "guardian"; *masa'*, "deer"); Sp. *el dueño de los venados*.

[32] One of the best known of these is called *tcur is t'ca'n* ("guard of the sweet potato vine"?), a few miles south of the *aldea* of Tunucó. This is also an abode of Chicchan.

they find out from him where deer are likely to be found. He is considered the owner of the animals and is responsible for their perpetuation.

The god of remedies,[33] who is the patron of herbalists, is said to own all wild and cultivated medicinal herbs and is angered if anyone wastes his remedies or uses them improperly. He is dual sexed, the male being responsible for the curing of women, and his female counterpart, for the curing of men. No ceremony, beyond the calling of his name by the herbalist or curer when treating a patient, is performed to this deity. He seems principally to be connected with wild medicinal plants and is responsible for their perpetuation and curative properties.

mer tcor[34] is said to be the special guardian of the milpas, and in this role he is somewhat confused with the earth-god, St. Manuel. He is said to be dual sexed and to live in the west, but nothing else is known of his function.

Every person, animal, and plant has a spirit, *u mein* ("its spirit"), which seems to represent its essential character, and possibly its life-principle.[35] Sleep is interpreted to mean that an individual's *mein* has left his body temporarily and is wandering around, dreams representing the experiences of one's *mein* while he is asleep.[36] Among the plants, only the spirits of maize and beans have known names, although every type of plant and animal is believed

---

[33] *ah wink-ir t'sak-ar* (*t'sak, t'sak-ar*, "remedy," "remedial plant"), or *ah wink-ir q'opot*; Sp. *el dueño del monte*. His saint name is San Antonio del Monte. At Mitla he is called San Antonio del Mundo (Parsons, 1936, p. 205).

[34] *mer*, meaning unknown; *tcor*, "milpa." This name may be Spanish *Merchór*, or *Melchór*, as the deity is sometimes called St. Merchór.

[35] The term refers also to the shadow cast by anything, since the shadow is vaguely believed to be equivalent to the spirit and to be its visible form.

[36] If a sleeper dreams of meeting other people, it means that his spirit met the spirits of those others, who were also sleeping at the time.

to have its *mein*.[37]   The individual's soul (Sp. *alma*) is called *p'ican*,[38] which is probably no more than the life-principle, since the Indians believe that it ceases to exist after death.[39]

The earth-god, *ihp'en*, is the native personification of the earth, the soil, plant growth, and riches and property in general. He is the special protector of families and their possessions, and his earthly form seems to be that of the family saints, who are usually Manuel and the Virgin.[40] He is both male and female, and it is the union of this pair which brings about the birth, or sprouting, of the cultivated plants, which are said to be their offspring.[41] Sacrifices of maize to the two earth-gods are buried in the milpas in the earth-god ceremony. *ihp'en*, as the passive spirit of maize, is said to be a single being and of male sex only. In this role he is the male consort of the female spirit of beans, *icq'anan*.[42] The deification of maize and beans in-

---

[37] The latter are referred to by general names, as *u mein ka kakau'* ("the spirit of our cacao"), *u mein ka un* ("the spirit of our avocados"), etc. The informants were not certain that post-Conquest animals and plants had spirits but believed they probably did.

[38] *p'ic*, "awake," "alive," "conscious." *p'ican* also refers to the pulse. The souls of the dead are called *pishan* in British Honduras (Gann, 1916, p. 40).

[39] The Indians have learned to speak of *la gloria* ("after-life," "eternity"), but there seems to be no association between this and the *p'ican*.

[40] The derivation of the Chorti name is unknown, although it is similar to *tcuhp'en* ("fireplace," "kitchen"). He is also called *tulunta'*, or *Señor tulunta'*, the derivation of which is not certain. *lun* may be *lum*, or *rum* ("earth," "soil"), and *ta'*, "increase." *p'en*, or *pen*, has no independent meaning. Förstemann (p. 563) gives *ben* as a Maya day name and says it means "reed," "rush," or "straw." He lists *cahgben* as meaning "dried cornstalk" in Tzental. *p'en* appears as a suffix in seven or eight Chorti compounds.

[41] Taken together they are called *u wink-ir-op' ka rum*, "the guardians of our soil" (or earth).

[42] Probably *ic-*, "female," *q'an*, "yellow," and *a'n*, "spring maize"; thus, "female of the yellow maize." *u wink-ir*, "her man," "her protector" (Sp. *su hombre*); *u nocip'*, "her husband." *Kanan* ("ripe maize") is the ancient name for one of the Maya days (Förstemann, p. 560).

dicates the supreme importance of these two foodstuffs, and their union symbolizes the fact they are always to be found together in the diet.[43] *cicimai*[44] is an evil spirit which devours *ihp'en*, the male spirit of maize. It seems to be female and is probably a personification of the weevil, as the latter is the principal destructive pest in the storehouses. It is said that, when the maize spirit is eaten, the maize itself disappears. In the storage ceremony, performed to guard against the entrance of this spirit, the protectors of the storage-house are stacked with the ears of maize and enjoined to guard the maize against *cicimai*. They are four in number, called *qu·m-ic*, *matulin*, *pastor*, and *salvador*,[45] and are made of copal wax, each in the form and size of a maize ear and wrapped in a white cloth.[46]

The *itakai*[47] are the spirits of high mountains and live only in the virgin forests. They are giants but resemble men and live as men do, planting milpas, pressing cane, keeping animals, living in houses, and having communal life. They are said to live in a single pueblo, which is made up of all the mountains, each mountain being the house of an *itakai*. They seem to have no relations with man.

The spirit of the dead, called *cerp'ax*,[48] seems to repre-

[43] Maize and beans are the only plant foods thus personified, and venison is the only meat food personified.

[44] The derivation may be *ic-*, "female," *icim*, "maize," and *ai* (unknown). *cic* means to pry open and may be used in reference to the boring of the weevil.

[45] *qu·m-ic*, "young," "small" (see n. 20). *Matulin* seems to be Chorti, but its derivation is unknown. *Pastor* and *Salvador* are Spanish.

[46] All four taken together are called *ah qohq nar*, "Maize Guardians." They are referred to as "copal maize ears" (Sp. *mazorcas de copal*; Ch. *na·k' uht's-up*) and are said to be the same as ears of hard ripe maize, but they seem to have no other character.

[47] Derivation unknown. The name resembles *xtabay*, who are female apparitions in Yucatan (see n. 57).

[48] Derivation unknown. *cer* means to rip open, and *p'ax* may be equivalent to *p'ahn*, "the body," "the self."

sent the continued existence of the individual after death.
It hovers in the house of the deceased for eight days after
death and forever after remains in the locality where the
deceased lived in life, although there is a belief that the
spirits finally go somewhere to the west. On the last day of
the funeral ceremony, as well as on the Day of the Dead,
food is placed on a table in the kitchen and is left for a few
hours for the spirit of the deceased to eat. The spirits of
the recently dead are much feared, as they are believed to
appear to persons in their sleep, especially to those who
were enemies of the deceased, and to frighten them into
extreme illness. The Indians dislike dreaming of the recently dead, as this is said to be a sign that the dead person's spirit is establishing contact with them, possibly to
harm them. A nightmare is attributed to the appearance
of an enemy's spirit, either in human form or in the guise
of a terrifying animal. Such appearances are guarded
against by avoiding the use of a dead person's name for
some time after death and by referring to him in a kindly
way and with the affectionate terms *compadre* and *comadre*
as a means of mollifying and flattering his spirit.

The apparitions[49] have a double role. They personify all
evil which is caused by human agency, in which role they
supplement the evil aspect of the Chicchans, who are responsible for all impersonal harm in nature, and they seem
to be personifications of certain natural phenomena. As assistants to the Devil who do his work on earth, they
frighten people, especially drunkards and unfaithful husbands and wives, out of their immorality, and they are the
"nursery bogies" of disobedient children, thus serving as
the enforcers of the moral life. They are all extremely evil

[49] *p'ahq' ut* ("frightful face"), "apparition," "fright," "terror" (Sp. *los espantos*).

and horrible to look at, and the fear of meeting them alone and in secluded spots is said to induce good behavior. They live in dark, mysterious localities, far from human habitation, and go around only at night. In the second role they personify the areas in which they live and seem to act as protectors of wild animals and plants.

The chief of the seven apparitions, as well as of all other detrimental deities, is Whirlwind,[50] the principal god of evil. The malignant beings are his "ministers" and do his bidding on earth, just as all the beneficial deities are God's ministers. Whirlwind is fused with the Devil. He is considered responsible for all evil, maledictions, and black magic, and he initiates sorcerers. As the personification of the whirlwind, the most evil of winds, he is called upon by sorcerers and enemies to carry illness and misfortune to others. The whirlwind, which carries more sickness than any other, is the protective covering which the Devil wears when traveling over the earth.[51] Women and girls wear cheap amulets as a protection against him and evil winds in general, and clasp them tightly when a whirlwind passes. This deity is said to be a hairy being, and his only visible part is a hand covered with long hair, terrible to behold. He appears to people in a blast of wind, shows his hand, and frightens them out of their senses. Another devil, *ah yacax*,[52] is called upon by sorcerers to send worms and flies into their victims' noses. He may be merely another aspect of the Christian Devil.

[50] Called in Spanish "the Devil" or "King Lucifer of Hell." This deity may be entirely a Catholic concept.

[51] At Mitla the top of a whirlwind contains a devil who is out to give sickness (Parsons, 1936, p. 215). Whirlwinds are feared by the Yucatecan Maya as liable to bring sickness (Redfield and Villa, 1934, pp. 119 and 164).

[52] *yacax*, generic term for fly. He is called in Spanish "King Fly of Hell."

The apparitions are Sisimite, Siguanaba, Duende, *u tcur witsir*, the Cadejos, and Lagarto.

Sisimite[53] is said to be both a giant and a dwarf of horrible aspect, his body covered with long hair reaching to the ground. Although he walks forward, his feet are turned backward on the ankles, and he takes long strides. The Sisimites are of both sexes, each sex usually living by itself, although they are sometimes said to live as man and wife. The male of the apparition deals with women, and the female, with men. They live in uninhabited hills and precipices and in dark secluded streams far from human habitations and are considered the guardians of rocky hills, precipices, and secluded spots. They are also the guardians of wild animal life, since all wild animals belong to them, and they are said to attack single hunters on lonely trails.[54] They go abroad only at night, especially at nightfall,[55] and drunken people hasten home before dark to avoid meeting the apparition, since it throws stones at them as they pass along the trails. Stones which roll down a mountain side at night are said to have been thrown by a Sisimite. They are believed to carry off children and to eat them, and will carry off adults if alone, the male carrying off women, and the female, men.

Siguanaba,[56] sometimes confused with Sisimite, as the

[53] Called in Chorti, *qetcux* (possibly *qetc*, "to carry off," and *ux*, substantivizer).

[54] The Sisimites are especially called the guardians of the hills and of wild animals. In the latter role they encroach somewhat on the realm of the deer-god, although the two beings are never confused.

[55] They have a horrible cry, *marikonet*, which can be heard a great distance and which is said to be terrifying. The derivation is not clear (possibly *on*, "we," and *et*, "you," but meaning of *marik* unknown), but the expression seems to have the meaning of "We'll get you!"

[56] Called in Chorti, *quhk*, or *ah quhk*. The term also refers to any sprout or shoot growing on a tree.

two are similar, is dual sexed, although usually a woman only, and each sex deals with people of the opposite sex. She has long hair and ugly fangs and wears a cloth around her mouth to hide her ugliness. She lives in dark spots in streams and is the protectress of such places and of fish. Fishermen are said to go out in groups to avoid being attacked by her. When the rivers rise, as during the rainy season, the deep spots have whirlpools, and the noise of these at night is said to be the bathing of Siguanaba. She carries off children, keeps them three days, and returns them insane. She meets men on the trail at night and attempts to embrace them, and, if they refuse, she scratches them with her long claws. She usually appears to an adult in the guise of his or her sweetheart, and the victim is deceived until she removes the cloth from her face, showing her fangs. He is so terrified that his legs swell and become so heavy he cannot lift them to run. She disappears, and the victim, as a result of his terror, is insane for the rest of his life.[57] Only immoral people, especially drunkards and unfaithful husbands, greatly fear her. A meeting with her is said to result always in insanity.[58]

[57] Siguanaba is very similar in name and description to the Matlasiwa at Mitla (Parsons, 1936, p. 230). Cf. the *xtabay* in Yucatan which, upon being embraced, changes from a beautiful maiden to a bundle filled with straw, leaving her victim ill (Saville, 1921, pp. 171–72). The *xtabay* are also reported by Gann from British Honduras (1918, p. 40) and by Tozzer (1907, p. 158).

[58] A story is told by the Indians and Ladinos of Jocotán about an Indian who, about thirty years ago, met Siguanaba on the trail when returning home from the pueblo after nightfall. She asked where he was going, and the man, greatly frightened, answered that he was going home. She told him to accompany her, took him to a deep well, and stood him close to it with his back to it. She told him to sit down, whereupon he fell to the bottom in water up to his neck. He shouted so loudly for help that many people came running with ropes with which they pulled him out. The man was frightened out of his senses and remained insane until his death a few years ago. The story seemed to be generally believed, although a few of the Ladinos suggested jokingly that the Indian may merely have been drunk.

Duende is a dwarf who is the god of hills and valleys, of domestic animals, especially cattle, and of property. Dual sexed, he is considered man and wife.[59] The female has long hair reaching to the ground and walks wherever she goes. The male has shorter hair and is on horseback. Both are dressed in green clothes, probably as a symbol of vegetation and increase. The deity lives in the center of any hill[60] and also near any group of cattle. The two go out only at night and make pacts with people, the male of the deity dealing with women, and the female, with men. If an individual wishes more property, he makes an agreement with Duende, written in blood, that for the increase in property he will give one of his sons to the deity. If the increase materializes, Duende returns at night after ten years to claim the son and takes him to his home in the hill to work as his servant.[61]

u tcur witsir[62] is an evil spirit, dual sexed, who also frightens immoral people on lonely trails at night. It has a

[59] He is called in Chorti, *mauh*, or *ah mauh* (possibly from *ma-*, negative, and *uh*, "good"; thus, "bad"); *mauh winik*, "male Duende," *mauh icik*, "female Duende." The Spanish name means "fairy" or "goblin."

[60] Especially a hill called *nonoh ha'* (*noh ha'*, "lake"; *nonoh ha'*, "Great Lake"), near Camotán.

[61] Another Duende, probably of Spanish origin, is a brother of *mauh*. He is about three feet high and wears an enormous hat. He represents the evil side of *mauh* and probably should be called an apparition. He desires women, and, presenting himself at a woman's house, he asks her to come with him to his home, a spot in a river or a cave in the mountains. If she agrees, her house the next morning is filled with fine things. Duende promises to return after a certain number of years, during which time the woman lives in luxury. He returns, takes her and the fine things home with him, and she is never seen again. Duende may present himself to a woman at any time or place. If she is in a public place, he is invisible to all except her. If she continues in the company of another man after Duende has obtained her promise, he hurls stones at this man as he passes along trails at night. This being is very similar to Big Hat, or Big Head, reported from Mitla (Parsons, 1936, p. 209).

[62] *u*, possessive; *tcur*, "guardian spirit"; *witsir*, "hill," "mountain."

horrible cry, the sound of which is so terrifying as to cause insanity. It seems to be the guardian of high mountains, while Sisimite is the guardian of the lower hills.

The Cadejos[63] are animal apparitions, resembling dogs or tigers, which live high up in the hills and rocky precipices. They have long black plaited hair and are fleet of foot. Like all apparitions, they have voracious appetites and eat everything.[64]

Lagarto[65] is a giant lizard spirit, probably of Spanish origin, which lives in the deep spots of streams and is the spirit of whirlpools.[66] He is invisible, his body consisting only of violently moving air, and is said to live wherever there is a turbulent spot in a stream. He has a large tail, the end of which is of bone and shaped like an ax. His mouth is extremely large, so that he swallows his victims whole. People who come to the spot to bathe, especially at night, are liable to be killed with the axlike tail and swallowed. The spirit eats everything edible and is said to be as large as a bull.

Characteristic in varying degrees of all the supernatural beings are (1) moral neutrality or duality, (2) sexual duality, (3) multiplicity, (4) bilocality in sky and earth, and (5) dual personality with native and catholic counterparts. The concept of duality is so strong that the Indian will ascribe it with little hesitation to any being, even where duality would seem to serve no purpose, in such cases stat-

[63] Ch. *tsuts*, or *p'ur-em tsuts* (*p'ur-em*, "black"; *tsuts*, "hair").

[64] Boys are told that, if they stay out late on the trails at night, the Cadejos will catch them and eat their testicles.

[65] Called in Chorti, *aihn*. The derivation is unknown but probably is *ah* agentive, plus an unknown stem which may have once referred to the lizard or alligator (possibly *yin*, since *ah yin* would be condensed into *aihn*). The Spanish term locally means alligator.

[66] *u wink-ir e sut-ur ha'*, "the guardian of the whirlpool."

ing that the being in question "must" be both male and female, good and bad, etc.

Moral duality is shown especially in the Chicchans, who send rain and make the maize grow, but who also cause floods, earthquakes, and other destructive phenomena.[67] In moral dualism the supernatural has two aspects, the one representing the good which is in opposition to the other which represents the bad, or has only one aspect, which is good, opposing a different supernatural being, which is bad. Sexual duality takes two forms: that in which a group of deities of one sex are related to a group of the opposite sex and that in which a single group is of dual sex, the male of the being affecting or dealing with women and the female affecting men. In the first type the male is placed in a relation of co-operation to a female, and the female is referred to as the "woman" or "companion" of her male consort. In the second the being is a single entity but can take on either sex at will, as the situation demands, and in some cases it has certain of the characteristics of both sexes in a single body. In either case the male form has relations with female people, and the female form, with male people.

Multiplicity is expressed in the belief that any supernatural being is to be found in a single locality, as a hill, spring, or precipice, but at the same time is everywhere at once, and innumerable in number. The Indians say it can be found in a particular sacred spot or that "it is wherever one wishes to find it." The most important deities are located in both earth and sky, each group having a somewhat different role and character. For example, the sky Chicchans produce rain and its accompanying sky phenomena,

[67] Moral duality seems to have characterized the ancient Maya deities (Thompson, 1927, p. 33).

while those of the earth produce floods, rainstorms, etc., and are the personifications of water, streams, springs, and the hills from which springs issue.

Most of the supernatural beings,[68] as previously mentioned, have their counterparts among the saints. In nearly every case the male aspect is represented by a male saint, and the female aspect, by the Virgin. The choice of the saint counterpart seems to have been determined by the function of the various saints in Catholic belief, although it is not certain that this is true in every case. The Virgin is the female consort of many of the deities who are associated with planting, the soil, fruit trees, family life, childbirth, and other elements in which the ideas of fertilization and growth are paramount. All life and growth proceed from her union with the male of the deity concerned.[69] None of the primarily destructive native deities has a saint or other Catholic equivalent, with the possible exception of the Devil, who is now said to be the same as the chief of the evil deities, Whirlwind. Those native deities who have

[68] It is difficult to state to what degree the Indians implicitly believe in the various supernaturals. They seem to be completely believed in as the producers of natural phenomena and in their roles as protectors of nature, although in these cases they seem to be thought of primarily as "saints" and only secondarily as native deities. The Working Men, for example, are, first of all, "angels" or "saints," at least individually, and collectively they are either angels or "working men," with both Spanish and Chorti names. There is obviously less belief in the apparitions. These are accepted as the protectors and personifications of nature, but there is a tendency to doubt their relations with man. The latter are usually referred to as "beliefs" (Sp. *creencias;* Ch. *na·t-ar-op'*). In relating the story of somebody's encounter with an apparition, the Indian seldom vouches for the truth of the event, usually adding "so they say" (Sp. *así dicen;* Ch. *kotce·ra u-y-a·r-e*), or "perhaps it happened that way, I don't know" (Ch. *xai-te' a-lo·k'-oy-ic kotce·ra ma·tci in-na·t-a*). The Ladinos refer to all the native religious beliefs of the Indians as merely "Indian beliefs" and laugh at them, although they are less inclined to doubt the Indian Catholic beliefs.

[69] She is by no means conceived of as a virgin, although such a conception is held by some of the other Middle American groups (cf. La Farge, 1927, p. 11, and Thompson, 1930, p. 50).

saint counterparts are so represented only on their beneficial side, since the saints in no way represent their harmful aspects. Because a given saint does not represent all his
native equivalent, the Indians often speak of a certain
saint and native deity as if they were entirely different,
when in reality the saint merely stands for the beneficial
aspect, and the native deity, for the harmful aspect, of the
same supernatural being. Thus, those saints who have become fused with native deities, and who are themselves
real deities, are all helpful to man, although the pueblo and
family patron saints, who are no more than semideities,
may send harm to their followers' enemies if petitioned to
do so.[70]

SAINTS AND CROSSES

The saints, as patrons and protectors, are associated
both with the pueblos and *municipios* and with the families, the former being community patrons, and the latter,
domestic patrons. They have some relation to all the
crosses, especially to the larger ones which are fixed permanently in the ground, but this is not clear. All the other
church saints, which do not have this patron function, are
considered unimportant by the Indians. Each of the pueblos of the department of Chiquimula has its patron saint.[71]
The Virgin, who is called his woman, or female companion,[72] is in every case his female aspect, or consort, and she
is said to help him as a wife helps her husband. The principal image of the patron is kept in the pueblo church in a
special niche, usually near the altar, with the smaller

[70] See pp. 419–20. Cf. the difference between the saints and the strictly
native deities at Chan Kom (Redfield and Villa, 1934, p. 111).

[71] *u tcur e tcinam* (*tcur*, "guard," "watcher"; *tcinam*, "pueblo"); *u santu-ir e
tcinam* (from Sp. *santo*, "saint").

[72] *u w ick-ar*, "his woman," "his wife"; *u p'ia'r icik*, "his female companion."

image of the Virgin standing beside him. Here he is worshiped on Sundays and especially on his festival day.

All the saints which have the same Spanish names are called brothers. Thus, San Juan Camotán, patron of Camotán, and San Juan Hermita, patron of the pueblo of the same name, are brothers. If two or more images of the patron saint are worshiped in the same pueblo, as at Quetzaltepeque, where the main patron, St. Francis, is kept in the church and a slightly lesser patron, called St. Francis the Conqueror, is kept in the *cofradía*, these are also called brothers, the *cofradía* image being the younger brother. There is a younger brother of the Jocotán patron saint in the Jocotán *cofradía* as well. The church image is called the elder brother of all his lesser prototypes.[73] Some of the Indian families keep miniature younger brothers of the pueblo patron as secondary family saints. The patron's protective power is exerted over both his pueblo and all the *aldeas* which belong in the same *municipio*. He belongs completely to his own *municipio*, and must on no occasion ever be taken out of it. He is said to be angered and to bring catastrophe to his own people if taken to another *municipio*, and especially if the people of the latter are permitted to worship him. It is the special duty of his own people to protect his image, keep it properly installed and dressed in the church, and celebrate him with a festival when his day of the year comes round. His power is localized, since he brings good fortune, or bad fortune, only to the people of his own *municipio*, or to those in whose *municipio* his image is actually present.[74]

[73] At Mitla, also, all saints of the same name are brothers (Parsons, 1936, p. 204).

[74] This relationship is illustrated by an event which occurred in Jocotán *municipio* in June, 1932. The rain was a month overdue, and the planted seed

Most of the Indians have their own family saints,[75]
which in nearly all cases are St. Manuel and the Virgin,
both of whom seem to be the equivalent of the dual-sexed
earth-god, *ihp'en*. Manuel is the principal of the two, the
Virgin being called his woman, or his companion. If a family has as its patron a saint other than Manuel, they explain that it is "just as powerful" and believe their saint to
be the particular one who is most able to help them in all
difficulties.[76] The image of Manuel is usually about eighteen inches high, stood up in a small wooden case. The
Virgin is either a small doll or a newspaper photograph of
a woman. Both images are entwined with colored crepe
paper, and Manuel is dressed to resemble his larger proto-
type in the church. They are made by the carpenters in
Esquipulas, usually of cedar. The two saints in their separate cases are kept always in one end of the storehouse on
the altar table or in a specially built altar-house, and next
to the family crosses. The case doors are kept shut when
no ceremony is being performed to them. The family
saints, although nearly all are images of Manuel and the
Virgin, are felt to have influence and power only for the

were dying. The patron saint of Jocotán had been taken by the Camotán Indians to Camotán pueblo and was being paraded through the pueblo in an effort
to bring on the rain there. They had previously paraded their own patron saint
but with no result. The Jocotán Indians were certain that rain had not come to
their area because their saint was away from his church, and so several hundred
of them angrily marched to Camotán, took their saint by force, and paraded
him in the streets and plaza of Jocotán. Two days later there was so great a
downpour of rain that the saint was brought out from the church and paraded
once more in order to stop the cloudbursts. The Jocotán saint, therefore, had to
be actually present in Jocotán *municipio* before he could bring rain to it. Before
this event, a number of Camotán Indians had been burning candles before the
saint in the Jocotán church, asking him to send rain to Camotán, but the informants stated that this could do no good so long as the saint was not physically
present in Camotán. A similar incident once occurred among the Mopan Maya
(Thompson, 1930, pp. 38–39).

[75] Cf. La Farge, 1927, p. 12.   [76] See Tozzer, 1907, p. 152.

families who own them. They are angered if taken off the land of the owning family and especially if another family should hold a celebration in their honor. Other families may attend such a celebration, but only as guests. Many families, especially those who have separate altar-houses in which their saints are kept, beat a tattoo on the altar drums for a few minutes every day at sunset in honor of their saints.[77]

The saints are the only deities of the Indians possessed in any material form. Their effigies in many cases are said to be so old that no one can remember their age or of what they are made, and the pueblo patrons especially are said to have come from God and to have appeared miraculously at the church in the distant past. The little brother of the Quetzaltepeque patron saint is kept in the *cofradía* and worshiped independently of the church. He is represented by a figure done in relief on a square of black stone and stands about two feet high. It is said that he fell from the skies one stormy night many years ago and was found next morning near the sacred springs which form the source of the Rio Conquista, the site at which the Quetzaltepeque rain-making ceremony is performed every year on April 25. The Jocotán patron saint, Santiago, is said to have appeared one night out of the sky during an electric storm ages ago and to have fallen behind the church, where he was found next morning and installed near the church altar. A few of the family saints, especially those obviously several generations old, are claimed by those who own them to have similar mysterious origins, but such claims are not made for the newer ones.

[77] A large and a small drum are for St. Manuel, called his drums, and a large and a small one are for the Virgin, called hers. The smaller drums have a higher tone and are beaten rapidly and in accompaniment to the large ones, resembling the beating of the two church bells in the pueblos.

The pueblo patron saint is formally worshiped every Sunday in the church, on his official day of the year and during any time of community crisis. The family saints are worshiped primarily in connection with rain-making, planting, the first fruits, the harvest, and hunting, and at any time of family crisis, as at birth, marriage, and death, and during sickness and poverty. The patron-saint festival[78] is the most important of the year in any *municipio*. It is held once a year on the patron's day and only in the particular pueblo of which he is patron. It lasts officially for four days, which include the saint's day, the two days preceding, and the day following. Prayers and masses are recited in the church by the Catholic priest, if he is available, for eight days preceding the saint's day, and sometimes for four days after, although most of the Indians take little part in this.[79] The Quetzaltepeque priest usually is able to get to the patron-saint festivals at the four or five churches in his district to recite mass, but he takes no part in the purely Indian celebration. The official four days are given over to individual prayers in the church before the saints, and especially before the patron, the carrying of the patron and his consort in processions around the plaza and through the pueblo streets, formal dancing, music, extensive trade in the plaza, drunkenness, and general merrymaking. A few Ladinos join in the celebration, although their participation is usually limited to watching and laughing at the Indian "antics" and to enjoying the brisk trade which the occasion brings.

The patron and family saints are much more involved with the religious and daily life of the Indians than are any of the other deities. The Chicchans and other purely na-

[78] *noh q'in,* "great festival." The Jocotán festival is described on pp. 449-53.

[79] Cf. Blom and La Farge, 1927, pp. 362-63; Thompson, 1930, pp. 82-83.

tive deities are exhorted merely to send rain and to aid in the growth of plant and animal life and are otherwise seldom approached. Thus, they are completely associated with the realm of nature, being both the essence and the cause of all natural phenomena. They have very little intimate contact with people and exert little direct influence over their personal lives. The saints, on the other hand, are especially asked to send rain and to stop cloudbursts and prolonged drought, but their influence extends far beyond this, since they are being continually exhorted throughout the year to protect families and communities from sorcery, to cure sickness, to insure a successful planting and plentiful harvest, and to bring general good fortune to families, *aldeas*, and pueblos. They are asked as well to send the opposites of these to enemies. During any family or community crisis it is vowed to the saint that, if he brings about a good result, he will be celebrated by the petitioners soon after. A man often does this when there is extreme sickness in his family, promising to carry the saint to his *aldea* for a special celebration, or to carry a certain amount of pine needles, flowers, and stones for several miles to place at the base of a wayside cross.

The saints are thought of in very personal terms, both because they can be approached individually, at any time, and for any crisis which may occur, and because they exist in material form and can thus be intimately handled, dressed up in finery, and carried from place to place wherever their help is needed. The relation between the Indians and the pueblo patron is somewhat formalized, since he represents an entire *municipio*, but the relation between the family and its own saint is extremely personal and intimate. The pueblo patron stands as a symbol of his *municipio* in its relations to other *municipios;* the Indians of the *municipio* claim a special right to his favors which does not extend to outsiders.[80] Indian and Ladino children are often named after him, in spite of the general rule that children should be named after the saint on whose day they were born. Many stories are told of how the patron appeared miraculously to individuals, often in dreams or in dark places at night, and helped them in times of necessity, cured their illness, informed them when the rain was to come, and brought about their success in farming or trading.

The patron saints seem to have some of the characteristics of semideities; they are sacred personages with great supernatural power, but they derive their power from God,[81] a superior being, and retain it only so long as God sees fit to grant it. If the patron does not send rain when it is badly needed, it may be that he is angry with his followers, in which case he is quickly celebrated at the pueblo *cofradía* and at the homes of many of the Indians. If there is still no rain, it may be assumed that he has temporarily lost his power, in which case an attempt may be made to secure the patron saint of another pueblo, bring him to their own pueblo, and beg him in a celebration to end the drought. The Camotán Indians took the Jocotán patron for this purpose, but only after repeated celebrations of their own patron had brought no results. This would be done only in cases of great emergency, since the neglected saint is angered if his followers celebrate another, and the latter is, of course, angered at his own people for permitting him to be taken away. The Indians do not know why a patron should temporarily lose his power. It is usually said

---

[80] Cf. Redfield, 1930, p. 201.

[81] *u-mor-i u q'eq'-on-er e ka tata'*, "He gets his power from God."

this happens because God "does not like him," although no one seemed to know why.[82]

The derived power of the patrons is also shown by the fact that in many prayers to them they are requested to ask God to bring about the desired results, although in just as many cases requests are made of them as if they were deities with an independent power of their own. All the beneficial native deities are now considered, at least nominally, as subservient to God and have been reduced to the role of his helpers, and the saints are similarly subservient. From their conversation about the roles and powers of the saints and native deities, it seems that the Indians primarily think of the Chicchans and Working Men as the supernatural beings actually responsible for rain, even though it is God who is asked in the prayers to order them to bring it, and of the patron and family saints who actually cure sickness, increase the crops, etc., even though they are usually asked to "work with God" to that end.

Aside from sexual dualism, the patron saints are characterized by moral dualism, since they are generally beneficial to those who keep them and whose duty it is to celebrate them, but, if requested, will send all manner of harm, sickness, and misfortune to their people's enemies.[83] This is considered appropriate, since it is said to be as much the proper function of one's patron to bring ill for-

[82] It is sometimes said that the patron has not lost any of his power but that, like the Camotán saint, he cannot bring rain because people elsewhere were no doubt praying to their saints to send a drought to the Camotán area, and since they probably had several saints working to that end, the Camotán saint was helpless. The Camotecos, therefore, decided to enlist one more saint on their side, in order to equal or exceed the power of the unknown saints who were working against them.

[83] At Mitla the saints may send evil to one's enemies, such as sickness and earthquake, although they are generally beneficial (Parsons, 1936, p. 206).

tune to his enemies as it is to bring good fortune to himself, the two being equivalent. The recipient of the misfortune is merely expected to go to his own saint to ask for protection, and possibly for the damnation of his enemy in return. He may ask for this from what he considers more powerful saints than those of his enemy or from a greater number of them.[84] Moral dualism is further shown in the fact that the patron will harm his own people if they fail to care for him, to protect his image, or to celebrate him properly. This is a punishment, however, and so indicates a personal relationship, whereas the ancient native deities cause harm to man in an entirely impersonal way.

The crosses[85] are made only of the wood of the *palo jiote* tree. These trees are planted all over the *municipios* of Jocotán and Olopa on Holy Cross Day, May 3, and are said never to be planted on any other day of the year. The branches used in making the crosses are also cut on May 3, as well as on the preceding Palm Sunday. At Quetzaltepeque and Esquipulas the Catholic priests bless the wood and limbs at the churches on these two days, after which the Indians carry them home and make them into crosses. In Jocotán and Olopa the wood is not consecrated, except perhaps at the family altars. Crosses are set up at the church, at various places within the pueblos, along the trails, in the family courtyards and houses, on the family altars, and over graves, and are carried for protection against all harm. They vary in length from an inch or two to about ten feet. The crosspiece of the larger ones is attached to the vertical piece by means of pegs and notching,

---

[84] This is the same line of reasoning followed in inflicting and protecting one's self against sorcery (see chap. xiii).

[85] *wa`r te'*, or *wa`r-om te'* (*wa'*, "stand up," "be erect"; *wa`r, wa`r-om*, "standing"; *te'*, "stick," "tree").

ROADSIDE CROSS ON THE TRAIL FROM JOCOTAN TO OLOPA

if made by the carpenters, or with any species of liana which is tied diagonally around the two pieces at the intersection. The carpenters make them of planed wood, although most of the Indians merely use unfinished limbs, and there is no attempt at decoration.

Every church has a large cross, about ten feet high, which stands in front of the plaza facing the church entrance and is sometimes referred to as the chief cross of the entire *municipio*. At Camotán and Olopa it is set in a foundation of stone rubble, about two feet high, and stands at about a hundred feet from the church door. The church cross is the largest in any *municipio*. On the trails, at the points of entrance to the pueblos, large crosses are set up in the ground, each in the center of its trail. Four important roads lead out of Jocotán toward the four cardinal points, and each of these has its cross at the point where it leaves the pueblo. The crosses are said to protect the pueblo from the entrance of evil spirits and apparitions, especially the Devil. They are stood up in the center of the trail so that the spirits, who theoretically could enter the pueblo only by way of the four trails, as people do, would be forced to pass over the crosses to gain entrance, and this would be impossible. The wayside crosses, each two to four feet high, are set up in mounds of loosely piled stones every mile or so along the mountain trails, especially at dangerous spots where the trails run along the edge of steep cliffs. The cross is stood on the outer side of the trail, so that an evil spirit would not be able to hurl a passer-by down the mountain side, since, in order to do this, it would have to push its victim over the cross—an impossible feat. Wayside crosses are also set up at the summit of long steep climbs, where the Indians are accustomed to stop for a short rest, leaving their offerings of flowers or vines before going on. A stone or two is often tossed on the pile in which the cross stands.[86] Many of these crosses are in pairs, a large and a small cross stood up a few feet apart in the same pile of stones, with long canes bent in a half-circle over the crosses and their ends stuck in the stones all around the pile, thus forming a roof over the crosses, as is done for the altars.

Crosses are perhaps most commonly used to protect families and their property from evil spirits and black magic. The courtyard cross is always stood up within the open courtyard near the group of houses, as near the sleeping-houses as possible. No family is without one, and some have three or four. It is usually made of limbs and is four or five feet high. Many of the families have growing yard crosses, the vertical piece consisting of a living *palo jiote* tree, and the crosspiece, of a small stick about two feet long which is bound to the tree trunk, six or seven feet above the ground.[87] These are said to be more powerful than artificial crosses, since they are not only alive but do not rot away, and so attain a greater age. Juliano Cervantes of Tunucó said that all yard crosses should be of this type. The four pueblo crosses in Jocotán are of living *palo jiote* trees. A large cross is often stood up on the floor inside the sleeping-house, at the head of the beds, and tied to the nearest upright post. This is said to protect individuals while sleeping.

[86] Some of the wayside crosses seem to have been much more venerated than others, as the stone piles at their base are now eight to ten feet high and covering an open space at the side of the trail several feet wide and ten or fifteen feet long.

[87] The family plants this tree on May 3, and while it is still young a notch is cut into one side of its trunk, into which the crosspiece is tightly fitted and bound with liana. As the tree grows, the upper and lower sides of the cut gradually close like a pair of lips over the stick, holding it in place without a tying material. If the crosspiece rots after many years, a new one is shaped to fit the notch and is inserted.

Each family altar has two crosses, a large and a small one, which are set up directly behind the altar itself, balanced against the altar table and resting on the ground. The large cross, six or seven feet high, is for St. Manuel, and the small one, about three feet high, is for the Virgin. Crosses are set up at the head end of all graves, usually about two feet high, and are said to protect the deceased from all evil spirits and black magic.[88] Tiny wooden crosses, made of a single piece and usually of wood, are hung as pendants on agave twine and worn by women, girls, and infants as a protection against all harm. They clutch them when they come in contact with any ritual object which might send magical sickness upon them. The cross protects the wearer against sorcery, the maledictions of an enemy, the harm of apparitions and evil spirits, and evil eye, for which reason infants and sick adults especially wear them.

The cross seems at times to be thought of as a deity rather than as a mere protective object and symbol, as much of the ceremonial behavior toward it is similar to that usually directed toward an active and personal deity. All the crosses have their special day to be reverenced (May 3), just as do the patron saints, and on that day they are adorned with a great variety of plants. The family crosses are decorated every time a family celebrates a saint, either their own or the patron saint of the pueblo, at their altar. These are hung with fresh maize ears, leaves, and stalks in July when the first spring maize of the year is ready to eat, as a sort of first-fruits ceremony, and ripe

[88] It is said that the grave cross, because of its protective power, also prevents the harmful *aigre* of the corpse (see p. 328) from escaping from the grave to contaminate living people. For this reason Indians are not afraid to approach graves which contain crosses, although they avoid those without crosses, especially if recently dug.

maize and beans are hung on them during the days when harvesting is going on. During sickness in the family they are usually garlanded with flowers and vines.

The crosses have a special relation to the saints, especially to the patron and family saints. All the wayside crosses of the *municipio* seem to be especially dedicated to the pueblo patron. He is said to live or to be present wherever they are set up, although his "real place"[89] is in his niche at the church. The wayside cross is sometimes said to "be" the patron saint. The patron is said to own all the church, pueblo, and wayside crosses, while the family saint owns the yard and altar crosses which his family have in their possession. But there seems to be no real notion of the crosses as being deities, with their own character and individuality, and with personal attributes such as the saints and native deities have. Although they are venerated and adorned, nothing is ever asked of them, and they are not treated as persons. None is named. Certain ones have more protective power than others, which power seems to increase with age, but they do not bring good fortune deliberately, as the saints do. They are merely sacred objects with protective power which is exerted over the spots where they are kept, so that everything near them is similarly protected from all nonnatural influences.[90]

[89] *u tur-tar* (*tur*, "to be," "to exist"; *tar*, "place"); Sp. *su verdadero lugar*.

[90] The cross is considered and worshiped as a personal deity at Chan Kom (Redfield and Villa, 1934, p. 110) and at Jacaltenango (La Farge and Byers, 1931, pp. 184–90). This faith in the protective power of the cross is strongly held by the Indians, who set them up in every imaginable spot where personal protection is desired. The Ladinos are much less certain that the cross is actually protective and usually refer to the notion as an Indian belief, but they seem to believe it somewhat, just as they prefer to believe that sorcery is merely another Indian belief but are obviously not free of the tendency to believe something like sorcery possible, especially in cases where they cannot hit upon rational and common-sense explanations of what occurred.

SACRED PLACES AND CONCEPTS

The sacred places consist of topographical features inhabited by supernatural beings, as well as places where ritual objects are kept and ceremonies and rituals performed. The degree of such sacredness varies, depending upon the nearness of the places to the various *aldeas* and upon their use throughout the year. There are many sacred bodies of water. All springs are in general sacred, since the Chicchans occupy the hills from which they issue during the dry season and enter the streams through them at the beginning of the rainy season. The most sacred of the springs are those used as depositories in the rain-making ceremonies, and from which sacred water is obtained for ceremonial purposes. All the springs are named. The water of hot springs is used medicinally to cure magical sickness. The deep spots in streams are said to be the abode of Lagarto, the giant lizard, as well as the home and bathing place of apparitions. The Indians avoid such places at night, and especially when bathing, as it is believed that an apparition would pull anyone into the water who came too close. Drowning at night is often thus explained.

Many of the rivers and lakes are the special habitats of earth Chicchans and so are very sacred spots, although any large body of water contains a Chicchan, who personifies the water itself and so has some sacredness. The four sky Chicchans live in lakes, each inhabiting one in his own direction. Crater lakes are especially sacred, as they are believed to be bottomless and fed from the hill itself and so are inhabited by giant Chicchans. All hills are sacred spots, since they are said to be inhabited by Chicchan during the dry season and by other supernatural beings, such as the deer-god, Duende, and the apparitions, throughout the year. The crests of hills are said to be the homes of mountain deities, each summit representing one of their houses. Many dark places in the forests, especially in the higher hills and far from human habitation, are the abodes of apparitions, such as Sisimite and Siguanaba, and to be avoided if possible. Dangerous places along the trails are inhabited by evil spirits and apparitions, one of whom may push a passer-by over the edge of the trail. Wayside crosses are set up in such spots to avoid this danger. Drunken and immoral people are especially liable to encounter apparitions in such places.

All burial places are sacred, since they contain corpses, which are ritual objects, and are inhabited by the death-god. A single grave has this sacredness, but a cemetery has much more of it, and the Indians usually visit them in groups. The land upon which any ceremonial house or wayside cross sits is considered a sacred spot and is not to be used for any secular purpose. The ceremonial house has a large space all around it, kept clean of vegetation by communal *aldea* labor, where the Indians congregate during ceremonies. No one is supposed to build a house, set up an oven, or graze pigs on such a spot. The site of the wayside cross is usually an area some twenty feet square and is used only as a spot to contain the stones brought to it by people who are making good a vow. On some of these sites stones are piled eight or ten feet high. The *municipio* patron saint is said to inhabit the space at times. The pueblo church is perhaps the most sacred object and place, especially the spaces within it occupied by the altar and the saints.[91]

The sacred concepts are those of time, direction, locality,

[91] The church is referred to as *u tur-tar e ka tata'* ("the place of Our Father"), or as *u y otot e ka tata'* ("the house of Our Father").

number, form, and color.[92] The sacred occasions are both beneficial and harmful to man. Sundays, saints' days, and the days or occasions on which calendric ceremonies and festivals are celebrated are "good" days. Several Indians thought that one's birthday was also a good day. The "bad" days of each week are Thursday and Friday, which are the days when sorcerers send black magic and when one is most liable to come upon evil spirits and apparitions. The sky deities inhabit each of the four world-directions, but they also inhabit intermediate positions between the cardinal points, thus forming the universe into a square as well as into a diamond. The east is said to be a good direction, and there is some belief that it is the source of all life and good in the world. A corpse is buried with the head toward the east so that it may see the setting sun in the west, the direction its soul took when it left the body at death. The west is a bad direction, as it is the abode of the spirits of the dead, which are harmful to man, and is the direction from which come most of the evil winds which bring sickness and death to persons, animals, and plants. Whenever possible, houses are built with the door facing the east, thus being oriented like the churches. North and south are seldom thought of and have no native names.

The concept of "up" is good, while that of "down" is evil. The beneficial deities live above, as in high hills or the skies, from which they are said to "come down" to help man, not from the Christian heaven but from what is called the "high," the "high places," or the "sky." The evil deities all seem to live below. Sisimite, for example, is always said to "come up from below" when he goes abroad, and the chief of the apparitions also "comes up" to do

---

[92] Most of the semisacred or magical concepts, principally used in connection with curing and sorcery, are described in chaps. xiii and xiv.

harm to people. The "below" refers to the low, dark, and secluded spots where evil deities live, and not to the Christian hell. In magical practices a candle, right side up, is left to burn in the church door to bring good fortune to one's self or friends, while one placed upside down, and lighted at its bottom end, brings harm to one's enemies. Copal fumes are said to be beneficial because they ascend; it is believed that if they go downward the copal should be thrown away, as it is bewitched by a sorcerer. The left leg is the evil leg, and sorcerers have their patron spirit in it, while curers and diviners, who are good people, have their patron spirit in their right leg, which is the good one. Sorcerers are said to stab the image of a victim with the left hand in order to make the pain more intense. The Devil makes his presence known to people by showing his horrible left hand.

Although nearly all the supernatural beings are universal in habitat and so are everywhere at once, they are also believed to inhabit certain spots, usually topographical features of importance which in many cases resemble the appearance or character of the beings which live in them. These spots are the places where the beings are usually to be found, and the Indians go to them if they wish to make immediate contact with supernaturals or avoid them if they wish to avoid supernaturals. The habitats consist of mountains, precipices, crests of hills, forests, dark and secluded places, lakes, streams, springs, whirlpools, and burial places, all of which are sacred and therefore avoided as a rule. The souls of the dead are said to go to the west, where they remain forever after.[93]

[93] Several Indians thought that the souls of newborn infants came from the east, but this did not seem to be a general belief. Other Indians were not sure of this but thought it quite possible, probably because it seemed fitting that the souls of infants should come from a "good" direction.

Nearly all the deities are considered both single and innumerable in number. The number "3" is of ritual significance for women probably because it is the number of stones contained in the fireplace. For example, women take medicine three times, or three days apart, and in many other ways make use of the number in all their ritual acts. Three is sometimes used by both sexes and in such cases may be the concept of the Catholic trinity. Four is of the greatest ritual significance for men, probably because it is the sum of the corners of a milpa where the men spend nearly all their time. It is also applied to the altar and the world, as both are in the form of squares. The men take medicine four times to effect a cure, or four days apart, etc. All festivals are supposed to last four days whether they actually do or not, and while the ceremonies usually last only a day and a night, it is said that they should last four days as well. Eight is important in the transition ceremonies especially and figures in nearly all ritual observances. Nine is not important and may be a Catholic concept. It is often used in medical practices. Thirteen is not of importance, although it is sometimes given as the number of days devoted to the annual patron-saint festival. Sixteen is used only where two eight-day periods, as of fasting, are lumped together, and all precede the ceremony, rather than eight days preceding and eight days following it.[94]

The conventional sacred forms are straight lines, zigzag lines, and squares. The snake and lightning are considered somewhat equivalent because of their similar shape, and so the producer of much natural phenomena is the giant

[94] Cf. the concept of "4," as applied to altars, milpas, and the world, in Chan Kom (Redfield and Villa, 1934, pp. 111–15). Thirteen happens to be the total number of the sky deities, but the Indians do not speak of this number in connection with them. It is probable that it had ritual significance in the past.

snake Chicchan. The zigzag line is equivalent to these and appears most often as a pottery decoration. The square is the only sacred plane, since it has the form of the milpa and the altar and has four corners. The milpa and altar represent the universe in miniature. The Indian sometimes refers to his altar as his little milpa, and to the world, as a great milpa. It is said that houses must be rectangular or square in order to be like milpas. The candles set up at the four corners of the altar are said to be both its corner posts (as if it were a house) and its boundary markers (as if it were a milpa). The movements of the participants in the pueblo rain-making ceremonies describe a square in that they march to each of the four cardinal points of the pueblo to pray to a Chicchan, to a Working Man, and to a saint at each of them. The Christian cross is an extremely sacred form, and the plants or objects which resemble it are considered sacred. The leaves of the *conte* vine, which have roughly the shape of a cross, are used medicinally and for adorning sacred objects.

The colors have special significance in many religious beliefs. White is associated with death, and the death-god is dressed in a long white robe said to be identical with that in which a corpse is dressed before burial. White candles are burned during the funeral ceremony and on the Day of the Dead, although black ones are used in other native ceremonies. White flowers seem to be preferred for decorating the corpse before burial. Usually only black turkeys and chickens are offered as sacrifices in ceremonies, and usually only black candles are burned on the native altars. The milk of a black cow has much medicinal value. Red represents power and force and is used to ward off disease, black magic, and the evil eye. Yellow represents value, sustenance, and fruition, and appears in the names of certain supernaturals. Yellow maize is fed to fighting cocks by the Ladinos to give them strength and courage. Green signifies vegetation, growth, propagation, and increase. Duende, who sometimes represents wild vegetation, is dressed in green clothes. Vegetation is also represented by the long hair worn by nearly all those supernaturals who personify wild vegetation in any way. Thus, Sisimite has long body hair, and Duende has long head hair dragging on the ground; the hair of both is said to be the same as wild vines and creepers.

Light seems to represent knowledge and is associated with the sun-god, who is the patron of wise men. Darkness is considered protective for sacred objects, for which reason they are usually kept in dark places, as by closing up the houses in which they are kept or by storing them in chests. Constant light is said to "hurt" the *santo*. Darkness is also considered effective in the performance of ceremonies, for which reason many of the esoteric professionals perform in dark rooms or in dark places in the forest. It is believed that the deities are more easily contacted in darkness, since darkness acts as a protective covering for them. Seclusion and secrecy are closely associated with darkness.

CHAPTER XVII

CEREMONIES AND FESTIVALS

CHARACTERISTICS OF RELIGIOUS OBSERVANCES

THE religious activity of the Indians consists of a series of calendric and noncalendric festivals celebrated throughout the year, the most important part of each being the one or two ceremonies performed in connection with it. The calendric observances are celebrated only once a year by all the Indians of one or several *municipios* on that date and are in every way community events. They are given in connection with the agricultural cycle and the bringing of rain, in honor of the Saints and Catholic deities, and for the souls of the dead. The noncalendric observances are not so much considered as community celebrations, since they have no official day or days on which they are held and since most of them are held and paid for by individual families. They are looked upon as primarily the concern of the family or group of families giving them, even though friends and relatives attend them.[1]

The festival is called *q'in*[2] (Sp. *fiesta*). The most important throughout the year in any *municipio* is that of its

[1] The important private ceremonies are the transition rites (chap. xii), the new-house festival (chap. vi), and the hunting ceremony (chap. iv). Private ceremonies connected with agriculture and maize storage are described below.

[2] This stem means "day," "sun," "time," or "season." In many cases, though not in all, it is prefixed to the name of the event to mean "day" or "festival," and suffixed to mean "season" or "time" of the year. Thus, the planting festival is usually *u q'in-ir e pa˙ q'-m-ar* ("its day" or "festival," "the planting"), and the planting time or season, *pa˙ q'-m-ar q'in*.

patron saint, called "great festival," or "his day the saint," and is usually referred to by all the *municipio* Indians as *the* festival. Other calendric festivals are called simply *q'in*, or *in-te' q'in* ("day," "*a* festival"). Most of the noncalendric festivals, especially those which are of importance only for a given family, are called *ut q'in*, "little festival" (Sp. *fiestita*). The formal ceremony is called *tca· n*.

The festival periods extend over four, eight, nine, or thirteen days, although for some of the festivals the Indians are not certain which period should hold. These numbers are often used indiscriminately in connection with all religious observances. The four-day period is the most commonly thought of and is considered by the Indians as the proper festival period. For calendric observances it includes the official day, the day preceding, and the two following, and for the noncalendric ones it either precedes or follows the event being celebrated. The eight-day period is used especially for the transition rite festivals, extending for eight days following the event, and in some cases to the ninth day, which is the principal day of feasting and the finale of the celebration. The church festivals, most of which are now co-ordinated with native ones, extend over thirteen days, the period including the official day, the eight days preceding, and the four following.[3]

The festival period is a time when no work is done, at least on those days when ceremonies are being performed. Some work is often done on the other days, as when planting and harvesting must be carried on, but it is said to be

---

[3] During the annual patron-saint festival, for example, prayers are made before the saint during the preceding eight days and to some extent during the following four, although even in this case the Indians seem to attach more importance to the four-day period, described above.

improper to work at all during a festival.[4] It is a time of general merrymaking, drunkenness, fighting, visiting with friends, and the extending of hospitality to neighbors. Every family puts aside several ollas of *chicha* to be properly fermented for drinking on these days, especially since it must be plentifully provided for visitors who call on the family. The occasion is looked forward to in the *aldeas* and is discussed for weeks in advance. Most of the annual festivals are celebrated by the Indians in their *aldea* homes, each family feasting, performing ceremonies, and extending hospitality in its own home, although groups of families combine for celebrating some of them. The patron-saint festival is the only important one of the year which is celebrated almost entirely in the pueblo and is the outstanding social, religious, and economic event of the year for all the *municipio* Indians. It is the most important marketing occasion and is certainly the most important religious event. It is the one time of the year when every Indian of the *municipio* gets to the pueblo to meet his *compadres* from other *aldeas*, to make new friends, and to visit in the plaza and in the *chicha* shop with old ones. Arguments are settled in the alcalde's office, and more serious disputes, usually of long standing and nearly always over married women or milpa land, terminate in fighting with machetes in the pueblo streets or along the trails to the *aldeas*.[5]

Ritual prohibitions are observed before, during, or after most of the ceremonies, the number of days being three, four, eight, or sixteen. The avoidances are sexual and social intercourse, sleep, and food. The directors of all cere-

[4] *ma' tci ka-patn-a tame' noh q'in,* "We do not work on a festival."

[5] It is said that more old scores are settled during this festival than during all the rest of the year.

monies, whether *padrinos* or the male heads of families, must abstain from sexual intercourse over a given period, or the ceremony itself will have no effect. The prohibition against sleep is especially observed during the consecration of the planting seed, in which all the participants must stay awake until midnight. A part of the rain-making ceremony is done secretly by the *padrino*, as otherwise its power would be lost. During most ceremonial occasions, usually for eight days preceding or following the ceremony, either the officiating *padrino*, the participants, or both eat nothing but maize foods, especially *chilate*, and particularly avoid condiments, like chili. The performer of a ceremony gets drunk on *chicha* made of maize and avoids *aguardiente*, which is not made of maize. The period of fasting on maize corresponds usually to the period of sexual abstention, the two being done together. Fasting is considered especially necessary during transition rite festivals, the family concerned eating only maize for eight days following the event.

The offering of sacrifice is made in almost every ceremony. Sacrifices consist only of sacred objects, especially maize, turkeys, and copal gum. The first two are offered principally to the native deities, and the third, to the saints, although all three are sometimes sacrificed together. Silver pesos are occasionally sacrificed. Maize is never offered in the crude state but is always cooked in some way, especially as *atol* and *chilate*. Turkeys, and occasionally chickens, are usually sacrificed without cooking, the blood being used along with the meat, but when used as gifts to other families they are first cooked, usually on the spit. Copal is sacrificed after being prepared into hard round pellets of the shape and size of either silver pesos or ears of maize and is either buried whole or burned in the incense burners on the family altars. The sacrifice seems to be con-

sidered an outright payment to the deity and is often
called "payment" in the prayers. The deity is told that
such and such a payment is being made to him, in return
for which he is expected to send what is asked.[6]

Nearly every ceremony contains a prayer, which is its
most important part. The prayer is spoken by the *padrino*
or the family male head, and only he is believed to be able
to recite it properly and with good effect. Most of the
prayers are in Chorti, especially the most important ones,
but a few are given entirely in Spanish, and nearly all contain a few Spanish words. A few have been taken over entirely from the Catholic priests, since they are recited altogether in Spanish and are made up of phrases used only
by the church. Feasting, drinking, and dancing are important parts of almost every ceremony and festival. The
principal festival foods are tamales, *tortillas, atol, chilate,*
and cacao, although many other foods are eaten to some
extent, and the principal festival drink is *chicha.* Nearly
everyone except children drinks during festival occasions,
and old grudges often break out into fighting. Music is provided by hired fiddlers, flutists, accordion players, and
drummers. The Indians dance singly and in pairs, and
there seems to be no preference for dancing with the opposite sex. The drinking and dancing usually continue until dawn.[7]

Despite its close connection with Catholic ideology and
ritual, the festival of the present-day Indians is probably
a development from purely native festivals of pre-Con-

[6] It is said that, if others make a greater and earlier payment, they will
receive the favors of the deities, and so it is sometimes stated in the prayers
that the payment being made is both the first and the best that anyone could
make and should therefore receive first consideration.

[7] The dance step is a sort of chaotic jumping about, with little attention to
rhythm.

quest times.[8] The church has proclaimed many festivals throughout the year in honor of various saints, but only those given in honor of saints who have native counterparts, as well as which could be made to coincide with important annual events in Indian life, have any significance for the Indians or are celebrated by them with any seriousness. The others are known to the Indians as being festival days but have not been incorporated into their religious life.

THE AGRICULTURAL CYCLE

The festival of St. Mark, from April 25 to May 3, marks the beginning of the ceremonial agricultural year. The rain-making ceremony ("great ceremony") is made on St. Mark's Day. It takes place in one of the *aldeas* of each *municipio*, and the following description is that of the Jocotán ceremony given in the *aldea* of Guaraquiche, about six miles northwest of Jocotán pueblo. On April 24 the *padrinos* choose four boys or girls and sometime four boys and four girls at the age of puberty and instruct them to go secretly at dawn the next day to a sacred spring to secure

---

[8] The ancient Maya filled the year with feast days, all of which were religious observances performed by the entire community or by certain groups within the community. In nearly all cases these festivals were held in honor of patron gods, such as the patrons of occupations, pueblos, vegetation, and natural phenomena. Early Catholic priests, finding they could not entirely displace the native pagan festivals, substituted for them certain Catholic celebrations. Thus, in the patron-saint festivals, folk dances from Spain took the place of native dances, and the characters and plots were taken from Christian history, such as the victory of the Christians over the Moors and of the Virgin Mary over the Devil. Similarly, other native festivals, like those connected with rain-making, planting, and harvesting, were made to coincide, or nearly so, with the celebrations of Christian deities and events. The changes were rendered less abrupt than they otherwise might have been by the fact that the priests were usually tactful enough not to attempt to change the dates on which the celebrations had been held in the past. Thus, little by little, the purely Indian festivals, whatever they were in the past, were converted into more or less Christian ones, and the Indians think of them now not only as primarily Christian but as being native to themselves (see La Farge, 1927, p. 17).

several jars of water.[9] No one else must know who are chosen, when they leave, or when they return. Each brings a jar of water and is especially careful to avoid meeting sorcerers, drought-makers, persons with evil eye, or anyone suffering from magical disease, since if such people looked at the water it would lose its sacredness. If a sorcerer or drought-maker should steal some of it, he could perform black magic over it and thus ruin the rain-making ceremony. The sacred water is used by the women in preparing the tamales, *atol*, *chilate*, and *tortillas* which are eaten after the ceremony.

Several weeks prior to this date most of the *municipio padrinos* have held a meeting at the church or other convenient place and chosen one of their number to act as leader[10] in the ceremony. He must abstain from sexual intercourse for eight days preceding and eight following the ceremony, or it is believed he will go crazy and die and his ceremony will have no effect in bringing rain. At sunrise on April 25 the leader secretly digs a hole at each corner inside the *aldea* ceremonial house and buries in each a cupful of *chilate* cooked with ground cacao and sugar. Shortly afterward, Indians from all over the *municipio* gather in the open space surrounding the house, bringing large quantities of chicken tamales, cacao, *chilate*, *atol*, fruits, and *chicha*. Each family contributes food and a peso or two until about one hundred are collected. The money and

[9] In the middle of April four men, picked by the *padrinos* of Chiquimula, journey secretly to a sacred river near Esquipulas and bring back several ollas of water to be used in the rain-making ceremony in that area. The *padrinos* derive income from the sale of this water to the Indians. The four men travel only at night and sleep in the forest during the day in order to avoid meeting dangerous persons who might destroy the sacredness of their water.

[10] *u t'cahn-ar*, "its leader" (*t'cahn-ar-i*, "to lead out," "to act as guide").

food are given to the leader as a payment for performing the ceremony. Each family brings additional food which is cooked by the women in the ceremonial house kitchen and eaten by everyone. All proceed with the *padrino* to the foot of the nearest sacred hill or to the nearest sacred spring, either of which is said to be the home of Chicchan during the dry season. The purpose of the ceremony is to induce the Chicchans to come forth and occupy the streams for the following five or six months, thus bringing the rain with them.

The leader digs a hole about two feet deep, into which he pours an olla of blood which was extracted the day before from the bodies of a male and female turkey and a male and female chicken. He then throws in the turkeys and chickens, the former on the side of the hole next to the spring or hill, and the latter on the opposite side. About two hundred pieces of copal in the form of pesos are thrown into the center between the fowls. This is the payment to the sky deities for the rain, while the animals and blood are an offering of food to the earth-god so that he and his consort may be able to give growth to the maize soon to be planted. The leader covers over the hole and smooths the surface in order to conceal its whereabouts from drought-makers and sorcerers. He then recites a prayer to all the deities who produce rain: the Chicchans, who churn the water in the sea and lakes and vaporize it; the wind-gods, who carry the vapor up into the sky; the Working Men, who beat the clouds into rain and who produce thunder and lightning; again the wind-gods, who carry the rain over the earth; and, finally, the earth-god, the personification of fertilization. The prayer is offered directly to God, asking that he "give permission" to all his "ministers" to

send rain.[11] The Indians then return to the ceremonial
house, where feasting, drinking, and dancing go on throughout the entire night. A large group of women prepare tamales, *atol*, *chilate*, *tortillas*, meats, and coffee, using the
sacred water for this purpose. This ceremony is performed
only once a year in the highlands, where there is only one
rainy season, but the lowland Indians perform it a second
time in order to ritualize their second planting of maize
at the beginning of the second rainy season. This time it
is directed to the Youthful Working Men.[12]

As a result of this ceremony, the rains are expected to
come not later than the first day after the end of the
festival, which is May 3, and during the eight-day period
the deities are said to be getting ready to send the rains
over the earth. Candles are burned before the church and
family saints, who are asked to assist in bringing the rain,
and all the family and wayside crosses are decorated with
flowers. All the families who can afford it give feasts in

---

[11] God is asked to send all his ministers over the earth and sky to produce the
rain and its accompaniments. He is asked to accept the people's payment for
the rain and not to accept that of the drought-makers and other evil people. He
is asked to send rain to all other people as well.

[12] In Quetzaltepeque *municipio* the Indians meet on April 24 at the source of
the Rio de la Conquista, about three miles north of Quetzaltepeque pueblo. The
padrinos pour the blood of a male and female turkey into the spring which is the
river's source, as an offering to the Chicchan who is living inside the spring and
hill. *Chilate* is then poured over the ground all around the spring. It is said that
formerly a giant Chicchan always reared its head out of the spring, grabbed the
turkeys out of the *padrino*'s hands, and pulled them under. The Chicchan does
not do this now, so only the blood is offered and the meat later made into
tamales. The *padrinos* then set up a small cross, about three feet high, near the
spring. Each year one is set up after the ceremony, all in the same spot, and
today there are about fifty still standing. The spot is called a cemetery by the
Indians. Prayers are said, and the entire throng, often five or six hundred,
march in a procession to the *cofradía*. The wife of the chief *padrino*, aided by
about fifty women, prepare *tortillas*, *chilate*, and tamales from the meat of the
two sacrificed turkeys mixed with the meat of a large number of others. Music,
feasting, dancing, and the drinking of *chicha* usually go on until dawn.

their houses, inviting everyone in their *aldeas* to come, and there is some exchange of presents, usually of ripe maize, among related and friendly families. If the rains have not come within a few days after May 3, the Indians of Jocotán *municipio* may meet at the church to parade the patron saint around the plaza to enlist his aid to bring on the rain.

May 3 marks the beginning of the planting festival, which continues for four days. This date is the Day of the Holy Cross and is the official day on which the first rains are to come. During the day and evening the planting ceremonies, which are the most important part of the festival, are performed. Their purpose is partly to protect the milpas and gardens from all harm but primarily to make a payment in the form of food to the dual-sexed earth-god for making the seed grow, as well as to consecrate the planting seed.[13] They are done usually by the milpa owner himself, although a *padrino* may be hired to do them for a fee of about one hundred pesos and a great quantity of foods, especially *chilate*. The latter is for the *padrino* to drink before performing the ceremonies, as a means of rendering himself sacred. In Jocotán *municipio* the performer must abstain from sexual intercourse for eight days preceding the planting, the day of planting, and seven days afterward, or the owner of the milpas will fall sick and his maize will be attacked by disease or pests and will not grow.[14]

At sunrise the milpa owner goes to his cleared milpas

---

[13] Before performing the planting ceremonies, the Indian says, *war in-t'oy-i e rum*, "I am going to pay the earth (earth-gods)."

[14] Around Camotán the period of abstention is the day of planting, two days preceding, and the day following. If violated, the owner will have violent pains in the neck and back from which he will die. The three-day period is found in Quetzaltepeque, although the penalty for violation is sickness brought by the evil winds. Around Tunucó, the period includes fifteen days preceding the planting, the planting day, and none afterward.

and digs a small hole at each corner of one of them. In each
he buries one fowl, preferably a turkey. The head is pulled
off and the neck gashed with a knife; the body is then held
over the hole so that the blood drips into it, after which
the body is thrown in and the hole smoothed over with
earth so it cannot be detected. This is done at each of the
four corners. He then digs a small hole in the center of the
same milpa and throws into it an olla of unsweetened
chilate. This and the fowls are food for the earth-god and
are said to protect the young maize plants from marauding
animals. On the north side of the center hole, and about
two feet from it, is dug an oblong one, about six inches
wide and a foot deep. In it is placed about two pounds of a
thick maize gruel. On the south side of the center hole, at
the same distance from it, a similar hole is dug, and in it is
placed a package of copal pesos, wrapped in a cloth. These
two offerings are the payment to the earth-god.[15] The Indian then recites four times each of two Spanish prayers,
the first to the male of the earth-god and the second to the
female.[16]

The three holes are covered over, and the Indian returns
to his house, where preparations are made for the festival
which is to be held until the end of May 6. Friends from
all over the *aldea* are invited. Tall lighted candles burn at
the four corners of the altar table before the family saints,
who are thus requested to assist in bringing on the rain
immediately. The day is spent in conversation and in eating tamales, *tortillas*, and meats, and in drinking *atol*,

[15] The maize gruel is called "maize paste *chilate*." The *chilate* is called the
companion of the copal, which relation may indicate their connection with the
idea of fertility, and therefore symbolizes the dual-sexed earth deities to whom
the ceremony is directed. It is believed that the maize plants are born of the
union of this two-sexed pair.

[16] These are entirely Catholic and are said never to be recited in Chorti.

chicha, and coffee, most of which are prepared by the women in the kitchen as the men consume them. At sunset of the same day the owner goes to his milpas alone and digs a hole about one foot in diameter and two feet deep in the center of one of them. He throws into it, bit by bit, a quantity of *tortillas* and *chilate*, at the same time reciting a prayer,[17] after which he covers over the hole.

The planting seed are consecrated[18] on the same evening. The consecration ceremony is directed to the family saints, or earth-gods, who are asked to accept the seed and to protect it from evil spirits and sorcerers until it sprouts. Fourteen candles are lighted on the family altar, seven for St. Manuel and seven for the Virgin. A large one also burns at each corner of the altar, the space inclosed by them being said to represent a milpa. The male head of the family, who performs it, invites a number of close men friends to assist him. The women remain in the kitchen, preparing the food the men will eat during the evening. After the candles are lighted, an incense burner is placed on the floor in front of the altar, about four feet from it, and between these two are set the ollas which contain the maize and bean seed to be planted the following morning. The men then burn copal in the censer, adding a peso of it every few minutes. One hundred pesos of copal are burned during the evening, fifty for St. Manuel and fifty for the Virgin. The prayers, in which the saints are asked to protect the seed and make it grow well, are in Spanish and are purely Catholic. The ceremony lasts until about eleven

[17] This is directed to the earth-gods, or family saints, who are offered payment for making the maize grow. They are asked to rise from the soil, bringing the maize plants with them, and to protect the family and its milpas from all evil people.

[18] There seems to be no Chorti name for this ceremony, although the consecration is sometimes referred to as "curing."

o'clock, when the candles are put out. Drinking sometimes
continues until early morning. The planting officially begins the next morning, May 4.[19]

The ceremony to the wind-gods is performed eight days
after the planting, when the maize and beans are usually
in the sprouting stage. May 11 is the official day for this,
although if the sprouting is late, many of the Indians wait
until a few sprouts have appeared before performing it.
The ceremony is meant to ask the wind-gods to bring rain
so that the plants will grow and to dissuade them from
blowing too strongly and from bringing evil winds which
will destroy the young plants. The head of the family goes
to one of his milpas at any time of the day and sets up in
the center of it a tall cane, six or seven feet high, attaching
a small wooden cross, about eight inches high, to its upper
end. About a dozen small pieces of cane are tied at right
angles to each arm of the cross-bar of the cross. No prayers
are spoken. Some of the families sprinkle sacred water,
brought from a sacred spring or river, in each of the four
corners of the same milpa, but this does not seem to be a
general practice. The crosses are said to propitiate the
wind-gods, and the sacred water, to keep all forms of evil
from entering the milpas. No offerings are placed with the
crosses. Many Indians said that a four-day festival followed this ceremony, but it seemed to be of no importance.[20]

[19] If the rain has actually not come by May 3, however, most of the
Indians wait until it does before planting. So great is their confidence in the
power of the rain-making ceremony, however, that some of the Indians start
planting on May 4, whether the rain has already arrived or not, believing that it
is bound to come in a day or two. But, as it sometimes happens that the rainy
season does not open until May 15 or later, the planting in such cases may have
to be done over again.

[20] This ceremony is called *u tca' n-ir ah yum ikar*. The cross is called the
San Pedro, which is the Catholic name for the chief of the wind-gods, and the

As soon as the first spring maize is ready to be eaten, around the middle of July in the lowlands and the first of August in the highlands, a first-fruits festival[21] is celebrated. It lasts either four or eight days and begins on the day when the first ears are cut. Ears and stalks, together with fresh beans and decorative flowers, are laid in profusion on the family altars as a votive offering to the saints for making the maize grow, and the family yard crosses are similarly hung with maize and bean stalks. Candles are burned on the family altars during the festival, and in some cases prayers of thanks and pellets of copal are offered to the saints. Offerings to the saints and crosses, however, are much more important in the harvest festival, described later. The Indians are especially joyful at this welcome change in the diet, send large gifts of maize to all their friends and relatives, and, for several weeks thereafter, eat almost nothing but roasted ears and *tortillas* made of fresh maize.

The first harvest of ripe maize and beans in the lowlands takes place around the first of September, and the second planting is done around the middle of the month. The harvest ceremony and festival, described later, are not celebrated until the final harvesting, which is done in both highlands and lowlands in November, although a rain-making ceremony is performed in the lowlands to the Youthful Working Men prior to the second planting. It is

---

small canes, his companions (*u p'ia'r-op' e San Pedro*). The cross is sometimes called *u hor ah yum ikar* ("their chief the wind-gods"). In Quetzaltepeque the materials used are blessed by the priest at that church on the previous Palm Sunday, and the Indians usually get their holy water from the church. A small cross is also set up at each corner of the milpa and left until the maize is grown. The four-day festival is called *quc nar q'in*, or *u q'in-ir e quc nar* (*quc*, "to be born," "to sprout").

[21] *a'n q'in*, or *u q'in-ir e a'n* (Sp. *la primicia, la primavera*).

performed by each family in its own milpas and somewhat resembles the ceremony of April 25, although it is not nearly so important. Many of the Indians have dispensed with it and merely burn candles on their altars and make offerings to their saints, asking them to send rain.

The harvest festival is celebrated by the highland families around the middle of November and by the lowland families at the end of that month. The maize ears and bean vines are brought from the milpas and piled in front of the family storehouses, where they are allowed to dry in the sun for four days, which is the period of the festival. For several days preceding, the women are busy in the kitchen preparing large quantities of ceremonial foods and *chicha*. The family male head invites all the members of his own family, as well as those of other families who assisted him in his harvesting work, and all feast and get drunk during the four-day celebration. Much visiting goes on among relatives and friends. It is during the harvest festival that the largest offerings are made to the crosses and family saints. These are heavily garlanded with ripe maize ears, bean stalks, pumpkins, cane stalks, and a great variety of flowering plants. The offerings are hung from the crosspiece of the crosses, spread on the ground at the base of the crosses, and piled high on the altar table around the saint's case. Four tall candles, one at each corner, are usually burned on the altar table during the four days.[22]

The storage ceremony is performed on the fourth day, at which time the storage begins, and is meant to protect the stacked ears and other stored foods from the evil spirit,

[22] *u q'in-ir e t'cam-w-ar*, or *u q'in-ir e t'cam nar*, "harvest festival" (*t'cam-w-ar*, "the harvest"; *t'cam nar*, "maize harvest"); Sp. *la fiesta de la cosecha*. The Indians say of their offerings to the saints and crosses, *ka-w-ahq'-u takar e santo*, "We give it to the saint," or *ka-w-ahq'-u takar e wa'r-om te'*, "We give it to the cross."

cicimai. Four pieces of copal, called *qu᠎ m-ic, matulin, pastor*, and *salvador*, are made in the form and size of maize ears and wrapped separately in cloths. After the ears are stacked to about a foot in height in the storehouse, the family male head places them, in the order named, in the corners of the house on the stacked maize, addressing a different prayer to each as he lays it down. The first prayer is to *qu᠎ m-ic;* the second, to *matulin;* and the third, to *pastor* and *salvador*, which are laid down together.[23] The stacking begins again and continues until the rows reach nearly to the eaves. The pieces of copal are left in place until the maize has been removed down to their level, when they are taken out and boiled down for further ceremonial use.

FESTIVALS OF SAINTS AND SOULS

The ceremonial year begins on April 25, which is called the beginning of the year, or the beginning of "winter" (the rainy season). The festival of St. Mark begins on this date and lasts for eight days, or until Holy Cross Day, which is celebrated on May 3. This is the most important ceremonial occasion of the year for the Indians as a whole, since it is celebrated in all the *municipios* which contain an Indian population. The most important part of this festival is the rain-making ceremony described above.

May 3, as the Catholic Day of the Holy Cross, is the day especially given over to the worship of the cross and is observed by decorating all the crosses, especially the family and wayside ones, with a variety of plants. Each family especially decorates its own yard cross, covering it up in a profusion of flowers, fruits, and vegetables so that it can hardly be seen. Gourds filled with water are often hung

---

[23] This ceremony is called *u tca᠎ n-ir e pe᠎ t's-w-ar*. The four guardians are enjoined to protect the stored maize against *cicimai*.

with agave twine to the crosspieces of the most important crosses. During the weeks around the Day of the Holy Cross travelers pick flowers, vines, and wild fruits as they walk along the trails and deposit them on the wayside crosses. A common way of venerating a cross is to lay a round, smooth stone on top of the pile upon which it rests, thus gradually building up the base year after year.[24] May 3 is the official day for planting the *palo jiote* trees, which are later made into the living crosses, and is also the day upon which all artificial crosses are to be set up. The Indians say that crosses are not set up on any other day of the year and that crosses are moved from one spot to another only on that day.[25]

The festival of St. John, patron saint of Camotán, is celebrated in that pueblo on June 24, when the "dance of the giants" is performed. Some trading goes on in the plaza, and candles are burned in the church, but the day is not important. This saint is also the patron of San Juan Hermita, in which pueblo his "day" is July 30; but on June 24 the Ladinos and a few of the Indians of San Juan perform a chicken-pull in the saint's honor.[26] This is principally a Ladino celebration, however.

[24] The *flor de la cruz* and *flor de mayo* flowers are especially used for adornment at this time. Every wayside cross along the trails has lying at its base a great pile of stones, and, clinging to the cross itself, the decaying remains of offerings of pine needles and flowers which may have been placed there many months before. This custom is observed among the Jacalteca (La Farge and Byers, 1931, p. 186) and in Yucatan (Tozzer, 1907, p. 152).

[25] Although most of the Indians seem to believe that Palm Sunday is the proper day for cutting the branches to be made into crosses, many do this on May 3, as well, probably because Palm Sunday is more Catholic than Indian and does not closely coincide with any important Indian activity.

[26] A group of men scout around during the morning in the hills near by, capturing roosters. A rope is stretched between two trees in the plaza, as high as a man can reach on muleback. The roosters are tied by the feet to this rope, head downward. The men ride by in turn, each trying to catch a rooster's head to

The festival of Santiago, patron saint of Jocotán, is celebrated in Jocotán on July 24 and is the most important saint festival which the Indians of Jocotán and neighboring *municipios* celebrate, since it closely coincides with the ripening of the first maize and beans of the year. Indians from all over the Chorti-speaking area attend it and seem to consider it a part of the general celebration of the first maize. It is held on the twenty-fourth, the two days preceding, and the day following. On the sixteenth, or eight days before the saint's day, the church is garlanded with flowers and hung with pine branches and vines which stretch from the walls, and its floor covered thickly with pine needles. The saints are dressed in freshly washed and starched clothes, and many are covered with crepe paper and flowers. Stalks of pine and cane are set up in the ground all over the plaza, especially in front of the church, at the cardinal points around the edge of the plaza, and at the spots where the four important trails enter the pueblo. During these eight days masses are said in the church on mornings, afternoons, and nights, and the church bells are constantly tolled by the *mayordomos*. During the evening of each day skyrockets are fired in the plaza, two after each three rosaries. This lasts from about seven to nine o'clock each evening. A group of about fifty women, appointed by the *mayordomos*, are busy at the *cofradía* making *chilate*, *atol*, coffee, and *tortillas* in the large ovens and fireplaces of the *cofradía* courtyard. Long benchlike tables are covered

---

jerk it from its body. After a number of fowls are decapitated, their bodies are carried to a house to be cooked and eaten. The Indians say this game represents the decapitation of the saint and that the feasters secure his good qualities by eating the fowls, which are his body. The Ladinos laugh at this notion. The celebration is attended principally by Ladinos, as not many Indians live in the *municipio*, and all bring their contributions of maize, beans, coffee, cacao, and money. Drinking and dancing continue for most of the night. The chicken-pull is played at Jacaltenango (La Farge and Byers, 1931, p. 95).

with gourd bowls filled with the *chilate*, which all the Indians drink free of charge. Most of the maize and coffee thus used is contributed by the Indians themselves, but a great quantity is purchased by the *mayordomos* with the contributions which had been left for the patron saint during the previous year.[27]

Indian merchants set up their palm-thatched stalls along the south side of the plaza, laying on good roofs and digging drainage ditches all around them, as the rainy season is already well advanced. The Ladino merchants, whose stores face the plaza, set up palm-thatched awnings in front of their stores.[28] Other merchants come from distant points of the republic, bringing Indian headpieces, skirts, shawls, blankets, pottery objects, jewelry, and other manufactures, mostly from the area around Guatemala City. Those who sell women's skirts, which they bring from the western part of the Republic, do a thriving business, as the Indian women almost never buy skirts at any other time of the year. By the twentieth of the month the plaza is full of Indians every day and evening, as all are especially anxious to be present by the twenty-second, which they consider to be the first day of the festival.[29] The *chichería*, located at the southern edge of the pueblo, enjoys its greatest business of the year and is full of Indians day and night. Drunkenness and street-fighting increase, and the Indian *regidors* are kept busy dragging drunken Indians to the jail, usually

---

[27] The festival foods, especially *chilate*, are always served gratis when the crops have been plentiful, but on bad years, as in 1931, they are given free only to the festival dancers.

[28] The alcalde requests this, but it is partly done to attract Indian customers during the rainy hours.

[29] Those who live in the nearer *aldeas* come every day and return home before night. Those of the remoter *aldeas* usually stay until the celebration is over, putting up in the houses of Indian or Ladino friends. A few Ladinos turn their homes into temporary inns in which Indians may stay for a peso or two a night.

in spread-eagle fashion. Many must be beaten until bloody and unconscious before they can be locked up.

During the official four days the patron saints are paraded in the plaza and along the pueblo streets several times each day, with a great tolling of the bells. The Catholic priest leads the processions if he is present, but, if not, this is done by the four *mayordomos*, who carry the saints on the wooden litter. Other Indians, mostly women and children, follow with burning candles, all praying and chanting in low voices. The procession, according to the usual procedure, comes out of the church door, which faces west, and proceeds to the southwest corner of the plaza, from there to the southeast corner, then to the northeast corner, and ends at the northwest corner.[30] The procession stops for a few minutes at each point before proceeding to the next. During the four days there is much individual praying and burning of candles before the various saints in their niches, who are asked to send all manner of good fortune to the petitioners, as well as much ill fortune to their enemies. Buying and selling go on in the plaza, families from many *aldeas* visit and gossip with one another, and a few of the women fight and quarrel continuously.

The dance of the Huaxtecs is given on the twenty-fourth and twenty-fifth, at about noon of each day. It is long and tedious and is given entirely in Spanish.[31] There are eight characters: two Huaxtecs, who wear black masks which resemble the face of a tiger; Graseco; the king; his daughter Malincia, who is the paramour of the captain; Hernán Cortéz, the captain; and two soldiers of Spain. Most of them wear high crowns, each with two arches transversed

---

[30] In some cases it goes to the four cardinal points, in the order of west, south, east, and north, and finishing at the church door, usually touching the points at which the streets enter the plaza. This seems to be more Indian.

[31] See La Farge, 1927, p. 18.

at the top and with a tiny bell hung in its center. The Huaxtecs, who are called Negroes, wear black masks, and Malincia is dressed entirely as a modern Indian woman and wears a pasty white mask resembling a woman's face. The other characters wear white masks and their ordinary clothing. The dance is performed in front of the church door, the two Huaxtecs standing in front of the rest of the group and doing nearly all the dancing. The step is a simple one, probably learned from the early priests. The few lines repeated are given in falsetto voice. The Huaxtecs are the principal actors, doing most of the speaking and dancing, and use rattlers made of small gourds which contain pebbles, shaking them in the right hand while dancing. Music is provided by the marimba player, who stands with his instrument in the church door. All the parts are played by men, the same ones taking part year after year. The director stands at one side and, as the dance goes on constantly, helps out with lines and directions. It draws a large crowd each time it is given. The older Indians look on sober faced and seem to take it seriously, but the younger ones and the Ladinos laugh uproariously at everything the characters do, especially at the light sex play which constantly goes on between the male characters and Malincia.

After dark on these two days, and amid a great shooting of skyrockets, the "bull" provides much fun and excitement. This is an Indian dressed in a framework which is made of sticks and covered with a cowhide to resemble a bull. Horns are attached in the proper place, and around the sides are tied revolving rockets and Roman candles which shoot off at unexpected intervals. The framework fits down to the man's waist, so that his legs are free for running. He runs wildly through the crowd, dispersing

CHARACTERS IN THE DANCE OF THE HUAXTECOS

Performed in front of the church in Jocotán every year on July 24, the patron saint's day

groups wherever he sees them, as everyone near him dashes for safety from the exploding rockets.[32]

The festival of St. John, patron of San Juan Hermita, is held in that pueblo on July 30 but is not attended by many Indians. In Chiquimula, on August 15, is celebrated the Feast of the Transition, as this is the day of the patron saint, the Virgin. This is said to be the most important market festival of the year in the entire Chorti-speaking area and is attended by a few Indians and Ladinos from all over the department.[33] The Jocotán festival on July 24 attracts more Indians, however. The festival of St. Louis, a purely Catholic celebration, is celebrated in San Juan Hermita on August 29, 30, and 31. The first day is in honor of this saint, although he is not the patron; the second, in honor of the "corpus," or body of Christ; and the third, for the souls of the dead.[34] St. Michael, patron saint of Gualán, is celebrated in that pueblo on September 25, but

[32] No Indian knew what a *Graseco* was supposed to be.

[33] For three days preceding, masses are said in the church, skyrockets are fired, and great business goes on in the plaza. On the fourteenth and fifteenth at about midday, the Moor dance is performed, first in the patio of the municipal building, after which the dancers parade through the streets looking for Moors to exterminate. The dance is then repeated in the street in front of the church. The twelve dancers include six Christians and six Moors, the former representing white Spaniards and wearing no masks, and the latter, who are said to be Negroes, wearing black masks. The crowns are similar to those worn in the Huaxtec dance, but are much more elaborate, and each has a small mirror placed in the crown. All the actors carry swords and face one another in two opposing lines, each man advancing toward a partner, a Christian and a Moor. The step somewhat resembles our Virginia reel, the partners alternately approaching and retreating from each other. The set speeches and answers are given entirely in Spanish, and in the usual falsetto. There is no action aside from the dance step. On the night of the fifteenth the saints and "angels" (the latter are young children dressed in white) are paraded through the streets. Thousands of people make up the procession, all carrying lighted candles, chanting, and singing.

[34] At each of the four corners of the plaza is set up a small palm-thatched structure, the side of each which faces the plaza being left uncovered. Each con-

the festival is not important to the Indians. This day is celebrated in Camotán as well. The festival of St. Francis, patron of La Unión, is celebrated on October 4 in La Unión and is the most important market occasion of the highland country in the north. Many Indians from Jocotán and Olopa *municipios* attend it.

The festival of the Day of the Dead[35] is celebrated by all the Indians on October 31 and November 1, although October 30 and November 2 are said to be included in the festival period. The celebration on October 31 is for those who died as children, and that on November 1, for those who died as adults, the ceremony on both days being the same. Old graves are covered with pine needles and a profusion of flowers, and the grave crosses especially are decorated. In the pueblos and those *aldeas* which have communal cemeteries, the festival ceremony is performed in the cemetery itself. In the forenoon the families gather at this spot and bring food which they lay out on the ground on plantain leaves. Several large crosses, each six or seven feet high, are set up in front of the food, and near these, set up on end, are dozens of tall lighted candles. The food is left untouched on the leaves for about two hours while the dead are supposed to be eating it; during this time rosaries are said in front of the crosses. By midday the feasting begins.

------

tains a table and is decorated inside with colored cloth and religious pictures. A long archway, ten or twelve feet wide, is built of carrizo stalks which are set up on each side and tied together at their tops. Each pair of stalks are five or six feet apart along the way, and with each is set a small branch of pine. As the church faces west, the archway runs from the church door to the four corners in the order of southwest, southeast, northeast, and northwest. The procession, which leaves from the church door, stops for a half-hour or so at each structure while rosaries are chanted. The priest usually attends this festival, and many local Ladinos take part in it.

[35] *si q'in, tcam-en q'in,* "the day of the dead." The meaning of *si* is unknown, although it resembles *si'*, "stick," "firewood." *tcam-ai,* "to die"; *tcam-en,* "dead," "dead person."

It is said that the people eat the food which the dead have left for them. The principal foods are tamales, *atol*, *chilate*, meats of all kinds, and fruits. *Chicha* is drunk until most of the adults are intoxicated.

In those *aldeas* which do not have cemeteries this ceremony is performed in the houses of the various families. Anyone may give a feast who wishes, and anyone may come without invitation. At about four o'clock in the afternoon the table in the house is spread with tamales, *atol*, *chilate*, coffee, and *tortillas*. These are left untouched for about two hours, so that the dead may eat them, while all the group are waiting outside. During this time the interior of the house is darkened, so that the spirits of the dead will not be afraid to enter. At about six o'clock a *padrino* comes and prays for about a half-hour to God, or Christ, and to the spirits of those who died during the past year, calling each of them by name. Afterward, the food is divided among all those present, most of which is taken home. In the early evening all return to the house for a night of drinking and dancing. By midnight everybody is drunk, and the celebration continues until daybreak.

On December 8, the feast of the Virgin Mary is celebrated in the Camotán church but is of no importance. St. Francis, patron saint of Quetzaltepeque, is celebrated in that pueblo on December 19 and is the best attended of the festivals of the southern highland region. Many Ladinos attend and take part in it, although most of the Indians consider the one at Olopa on March 15 as more important. The most important part of the Quetzaltepeque festival is the installation of the patron saint in the home of the newly appointed captain.[36] The Christmas festival

[36] At about ten o'clock in the morning the outgoing captain and a group of his friends transport the saint, who is a "brother" of the church patron, on a litter to the house of the new captain. Many Indians come in from the surrounding

is celebrated in most of the churches, but the Indians give little attention to it. It seems to be considered primarily a Ladino celebration. The festival of the Virgin, patron of Olopa, is celebrated in that pueblo on March 15 and is the most important social and economic occasion of the dry season in the Jocotán and Olopa *municipios*. It is attended by many Indians from other *municipios* of the area and is looked forward to as a relief from the tedium of the dry nonagricultural months, during which there is little other social and economic activity. It is celebrated like the festival in Jocotán but not on so grand a scale, probably because Olopa, being at a cold, high altitude, is more difficult to reach and contains a smaller Indian population around it. The Devil dance, which seems to be of Catholic origin, is performed, in which the Devil becomes envious of the power of the Virgin and tries to steal it, but in the end the Virgin is victorious. The festival of St. Joseph, patron of Copan, is celebrated on March 19 and is an important market day for the Indians for the Copan region, but Copan is too distant to draw many Indians from other *municipios*.

Palm Sunday is celebrated somewhat as a festival and extends over the first four days of Easter week. This, together with the Easter festival, described below, coincides closely with the burning of the cut and dried vegetation in the milpas, preparatory to the first planting of the year in May, for which reason the continuous eight-day period of the two festivals, from Palm Sunday to Easter Sunday,

---

aldeas to march in the procession. Upon their arrival at the new house, skyrockets are shot off, and rosaries are recited at the house altar after the installation. The altar is decorated in the usual manner with crepe paper, flowers, pine needles, maize leaves, etc. The priest usually officiates. A box is placed on the altar, in which Indians who come to do homage to the patron may place offerings. At the end of the year the captain uses these to pay the expenses of the next festival.

seems to be considered by the Indians as a single festival. It is said that all the timbers and branches which are to be made into crosses should be cut on Palm Sunday, although many Indians cut their cross materials on Holy Cross Day as well. Most, however, seem to believe that Palm Sunday is the proper time for cutting and collecting the materials, while Holy Cross Day is proper for making them and setting them up. In Esquipulas and Quetzaltepeque, where there are resident Catholic priests, these branches are blessed with holy water by the priests on Palm Sunday. In Esquipulas not only branches but the produce of the milpas and gardens is said to be brought to the church to be blessed, such as cakes of native sugar, stalks of cane, ollas of beans, maize, and fruit, and other foods. This is also done during Easter week in Esquipulas. In Jocotán and Olopa *municipios*, where there are no Catholic priests, no blessings are given at the churches, although the custom was observed in the past during those times when permanent priests were stationed there. Many of these Indians cut branches for cross-making on Palm Sunday and leave them piled in the family altar-house or on top of the altar table until they are made into crosses on Holy Cross Day. On Palm Sunday the Indians decorate many of their yard and wayside crosses and burn candles before the family and pueblo saints.

The Easter festival, which includes Easter Sunday and the three days preceding it, is the only festival given in honor of Christ as an active deity. Candles are burned before the saints, as usual, and the wayside crosses are decorated with flowers. Many Indian families give feasts in their houses, inviting friends from their own and near-by *aldeas*. During this celebration branches and leaves of the *mano de león* plant are tied by the Indians to the upright posts of their houses as well as to the walls of the churches.

It is said that Christ hides in these during that time, so that the Jews cannot find him.[37] The Jew dance is performed at Quetzaltepeque and is a representation of the Crucifixion, with actors dressed to represent Jews, Roman soldiers, and Christians. It is now rarely given in Jocotán and Olopa. After Easter the burning in the milpas is usually completed, and there is no more festival activity until the rain festival is celebrated on April 25 to usher in the new year.

Noncalendric ceremonies connected with the saints include the regular church worship of the saints and the celebration of the saints during times of family and community crisis. The Indians have no form of regular worship inside the church other than that of burning candles and praying before the various saints on Sundays and saints' days. Sunday is market day, and the Indian usually proceeds to the church as soon as he arrives with the goods he intends to sell. If he comes to the pueblo with his wife, each visits the church while the other watches and sells their wares. He buys his candle from the candle-seller at the church door as he enters, lights it, and sets it upon the floor in front of the image, and, on his knees, but with body erect, he prays to the saint in a faintly audible voice. The mumbling goes on for about a half-hour, during which time he asks the saint to send all sorts of favors, such as rain, good crops, and health to his family. He concludes often by asking that harm be sent upon his enemies. The men kneel and pray in the same way before the church altar, while the women lean backward when praying, resting the body on their heels. The worshiper always sets up a lighted candle beside him on the floor. It is usually white, as white candles are said to be preferred for church wor-

[37] There is a story at Jacaltenango of Christ being pursued by the "Judases" and of his hiding in a ceiba tree (La Farge and Byers, 1931, p. 192).

shiping. When praying at the altar the women usually go forward, while the men remain in the background.

During any community crisis throughout the year the Indians and a few of the Ladinos celebrate the patron saint with a four-day festival for the purpose of enlisting his aid. Such a crisis may be caused by drought, excessive rainfall, the spread of contagious disease, and any danger from outside the *municipio*.[38] The Indians meet at the church on a day appointed by the *mayordomos* or the priest and prepare to march in a procession through the plaza and the pueblo streets. The priest takes charge if he is present, but, if not, the *mayordomos* recite the prayers and lead the procession, sometimes carrying the saints. The images of the patron and the Virgin are stood upright in the center of the wooden carrier and thus placed before the altar. Prayers are said over them inside the church, and the four men who carry the images march out from the altar with the group following. The saint-bearers usually transport the carrier in their hands, but, if many Indians are present, they carry it on their shoulders in order to lift the images above the crowd.

Most of the marchers are Indians, although a number of the more Catholic Ladino women and children take part. Many carry lighted candles and chant Catholic prayers to the two saints as they walk along. The saint-bearers lead the way slowly to one end of the pueblo, usually the north, and there stop for a few minutes for rosaries. They then proceed to the west, stop again for rosaries, then to the south, and finally back to the church, where everyone enters to watch the installation of the saints and to set their

[38] According to several older Ladinos in Jocotán, the patron saints of Jocotán, Olopa, and Copan were much paraded in this way during a smallpox epidemic in the Copan region some fifty or sixty years ago. This was also done in the past when there was danger that soldiers from Honduras might cross the frontier and overrun eastern Guatemala.

lighted candles before them. This is done once a day for four days, and if necessary the period is extended to eight days. The principal purpose of the ceremony is to enlist the aid of the saint in the crisis. If performed because of drought, it is said that by parading the saint bareheaded in the sun for several hours he is thus made to realize how hot and dry it is and so may be persuaded to ask God and the native deities to send rain. If because of excessive rain, he is thus shown the necessity for stopping the rains.[39]

During any family crisis the patron's image is borrowed by a family from the church or *cofradía*, carried in his case to their home in the *aldea*,[40] and celebrated with a four-day festival on their family altar.[41] The image in its case is placed in the rear center of the altar table, next to the family's saints, and the altar and cross are adorned with *conte* leaves, pine needles, and flowers. Various maize foods are prepared in the kitchen for the feasting. During the day of the ceremony a few rosaries and prayers are recited. During the afternoon and early evening friends of the family arrive, and at about six o'clock all gather in the sleeping-house to feast on tamales, coffee, *atol*, and the usual *chicha*. A little later the group gathers around the altar-house to say the rosaries, and four men, stationed some distance away, make ready to shoot off skyrockets. The

[39] Thompson (1930, pp. 38–39) describes a similar ceremony among the Mopan Maya of British Honduras. He assumes that it is of pre-Columbian origin and that, prior to the influence of the church, some native deity was probably accorded similar treatment.

[40] Only women carry the saint both from the church and from house to house, since it is said that only women carry infants both before and after birth. Men are often seen on the trails with saint cases on their backs, but this is said to occur only when no women of the family are available to carry them.

[41] This is called the "watching of the saint." Usually the saint is celebrated for only a day and a night, although a few of the wealthier families celebrate him for four days. In any case the festival in his honor theoretically lasts four days.

group inside, most of whom are women, begin the rosaries and prayers to the saints, as the men outside send up two skyrockets, each about five minutes apart. More rockets are sent up during the middle of the cememony, and the last are fired as the rosaries are being finished. All this lasts about two hours. Everyone soon begins drinking *chicha*, until most of the adults are drunk; the musicians start playing, and the dancing and drinking usually continue for most of the night.

Each person who comes contributes a peso or two, and the next day the saint is carried to the house of the next family who wishes to celebrate him. The round is made throughout the *aldea*, and the saint returned to the church. Before long another round is made, and all the contributions are turned over to the *mayordomos*, who use them to defray the expenses of the saint's annual festival when his day comes round. Any saint may be borrowed from the church to be thus celebrated, but the patron saint is the most popular, since he is considered the most powerful of saints within his own *municipio*.[42] The purpose of the festival may be to insure a good harvest, a successful planting, a plentiful rainfall, to cure sickness, or to protect one's family from sorcery. In the prayers the saint is told how sick the family is, how poorly the crops are going to turn out, or how dry the weather has been, and he is asked to intercede with God and all the deities. He is told how he is loved by all the people and how necessary it is that he help them. In some cases copal money is sacrificed to the saint as a payment for his help. The alcalde's office collects a fee each time the saint is borrowed.

---

[42] In Quetzaltepeque, where the patron saint is kept at all times in the church, his "brother" is borrowed from the *cofradía* for this purpose.

CHAPTER XVIII

SUMMARY: THE ANNUAL CYCLE

THE social, religious, and economic year may be said to begin with the rainy season, usually in the latter part of April or in the early part of May. The official day of its beginning is April 25, St. Mark's Day, which is the first day of the rain-making festival, sometimes called St. Mark's festival. This date, called the "beginning of the year," or, more commonly, the "beginning of winter," is noted primarily as the beginning of the rainy season, which is by far the most important season of the year for the Indians, and secondarily as the beginning of the year itself. For several months preceding there has been almost no agriculture of any kind and very little traveling and social life. Many of the families have eked out a bare living on the maize from the last harvest remaining in their storehouses and on the few edible shoots, leaves, and fruits not too tough and tasteless to be eaten. The poorer families often run out of maize by February and subsist almost wholly on tough greens, mangoes, *pacayas*, and plantains until the first rains produce once more an abundance of wild greens and fruits, and, about two months later, the first and long-awaited crop of spring maize.

By the beginning of April all the fields and gardens have been finally cleaned of wild vegetation, and the latter has been heaped together in small piles to dry in the sun. By the middle of the month these piles are fired, and the ashes left on the soil to serve as fertilizer for the crop soon to be planted. The heat of the fire dries the sap in the large trees, which have been left standing, after which they are cut down to be used or sold as firewood. The harvesting of tobacco, which was planted several months previously, is started, and continues until the end of the month. Deer-hunting, which began the previous February, comes to an end with April. The manufacturing of the dry season, which started the previous November, gradually ceases as the dry season ends. All the Indians make ready for the annual rain-making ceremony and festival which are celebrated to bring on the first rains of the year, so that the all-important crops of maize and beans can be planted. The ceremony itself is held on April 25, and the festival continues for eight days, until May 2. During these eight days all the crosses are decorated with flowers, and the family saints are asked in prayers to assist God and the native deities in bringing on the rain. During this month, because of the shortage of maize and beans from last year's harvest, the diet consists largely of mangoes, bananas, plantains, wild fruits, a few wild greens, and an occasional meal of venison.

The rain-making ceremony is expected to bring on the first rain by May 3. This is the Day of the Holy Cross, as well as the first day of the planting festival, and on this day the families perform ceremonies in their milpas in which the earth-gods are asked to enrich the soil and make the seed grow. Ceremonies are performed to the saints, as well, for the purpose of consecrating the seed before planting, and, with this, all the ritual preparations in connection with the planting are concluded. If the rains have come, planting begins on the next day, May 4, which is the official day for starting it, but otherwise the Indians usually wait until the first shower, which seldom comes later than the first week of May, and then start planting. Planting lasts from one to two weeks, and there is much co-operative labor among most of the families in each *aldea* at this work. Vine beans and other vegetables are planted in the same milpas so that later they may grow around the maize stalks. The rainy-season garden vegetables are planted as soon as the maize-planting is out of the way. Rice is planted in the highlands at this time. On or around May 11 the families hold ceremonies in their milpas to the wind-gods, the purpose of which is to ask the latter to bring rain-bearing wind and to blow gently over the milpas so as not to destroy the young plants. At this time the milpas are replanted in those spots where no sprouts have appeared. With planting out of the way, firewood and hay are brought into the markets in large quantities for sale.

At the beginning of June the occupation of rainy-season fishing, by means of nets and traps, gets underway. The rains have been falling for nearly a month, and the rising rivers contain great numbers of fish. The hunting of small game begins and continues until the end of September. The first cleaning of weeds from the milpas and gardens is done at this time, so that the young sprouts will survive. The last cleaning is done at the end of the month, after which the plants are considered hardy enough to compete unaided with the wild vegetation. Fishing and game-hunting supply the only meat foods available, although some pork and beef are sold in the markets, and the wealthier Indians eat chickens. St. John, patron saint of Camotán, is celebrated on June 24 in San Juan Hermita. A few of the Indians attend this for marketing and especially to watch the Ladino chicken-pull.

Around the middle of July the first roasting ears are gathered in the lowlands, and this is the first fresh maize of the year. Gifts of it are sent or carried to highland friends in Olopa *municipio*, every family in Jocotán starts eating it to the exclusion of almost everything else, and a little is sold in the markets. The Indians are especially joyful for this welcome change from the monotonous dry-season diet and particularly for the fresh-maize *tortillas*, which have been looked forward to for months. A first-fruits festival is celebrated as soon as the first ears are gathered and continues for several days with feasting and *chicha* drinking. On the twenty-fourth the Jocotán Indians celebrate their patron saint in the pueblo. This is the most important social and marketing event in Jocotán *municipio* during the whole year, and every Indian attends during most of the thirteen-day celebration. It is the one day of the year on which the patron saint is celebrated by the *municipio* as a group and so is referred to as a religious event, although it is mainly a time for trading, social participation, and much drinking and merrymaking. It is the most important event during the rainy season for the Indians of surrounding *municipios*, as well, owing to the importance of Jocotán as a trading center and to the fact that it is celebrated shortly after the first maize, when all the Indians are in a holiday mood. Fishing and game-hunting continue through July. Because of the heavy rains the trails and streams become more and more impassable, and market attendance on Sundays falls off. There is little interest in buying and selling, since at this time of the year there are not many manufactured articles to trade and since all the Indians are producing their own foodstuffs. Added to this, everyone is too busy with agriculture to take the time to travel to the pueblos. The festival of St. John, patron saint of San Juan Hermita, is held in that pueblo on July 30, but very few Indians attend it.

At the beginning of August the first fresh maize and beans of the highlands are gathered. The happiness and elation of the Olopa Indians at this event is manifested by their sudden participation in dancing, feasting, drinking, and merrymaking in all the *aldeas*. They return gifts of their maize and beans to their lowland friends and visit at their homes. Toward the end of the month the cleaning of wild vegetation from new milpas is done in the lowlands, in preparation for the second maize-planting, which is done in the middle of September. The diet consists now almost entirely of fresh-maize and bean preparations and continues so until the end of the month. The patron saint of Chiquimula is celebrated in that city on August 15 and is attended by a few Indians and all the Ladinos from all over the department. This is the most important social and marketing event of the year for the Ladinos of the *municipios*, all of whom look to Chiquimula as their urban capital, but that city is too far removed culturally and geographically from Indian life for the Indians to participate much in its social and economic activity. The festival of St. Louis is celebrated in San Juan Hermita on August 29, 30, and 31. A few of the Jocotán and Olopa Indians attend it for marketing, but it is primarily a Ladino celebration. In the latter part of August the first lowland crop of maize ripens and is ready to be harvested. The stalks are cut partially in two, and the ears bent downward to dry during the following two weeks.

At the beginning of September the tobacco fields are cleaned of wild vegetation in the highlands and are made ready for the planting which is done a month or so later. In the middle highlands the planting of sugar cane is started and lasts until the middle of the month. At this time the second crop of beans is planted in the highlands.

The lowland maize, which by now is sufficiently dry for harvesting, is gathered at the beginning of the month and immediately placed in the storehouses. A brief dry spell, called the *canícula*, facilitates the harvest work. Immediately afterward, the second lowland maize crop is planted, prior to which the families individually perform the second rain-making ceremony in their milpas to a group of native deities and burn candles before their family saints, asking that the rainy season continue until this second crop matures. Toward the end of the month the cane fields in the middle highlands are cleaned of weeds for the first time, and this work goes on intermittently until the middle of October. Wet-season fishing tends to die out as an important activity, since the rains, especially in the highlands, are growing less and less heavy, and the streams contain too few fish. Besides, fish are not in great demand, there being sufficient maize and vegetables for everybody. Game-hunting also falls off in importance. The festival of St. Michael is celebrated in Camotán and Gualán on September 25 but attracts very few of the Indians.

The festival of St. Francis, patron saint of La Unión, is celebrated in that pueblo on October 4 and is the most important marketing event of the year in the northern highlands. Many Jocotán and Camotán Indians attend it. At the beginning of October the dry-season crop of tobacco is planted in the highlands, to be harvested in the following April. From the middle to the end of this month the milpas in the lowlands, which are now yielding the second crop, are being daily cleaned of weeds, and the young plants are protected from pests. At this time the harvesting and pressing of sugar cane are started in the middle highlands. This is the crop which was planted over a year before, since cane requires a year to ripen. The pressing goes on in the *aldeas* of the middle-highland regions until April. The festival for the souls of the dead is celebrated in all the *aldeas* and churches on October 31 and November 1, on which days the dead are prayed for and given feasts to eat, the families feast in their houses and in the burial grounds, and the saints and crosses are venerated.

In November the rainy season is definitely over in the highlands, and the near-dry season, which lasts until February, begins. At the beginning of the month the maize ears in the highlands are dried in the milpas, and by the middle of the month the harvesting of maize, rice, and all wet-season vegetables except beans is started in that area and continues, along with the harvesting festival and ceremonies, for the following ten or fifteen days. The vegetables, as well as the seed maize for the next year's planting, are stored in the kitchen, and the bulk of the hard ripe maize is placed in the storehouses to be consumed during the approaching dry season. Toward the end of the month the second crop of maize is harvested in the lowlands. In both areas a harvest festival is celebrated with much feasting, drinking, and dancing in the Indian homes, during which time votive offerings are made to the saints for the abundant harvest and a special ceremony is performed in the storehouses to guard the spirit of the stored maize from destruction by evil spirits and sorcerers. With this, the wet-season agriculture of all the Indians is concluded.

The near-dry season begins with November, and at this time irrigation is started, as the rainfall is slight. The beginning of November sees the inauguration of the manufacturing activities, which are the economic mainstays of the Indians during the long dry season, when the soil is largely unproductive. The tobacco fields are cleaned of weeds and grass for the first time, agave leaves are cut, sedge is brought in from the gardens and stream banks, palm fronds are gathered, and limestone and clay brought in from the hills, all of which are collected in the houses where the manufacturing processes begin. From this time until the following May the principal activities are the manufacturing of pottery, woven and netted articles, sugar, lime, wooden objects, soap, charcoal, dyes, candles, medicines, and many other trade articles. The climate becomes increasingly colder, with occasional frost in the highlands but never snow, and the rains are light and rare. Maize, beans, cultivated vegetables, and occasional fruits form the general diet. Wild greens soon become too tough to be eaten once the rains have ceased.

Manufacturing continues throughout December. At this time, because of the accumulated surplus of manufactured goods, as well as the improved condition of the trails and the shallowness of the streams, marketing takes on new life. As the rains become lighter and the streams gradually decrease in size, dry-season fishing, which is done by poisoning the low streams, is started and continues until April. All the near-dry season crops of vegetables are being irrigated and tended and are usually harvested by the end of the month. Fresh beans are then once more eaten, which, together with ripe maize, comprise almost the entire diet. The feast of the Virgin Mary is celebrated in Camotán on December 8 but is accompanied with very little marketing and seems to be of importance only to the Indians who live in that pueblo. St. Francis, the patron saint of Quetzaltepeque, is celebrated in that municipio on December 19 and is the most important event in that and neighboring *municipios* during the near-dry season. Many Jocotán and Olopa Indians attend it for marketing and visiting with their friends and relatives who live in that part of the Chorti-speaking area.

The first part of January sees the end of the agricultural

year, once the second annual crop of beans is harvested and stored. From this time until May 1 there is almost no rain, and the nights are fairly cold. By the middle of the month all the milpas and vegetable gardens are first cleaned of wild vegetation, the latter being left where cut to dry in the sun. This work is rather occasional and intermittent, since there is plenty of time to get the cleaning done before the May planting, and since many of the Indians are devoting most of their time to such manufacturing as provides them with income. During this month a few of the Indian families are without maize, having already consumed the last harvest, and, if they eat maize, it must be bought in the markets from the wealthier Indians who had planted a surplus and who now begin to sell it at a high price.

February and March are not characterized by any important activities. Most houses are built in the months when there is not much else to do. This is also the time for lime-making, since it is possible to work outdoors and since firewood is plentiful. The trails are also repaired during this season, when they are dry and have little vegetation. Dry-season hunting and fishing continue from January and come to an end with April. Because of the drought the animals are said to come down from the extreme highlands in search of food, so that deer-hunting at this time is less difficult than at other times of the year. Thus, as during the rainy season, fishing and hunting continue to supply most of the meat foods which supplement the maize and vegetable diet; but what slaughtering of domestic animals there is is done in the dry season. The supply of food available during the dry season is much limited in amount and variety in comparison with that during the rainy season, as the Indians are much more adept at agriculture than at food-collecting. This is the time when groups of men make long trips to gather fruits, especially mangoes, to eat in lieu of maize. Principally because of the shortage of food, the general mood during the dry season is not a happy one. There is no elation or excitement but rather an emotional depression, and the Indians seldom come together for purely social intercourse. The stealing of maize is the principal antisocial act during this time. The festival of the Virgin, patron saint of Olopa, is celebrated in that pueblo on March 15. This is the only important event in Olopa and other *municipios* throughout the dry months and is much welcomed by all the Indians as a change from the tedium of life in the *aldeas*, where no excitement is to be had. Many Indians attend it from as far away as La Unión and Copan. St. Joseph is celebrated in Copan on March 19, but this festival does not attract many Indians outside the Copan region.

By the end of March manufacturing, fishing, and hunting begin to cease, for in a few days more the milpas must be finally cut of their dry vegetation, burned, and made ready for the rainy-season planting, the first of the new economic year. Near the beginning of April the tobacco crop is harvested in the highlands. With all the dry-season crops out of the way, the milpas are burned everywhere, and the ashes left on the ground as fertilizer. This closely coincides with the celebration of Palm Sunday and Easter in all the *municipios*. The rain-making festival and ceremonies are held at the end of April to usher in the new rainy season, and the social and economic year begins once more.

GLOSSARY

[Plant identifications were made by Paul Standley, of the Field Museum of Natural History, both from my descriptions and from his own knowledge of Guatemalan plants and plant names. Unfortunately, I did not collect any plant specimens. In some cases he was not certain of his identification, and in a few cases no identification could be made.]

ACEITUNA—Simarubaceae, *Simaruba glauca* DC.
AGUARDIENTE—A distilled alcoholic liquor.
AGUJA DE AREA—Flacourtiaceae, *Xylosma hemsleyana* Standl.
AIGRE—Air, wind, disease.
ALCALDE—Municipal office corresponding to that of mayor.
ALDEA—A rural settlement.
AMATE—Moraceae, *Ficus* sp.
APACINA—Phytolaccaceae, *Petiveria aliacea* L.
APODO—Nickname; extended-family name.
ARBEJA—Synonym for *alberja*.
ARBOL DE CERA—Synonym for *cera vegetal*.
ATOL—A gruel of maize.
AUXILIAR—An *aldea* office, subordinate to alcalde.

BARBASCO—A vine: Sapindacea, *Paulinia* sp.?
BARCO—A gourd vine: Cucurbitaceae, *Lagenaria leucantha* Rusby.
BEJUCO DE BARBASCO—Synonym for *barbasco*.
BONGO—Olla used in making *chicha*.
BUTACA—A kind of chair with leather seat.

CABALLERO—An unidentified bird.
CACASTE—Carrying crate.
CAMOTILLO—Cycadaceae, *Zamia furfuracea* L.F.
CANÍCULA—A dry spell in the rainy season.
CANTÁRIDA—A fly.
CÁNTARO—Earthenware water jar.
CAPULÍN—Elaeocarpaceae, *Muntingia calabura* L.
CARRIZO—Poaceae, *Arundo donax* L.
CASERÍO—A small rural settlement without local government.
CAULOTE—Sterculiaceae, *Guazuma ulmifolia* Lamarck.
CHACHA—A bird.
CHAPERNA—Leguminosae, *Lonchocarpus minimiflorus* Donn. Smith?
CHAYO—Synonym for *copapayo*.
CHICCHAN—A native deity.
CHICHA—A fermented beverage of sugar cane.
CHICHERÍA—A place where *chicha* is sold.

473

CHILATE—A maize gruel.
CHILE CHILTEPE—Solanaceae, *Capsicum baccatum* L.
CHILE LENGUA DE GALLINA—A variety of chili.
CHILILLO—Solanaceae.
CHIPILÍN—Leguminosae, *Crotalaria longirostrata* Hook. and Arn.
CHUCTE—Lauraceae, *Persea schiedeana* Nees.
CIGUAPACTE—Compositae.
CILACAYOTE—Cucurbitaceae, *Cucurbita ficifolia* Bouché.
COFRADÍA—House in which community saint is kept.
COMAL—Earthenware griddle.
COMANDANCIA—Headquarters of the *comandante*.
COMANDANTE—Military official in each town.
CONACASTE—Leguminosae, *Enterolobium cyclocarpum* (Jacquin) Grisebach.
CONTE—Araceae, *Syngonum* sp.?
COPAL—A tree: Burseraceae, *Bursera* sp.; also, a kind of incense made of the
    gum of the tree.
CORTÉZ (WHITE)—Bignoniaceae, *Tabebuia Donnel-Smithii* Rose.
CORTÉZ (YELLOW)—Bignoniaceae, *Tabebuia chrysantha* (Jacquin) Urban.
CORTÉZ COYOTE—Bignoniaceae, *Tabebuia* sp.
CUAJATINTA—Boraginaceae, *Cordia cana* Martens and Galeotti?
CUARTA—Measure equivalent to the English span.
CUCARACHO—Unidentified plant.
CUJE—Leguminosae, *Inga* sp.
CUJINICUIL—Synonym for *cuje*.

ELOTE—Maize before it is ripe and hard.
ESPINA DE TEJER—synonym for *pitahaya*.

FLOR AMARILLA—Bignoniaceae, *Tecoma stans* (D.) H.B.K.
FLOR DE LA CRUZ—Apocynaceae, *Plumeria rubra* L.
FLOR DE MAYO—Apocynaceae, *Plumeria* sp.

GARRAPATA—Tick.
GUACAL—A gourd from the calabash tree; utensil made of such a gourd.
GUACHIPILÍN—Fagaceae, *Diphysa* sp.
GUAJE—Synonym for *nacascahuite*.
GUALMECO—Unidentified plant.
GUAMA—Leguminosae, *Inga* sp.
GUAPITO—Solanaceae.

HIERBA DE TINTA—Synonym for *tinta de monte*.
HIJILLO—An *aigre* (or disease) contracted from certain special agents.
HIPERICÓN—Hypericaceae, *Hypericum* sp.
HOGAR—Dwelling-place, home.
HOJA DEL AIRE—Crassulaceae, *Bryophyllum pinnatum* (L.) Kurz.
HOJA DE CONTE—Synonym for *conte*.
HUISQUIL—Cucurbitaceae, *Sechium edule* Swartz.

IZOTE—Liliaceae, *Yucca elephantipes* Regel.

Jefe político—The highest official of a department, corresponding to a governor.

Jícaro—Calabash tree (Bignoniaceae, *Crescentia cujete* L.); the gourd of the tree; a utensil made of the gourd.

Jiote—Synonym for *palo jiote.*

Jiquilite—Leguminosae, *Indigofera suffruticosa* Miller.

Jocote—Any of a variety of Spanish plum (Anacardiaceae, *Spondias purpurea* L.).

Jurgáy—Sapindaceae, *Talisia olivaeformis* (H.B.K.) Radlkofer.

Jute—A shellfish.

Juzgado—The town hall and courthouse of the *municipio.*

Ladino—A non-Indian; a class of people of Spanish language and relatively occidental culture.

Lenguajero—A Chorti-speaking Indian.

Loroco—Apocynaceae, *Urechites karwinskii* Mueller.

Machete—Agricultural and woodworking implement.

Madre cacao—Leguminoseae, *Gliricidia sepium* (Jacquin) Steudel.

Maguey—Agave.

Maicillo—Graminae, *Holcus sorghum* L.

Maicillo montés—Wild *maicillo,* Gramineae.

Mango—Anacardiaceae, *Mangifera indica* L.

Mano—Handstone used with the metate.

Manzanilla—Malaceae, *Malvaviscus* sp.

Marimba—A musical instrument similar to the xylophone.

Mashaste—Bignoniaceae, *Arrabidaea* sp.?

Mayordomo—Indian religious official.

Mecate—Ulmaceae, *Chaeloptelea mexicana* Liebmann.

Mein—The spirit of an animate or inanimate object.

Melocotón—Cucurbitaceae, *Sicana odorifera* (Vill.) Naudin.

Metate—Grinding-stone.

Micoleón—Unidentified animal.

Milpa—Field of maize and associated crops.

Monte—Wild vegetation, forest.

Moronga—Blood sausage.

Morro—Bignoniaceae, *Crescentia alata* H.B.K.; kitchen utensil or rattler made of the dried fruit of this tree.

Mozo—Day laborer.

Municipio—Township; a municipal territory.

Murul—Bombacaceae.

Nistamal—Maize that has been boiled with lime for use as food.

Ocote—A variety of resinous pine (*Pinus oocarpa* Schiede); a torch of the wood.

Oficio—Profession, trade.

Olla—Earthenware cooking pot.

Orchata—Any uncooked beverage, drunk cold.

ORÉGANO—Cactaceae, *Cereus* sp.
ORÉGANO MONTÉS—Verbenaceae, *Lippia* sp.?
OREJUELA DE RATÓN—Synonym for *hierba del ratón.*

PACAYA—Palmae, *Chamaedorea* sp.; edible shoot growing on any of several palms.
PADRINO—Godfather; an Indian priest or "wise man."
PALO JIOTE—Burseraceae, *Bursera simaruba* (L.) Sarg.
PAPAYA DE MONTAÑA—Caricaceae, *Carica* sp.
PARPÁR—Synonym for *zacate parpár.*
PEINE DE MICO—Bignoniaceae, *Pithecoctenium echinatum* (Jacquin) Schumann.
PESO—Small Guatemalan coin worth one-sixtieth of a dollar or a quetzal.
PIMIENTA GORDA—Myrtaceae, *Pimenta officinalis* Lindley.
PIMIENTO—Piperaceae, *Piper* sp.
PINOL—A maize gruel.
PIÑUELA—Bromeliaceae, *Bromelia pinguin* L.
PIZOTE—Unidentified animal.
PLAZA—The market place in a town.
PUEBLO—Town; the capital of a *municipio.*

QUESO—Cheese (Sp.).
QUETZAL—A bird; Guatemalan monetary unit.
QUILETE ROJO—Synonym for *bledo rojo.*

RANCHO—Home establishment, including fields.
REGIDOR—A municipal official.

SABIO—Wise man, especially priests, curers, etc...
SACATINTA—Synonym for *tinta de monte.*
SAHURÍN—Power possessed by "wise men."
SANTA MARÍA—Piperaceae, *Piper umbellatum* L.
SARAQUE—Gramineae, *Panicum* sp.
SENSITIVA—Leguminosae, *Mimosa pudica* L.
SHAGUÁY—Leguminosae.
SHEPE—A kind of tamale.
SONANZA—A musical instrument with metal rattlers.
SUBÍN—Leguminosae, *Acacia farnesiana* (L.) Willd?

TABACO DEL RATÓN—Synonym for *hierba del ratón.*
TALNETE—A wild black bee.
TALTUZA—Unidentified animal.
TAMALE—A maize dumpling (with other ingredients) wrapped and cooked in leaves.
TAREA—A unit of work; a stint.
TASHISTE—Compositae, *Compositae* sp.?
TECOMATE—A gourd vessel; also a calabash vine.
TEMPISQUE—Sapotaceae, *Sideroxylon tempisque* Pittier.
TEPONAGUA—A kind of drum.
TINTA DE MONTE—Acanthaceae, *Jacobinia spicigera* (Schlecht.) Bailey.

Tomatillo—A small tomato.

Tortilla—A kind of griddle cake of maize dough.

Totoposte—A thin, toasted *tortilla*.

Tun—A kind of drum.

Vara de bambú—A cane: Gramineae, *Bambusa* sp.

Vara de canasto—Graminacae, *Panicum* sp.

Vara de escoba—A cane: Gramineae.

Yagual—A hanger for holding food and objects.

Yupáy—Boraginaceae, *Cordia alba* (Jacquin) Roemer and Schultes.

Zacate—Any of a variety of grasses (Gramineae *Panicum barbinode* Trinius), including the *amargo, camalote, conejo, coronita, habanero, mozote, pará, parpár, pelo de mico,* and *teozinte.*

Zapote—Sapotaceae, *Calocarpum mammosum* (L.) Pierre.

Zarza dormilona—Synonym for *sensitiva.*

Zunzapote—Amygdalaceae, *Licania platypus* (Hemsley) Fritsch.

Zunza—Synonym for *zunzapote.*

BIBLIOGRAPHY

BLOM, FRANS. *Commerce, Trade, and Monetary Units of the Maya.* "Middle American Research Series," Pub. 4. New Orleans: Tulane University, 1932.

BLOM, FRANS, and LA FARGE, OLIVER. *Tribes and Temples.* 2 vols. New Orleans: Tulane University, 1927.

COOK, O. F. "Milpa Agriculture: A Primitive Tropical System," *Smithsonian Institution Annual Report,* pp. 307–26. Washington, 1919.

EGGAN, Fred. "The Maya Kinship System and Cross-Cousin Marriage," *American Anthropologist,* XXXVI, No. 2 (new ser.; April–June, 1934), 188–203.

FORSTEMANN, E. *The Day Gods of the Mayas.* Bureau of American Ethnology Bull. 28, pp. 559–72. Washington, 1904.

GANN, T. W. F. *The Maya Indians of Southern Yucatan and Northern British Honduras.* Bureau of American Ethnology Bull. 64. Washington, 1918.

GANN, T. W. F., and THOMPSON, J. ERIC. *A History of the Maya.* New York, 1935.

GATES, WILLIAM. *Distribution of the Several Branches of the Mayence Linguistic Stock.* Carnegie Institution of Washington Pub. 219, pp. 605–15. Washington, 1920.

LA FARGE, OLIVER. "Adaptations of Christianity among the Jacalteca Indians of Guatemala," *Thought* (New York), II, No. 3 (1927), 476–95.

LA FARGE, OLIVER, and BYERS, DOUGLAS. *The Year Bearer's People.* "Middle American Research Series," Pub. 3. New Orleans: Tulane University, 1931.

McBRYDE, WEBSTER. *Solólá.* "Middle American Research Series," Pub. 5. New Orleans: Tulane University, 1933.

MORAN, FRANCISCO. *Arte de lengua Cholti* (copy in Department of Middle American Research, Tulane University, New Orleans).

MORLEY, S. G., *The Inscriptions at Copan.* Carnegie Institution of Washington Pub. 219. Washington, 1920.

———. *An Introduction to the Study of the Maya Hieroglyphs.* Bureau of American Ethnology Bull. 57. Washington, 1915.

Motul Dictionary (copy in Department of Middle American Research, Tulane University, New Orleans).

PARSONS, E. C. *Mitla: Town of the Souls.* "University of Chicago Publications in Anthropology." Chicago: University of Chicago Press, 1936.

——. *Pueblo Indian Religion.* 2 vols. "University of Chicago Publications in Anthropology." Chicago: University of Chicago Press, 1939.

POPENOE, WILSON. "The Useful Plants of Copan," *American Anthropologist*, XXI, No. 2 (new ser.; April–June, 1919), 125–39.

——. *Manual of Tropical and Subtropical Fruits.* New York, 1920.

REDFIELD, ROBERT, *Tepoztlán.* "University of Chicago Publications in Anthropology." Chicago: University of Chicago Press, 1930.

REDFIELD, ROBERT, and PARK, MARGARET. *Disease and Its Treatment, in Dzitas, Yucatan.* Carnegie Institution of Washington Pub. 523, Contribution No. 32. Washington, 1940.

REDFIELD, ROBERT, and VILLA, ALFONSO. *Chan Kom: A Maya Village.* Carnegie Institution of Washington Pub. 448. Washington, 1934.

SAVILLE, M. E. *Reports on the Maya Indians of Yucatan.* "Indian Notes and Monographs," Vol. IX, No. 3. New York: Museum of the American Indian, Heye Foundation, 1921.

SELER, EDWARD. *Antiquities of Guatemala.* Bureau of American Ethnology Bull. 28, pp. 77–121. Washington, 1904.

STARR, FREDERICK. "Notes upon the Ethnography of Southern Mexico," *Proceedings of the Davenport Academy of Sciences*, Vol. VIII, 1899–1900.

STEPHENS, J. L. *Incidents of Travel in Central America, Chiapas, and Yucatan*, Vol. I. New York, 1842.

TAX, SOL. "The *Municipios* of the Midwestern Highlands of Guatemala," *American Anthropologist*, XXXIX, No. 3 (new ser.; July–September, 1937), 423–45.

THOMPSON, J. ERIC. *Ethnology of the Maya of Southern and Central British Honduras.* Field Museum of Natural History Pub. 274. Chicago, 1930.

——. *Civilization of the Mayas.* Field Museum of Natural History Pub. 25. Chicago, 1927.

——. "Sixteenth and Seventeenth Century Reports on the Chol Mayas," *American Anthropologist*, XL, No. 4 (new ser.; October–December, 1938), 584–605.

——. *Mexico before Cortez.* New York, 1933.

TOZZER, A. M. *A Comparative Study of the Mayas and Lacandones.* New York, 1907.

INDEX

Abortion, 286

Accordion, 296–97, 300

Aceituna, 85 (n. 34), 182 (n. 32)

Achiote, 64, 91, 289, 366

Adoption of children, 247 (n. 5)

Adultery, 256

Adz, 174

Agave, 64, 152–53, 288

Age and status groups, 195–96

Agriculture, 39–50; cycle of, 437–47; deities of, 391, 400; implements used, 172–74

Aguardiente, 96 (n. 12), 105, 185, 300, 352

Aigre, 285, 308–9, 317–26

Alcalde, 230–32, 299

Aldeas: ceremonies of, 237; co-operative work in, 237–45; description, 18, 216–22; languages spoken in, 7; location, 2; names, 217–18; officials, 233–35; population, 219; trails, 206–7

Aloe, 294, 351 (n. 20), 366

Altars: description, 147 (n. 36), 382–84; for funeral festival, 305–6; structures containing, 384–86

Amate tree, 353

Anatomical beliefs, 307–8

Animals. *See* Domestic animals; Wild animals

Anise, 185, 294

Annona, 21, 60, 85, 101 (n. 21), 356

Annual cycle, 462–71

Apacina, 286–87, 289 (n. 12), 351 (n. 20)

Apparitions, 390–91, 404–9

Artemisia, 331, 347, 349

Ashes, use of, 108–9, 154, 181, 331–32

Atol, atolágrio, 90–91

Avocado, 20, 61–62, 85 (n. 34), 104 (n. 24)

Ax: of iron, 39, 173–74; of stone, 382, 396

Bags, 26, 33–34; of agave, 160–61; of leather, 179–80; of mats, 164–65

Banana, 21, 59, 96, 123 (n. 12), 167

Baptism, 291–93

Baskets, 21, 26, 35 (n. 19); making of, 161–64

Bay tree, 63, 129 (n. 18)

Beans, 20, 35; amount eaten, 98; cooking of, 93; harvesting, 50; medicinal use, 286 (n. 7); preservation and storage, 107–12; spirit of, 402–3; varieties, 41–42

Bed structure, 132, 134

Bees, 68–69, 183, 351, 360

Benches and stools, 136

Beverages, 31, 91, 93, 94, 96

Bindweeds, 123

Birds, 47 (n. 17), 74 (nn. 20, 21); trap used for, 77

Blacksmiths, 172

Blowgun, 70

Bow and arrow, 70, 296

Bowls: of gourds, 144–45; of pottery, 139–40

Braiding of textiles, 158–60

Brazil tree, 123 (n. 11), 136 (n. 27), 154–55, 163

Date Due			
Ap 24 '56			
Ap 30 '57			
Jl 3 '59			
Fe 22 '68			
Sep 26 70			
Demco 293-5			